Crashing Through Constellations

Crashing Through Constellations

Tony Craven

First Published in United Kingdom 2014
© Tony Craven

Douglas Foote

ISBN 978-1-909381-04-9

www.douglasfoote.com

For Edward

Acknowledgements

To every fellow traveller - not mentioned in these pages, but whose orbit has met with mine over the years, and added exhilaration to the ride.

With special thanks to Hazel Douglas and Brenda Nickson, who kindly ploughed through the manuscript early on and provided invaluable insight and encouragement; to Jean Kent, whose common sense and unbridled enthusiasm for the book never wavered, but who – sadly – never lived to see the final result; to Michael Thornton, for his wisdom and positive thinking, which so much helped to ensure that I never gave up; to Liz Moscrop who suggested the trajectory; and to Alan Russell for inviting me onto the all-important launch pad.

I owe an enormous debt of gratitude to my mother for (amongst all the other things) her meticulous compilation of so many scrapbooks over the years, which I have been able to resort to on a number of occasions to check dates, names and places and to confirm (or challenge) the accuracy of my memories. Any errors are, of course, my own.

I want to thank Douglas Foote, whose unerring patience and expertise I have come to rely on, and without whom this story would contain a multitude of exclamation marks!

And, finally, remembering Pat Edwards: 1931-2013

PART ONE

Landings & Take-Offs

On July 20th, 1969, Man landed on the moon. And I landed in Birmingham. Without a doubt, my arrival failed to attract the same degree of worldwide attention, and my journey, from the family home in leafy Buckinghamshire, was a great deal shorter. However, the road I took was to lead, ultimately, around the world to meet with Hollywood legends, rock stars, leading players from stage and screen, musicians, prime ministers, royalty, and a sprinkling of oddballs quaintly known as "national treasures".

J.R.R.Tolkien (yes, the old Prof himself) had told me over tea that, "fantasy is the true reality." He had come to my university college to talk to one of our literary societies and the committee thought it was a good idea to entertain him first. I had only recently begun reading *The Lord of the Rings*, but the man turned out to be so pompous and self opinionated that the rest of his book somehow lost interest for me.

So whether he was right or not about fantasy and reality, this at least is a true story.

Whilst Man hopped about on the moon, I was headed for the stars. A veritable galaxy twinkled above me and a tangle of pathways beckoned. Each promised adventure and excitement. I might be treated rough, but there could be treats in store. Believe me, and I hope you will, over the next 40 years, I just about covered it all.

But first there had to be an apprenticeship. I'd come from the world of the concert pianist - not exactly as an infant prodigy, but certainly as an early starter. At the age of four, I perched on the piano stool. Stubbornly I kept returning to it, until my mother took me by the hand and delivered me to the front door of a local piano teacher. Once across the threshold, I discovered the musty world of Mrs Brotherton, together with her cardigans and skirts and ancient bosom. The latter (though not as well-fingered, I imagine) was as solid and upright as her own piano, and always seemed to hover on the edge of my eye-line, as I investigated – for the first time – the thrill of scales and arpeggios, of rubato and allegro.

Any Requests?

Within time, there was a mellowing of my view of Mrs Bro. My initial foreboding evolved into an affectionate and gentle respect, and my twice weekly visits became something to look forward to. I discovered the twinkle in her eye and the love of her subject, as we explored together the fascinating repertoire of early studies, etudes, sonatas, fugues and musical jokes.

One day, as the lesson came to an end, however, Mrs Bro looked at me with an odd mix of sadness and admiration. "There's nothing more I can do for you. Your parents must find somebody who can take you further – somebody who is able to stretch your musical talents to the full."

I was devastated. To think that I would never again arrive at that door; that my sessions with Mrs Bro were finished; and that I was to be moved on – to perform under the eyes of a stranger.

My mother, who also played the piano, was already aware of the progress that I was making. In fact, she and I could often be found – side by side on a double piano stool – vamping our way through a vast collection of duets and "chopstick"-type trivialities and having enormous fun. And it was my mother who arranged for the next step up.

I became a regular visitor to Cookham and Pinner, homes of the Childs Academy. Here, there were sleek grand pianos and more than a touch of professionalism. Valerie Childs was a concert pianist who had studied with the great Claudio Arrau and, together with her mother, Elsie, she set about establishing a stable of musical talents. We were pushed to practice for hours at a time, our technique honed and polished, our backs straightened and our fingers curved. And then – like rows of little pottery prodigies – we were unveiled and presented to the outside world.

I worked so hard that much of my childhood disappeared as I went from a round of music festivals to concert platforms; recitals to competitions; from the recording studio to… *Opportunity Knocks.*

This was the forerunner and defining template for *Britain's Got Talent*, and it was with great excitement that I travelled to Manchester and the old Didsbury Studios. Within a short time, I emerged from wardrobe dressed in a vile puce-green shirt. In those days, apparently, the camera translated this into a brilliant white on the television screen. I was then hoisted to a grand piano mounted on a rostrum, to perform Liszt's Hungarian Rhapsody Nº 2.

A day and a half of rehearsals followed. I was joined by three others from the Childs' fraternity - this was eight hands, on two pianos – to deliver our bizarre display of virtuosity over and over. Word came from the gallery: "Play faster! It's too long!" Breathless with a continuous and idiotic pummeling of the keyboard, we raced through this Rhapsody time and again. Still we were running over. Could the piece be edited?

And, all the while, we awaited the arrival of our Master of Ceremonies himself - Hughie Green. Or, as we contestants called him, "Who He? Green." We hadn't met at the audition, and he didn't appear until the final run-through. Even then,

Camera Rehearsal, Opportunity Knocks·

*ABC Television Picture

he struck me as smarmy and insincere. He never spoke to any of us and, even though "you good people at home" were meant to decide the lucky winner, it seemed to me that it was he who made the decision - announcing it to his aides, immediately following the camera rehearsal, as to who should come out on top and return the following week. Even the famous clapometer broke down on that particular show.

But, having mangled Liszt, it seemed perhaps only appropriate that we should be beaten into second place by a fire-eater.

I'd had it with the piano. I, who not long before had worked with the famous Richard Rodney Bennett, on the première of a work by the celebrated composer, Malcolm Williamson (two pianos and wind quintet), though I suspect the performers had more fun than the poor unfortunate listeners.

Never mind. I put the indignity behind me, and…

So it was that, on that Monday morning in July, bright-eyed and bushy-tailed, I walked along Station Street, and round to the stage door of the old Birmingham Repertory Theatre anxious to start my new job as an ASM (assistant stage manager). The glamour, the magic and the sheer exhilaration of a life in the Theatre was waiting for me on the other side of that door. Or so I thought.

Instead since they had been up all night watching the moon landing, most people were slumped in various corners of the building, yawning, snoring or just drinking coffee.

The Stage Manager, a humourless curiosity called Alison Symington, got so embarrassed by my overwhelming eagerness to work and having nothing for me to do, she eventually sent me out to buy ring binder strengtheners for the prompt book. My recently acquired Honours Degree from London University surely entitled me to a more prestigious beginning?

And yet it was there, at Royal Holloway College, that my yearnings for a career in the Theatre had begun. Though, in truth, it might have been earlier. Maybe the seeds had been sown at Primary School, in an improvised production of *Peter Pan*. Cast as Captain Hook, I evidently scoured the local butchers for a suitably threatening appendage. A monster hook it was, too, and I couldn't resist

A Pious-looking Thomas More

5

reappearing on stage to brandish it at the audience long after I'd been swallowed by the crocodile and the plot had moved on.

Later, I was found in the stocks as Watt Tyler and, in December, 1965 took the school by storm as Sir Thomas More, in *A Man For All Seasons*. According to the local newspaper, I had "conveyed the mixture of wit, humility, nonchalance and fervent adherence to principle that characterized the man." Certainly my mother was convinced. Legend has it that, as I climbed the scaffold to my death, she gave audible vent to her feelings, "You can't. That's my son!"

But in Birmingham I was there to learn. I had not come for the money. In my feverish brain, when the Production Manager had fixed my salary at "twelve ten," this translated into twelve hundred and ten per year. It took my father's pragmatic input to reduce that to its true value: twelve pounds, ten shillings a week.

Had I made the right decision: to start at the bottom, in the Theatre, rather than go for one of the Trainee Director Courses that were being offered at that time in Television? Because it was as a DIRECTOR that I now saw myself.

Early Filming at University

In my first year at University, a notice had gone up asking for volunteers to direct the college entry for London University's One Act Play competition. I remember a discussion in the bar, during which I had mercilessly scoffed at the idea. Ordering people around the stage? Easy. Bets were laid.

Before I knew it, I was directing my first production, *Getting & Spending*, by David Campton, and I learned two things: firstly, that it was very, very far from being easy; and, secondly, that I hadn't enjoyed anything so much since I was playing the piano. And we won the competition.

From then on, much of my time (probably too much) was spent conducting a passionate affair with the college's Drama Society. Together we experimented with every theatrical position. I acted, wrote, I sat on committees, I made a couple of films and directed anything I could. The course was set - first stop, Birmingham.

But it was to be a while before I saw the words, "Directed by Tony Craven." In fact, in 1969 I didn't even know who Tony Craven was. I'd never met him. My passport bore the name Anthony Thornton.

It seems odd, looking back now, that I was able to work for half a year in a major repertory company without joining the union, Equity. It had been mentioned a couple of times, but there was certainly no pressure and it wasn't until the early part of 1970 that I looked at the issue seriously. When I did, I was told to change my name.

Another Equity member existed with the name 'Tony Thawnton', bad enough that he spelled his surname differently, but it was particularly galling that the individual for whom I would have to sacrifice my identity was not an actor, not even a stage manager, but a conjuror. In Manchester, I'd been pushed into second place by a fire-eater, and now I was forced to forgo the name I had carried for nearly 22 years by a prestidigitator.

This was not trivial stuff. A name is important. And a change can cause problems. When it concerns an Equity member's passport, confusion and near disaster are never far away.

A salutary lesson of the dangers of names was garnered by an actor I worked with in the early 1980s. Quite new to the business of acting when I employed him, Mark Lindsay was a delightful young man, eager to learn, good-looking, with a strong voice and strong, if raw, talent. I reckoned he could go far, and it looked at one moment as though it would happen soon.

An American company was making a film about the life of John Lennon and Mark was in the frame to play the lead. He went through endless auditions and meetings and, each time, advanced further. He flew to America for a screen-test and the shortlist was reduced to two. Finally, he was offered the part and I was thrilled for him. He was tremendously excited, dreaming already of life beyond this breakthrough. And then the call came.

He was NOT going to be playing the part. Yoko Ono had stepped in and refused her consent. And why? Because she had discovered Mark Lindsay's real name. And that name was Mark Chapman.

Of course, Mark Chapman was the name of John Lennon's assassin.

I'm happy to say that Mark did play Lennon many years later, and enjoys a successful career in the US as Mark Lindsay Chapman.

The name Craven was hijacked from another branch of my own family, and I have lived with it for most of my adult life. But that was all a distant prospect as I returned with a fresh packet of ring binder strengtheners to find a company of actors now lively, awake and going through their paces.

Rehearsals had started on a new musical, *Quick, Quick, Slow*. Written by David Turner and set in Birmingham, this was a satire on the world of ballroom dancing. Music was by Monty Norman famous for the James Bond *Dr. No* theme and the lyricist was Julian More. Together, they were responsible for a number of hit musicals, including *Irma la Douce* and *Expresso Bongo*, and expectations were high that *Quick, Quick, Slow* would enjoy a similar success.

The leading lady, the first of dozens for me, was called Stella Moray. She was always chasing me up the stairs, ready to pinch my bottom or appearing around corners, with a lewd remark. The Musical Director developed a crush on me and offered work and a few other things in London. He was fond of champagne at lunchtime, which led on occasion to our choreographer, Virginia, delivering the dreaded line to me: "YOU play the piano, don't you?" at the start of the afternoon session.

Virginia, by the way, was wickedly referred to by the stage-management team as 'Vagina', on account of the fact that she was conducting an affair with a leading member of the company, and each morning they would share with us the intimate details of their nocturnal activities. Apparently, at the conclusion of each display of dazzling virtuosity from him, she would sit at the foot of the bed to applaud. We assumed that the length and intensity of her hand clapping reflected accurately on what had gone before, and she must surely have called for the occasional encore.

There was a lad in that company called Paul Henry. If the name sounds familiar, it would be because he went on to find fame as Benny in *Crossroads* and made huge numbers of fans. At Birmingham, however in less politically correct days he was known to us all as 'Gyppo', in reference to his Romany background. Paul had no problem with that. He was extremely popular, as I recall, and we all attended his wedding in the autumn, and celebrated in style. Those who made up the audience that evening may have been aware that the performance was a little... shall we say, slurry and unfocused.

Jane Freeman was another actress on that Birmingham stage who went on to enjoy considerable success in a television series. As the café owner Ivy in *Last of the Summer Wine*, she was in the very first episode shot in 1973, I believe, and stayed with the show until its penultimate episode, in 2010.

Jane became a great friend and, in fact, I was Best Man at her wedding to Michael Simpson, who was then the Associate Director at Birmingham. I directed them both in a scene from *Who's Afraid of Virginia Woolf*, in a Sunday night anthology programme. How brave they must have been to share my first tentative steps towards becoming a professional director.

Meanwhile, *Quick, Quick, Slow* went from quick to quicker to frantic. Capacity houses brought a stream of curious visitors from London and, after the final performance and 14 curtain calls, there was much talk of a transfer. Everyone was full of the news that "a chap called Pilbrow, who owns a lot of London theatres" was so delighted with the show that he had bought it on the spot and was taking it to the West End.

Jimmy Edwards and Sheila Hancock were to nudge John Baddeley and Jane Freeman aside to star in the London production. Glamour was finally making her entrance, it seemed. Yet, coy as ever, she remained in the wings a little longer. The transfer never materialized and it was back to the daily routine of production. With one slight adjustment. The way was beginning to open up to my first stumbling attempts at directing.

It is time to introduce you to my mentor.

*   *   *   *   *

Man in the shape of those American astronauts was well and truly earthbound again before I was even able to meet my new employer. Rumours swirled around the Rep's Artistic Director that, with his fierce some temper and terrifying bark both of which could erupt at any moment, he could make a building tremble together with its occupants.

It was said that he once hit a young actor with a prop goblet from 40 paces. And word had it that, during the rehearsal period for *Hamlet* the year before, he had turned up in Richard Chamberlain's hotel room in the middle of the night, and very nearly made it into his bed before being ejected by the hotel security staff.

Princess Margaret's technique was very different, but equally unsuccessful.

We are now in fast-forward mode to 1971. The lady was due in Birmingham to attend a Gala Performance to mark the opening of the gleaming new theatre, in Broad Street. Her appearance was in doubt until the last minute, however. She had a throat infection; she'd lost her voice; she might cancel. We received almost daily bulletins.

In the event, the lady arrived. And the lady was late. Not for her afternoon tour of the theatre, which took place as scheduled. Her planned itinerary was for a full day in the city, taking in one or two other venues as well. But the evening was set aside for the Gala Performance.

And we waited.

Backstage, of course, it was very nerve-wracking and all we could do was pace and check, over and over, that everything was in readiness. On the other side of the curtain, we sensed a growing impatience in the auditorium.

Some 20 minutes after the scheduled start time, we heard applause, which like a 'Mexican Wave' rose and tumbled towards us. The lady had clearly arrived. After a cue from front of house, the orchestra struck up the overture.

We knew that there were a lot of "big names" out front, and everyone involved, both on stage and behind the scenes, was determined to give of their best. And all went well.

Presented to Princess Margaret by Peter Dews. With Isla Donald and, far right Paul Henry.

*Picture by Willoughby Gullachsen

Afterwards, as arranged, we lined up behind the huge curtains and waited once more for our distinguished visitor to arrive and for us each to be presented. I was struck by how pretty she looked and how genuine she seemed to be in her praise for everyone, as she made her way down the line. Her voice was a little croaky, but she and I managed a brief chat. And then it was all over.

A car was scheduled to arrive at 10.30 and, as far as we were all concerned, it had duly whisked the lady away. HRH, on the other hand, had different plans.

Within minutes, word came that an impromptu party had been requested. Bottles and glasses were rushed to the space that would become in time our Studio Theatre. We and our guests were all invited to this spontaneous jamboree. And it was great fun.

Amongst the sprinkling of celebrities, one figure stood out - tall, distinguished, and with a heavy beard. Obviously in readiness for a part in film or television, the hirsute expression could nevertheless not disguise Richard Chamberlain from us, and Princess Margaret was attracted like a magnet.

Firstly, of course, she mingled, as she drained a few glasses - all merriment and laughter, and then I was drawn to the sight of this very petite figure, standing alongside the tall, imposing actor. The lady's expression (aided possibly by a degree of alcohol) was determined and decidedly 'smitten'.

Time past, and it was just before midnight and after the bar stocks had been replenished more than once that our special guest took her leave. The mood was one of elation, relief and a genuine thrill that all had gone so spectacularly well. But then we had been told to expect the unexpected from the lady...

I was one of those, I think there were three of us, who escorted her to the stage door and the car that awaited her. As we arrived, she turned to me with a new and utterly imperious quality to croak the memorable words: "Thank you for a delightfully BORING evening!" And she was gone.

Perhaps Richard Chamberlain had not succumbed to her charms. Perhaps she had truly hated the show. And perhaps she just wanted to remind us of who she was.

Her mother was so much wittier. But for that we'd have to rewind past our starting point and I must concentrate and finally introduce my mentor.

One full week into my new career, and I was about to meet Peter Dews. He had been at the helm at Birmingham for 3 years and with him as Artistic Director the company was making waves. *Hadrian VII* had premiered there and emptied the theatre before becoming a smash hit in London and on Broadway. As a result, Peter had won an award for Best Director on Broadway in 1968, and he was now gaining a great deal of attention for his work at the Chichester Festival Theatre. His production of *Antony & Cleopatra,* with Margaret Leighton, had just received stunning reviews. And all of this was in addition to his fabled string of Shakespeare productions, *The Age of Kings* for television.

Peter was a Bradford man and a former school teacher. He would not tolerate foolishness, laziness or unprofessionalism of any sort, and woe betide the individual who dared to transgress on any of those counts.

At the same time, and at the age of 40, Peter saw himself as a father figure to the company, and could be extremely kind, caring and compassionate especially, it has to be said, to the younger male members.

Married to Anne, an ex-hairdresser, one of the complexities of Peter's character was his affection for, and passionate loyalty towards, his group of "Dewsy Boys." He discovered many of them and took them under his wing and, for as long as they remained within the bounds of his definition of good behaviour both on and off the stage, he stood by them and gave them opportunities.

As a director, Peter Dews was also complicated. He confided in me once that his ambition was to be the "best comic in rehearsal since Guthrie," and he was certainly always full of anecdotes and jokes. A lot of time was wasted whilst he recounted tales of people he'd worked with, good and often enjoyable, but tediously repetitive.

On some days, 40% of the rehearsal time was taken up in this way. 40% would then be spent on the mundane business of blocking, interpreting and running sections. But there was usually 20%, more on a good day, that was sheer brilliance and genius at work. As an aspiring director myself, these were the sessions I drank up and from which I learned invaluable lessons.

I remember Peter's entrance into the auditorium on that day in July, 1969 very vividly. We had all congregated in the first couple of rows, nursing our cups of coffee and chatting nervously, whilst sitting in anxious expectation of the great arrival.

My first sight of that magnificent theatrical force was probably an anticlimax. A round, ruddy faced and rather ill dressed and tubby figure came through the doors, fully aware of the effect his return was having and glorying in the manner in which everyone had snapped to attention. He was received with tremendous respect and awe, with just a sprinkling of fear mixed in.

In fact, for the next six months, I viewed The Director, Peter especially, as The Boss. His word was law and he, in every sense, directed what happened on the stage. Then one day I suddenly saw him challenged. I witnessed a colossal battle of wills between Director and Star that is not in any way uncommon, but which in early 1970 was, for me, an eye-opener.

I am already reminded of the story of a superstar leading lady, who clearly had very little respect for her director. On the first day of blocking, he tried to accommodate her wishes.

Director: Now, I'd like you to enter upstage centre, and move towards the down left corner.

Superstar: No. I don't want to do that.

Director (after a pause): OK. Er… why not try entering upstage and then move towards the down right corner.

Superstar: No. I don't want to do that.

Director (after a longer pause, and deciding to do the obvious): Alright, darling. Just come in at the back and walk downstage centre.

Superstar: No. I don't think so.

Director (utterly exasperated): Right! What would you LIKE to do?

Superstar (sweetly): Well, I don't know. You're the Director. You tell me.

Apocryphal or not, the story is a plausible one.

Peter met his hard rock on the production of a new play called *The Sorrows of Frederick*. What a contrast with the *Hamlet* he'd just directed with the gentlemanly Alec McCowen and the delightful Anna Massey, utterly engrossing and riveting to watch.

Not only did the rehearsal atmosphere undergo a huge change between *Hamlet* and *Frederick* but I, too, was raised to the dizzy heights of Stage Manager with a corresponding lift in salary to the commanding sum of 17 pounds a week. I also moved from Handsworth Wood to

Edgbaston – from my own tiny flat to the more lavish apartment of our DSM (Deputy Stage Manager), Isla Donald. Phenomenally good at her job, Isla was also a powerhouse of fun and irreverence and we had already become platonically very close. Even though she married and left the business whilst I was still at Birmingham, my friendship with her remains amongst the most enduring of those I have made over the years in the Theatre.

Briefly, I revisited the world of Anthony Thornton, however. In May 1970, I travelled to the Royal Albert Hall to receive my University Degree from our Chancellor, the Queen Mother. This was not my first encounter with that impressive figure. A few years earlier, I witnessed her deft ability to defuse an awkward situation.

A great friend of mine was a member of the National Youth Orchestra as a flautist and he invited me to a concert at the Festival Hall, given in the presence of the orchestra's Patron, the Queen Mother. Afterwards, she descended the staircase to meet the players, as I stood in front to watch.

As she was performing her duties, a sound was heard from further along the receiving line. One nervous musician had let out the most enormous fart. Everyone heard it, and most people gasped. The Patron, however, appeared oblivious and continued on her way - smiling, chatting and shaking hands.

As she approached the offending youth, his face turned a deeper shade of crimson and the line visibly tensed. The Queen Mother finally arrived in front of him. Her cherubic smile remained in place, as she raised her voice almost imperceptibly. "Ah!" she said. "This must be the wind section."

I remembered the occasion – with a grin – as I took my place with hundreds of other graduates at the Albert Hall, on that afternoon in May 1970. In the programme, in red letters: 'The Chancellor has graciously expressed the wish that the audience remain seated'. Already in her 70th year, 'The Chancellor' herself remained standing throughout, however, and I well remember the sense – as I received my 'scroll' – that, for her, I was the most important graduate of all.

But I digress.

Strictly speaking *The Sorrows of Frederick* was not a new play. Written by the American, Romulus Linney, it had already been produced in Los Angeles, Düsseldorf and Vienna, but coming into Peter's orbit at that time there was a sense that this would become his next West End/Broadway success. It was essentially about Frederick the Great and, to a lesser extent, Voltaire. What it lacked in solid dramatic writing, it more than made up for in Theatre and spectacle, and this was a gift for Peter Dews.

Voltaire was played by the French Canadian actor, Peter Jobin, but the towering figure of Frederick himself who dominated the piece was given to the film and stage actor, John Wood.

The production involved hundreds of sound, light and effects cues. There was smoke, there were maroons, and there were vast contraptions that had to be manoeuvred across the stage on cue. There were also pyrotechnics between Peter and John. From the very first day, it seemed that they were determined to cross one another.

John, who had a monumental job to do as Frederick, would voice disagreement with Peter at virtually every turn; and Peter, who always had a total vision of how a part should be played and a production mounted, would bark back at him and join combat on the seemingly most trivial of issues. The atmosphere throughout rehearsals was extremely tense and volatile.

Ironically, Peter Dews was creating a memorable, exciting production, whilst John Wood was building a brilliant tour-de-force performance. The final result would be astonishing, but there was never a moment's letup or rapport between these two men.

My sympathies were with Peter through a sense of loyalty, but also as the Director. And I could not warm to John Wood on a personal level. Even socially, he continued to challenge.

I remember, on one occasion at a party at Isla's flat where there was a grand piano, he took me, personally, to task over a passing comment as to the best way to clean piano keys. John wouldn't, couldn't agree. He always had to be right, and always had to know.

The first night of Frederick, on March 11th 1970, was thrilling. We were all exhausted at the end, but it couldn't have gone better. Rightly so, everybody congratulated each other but, between Director and Star there was only iciness.

John muttered that as soon as Peter was away, (he was leaving for another production at Chichester), he John Wood would do things his way. At the same time, Peter confident of a transfer to London and New York was already sounding out a replacement leading man, in the person of Christopher Plummer.

The transfer never materialized but, from all reports, I doubt that Peter would have fared any better with that particular choice. He would certainly not have got a better performance.

But there is an intriguing twist to this tale. Not long afterwards, Peter invited me to spend a couple of days with him and Anne at their cottage near Chichester. Drama started from the moment I arrived at the theatre.

Laurence Harvey had had an accident and was hospitalised. He was one of the stars of the season and the desperate hunt for a replacement was on. With less than appropriate timing, I wandered into the building and proudly asked for Peter. To his credit, he came to greet me, but then instantly bundled me into Sir John Clements's office, Artistic Director at that time, whilst the business of phoning agents and checking availabilities went on. It was a very bemused John Clements, who arrived to discover this unexpected and embarrassed young man sitting in front of his desk. Without turning a hair, he merely opened the drinks cabinet and plied me with scotch and soda.

In the midst of the frenzy of that day's crisis, Peter appeared in the office, with a wicked grin on his face and a piece of paper in his hand. It was a telegram, and he read it out loud: "Available and Ready STOP. Waiting for your Call STOP. John."

With all the chutzpah and gall at his command, John Wood was putting himself forward to replace Laurence Harvey. And, equally, with all the sweetness and pettiness of the revenge so eagerly awaited, Peter was happily refusing an offer that might have made very good sense.

For my part, it turned out that I had been summoned to Chichester for a different purpose altogether.

*   *   *   *   *

One crisis dealt with in a day, that evening, over coffee and cognac whilst Anne busied herself in the kitchen, the spotlight was turned on me. Here was a clue to the extraordinary ambivalence of Peter Dews's personality and the way that he ran his theatre in Birmingham. In the midst of rehearsals in Chichester, and even whilst gathering further kudos and international reputation as a director, he had summoned his stage manager for a purpose.

It had come to his attention that I was conducting an affair with someone in the administration (true), and that this was having an adverse effect, (possibly) on the cuckolded partner, a key and leading member of that administration. I must, Peter said, "cease forthwith."

That edict came as a surprise. Never mind that I felt hurt and humiliated, manipulated, as my private life now was by the Artistic Director of the company. In the Dews family we all had our responsibilities, and we were all answerable to the father figure who employed us. I grudgingly gave my word.

It seemed as though my future hung in the balance. My copybook looked to be permanently blotted. Yet the feeling only lasted a moment. The second part of the plan followed.

"So, luvvy," in that broad Yorkshire accent, and with an even broader grin, "I understand you want to be a Director. We'll have to see what we can do about it, won't we?" And Peter, unlike me on that occasion, was true to his word.

Did I mention that we were moving to a new theatre?

The old Rep theatre was cramped, over stretched and creaked more and more under the weight of all that it was expected to contain and sustain. It was also steeped in history and flickered with shadows of actors from the past. It wasn't hard to believe tales of a ghost, even if you never got to experience a sighting.

The original Birmingham Repertory Theatre company evolved from The Pilgrim Players, who presented their first production in 1907 and continued at various venues until 1912. It was then that they announced plans to build their own theatre, in Station Street. Barry Jackson who engineered the move opened the new building in February, 1913 and still, in 1970, people spoke of seeing him around. But I can testify to another presence. After all, it's not unusual for elderly theatre buildings to play host to their own ghosts.

I first became aware of something, late at night, when I was the last person to leave. There was a passageway that ran underneath the auditorium, emerging at a street entrance, where a key was turned and the building left secure. That passageway was as dimly lit as my memory, as to why on this one occasion I was entrusted to lock up. But there I was, and having checked that nobody was left backstage or in the dressing rooms and that I was truly alone, I switched off the lights and made my way below.

Empty theatres can be spooky at the best of times and, halfway along that darkened eerie passageway, I became aware of the sound of footsteps behind me. I stopped to listen, but instead of turning back to investigate, I walked faster towards the door at the far end. The footsteps behind me appeared to increase their pace shortly after.

When I reached the safety of the street, I called back and waited. There was a loud 'clunk' and then silence. Nobody emerged from the darkness and nobody answered my calls. Eventually, I closed and locked the door. The following day, I was relieved not to hear of any actor accidentally incarcerated overnight, and when I recounted my tale to others, heads nodded: "The Ghost."

Later, I got the sighting. It was during a performance and I was seated in the prompt corner, as usual. There wasn't a lot of light coming into the wings and I knew there was a good 10 minutes before I was due to call the next entrance. Behind me, and around a corner between myself and the pass door from the dressing rooms sat the DSM (Isla Donald), at the sound desk, the 'pan'.

There were no cues and I was pretty relaxed about the way things were going, when suddenly a figure was standing alongside me. I assumed that one of the actors had come to watch the scene in progress, and I turned to acknowledge her. But this was no actor.

She wore long clothes from an altogether different century and her face was masked by long hair that looked silver in the light. I flicked my attention back to the stage and to the script, before turning once more to check out exactly who had come into the wings. There was no one there.

Since everyone had to pass the 'pan' to get to the wings, I left the corner to ask Isla: "Who had come through? and why?" She shrugged her shoulders. She'd seen no one and didn't understand what I was talking about. My visitor had been… "The Ghost."

But now the clock was ticking. The foundation stone for a new building had already been laid by Jenny Lee, the then Arts Minister. From April 1971, we would all be out of a job for several months at least.

Meanwhile, half the company had high tailed off to Chicago and the Ravinia Festival. I, and my team, were left to hold the fort in Birmingham. It was a severe disappointment to me at the time. The idea of travelling to different parts of the world, and being paid to go, was very appealing… but I had to wait a little longer for that.

At the coalface, those of us who were left continued to work hard. Almost always we rehearsed on stage, so that part of the set had to be struck every night after the performance including furniture and props and then reset at the end of the day's rehearsals. As stage management, it was our job to tape out the outlines of the new set (a tedious job); organise rehearsal props; make coffee for the actors and director; keep the prompt script updated with moves, cuts in the script, or special requests; keep notes in rehearsal to send to every department; prompt (of course); laugh at jokes (funny or not); and generally look after everybody's well being.

Then, we would grab a quick snack or sandwich and turn our attention to the evening performance, check props, sound, lights, dressing rooms, etc., etc.. We were rarely away before 11.00pm assuming there was no late night show and it was only then that we might get to a restaurant and enjoy something more substantial to eat.

After the Chicago company returned to Station Street in triumph, I was summoned to Peter Dews's office, the "inner sanctum". Of course, I'd been there many times but, on this occasion, it all had the air of something very serious as I climbed the stairs and threaded my way through the reception area and other offices. When I emerged a short time after, I was stunned.

I knew that the Christmas production and the show that would see us into the New Year and out of the old building was going to be the Reginald Arkell/Alfred Reynolds musical romp through history, *1066 & All That*. Only one stage manager was required and as head of the junior team I would again lose out. Would I be leaving before everyone else?

In the event, it was decided that not for the first time my piano playing skills would be dusted off and I would be put in the pit, as Assistant MD, on second piano. Had I really progressed in 18 months? Yet why, after leaving Peter's office, did I walk through the theatre on air, believing that from here on in I was on my way up?

It was well known that Peter was planning something special for the closure of the old Rep, an announcement had already been made in the Press. Since so many actors now at the very top of their profession had trod the boards in Station Street through its history, it was decided to invite many of them to return for the theatre's closure.

An anthology had been devised, celebrating that history, and to be presented by those star actors on the last night. As Peter was going to be rehearsing in Chichester for much of the week or two before, he needed a co-director. Would I be interested?

The cast list for the show was beginning to gather momentum: Sir Felix Aylmer, Margaret Leighton, Michael Wilding, Rosemary Leach, Alfred Burke, Anna Calder-Marshall, Elizabeth Spriggs, Brenda Bruce, Geoffrey Bayldon, Hubert Gregg, Isobel Black... I was on Cloud Nine.

But, before that, I was in the pit, on second piano. Having decided at the age of 18 not to touch those black and white keys again professionally, I had played them a lot in Birmingham, and I had even written incidental music for one or two late night shows.

Most notably as a pianist, in May 1970, I was one of two musicians in a production of *The Hollow Crown*. I shared the billing with a young guitarist who is now one of the most sought after and successful composers of TV, film and incidental music in the world, and there can be very few people who have gone through life without listening to and appreciating some of his music. His name is George Fenton.

For *1066 & All That*, I shared honours with another musician who went on to make a bit of a name for himself. In fact, he left during the run, promoting me to Musical Director, in order to fulfil his contract with *Coronation Street*. That was Stephen Hancock, and he went off to begin his life leading to a premature death, as Ernie Bishop, husband of Emily.

As I drove back to Bucks that Christmas, I couldn't believe my luck. And, as I drove, it seemed as though I was in one of those sentimental

Hollywood films that always seem to coincide with the festive season. It was Christmas Eve, and we had done two performances that day of *1066*. Just as I approached Banbury, the church bells began to ring for the midnight service; snowflakes began to fall; and the streets began to fill with carol singers and families on their way to church. It was a magical moment, and I looked forward with eagerness to the coming year.

On Saturday, April 3rd 1971 - coincidentally 10 years to the day since the death of Sir Barry Jackson - a Gala Performance of *1066 & All That* was preceded by *The Mighty Line*. I was thrilled to see the special programme issued for the event:

The Mighty Line.
Devised by Peter Dews.
Directed by Peter Dews & Tony Craven.

When the final curtain fell, there were quite a few lumps in the throat. It had been a totally absorbing and humbling experience. To hear Sir Felix Aylmer speak the same opening lines, after 58 years: "If music be the food of love..." and then for him to whisper in my ear, "Thanks, old boy," as he sat down in the wings to watch the rest of the performance, these were rewards enough. At that moment, Theatre embodied all the glamour and magic that I had hoped for as I walked down Station Street more than 18 months before.

And, afterwards, we all got very drunk. There seemed to be an excess of champagne. One particular buddy for the evening was Elizabeth Spriggs. In full evening dress, we both staggered into the car park behind the theatre, champagne glasses clutched tightly in our hands to search for her car. Between us, we must have pulled at the doors of half a dozen or more, and tried with full and earnest concentration to fit her key into the lock of someone else's vehicle.

But, since we continued to giggle, I guess we were very happy. And emotional. I felt part of a great family and, to this day, I have hundreds of distant relatives spread out across the globe.

But where was Home now? Once the doors were locked on the Station Street premises? The new theatre wasn't due to open before the autumn and I needed a job in the interim. Let me introduce Peggy Mount.

When I eventually made it to the New Birmingham Rep, I was also promoted to Company Stage Manager in charge of the entire stage management personnel and with the additional responsibility of looking after the actors. For some reason, I also became the first port of call for any unexpected visitors.

I was barely installed in the new building, when I got a call from the stage door to say that Peggy Mount had arrived "on the off chance" that a tour of the place might be possible. I was intrigued to meet her, partly because of her television fame at that time, but also because, in my school days, I had seen her on stage at the Old Vic, in Zeffirelli's production of *Romeo & Juliet* playing the Nurse, and had been bowled over by the whole experience. Naturally, I dropped what I was doing, and made my way very quickly downstairs.

As we walked around the backstage and technical areas, however, she was subdued and clearly disinterested and conversation was, frankly, difficult. But, as we entered the auditorium, and went through the pass door, her face lit up in an enormous smile. She walked to the centre of the stage and looked out, beaming.

After a while, as I was about to suggest that we move on, her eyes, so tragically blinded later in life, welled up with tears, and that famous gravelly voice rang out, proudly: "At last I can tell myself that I have stood on the stage of the Birmingham Repertory Theatre!" As we made our way out, she told me that I had helped her to achieve a long standing ambition.

She was playing the Alexandra Theatre for a week, and that was where I had spent the summer, as Stage Manager. I had enjoyed it, but it felt as though I'd been relocated from the Classics to Easy Listening. It was not the Rep, and the Rep was something special. Nevertheless, for much of the year, the Alex was a touring theatre, and there were new people arriving every week. I revisited several times afterwards, never knowing quite whom I would encounter. I once came face-to-face with the gentlemanly Michael Denison, whilst his wife and regular colleague Dulcie Gray was audibly turning the air upstairs blue. I also watched a blonde haired lady in blue jeans trotting up the stairs. It was the legendary Marlene Dietrich.

Backstage, the place was buzzing with news of an unfolding drama. Ms Dietrich had apparently inspected the stage and reported that it was not clean. The stage carpenter had been called at home, I forget his name, let's call him 'Jim', and he had indignantly reported that, as far as he was concerned, that stage had been left spotless. There was an impasse, and Ms Dietrich was threatening to get down on her hands and knees and scrub the stage herself.

'Jim' was summoned back to the theatre. My arrival coincided with the wait for his.

Now it has to be said that it was not unknown at that time for Marlene Dietrich to mop her own stage but, clearly, the management at the Alex were keen that she should not be compelled to do so in Birmingham. Nevertheless, 'high noon' was approaching.

'Jim' was a big, burly Brummie and stubborn to-boot. We did not expect him to back down.

He arrived in a lather, effing and blinding, and marched onto his stage to prove his point. In truth, we could probably all have eaten our dinner off it, but he was sent upstairs to convince the lady herself. I watched him as he went slower than MD, and in jeans several sizes larger but with an ever determined air.

We listened, as he knocked on the dressing room door. After a few moments: "Good afternoon, Miss Deertritch. What's this I hear about a dirty stage?" All we heard in reply, was a quiet, "Won't you come in, please?" The door closed. Silence.

I have always been surprised at the youthful energy displayed by Marlene Dietrich, as she swung up those stairs. After all, it was said only a short while after that a special rostrum had to be constructed at the side of the stage for her. With the correct degree of propulsion from a well rehearsed assistant, a single push would deliver her to centre stage, and no further. Whether such freewheeling really did become necessary, I don't know. What I do know is that, after some 15-20 minutes, 'Jim' emerged from that dressing room and like a lamb went straight to the stage and cleaned it again, thoroughly. What took place between those two very different people…

I don't know how I could have been so lucky, but the Alex was starting a summer season around the time I was skipping around the Station Street carpark with Elizabeth Spriggs, and I was offered the job of Stage Manager beginning immediately. The Alex was positioned between the old Rep and the new Rep, and so it was fitting that I should call in there for a few months en route, so to speak.

But then I continued on and, in the late summer of 1971, took up residence at the new theatre, which boasted the second largest stage in the country after the Coliseum, in London. The next 18 months were memorable indeed.

For a brief period, the moon was now our balloon, and people landed on it at regular intervals. Even the Prime Minister of the day Edward Heath came to visit. In one of those intensely artificial moments, we pretended to rehearse, whilst he feigned interest. He stood and watched - the spitting image of his on-screen puppet, as a distinctly self-conscious smile cracked across his face.

He was brought forward to chat to us; gave me an up-and-downer; and thrust out his hand. I was transported back to my teens, and an occasion that also stayed with me.

I had won a particular piano competition and was thrilled to have a very splendid cup presented to me by the legendary English pianist, John Ogdon. A big bear of a man he was at that time, and I felt the full force of his stature as I arrived on the platform to receive his congratulations, but the shake of his hand was completely incompatible with the delicacy of his keyboard touch. With supreme confidence, I might have betted that day that never again would I reach out to take such a cold, fish-like slab.

But I reckoned without Edward Heath, and the handshake that he brought with him to Birmingham. After stiffly thanking us and with heaving shoulders, wishing us well he left.

For the meantime, we were all proudly discovering our new home - gleaming and new, fully high-tech and spacious. Wheeled out of the hangar, we stood on the tarmac awaiting our maiden flight. For this, Peter Dews had chosen to open with the British première of an American musical. The sun was shining that September, as the cast arrived for rehearsals. In typical fashion, the management laid on champagne. The Press were invited to join in. And Cheryl Kennedy one of the leading actors announced, "I don't think any of us could wish for a better start than this."

In retrospect, we might have been playing the opening scenes of one of those airline disaster movies. I had grown used to hard work rewarded with smooth running production. What minor hiccups there had been were usually sorted quickly and forgotten. On occasion, they were laughable - just a bumpy ride, with seat belts fastened. So I was not prepared for the full scale turbulence that lay ahead, especially when forgetting to keep up all appearances of dignity Patricia Routledge whipped up the head winds still further.

Let me try to mark the contrast between a little choppiness and being in the eye of a storm. Between Agatha Christie and Jane Austen.

My season at the Alex had introduced me briefly to the joys of touring and the banalities of Agatha Christie's, *Love From A Stranger*. Our few nights at the Malvern Festival Theatre were idyllic and our days were spent walking in the hills, humming Elgar to each other.

But before that, our first stop was the Empire Theatre, in Sunderland where some of the facilities left a great deal to be desired. Unlike my digs. These, it has to be said, were magnificent. The house was run by a pair of musicians who - after a few years of life "on the road", enduring their fair share of dog-eared attic rooms in damp and unwelcoming boarding-houses - decided to create the ideal 'home from home' for their fellow professionals to rest their weary heads. Every room had a television and a comfortable bed; breakfast was available until teatime; and the aroma of home baked bread and freshly ground coffee seemed to waft through the house in the most delightful way.

But not so fresh were conditions backstage at the Empire. The show relay system for the cast to follow the performance and receive their cues comprised a single speaker that crackled away in the corridor and was meant to be heard in every dressing room.

As the drama on stage headed relentlessly towards its dénouement, the heroine's desperate plight intensified by its being played out in a remote country cottage, the murder was about to be committed. A deadline was set, its approach made only too clear to the audience by a clock, visible on the set, where the hands moved inexorably towards 10.00 - moved by a very patient ASM positioned behind the flat. Just in time would the police arrive and break in through the French windows.

Unfortunately, one night the police were too immersed in a card playing session upstairs to hear their call. Little did they know what havoc their lack of concentration was causing on stage. Firstly, the villain chased the heroine. Then, with a frantic eye on the French windows, she turned and pursued her reluctant killer. Meanwhile, as a galvanized stage management team dashed to the dressing rooms, even Time mysteriously stopped. The clock abandoned by the on duty ASM. Ultimately, the exhausted and angry actress simply gave up, opened the windows and made her own escape, so that the dishevelled coppers, wearing less than full uniform when they did turn up found an out of breath actor, sitting down and begging to be arrested.

I doubt the audience even noticed. Certainly the dear old fellow who played the gardener and who spent much of the show in the wings nursing a hip flask, was not aware of anything amiss.

All was very different, however, one memorable night at the new Rep.

The very first show was called *First Impressions*, and the array of credits it carried should have been warning enough:

Adapted by Abe Burrows, from Helen Jerome's dramatization of Jane Austen's novel, *Pride and Prejudice* with music and lyrics by Robert Goldman, Glenn Paxton and George Weiss.

This was the show that HRH arrived late for and found so "delightfully boring," but it was rather different for a full house that attended an early performance.

First Impressions starred Patricia Routledge, Cheryl Kennedy, Francis Matthews (hot from the extremely successful *Paul Temple* series), with his wife, Angela Browne, a young Gemma Craven (no relation), and an even younger Mary Tamm. In the pit was my old musical comrade Stephen Hancock a.k.a. Ernie Bishop.

The set was designed by a fussy Scot, called Finlay James, and was a mass of filigree - we called him Filigree Finlay. He had a vast stage to fill and cleverly removed part of it, so that he could install a huge staircase in the centre.

The second scene of this extravaganza was played before a front cloth and was all about the arrival of Mr Darcy, Fran Matthews. Whilst the Bennets and assembled townsfolk gathered downstage to sing an interminable number called *Have You Heard The News?* (for which the lyric mostly comprised a repetition of "Welcome, Welcome!"), behind the cloth, the stage was being set for a sumptuous and grand ballroom scene.

As the Darcys, in their carriage, were hustled off on one side by the excited villagers, the front cloth was flown out to reveal the breathtaking spectacle of several pairs of elegantly dancing couples gliding effortlessly up the central staircase, from below the stage, to fill the dazzling ballroom that became Scene Three. Thus, the rapturous applause that followed *Have You Heard The News?* rose to a crescendo as the music changed.

On this particular night, however, there was a fly in the ointment. Or rather, a pony on stage.

Every day, this pony was delivered by its owner to the stage door much to the wonderment of various local children who, never having seen a pony, came to watch the big dog. The animal was then led to the wings and positioned in front of Darcy's carriage, to await its entrance. Francis Matthews and Angela Browne would gamely step into the trap, during the opening bars of *Have You Heard The News?* As the pony trotted off, and the carriage lurched forward, Fran stood up and adopted an imperious smile of condescension at his welcome. Centre stage, the pony and vehicle stopped, whilst its occupants received their thunderous musical acclaim.

At this very moment, on this particular evening, the animal started to relieve itself. It was as though somebody had turned on a tap, and the musicians witnessing this at eye level were the first to become aware. One or two instruments spluttered and stopped. But there was more to come.

The beginnings of what would quickly become a large pile of steaming pony business were spotted now by chorus members and leading actors on stage, many of whom failed to maintain their harmonies. It scarcely mattered, though, because the audience reaction now drowned out much of the singing as the pile grew larger. The only two people in that theatre who were blissfully unaware of precisely what was happening beneath them were Fran and Angela. That song had never seemed so interminable, I am sure.

To complete the chaos, the fly crew decided to go ahead without a cue and take out the cloth. Try to imagine the looks of disbelief on the faces of those beautifully clad ballroom guests, as they swirled up from below the stage - at first, unaware of what awaited them - and then came, literally, face to face with the steaming pile.

All the rehearsed choreography was set aside, as instinct drove each couple to take whatever avoiding action was necessary. Unable to stop, with more guests ascending behind them, they spread out and slithered and slid to the music.

Backstage, things had quickly livened up. I well remember a crimson faced banshee of a Pat Routledge screaming and yelling at me: "Do something!" And there was only one course of action that I could take.

In attendance were two ASMs in flunkey costume, ready to make an occasional appearance and to help dress the stage. However, they were not equipped with any period cleaning implements. And so it was that they were sent onto that vast stage, beating a path through an array of bemused dancers, to reach the offending pile. One of them - Harris Deans, as he was called then - carried in his hands a regular 20th century dustpan and brush. He could be forgiven, as he completed his task, the huge grin and deep bow that he delivered, brought on by the biggest ovation of the evening.

Appropriately perhaps, the ballroom number was entitled, *A Perfect Evening*. Oh, Princess Margaret, why weren't you there?

The shine was coming off very quickly. The Press was kind to the theatre, and to Peter, but we could all read between the lines. He'd got it wrong. Despite the lavishness of the set and costumes, and the impressive scale of the staging, the adaptation was heavy and the music unmemorable. This was not the start we had hoped for, and the second production of the season was pretty dire. On the horizon, though, was the arrival at the end of the year of Ronnie Barker and Joan Sims.

Another musical, but this was something with class. *Good Time Johnny*, it was called, and was based on *The Merry Wives of Windsor*. Music, book and lyric credits were shared by James Gilbert and Julian More, and the director/choreographer was Alan Lund (Canadian, I believe).

To my mind, it was streets ahead of the opener, with some dazzling routines and wonderfully comic performances from the two stars. Unfortunately, however, and through no fault of its own, this was also plagued from the start.

*   *   *   *   *

There's often a great buzz in the Green Room through rehearsals and, when things are going really well, you can't wait to start the day's work. Of course, a great deal depends on the personalities involved. In my last year as a Company Stage Manager, I witnessed the torment that comes when a toxic mix of ill tempered and unhappy individuals get together. But by that time, the elephant that was the new Rep was already beginning to take on a clear shade of white. And we all looked back nostalgically to Station Street days.

At the end of 1971, however, I couldn't have asked for better. Despite a frosty start (all down to a misunderstanding), Joan Sims and I became firm friends. And Ronnie Barker lit up the rehearsal room the moment he arrived. He was a delightful man and a truly professional performer. I have worked with comics and comic actors since and you will read further on about their darker sides but I never saw such a side to Ronnie Barker. But then I didn't know him for very long.

Early on, he had to withdraw from the show. He contracted some kind of throat infection and was told that, if he carried on, his voice would be irrevocably damaged. It was an immense blow to everyone, and I know that Ronnie was deeply saddened and affected by the decision that he had to take. However spirited his replacement John Baddeley was, a huge hole had been blown in the show. But there were further squalls to come.

A mystery virus hit the cast and, day after day, last minute understudies and replacements had to be organised and rehearsed and regular announcements made to the audience.

A steady trouper almost to the end was Joanie Sims. I can honestly say that I have rarely worked with anyone who could bring a smile to my face so instantly, whenever I was in her company. I always gravitated to Joan's dressing room after the show, and we invariably moved on to the flat that she occupied at the top of the building.

There, we would talk long into the night about the *Carry On* films, her co-stars and her RADA experience. She very much wanted to be taken seriously as an actress and, to my mind, she was capable of being so good, but was rarely given the chance to prove it. That depressed her, of course, and maybe went some way to explaining her heavy drinking.

One day, she called me and said that she had totally given up cigarettes and alcohol. "I think they're bad for me," she said. Of course, I was enormously impressed until I went to her dressing room after the show, that very same day. The air was thick with tobacco smoke, and there was a half bottle of gin on the table. "Only before the show!" she giggled, when I reminded her of her earlier announcement.

The *Carry On* producer, Peter Rogers, never once raised her two and half thousand pound fee, despite the dozens of films she made for him, and she did struggle to make money.

It was upsetting to see how frustrated she was at having to go to London on a Sunday during the run, for a film première. She wanted just to be able to catch a bus and turn up as any other audience member might. But, because she was a celebrity, she needed to spend money on an outfit; a driver to collect her; and then to wait and whisk her away again at the end of the night; together with all the other extras. She needed, she said, to be seen to be generous. "Otherwise, they just think you're on your way down."

Kenneth Williams had suggested they got married, but she just laughed. "You won't even let me share your taxi home!" she retorted. Maybe he needed the feel good factor that, in my experience, Joan Sims always provided. Even when she finally succumbed to the dreaded virus and had to take to her bed during the last few performances of *Good Time Johnny*, she didn't stop giggling whenever any of us went to visit.

Afterwards, we stayed in touch and I went to her house in Fulham, at every available opportunity.

Once the light that she and Ronnie Barker had brought to Birmingham moved on, however, the theatre hit the kind of turbulence that, in my time there at least, left it irrevocably damaged.

Now, I'm well aware that it's nearly time to change the set. After all, I've written the word 'Birmingham' ad nauseam and so many characters and personalities have passed through and gone on to other things. Even Peter Dews will shortly leave after impersonating Derek Jacobi. By rights, he should have taken over at Chichester when the Artistic Director's job became vacant again, and when he was at the peak of his success. But good sense was replaced by commercialism as so often happens and the post went to Keith Michell instead.

Anne was, as they say, already measuring the curtains but, by the time the job did come Peter's way, his health failed; he had a stroke; and he wrote to me to say he'd been told it would take a minimum of 2 years for him to effect a full recovery. The damage was done.

There is a pernicious streak in this business that seems to gloat at the sight of a career in free fall. Ironically and sadly, Peter finally ended up in Birmingham again - this time, guesting at the rather dismal drama school there, and died in 1997.

But in this story we're not quite ready to move on, not whilst such luminaries as the aforementioned Derek Jacobi, Patrick Mower and Keith Baxter are waiting in the wings. And even though I should also be changing costume by now and slipping at last into the role of Director, Fate it seemed had another interim part for me. I was taken for a while into a different area of life altogether.

In less than 3 years in the crazy world we call Theatre, I had risen through the ranks, from ASM (not quite the bottom, there were Student ASMs in those days, on a pound a week) to Stage Manager; to Company Stage Manager; and now suddenly I was made Concerts & Events Manager. In their wisdom, the powers that be had decided that we needed Sunday night entertainment. A small budget was provided and I couldn't believe my luck - the Concerts & Events Manager had carte blanche to book whatever artistes he wanted.

Within days, it became clear that the money wasn't going to stretch very far and so I decided that a couple of cheap acts might help to pay for something a little bit special.

Nevertheless, everyone seemed delighted when we kicked off with musicians from the City of Birmingham Symphony Orchestra, in a *Mozart Serenade*. That was followed by *An Evening With Jake Thackray* - a ubiquitous performer at the time whose talents I could never personally appreciate, but who turned out to be a popular choice, and saved me some money so that we could move up a gear.

We had a fantastically exciting Sunday night with Kenny Ball and his jazz musicians, who almost lifted the roof off the place and which led to calls in the papers for more regular jazz events. I was also thrilled to organise a show with Georgie Fame (affable and co-operative) and Alan Price (sullen and awkward), and I have to say that they both delivered an electrifying two hours or so, both as soloists and in their famous duo form together with *The Armpit Jug Band*.

Another clear triumph was to persuade the Festival Chamber Orchestra of London to perform all six of Bach's *Brandenburg Concertos* in one programme - a rare event.

There were two ladies from that series, however, that remain especially memorable for me, and for very different reasons. It is also no exaggeration to admit that, for both of them, I took my job above and well beyond the call of duty.

The first brought a mix of Politics, the Arts and a touch of Royalty. This was Moura Lympany, the concert pianist. I'd been a fan of hers for some time and, although it was stretching the budget, I arranged for her to travel to Birmingham, on November 26th 1972, to give a recital. And the tickets sold well.

The weather was cold and misty, but our guest arrived well in advance and spent some time at the piano, getting used to the acoustics and running through passages from her programme. We had taken delivery that morning of her own piano from Steinway's, the particular instrument that she favoured, and which followed her around the country. It was the venue's responsibility to hire it and deal with its safe delivery and return.

After satisfying herself that all was well, Ms Lympany retired to her dressing room, to rest. Before her lie down, however, she asked if I might accord her a special favour. She had absolutely promised that she would arrive, albeit late, at the Savoy Hotel, in London, to join a private reception given by the Prime Minister, (the one with the fish hands). In order to honour that promise, she needed somebody "to whisk her down the M1" immediately after the performance.

From the look in her eyes, I knew instantly that there was only one person in line for this job.

And so it was that on that cold November night, this 24 year old (Yours Truly) opened the door of his somewhat battered old vehicle, so that Moura Lympany could be sped to the Savoy Hotel and have drinks with the Right Honourable Edward Heath.

She and I had already grown close. Earlier, I had led her to the side of the stage from her dressing room; taken into safe keeping her mink lined muff which contained a tiny hot water bottle; and listened to her entire programme of Schumann, Brahms, Rachmaninov and others. I had waited through the applause and a couple of encores. How could I refuse the after show trek?

What we talked about on the drive I can't remember. Initially, I was in dread of the car breaking down, or running out of petrol, or suffering a blow out somewhere on the motorway. But the company was so easy and relaxed that, by the time I pulled up on the Embankment so that she could slip through the backdoor of the hotel, it felt as if I was dropping off an old friend. The return journey was much more of a chore, and seemed a good deal longer.

The following morning, I got a call in my office from the Mayfair home of… guess who? She wanted to thank me again for making it possible for her to get to the reception which she had enjoyed. She was anxious to know that I had got home safely, and particularly keen to tell me of the matchmaking she had done at the Savoy.

She had sprinkled a little magic dust on Jeremy Thorpe who was then the leader of the Liberal Party and Marion Harewood ex-wife of the Queen's cousin, and herself an accomplished concert pianist.

Thorpe's first wife, Caroline, had been killed in a car accident. Marion née Stein was from a Viennese musical family. And some time later it was announced that Jeremy Thorpe would marry Marion Harewood. I often wonder whether any part of our political history might have been different if Moura Lympany had not attended the Prime Minister's reception that evening.

But then there was Juliette Greco.

This was an engagement that I worked very hard to bring about. The appearance of this French legend was certain to bring real class to the Sunday evening concert series. But the problem was… money.

She wouldn't give any concert without her own musicians in

Mlle. Greco - Louche and sexy

attendance, and the cost of transporting them all from Paris, in addition to fees and payments, was in my limited budgetary terms astronomical. But I could not let this prospect go.

The breakthrough came in a call from her agent. Juliette Greco had been booked on the Parkinson Show to promote her new album. In order to sing one of the songs from that album, she would need her musicians. The television company was happy to pick up the expenses and, since she would now be in England anyway, getting her to Birmingham could finally be an affordable proposition. Furthermore, I could legitimately bill this: The Only UK Stage Appearance of the Year. We had a deal.

I was ecstatic, and raced to tell anyone who would listen. However, as the date of the show approached, it became clear that Juliet Greco was not a big draw in Birmingham even if it was her "only UK stage appearance". Some people did travel from London, but ticket sales were desperately disappointing. The auditorium, which could resemble the north face of the Eiger on such occasions, was going to look depressingly bare.

With a deep sense of embarrassment, I waited at the stage door for Ms Greco to arrive and, with some crazy idea that it might just make the news a little more palatable, I used my hesitant French to explain that there would be only a small house. I was awed by this glamorous figure in black, and it all seemed so cruel.

Of course, a shadow of disappointment crossed her face, but it was quickly chased off by a flirtatious smile and that hoary old chestnut:

35

"Well, we must make it even more worthwhile for those who are here." She did seem to mean it at the time, and she gave a tremendous show that evening. Those who stayed at home missed a rare treat. And for me, an even rarer treat was waiting.

Her manager asked if I would have dinner with them both after the show, in the restaurant of their overnight hotel. They had enjoyed their visit and appreciated all of my efforts, and we had a very lively time over the meal. As the evening was coming to an end, however, Juliette Greco flagged a very overt proposition to me. If accepted, it would have meant not seeing my own bed for several more hours yet.

I remember how my heart raced, the night I drove, in the early hours in madcap fashion, round and round the Arc de Triomphe, in Paris. I felt liberated, exhilarated and happy to be alive.

I was on a high. I'd been to see another extraordinary French performer, at the Casino de Paris. This was a revue choreographed by Roland Petit; with songs by Serge Gainsbourg; and starring the amazing Zizi Jeanmaire. I knew two people in the show - Jay Benedict and Richard Denning - and I stayed with Richard.

But the show took my breath away from the opening number, *Zizi t'as pas d'sosie*, when I swear a full jumbo jet flew across the auditorium and landed on stage. Steps were put in place, the doors opened and an immense chorus of stewards and stewardesses came down in advance of the emergence of the star, petite, charismatic and totally over the top. I was lucky enough to meet Jeanmaire after the show, and was not disappointed. The revue was called *Zizi Je T'Aime*, and I felt it was not inappropriate.

Looking into the eyes of Juliette Greco that night, at the Albany Hotel in Birmingham, I had the same feeling. Fortunately, perhaps, her manager, who had no doubt seen it all before, stepped in and vetoed any plans the star might have had. Nevertheless, I was given the lady's address in Paris to look her up, if ever I was, etc., etc..

When I was next in France, it was far too long after the event for me to even consider it. But, to this day, I have an LP signed and inscribed, in heavy black felt tip: *avec merci et tendresse, to Tony. GRECO.* signed with her trademark love heart.

She flew away, and I began to harbour thoughts of doing the same.

I was gathering some directing experience; I'd done a few late night shows and anthologies; I'd helped Peter Dews with *The Mighty Line*; and I eventually got to direct my first full length play *Dingo*, by Charles Wood in the newly opened Studio Theatre.

I had also witnessed directors at work both good and bad. None of them came up to Peter's standards of brilliance. One of them arrived on the first day of rehearsal, to suggest a read through, "because I haven't had a chance to look at the script yet"; one of them cried on my shoulder because he couldn't cope with life in rehearsal; and one of them had the temerity to ignore Mary Tamm and then immediately regretted it.

Peter's successor was nothing but a pale shadow of that man and in my last months at the Rep things, literally, began to fall apart.

*   *   *   *   *

The director's chair can be a dark and lonely place, and I have often felt cause to be grateful for some of the lessons learned whilst watching other people. That luxury is not available once you move into the job yourself.

First lesson: do something. My mentor once said to me, "Don't hesitate to answer a question. The important thing is to give an answer. If you're wrong, you can always change your mind later."

It is true that, from time to time, an actor finds himself/herself miscast and spends a confused and bewildering time in rehearsal wondering why things are not going as planned. It's important for the director, ultimately responsible, to be at his most enlightening and supportive as well as providing justification for offering the part in the first place.

But there are other times when an actor well cast spends the rehearsal period confused and unhappy for a very different reason.

At the start of 1972, Patrick Mower and Jennifer Hilary arrived at the Rep to star in Shaw's, *Man & Superman*. Jennifer was already hugely experienced, and Patrick was particularly well known at that time for the TV series, *Callan* (though, of course, he has recently moved into soap territory), and was a glamorous and exciting choice for Tanner. The anticipation that we all felt quickly evaporated, however, as our leading actors found themselves marooned, without anchor, and drifting towards disaster.

It's quite possible that those two, with different theatrical backgrounds and with a very different approach to their work, might have been at odds throughout the production. Patrick's vanity and Jenny's quick witted humour might have collided except that they faced the same battle. They were lost and needed help, and to their credit managed to keep their frustration in check for much of the working day. But the director was giving them nothing.

Shrewdly, the two leads worked together after hours to solve their problems. Not having an evening show to perform made it possible. Different corners and unoccupied rooms of the building were sought out, and they would ask for my assistance, as they struggled to make sense of the scenes they had together.

Initially, of course, I was asked as the keeper of the book to feed them the lines and the moves but, increasingly, they used me as a sounding board, even soliciting my opinion, and I like to feel that I provided them with some much needed and productive feedback and suggestion.

It certainly fed a hunger in me. Forced to sit in rehearsal during the day and watch the agonising tedium of a production going nowhere, I at least got an opportunity to voice my own would-be director's opinion. When it was taken up with respect and very often acted upon by two highly talented and professional actors, I began to achieve confidence, and ask myself more strongly: "When will I be able to do this legitimately?"

It was a turning point for me. It was also a significant time, I believe, for Mary Tamm.

Somebody will correct me, I'm sure, and prove otherwise, but I am convinced that *Man & Superman* marked Mary's professional acting début. As indeed, I remember her as a fun-loving, down-to-earth Yorkshire lass. She certainly had spunk.

The part she played in the show was undoubtedly a minor one, a Maid, but Mary was determined to make the most of her entrance and get it right. Each time the scene was rehearsed, her contribution was ignored.

She tried different accents; she attempted a slightly skittish movement; she even developed a heavily asthmatic delivery; but nothing she did invoked any kind of reaction from the director, and Mary began to feel that she was proving desperately inadequate.

Matters came to a head at the Technical Rehearsal, often a tense and difficult time, but this was a production that was not particularly technical. Mary Tamm was emphatic that she would grab her last opportunity to get a note from the director. She made a slow and lengthy entrance, for which, on this occasion, her character had developed an awesome and exaggerated limp.

Once again, not a word came from the auditorium.

Unable to mask her frustration and disappointment any longer, Mary turned towards where the director was sitting. "Excuse me. Is what I'm doing alright?"

"What?"

"Well, I don't know whether you've noticed, but I have changed my background, my breathing and now my gait, and you have said absolutely nothing to me."

The director's reply rang out. "I'm sorry, darling, but your part is just too small for me to direct."

Patrick and Jennifer, with nothing to lose, immediately jumped to Mary's defence, and the director finally realised that he had long since lost all control and respect. I must have shaken my head in disbelief.

Now consider Lesson Two: and that is, once you've mastered your own job, let the actors do theirs.

One or two confessions appear along the way in this story - some more difficult to acknowledge than others - but it is true that I have never been one for writing fan letters. However, I happily confess to sending one in 1983.

Of all the plays that I would like to have directed in my career but never did, I guess *Cyrano de Bergerac* would rate high on the list. It's not often done, it's very expensive, and needs a large cast. So, when I heard that the Royal Shakespeare Company were doing it, I had to book seats, though I went along in trepidation that I was going to hate it. Derek Jacobi was playing the lead role, and I confess (note: so soon after the first confession) that I was not sure that he would be up to it.

In the event, he turned out to be more than that. He was wonderful, and afterwards I couldn't resist writing to tell him so. I should point out that we had worked together at Birmingham, and so it was not such an audacious act as it might sound. In characteristic style, he replied.

To play Cyrano, he wrote, was "such a thrill; to earn the approval of my peers is an added honour. Bless you and thank you." He didn't need to thank me, my letter to him had talked of witnessing the "natural successor to Olivier" that night, and I meant it. And the Laurence Olivier connection was a strong one.

A decade earlier, Derek had arrived in Birmingham to emulate Olivier's outrageous achievement 27 years before that of playing, in one evening, Oedipus in the tragedy of Sophocles's, *Oedipus Rex*, and Mr Puff in Sheridan's, *The Critic*. Larry's performance, at the Old Vic, had become the stuff of theatrical legend, and understandably so.

In the brief space of a 15 minute interval, the centre of the Greek tragedy of King Oedipus is transformed into the highly theatrical, high camp, bewigged, made-up and perfumed fop that is Mr Puff. And Derek was brilliant. Since that time, I haven't always been moved by his work but, when he hits the target as often as he did in Birmingham, he can rate with the very best.

Of course, he was a young man then bristling with energy, popular with the company, and up for anything. My image remains of an actor who was such FUN. After his nightly tour-de-force performances, he would often arrive at the stage door ready to hit the town, do the clubs with us, and generally unwind. His hair sometimes changed colour as well, from an outrageous rinse that he would use.

And then one night it seemed that tragedy had struck.

I should mention here that Jocasta was being played by Margaretta Scott, an actress I found vulgar and demanding. She occupied one of the theatre flats for the rehearsal period (the one where I spent such happy times with Joan Sims), and had to be evicted by the Theatre Manager when she refused to move out on the agreed and contracted date. There were some unpleasant scenes upstairs when she finally complied - with bad grace it has to be said.

Her appearance in Oedipus was over the top of a huge rostrum and looked, for all the world, like Judy Garland, staggering on to perform in her later years. Peggy Scott was dressed in a cabaret style, black sequined number, that must have brought tears to Derek Jacobi's eyes whenever he caught sight of her. Maybe it was this that caused him at one memorable performance to fall from the rostrum.

He managed the rest of that evening, but it was uncertain whether he would be fit enough to appear again. Fortunately, the plays being in repertoire, we had a few days grace during which we hoped - we prayed - he would recover. The alternative was something we couldn't bear to contemplate.

This was the last production to be overseen as Artistic Director by Peter Dews. This will be his last, his very last, appearance. One of Peter's abiding weaknesses was his readiness to take to the stage in a crisis in a trice.

Long before Derek and I worked together, and whilst I was still in the pit in Station Street, pounding the piano keys with an eye on Ernie Bishop across the way from me, I watched in horror and then open amusement at another of those calamitous occasions.

Although company member Jacquie Ann Carr was credited as choreographer on *1066 & All That*, there was one routine that was going to be very much a Dews routine. The Roman Soldiers, as they sang their way through the opening number, *We're Going Home*, were drilled and rehearsed for hours.

Peter would stand in the auditorium and bark his orders, scream at anyone who didn't master the simple marching routine until even he was hoarse. They marched to the left; they marched to the right; they went into formation; and then they turned the other way all in time to the music, whilst singing a crass and ludicrous set of lyrics. It quite simply set the tone for the evening.

Once the show was in performance, and one of the company was off sick, Peter's moment had come.

If you took one of the pieces from that opening jigsaw, it would suffer. But to replace it with a stocky, balding Yorkshire man, who could barely fit into his toga and helmet, was tempting the Fates to their limit. Seated at my piano in the pit, I got a perfect view of the carnage on stage that night.

The precision of the routine, drilled over weeks, simply fell apart as a certain Roman soldier made one wrong turn after another. He trod on other actors; he collided with all of his men; and, as they all toppled like dominos, our steady thump on the piano keys was drowned by the laughter around us.

To his credit, Peter very much saw and enjoyed the joke, and never donned that toga again. And a Roman Soldier in a light hearted romp at Christmas is one thing. But Oedipus?

I'm sure Derek Jacobi did all in his power to recover in time, but was advised to wait just one more day - this was just a matinee, after all. The call had come, and Peter disappeared into the dressing room. He had prepared, as we all knew. He would have to carry the script with him, of course, and we jokingly suggested that, after the character's blinding, the book would have to be in Braille.

Those of us who were available (and in a spirit of solidarity, I am sure) rushed to the stalls to take our seats.

I admire to this day Peter's composure, as he appeared at the top of the rostrum and held out his hand (the bookless one). It was a gesture of Derek's, but with only one hand Peter's looked alarmingly like a Nazi salute. He struggled manfully through the performance, as we in the stalls struggled to maintain our supportive expressions. That is, until Judy Garland forgot what was happening.

There was a moving moment in the production when Derek used to sit at Peggy's feet and bury his face in her lap. Through her next speech, she would then run her hands through his hair, with the full intensity of a mother's love for her son. Perhaps by this point in the afternoon we had become accustomed to the image of Oedipus as a stocky, round, ruddy faced Yorkshire man with a book in his hand. But, as he dropped to his knees and sought out his mother's lap, it became too much for us to watch.

Jocasta first stroked, then looked in horror at, before recoiling from, the sweating bald head that she had inadvertently begun to run her hands over. Audience numbers were quickly reduced by at least three, as we dashed to the nearest exit.

*　　　　*　　　　*　　　　*　　　　*

I'm sorry to head for the end of Part One with a report of major tragedy, but what happened when *Macbeth* came into the following season's programme provided at least a dozen lessons for any aspiring director in just exactly what to avoid.

It's a play that traditionally flirts with the Fates and brings bad luck. But there was nothing so mystical, nor intriguing, about this production. It was, truly, a mess. And so much of it could have been avoided. All the different personalities involved seemed to tug in different directions from the very first day, and it was obvious that nobody even liked each other. In fact, in whatever permutation you put those leading figures, I doubt that you would have come up with any combination that wasn't riddled with distrust, disagreement and a lack of respect.

So as this is a developing tragedy, in every particular, let me first provide a cast list of the leading characters.

John Napier, the designer, is a man who has done remarkable work since that time, and has become one of the most respected in his field. His contribution to this particular Shakespeare production, however, was dire.

Keith Baxter, the leading man, arrived in Broad Street with his dogs and his vanity and was allowed to turn Shakespeare's shortest play into the longest and most tedious of any that I can think of.

Sara Kestelman, the leading lady, whom I hardly saw smile through-out her time in Birmingham, and who remains in my memory, more than anything else, for a particularly insensitive remark she made.

Derek Goldby, the director, who had come to prominence for the première production of Stoppard's *Rosencrantz & Guildenstern are Dead* - though it is often rumoured that the responsibility for that play's success lay elsewhere.

Del Henney, cast as Macduff, but who seemed to lose the will very early on.

David King, one of the actors involved, whose chief appearance comes later, but whose canine comrade came into direct conflict with Keith Baxter's hounds.

Everybody gathered on the opening day of rehearsal with high expectations as is so often the case and, as the costume designs were displayed, there was no doubting that they looked impressive. Visually, they conjured up a world of chilling barbarism and primitive living, and the imagery they inspired of raw tribal conflict resonated excitedly around the assembled group of actors.

Costume designs are often unveiled as miniature works of art, and John's were exceptionally detailed, bold in both concept and execution. However, there were some who were quick to question their practicality.

Nevertheless, as we turned to regard the set design, there were whistles of astonishment, at the audacity of what was being proposed. Once again, it looked extraordinarily dramatic, a huge, elliptical crater, raised at the upstage end and dominating the entire length of the playing area. Upon this, sword fights, battles, witchcraft and tragedy were to be played out over a period of weeks, but which would also have to make way at regular intervals for other productions in the repertoire. I think that some of the whistles were an acknowledgement of the scale of problems to come.

Cast in the role of Macbeth was Keith Baxter, a man who took himself extremely seriously. The laborious and self indulgent manner in which he delivered the verse contorted each performance into a marathon of concentration for those of us who had to listen. Keith is a hugely likeable and talented actor, but on this occasion needed a rod of iron on his back, in the shape of a Director.

This task fell to Derek Goldby, and he was very far from being up to it. It seemed to me that he was so obsessed with the problems and misunderstood intricacies of his own role that he proved incapable of helping anyone else with theirs.

There is an entire breed of director who finds it hard, after the initial blocking and superficial interpretation of a script, to advance any further. He (or she) will then fill the time by running sections endlessly, until they have been drained of any spontaneity, thrill or danger that might have lurked there in the first place.

I remember countless sessions, in a dingy rehearsal hall in Digbeth, watching Derek and Sara (Lady Macbeth) go through their paces. Again and again, Sara would deliver her, "Unsex me here" speech and each time after a pause, Derek's response would be: "Fine. (Another pause) Let's just do it one more time."

Meanwhile, Del Henney, a gritty and virile Macduff, was left on his own to sink or swim and, like Macbeth himself, with little control over his own destiny. He very quickly lost the battle.

As rehearsals ground along, and at the end of each day's work, a painful routine developed. I would be summoned to see the director. He was staying in the same flat that was so reluctantly vacated by Margaretta Scott, and in which I had sat so many times whilst helping Joan Sims to empty another gin bottle, as we gossiped about stars of stage and screen.

Through Macbeth rehearsals, I climbed the stairs to that top corridor very much more slowly. It became my job to bolster, encourage, lift morale and listen to bouts of rage against every member of the cast. Or, more usually, just to witness uncomprehending tears as they cascaded onto my young shoulders.

Finally, we reached the production week. It was already becoming clear that the costumes over which everyone had ooh-d and ah-d a few weeks before were far too heavy and cumbersome. Rather than help the performances, they hindered them.

At the nightmare technical rehearsal, the set broke apart into pieces on a regular basis, stranding any actor who happened to be struggling with its contours at the time. Tempers frayed; insecurities and egos surfaced; and the director sulked. Occasionally, (very occasionally) major technical problems are righted. Ultimately, however, this whole production was a disgrace, and we dreaded its every return to the repertoire, along with the monumental difficulties of striking and resetting the John Napier design.

The nadir was reached at a schools matinée, on one damp and grey Wednesday afternoon. The visions, the spookery and the witchcraft elements of the production were risible at the best of times. Sniggers and whistles were audible, and then the kids got bored and restless. The rule, on such occasions, is just to carry on, persevere and get through it. But Keith Baxter had other plans.

He was angered by the lack of respect that his performance was receiving. The constant chatter, the odd boo or wolf whistle, these disturbed him so much that he was threatening to stop the show. We warned him to remain patient and focused, but he finally interrupted proceedings and stepped to the front of the stage. Children love these moments, when they feel they have made an impact.

Keith gave the audience two minutes to decide whether they wanted to remain in the theatre - in which case, they should be silent - or whether they preferred to leave. As the two minute silence ticked by, Sara Kestelman retreated to the wings for a cigarette.

Of course, nobody left. How could they? Most of the audience was made up of school parties, with coaches arriving at the scheduled finishing time. Furthermore, they were not independent. There were teachers in tow, to make decisions on their behalf. Those two minutes were wasted.

When everything started again, it was a full 30 seconds before Lady Macbeth realised she was still holding a lighted cigarette in her hand.

To make matters worse, and to make the afternoon especially memorable, the set performed its usual trick of collapsing in the middle of the final act, as swords clashed feebly around the perimeter. Keith achieved his aim, however. Those school kids remained silent for the rest of the show. And they continued to sit on their hands throughout the entire curtain call.

But where was David King and his dog and why did I mention them at all?

*   *   *   *   *

When I was in my teens, and my world seemed to be full of music and piano practice and scales and rulers laid on the back of my hands and recitals and lessons and committing pieces to memory, I had two narrow escapes in one day.

Since then, and when people talk about being run over by a bus and laugh, because it never happens, I give a wry smile. It's a little like slipping on a banana skin: have you ever seen it happen? Well, it happened to me and it wasn't funny, and I was very nearly, as it seemed at the time, run over by a bus – a 209, to be precise.

I was on my way to give a recital, and my mind was very definitely elsewhere. As it turned out, I don't think it was even focused on what I was doing that evening. After all, I had played that particular piece, a Chopin Scherzo, many times before. But it wasn't my day.

As I walked onto the platform and sat down at the piano (a very nice Blüthner, as I recall), I raised my hands and… nothing. I couldn't remember the first note, not where to start, or even how to approach it. I was very aware of the silence out front, and pretended to adjust the height of the stool - something I've seen many times since, and which must have looked very impressive at the time. However, my mind remained stubbornly blank, as I heard the dreaded sounds of polite little coughs echoing round the hall.

There was only one option, and it felt like a humiliating one. I stood up, turned around, and retraced my steps across the stage. I hadn't realised that I'd walked so far to the piano. Fortunately, my music was in the wings. All I needed was the first note. Having consulted with the score, I lifted my head, and began the return journey to the Blüthner. Now there were whispers from the audience. Never mind. I was in control again. And all went well.

That day, nevertheless, started a slow erosion of my confidence on the concert platform and a gradual loss of nerve. Surely it was Hughie Green and his clapometer that finally broke the camel's back but by then I had fallen out of love with the piano. And it was 15 years before I regained my nerve.

Let me reintroduce you to David King. He had a faithful companion forever at his side and, because I've been friends with many dogs in my time, forgive me that I have forgotten the name of David's. He was a superbly intelligent animal. Even if you took David's assertion for real that the dog was bilingual - he spoke to him all the time in French - there were other pointers to his general understanding.

In the days when dogs were allowed to be in dressing rooms, 'Max' (I must give him a name) waited patiently there listening to his master's performance over the show relay system. As David's exit approached, Max excitedly made his way to the pass door, where he sat until David came through.

This was a very popular dog until Keith Baxter arrived, and whose hounds took very great exception. David, however, was a lonely man and Max was his lifelong friend, companion and true love. When Max finally died, David was not long in following.

David King was also a pianist, and he and I often sight read our way through a pile of duets. It was one afternoon, between shows, that Sara

Kestelman gave her insensitive cry: "Can someone tell those two to stop that bloody awful row!" Well, maybe we were still getting to grips with *The Arrival of the Queen of Sheba*, but I didn't think we were that bad. Could things get any worse? Yes, they could.

One day, the Theatregoers' Association approached David to ask if he and I would be prepared to give a concert for their members. David replied that we would be delighted. Furthermore, we would perform on two grand pianos, on the Rep stage, to an audience of up to 900 people.

The first I heard about it was when David arrived with a sheaf of music and a rehearsal/practice schedule. Given the fact that he had more spare time than I did, I found myself stretched in several directions.

David was a big man, a larger than life character, who attacked everything with a bravado and gusto that I was neither willing, nor able, to match. After one particularly gruelling practice session and, as he dropped me off at the flat, I suggested a cup of tea and a chance to talk about how things were going.

The scene remains very clear in my mind. As I carried the tea things into the living room, I was trying to decide how best to introduce the theme of, "should we perhaps reconsider?" and, as I left on the pretext of getting some biscuits together, I was aware of David excitedly 'tum-tum-tumming' some notes that vaguely belonged to a piece of Mozart we had been rehearsing.

I returned and sat down opposite him, wondering how he would react to the idea at the very least of a postponement. I barely had a chance to speak.

Without any hesitation, David was suddenly off his chair and on his knees in front of me. I remember thinking how large his face was, as he looked up at me, his eyes glistening, and declared a passionate love that he could no longer keep to himself.

Thoughts crowded in. The excitement of all my days at Birmingham, all I had learned and witnessed, the steady tread towards one day being a director myself. I thought of all the wonderful actors I had already met and worked with, and how much respect and admiration I had held them in. Yet, suddenly in the space of a few short weeks I had watched directors struggling to make sense of their own impotence and actors weighed down by their own egos.

Now, to top it all, one of the leading members of the company was embarrassing both of us on his knees in front of me, shedding tears of a schoolboy infatuation.

Like the piano, was a slow erosion of confidence in the whole profession setting in? Would I lose my nerve? Would I, ultimately, fall out of love with it?

I wasn't prepared to let that happen and I think I decided there and then that I would take the bull by the horns and leave Birmingham as soon as I could.

The situation in my flat was more delicate, however. I mumbled a few words. It was a shock and it was embarrassing, but I think we both extricated ourselves from the moment with dignity, and from then on it wasn't much referred to. As I have discovered, over and over since, relationships within companies can develop in very complex and unexpected ways.

In the event, David and I continued to prepare for our *Two Piano Recital*, but I felt hopelessly unprepared when we both trooped onto the stage, at 7.00pm, on March 18th. I still have a recording of the 2 hours that followed, and listen to it with mixed emotions.

David tended to pound the keyboard and, together with the wrong notes that I hit that evening, I reckon it was all a bit of a shambles. We positively slaughtered a movement from Stravinsky's *Petrouchka* to close the first half. We did better after the break, but I was more than delighted when we ended a rousing version of Saint-Saëns's, *Danse Macabre*, more or less hitting the last notes at the same time, and rose to take our bows.

Before long, I had handed in my resignation and prepared to take my leave. But I can't finally depart this location without mentioning one more name - that of a lady who has probably never realised how much she affected the course of my life from this point on.

Felicite Gillham, or Gilly, was a partner in 'Gilly Wigs', a company whose strong selling point was that they remained in residence at the theatre right through the production weekend to opening night - a reassuring presence, at a tricky time, for everyone involved. Before this time, wig fittings usually entailed a one-off trip to London for the actor involved. The wig was then dressed and dispatched by train, in time for a quick reset by the wardrobe department and subsequent maintenance throughout the run.

Gilly and I quietly became firm friends. She would stay in one of those theatre flats and, when the day's work was done, I would once more find myself on that upper corridor route to a glass of wine, a sandwich and long, long chats. If we were still there in the small hours, she sometimes offered the keys to her Volvo Estate for me to drive back to Moseley (yes, I'd moved again). I could then sit back and drive through the quiet streets and think about the production in hand. I usually picked out one of Gilly's tapes to listen to - nearly always Andy Williams.

One night, I was pulled in by a police vehicle for a failed rear light. Since it was not my car, and I could not remember the registration number; since the name and address on my driving licence did not tally with those I had sleepily given, (Equity confusions again) some suspicions were naturally aroused, and I was hauled out of the car for further examination.

The officer was asking me why I was out so late when both our heads turned - mine, in horror; his, in disbelief - as Gilly's Volvo Estate slowly rolled backwards down the street, Andy Williams still crooning inside. In my tired and distracted state, I had forgotten the hand brake.

These were the final weeks of my life as a company manager. The deed was done. I had made myself redundant, with no prospects. But I was ready to cut loose and blast off once more albeit into completely unknown territory. The difference was that this time, for better or worse, I would call myself a Professional Director.

PART TWO

A Distant Planet

R eckless Youth. In the summer of 1973, a rhymed couplet tells it all:

> Out of a job and nowhere to stay
> I packed my bags for St. Tropez

I was always a bit of a Francophile, and crossed the Channel far too often in my teens, no doubt getting up to no good. So it was inevitable that having worked intensely for four years, and reckoning that I deserved a bit of a break, I should blow my meagre savings on a 3-week trip to the south of France. Assuredly, my appetite was whetted by recent encounters with Juliette Greco and Zizi Jeanmaire, but I decided this time to bypass Paris and head for the beach.

Although very definitely out of a job, it's not strictly true that I had nowhere to stay. I first headed for London and a flat in Coptic Street just round the corner from the British Museum. The flat belonged to a friend of mine from the old Rep. We'd first met up when I was an ASM, studying the work of various directors, and he was a stagehand, with aspirations to becoming an actor. He notably achieved his ambition first, but was now on hand to help me as I made my own transition.

We caught up with each other in the theatre bar, just as I was cutting the umbilical cord at Birmingham, and immediately renewed our friendship. Over a few drinks, and in true Hollywood let's put on a show tradition, we laid our plans for taking London by storm. It would be another 3 years before I made it to the West End and, even then, I'd be 5,000 miles away but, in a burst of pragmatic realism, we set our sights that evening on the Fringe.

My friend's name was Rayner Bourton and he'd just spent a season with the controversial Glasgow Citizens' company. There, the look was all-important and actors were groomed to believe in themselves as stars, so that vanity was lauded (or so it seemed to me). As a consequence, Rayner was now more confident, more self-aware, and as I quickly discovered distinctly more garrulous.

But he had lost none of his charm, and his enthusiasm became very contagious. Before we'd drained our last glass, and after dismissing a number of equally ambitious and expensive proposals, we settled on a London Fringe show, based on Jean Genet's novel, *The Thief's Journal*.

To complicate matters, Rayner was already about to start rehearsals for a new musical. Nobody knew it yet, but that show was destined to make instant theatrical history. However, our own plans made that evening seemed much more exciting, or so I thought, as I made my way into the murky depths of Soho to make them a reality.

The Fringe, in the early 70s, was growing apace, and back rooms and basements and vacant attics above pubs all over the capital were being turned into hotbeds of experimental theatre. To check out the venue that was to launch my own directing career, I stood on the pavement of Old Compton Street and looked up.

We were booked in to the Play Room, run by the 60s icon, Mike Sarne, above The Swiss Tavern, now renamed. This was an off-off-Broadway style space, in the heart of a London that was still pulsating from the swinging revolution of the previous decade. To be making my freelance début in this way was a cool introduction to the life, and I found it exhilarating.

However, I was also appalled by the basic nature of the Play Room and its lack of any useful facilities. It was little more than a blacked out room, with a few power points. It suddenly dawned that nothing would be done unless we did it. At that stage, there was no designer, no lighting, no sound, no stage management, and there would be no audience, unless we advertised the show.

The cast was kept to four including Rayner, who was now already in the throes of rehearsing the new musical. It would open at the Royal Court Theatre Upstairs, in Sloane Square, and all I knew about it at the time was based on reports that Rayner brought back with him at the end of each day. It was called, *The Rocky Horror Show* and he was cast as Rocky.

The Rocky Horror Show was going to cause problems for our own rehearsal plans. It had already been rescheduled for a late-night slot at the Court, after it became clear that the sound would be too intrusive for the Main House, currently preparing Edward Bond's, *The Sea.*

The omens were not especially good for the opening, either, after it was put back a couple of nights. I arrived to take my seat, with a degree of apprehension for Rayner and the whole cast. Nobody knew how the audience would react and to be honest it was a tentative start. It felt as though the show was heading for disaster.

All doubts were dispelled, however, as soon as Tim Curry made that explosive entrance as Frank'n'furter, at which point the show just took off. We all knew there and then that we were present at one of those landmark events that go down in the annals, and the atmosphere that night in that cramped upstairs space became electric. I'm told that Tim Curry will barely acknowledge his presence in that show these days, which is an inexplicable shame.

Back in my own cramped upstairs space, there seemed to be a lot of nudity to deal with. Characters always seemed to be taking their clothes off, or taking somebody else's clothes off, or simply appearing undressed.

We decided to promote the piece as frank, provocative and honest, and play up the decadent aspect of Genet's work. Immediately, of course, we had a hot line to all the gay press and a ton of free coverage. One magazine sent a photographer to get a 5 page spread together which, unfortunately, appeared too late to help very much.

Meantime, in stark contrast, we grappled with the meaning of *The Thief's Journal.* In between trying to interpret some of the lengthy speeches lifted directly from the book, I was also trying to stage some more theatrical visuals - not too difficult to do with Genet. More nudity seemed inevitable, but thanks directly to *The Rocky Horror Show* we were restrained.

Nakedness on stage requires careful handling by the director, as I've learned many times since. Most actors can't wait to get into drag, but are more reticent about getting their kit off. Some are laid back about it - positively enthusiastic, sometimes - but many are resistant, until they get used to it and then they won't get their clothes back on.

Rayner, however, had his own problems with it.

For anyone who saw *The Rocky Horror Show* in Sloane Square, they will remember just how campily theatrical and extrovert it all was. Rayner's character became a very glittery hunk, glitter dust and makeup was everywhere. Probably with the director's encouragement, and certainly with Glasgow's influence, Rayner was happy to keep heaping on that glitter.

Every night, he tried in vain to shed it all, after the show, but the stuff gradually seeped into his groin area and caused irritation and a rash. He came to my room in agony, one day, and displayed one very good reason why he would not be able to go naked for Genet. I had to agree. His fan base would certainly have suffered.

We called the show, *Beggar My Neighbour*, and we opened on July 8th for six performances. Given all the obstacles, we had a show to present, though I think it was a mass of contradictions. Pompously, we wrote: … inspired by the serious writings of a few literary giants, on the plight of many less able to speak their feelings… the play attempts a frank and honest appraisal of one form of existence. For good measure, we had thrown in bits of James Baldwin and Henry Miller.

And what of the reaction? There were those who, unsurprisingly, fell asleep through the more turgid literary sections; one lady even complained that the lighting was so bad that she couldn't read her book; there were those who found a theatrical freshness and originality to the visual imagery; and there were those who were only present to look at naked actors.

In all, it was okay for its time and place, and at least it made me forget for a time that I was unemployed.

Three days before the show finished - like a madcap Mr Micawber, desperately hoping that something would turn up on my return - I was packing for France. And then came the call.

The telephone's a strange thing. We spend a great deal of time, especially early on in our career, waiting for it to ring and, of course, it rarely does. Unexpectedly and perversely, on the other hand when it's out of mind altogether, it will give forth its persistent sound. On those occasions, take a deep breath. Your life may be about to change direction altogether.

As I dropped the latest trendy pair of shorts into a bag and checked my airline ticket, the phone rang. At the other end of the line was Gareth Morgan, the Artistic Director of the Tyneside Theatre Company, in Newcastle. His Associate Director, Michael Bogdanov, was leaving and he needed a replacement. He would be taking a risk, he said, but if I wanted the job it was mine.

I couldn't believe it. Here was the chance to go from resident Company Manager to resident Associate Director within a few short weeks and I said, "No."

My ambition had been achieved, but I heard myself answering; "I can't. I'm flying to Nice on Saturday."

There was the briefest of pauses, and then: "How long for?"

"Three weeks."

"Fine. You can start here the following Monday."

From Jean Genet to St Tropez. The south of France seemed particularly enjoyable that year. It's worth mentioning here that I became a devoted Francophile at an early age. I put it down, in part, to a dazzling gesture of indulgence given by my parents. Still in my mid-teens, I calmly suggested to them that I disappear – on my own – for a few days in Paris, on the slightly wobbly pretext that it might add some impetus to my school French lessons.

In a sudden burst of sixties liberalism, they agreed and – before I knew it – I was on a plane to Le Bourget, with accommodation pre-booked at an address near to the Luxembourg Gardens. I remember it well. The street was called Rue de l'Abée de l'Epée, and it seemed wonderfully exotic.

As I fastened my seat-belt on the tarmac at Heathrow, a degree of trepidation caught up with me, but I was determined to be grown-up and mature. Adopting the kind of nonchalant insouciance of one who was highly accustomed to jetting his way around the continent, I turned to the man sitting next to me and smiled. I don't think my performance convinced him.

He was Japanese, as I recall – a smartly dressed businessman – but his own features took on a bemused look, as he politely enquired what I might be doing, once in the French capital. Adopting my best schoolboy accent, I announced that I would be staying on the Rue de l'Abée de l'Epée, adding for good measure that it was situated on the Left Bank.

He then asked how I intended to get to the city from the airport, to which I replied that I would take the bus. "Come with me", he said, "My driver will be very happy to drop you off at your hotel."

Of course, these days many people might be appalled at the idea of a young lad agreeing to such a proposal, but it sounded good to me. In the event, he was true to his word and I disembarked from his limousine, unharmed, at the entrance to the said "Rue". My introduction to Paris remained a charmed one, and I had a wonderful week.

Whether or not my French improved, I can't say, but I was determined to return in the near future. On that occasion I took my sister, Lynne, with me and we both checked into the Hotel Nêvers. We were there to celebrate Lynne's birthday but, this time, my parents had cause to regret their indulgence.

On our second day, my sister foolishly allowed her bag, together with all her money, to be stolen from a park bench where we were sitting. Gallant to the end, I assured her that we could live off my own stash of francs. For the next 48 hours, we led a meagre existence – tramping the city streets on foot, and maintaining a diet of *croques monsieur* (a kind of toasted sandwich) so as to avoid the indignity of calling for help.

But then our resistance crumbled, and – following a hastily convened summit conference in my room – we got in touch with our parents. In the early 60s, there was a very tight limit on the amount of cash that could be taken out of the country, but my father responded to our SOS as though he had years of CIA training behind him.

Within hours, we were directed to a metro station for a meeting with a Paris-based colleague of his. An apparition appeared, dressed straight out of Central Casting in a long, sinister trench coat and who handed over a plain brown envelope containing our rescue fund.

That night, we celebrated with extra *frites*.

In 1973, my stay in St. Tropez was equally charmed, thanks to the intervention in my career by Gareth Morgan. I was now heading up the A1 to Newcastle-upon-Tyne, and Jesmond Dene.

Of course, this was not all a complete surprise and, if I've given that impression, then I apologise. But I had long since dismissed the idea at the time as nothing more than a long shot.

I had already been to the University Theatre, as it was then called, by invitation. My first impressions were that it was not dissimilar to a lecture hall. It had a wide auditorium, steeply raked, but with no upper gallery or circle. Instead at the top, and on either side, were broad landing areas where it was easy to come and go and watch the performance, and where occasional lunchtime productions were staged.

On my first visit, I had stayed overnight, so as to watch the evening show. *Close the Coal House Door* was a hugely popular and successful musical, steeped in the Tyneside culture, and bursting with affection for the place. It couldn't fail with the local audience and, after almost 4 years in the Midlands, I was carried away by the sheer exuberance and unfettered joy of those around me.

I'm told that Leicester audiences are the worst to play to, though I'm sure that those on the south coast must be up there with them.

At Newcastle, I hadn't heard such waves of spontaneous, full throated laughter in a long time and, even though there was much of it I couldn't relate to or even understand, I was mightily impressed and wanted to be part of it.

But there was no vacancy.

This is where Gilly of 'Gilly Wigs' makes her star entrance - a cameo performance, if you like, because it seems so inconsequential. But not at all.

An actor can at least audition to display his talents; a musician can strum his guitar or sing his show stopping piece; and a designer can open his portfolio and leaf through his sketches. But a director can only convince by doing the full thing or be left repeating his mantra, "I believe I can direct." Somebody then has to take his word and entrust a full budget to his safe-keeping. That takes some courage.

Gilly was an old friend of Gareth's, and she wrote to him about

Gilly - Outside the New Birmingham Rep

me and about what I wanted to do, about my passion for the Theatre, and because she had an instinct about me. She believed in me. And Gareth kindly invited me to Newcastle to look around. But at that time there was no vacancy.

Now, suddenly tanned and rested from my Riviera break, here I was. Lodged temporarily in Jesmond Dene and tackling Bertold Brecht. For some reason, in pseudo-Brechtian experimental style (well, this was the 70s), three of us worked on *The Caucasian Chalk Circle* and I was put in charge of the romantic element of the play, working with such future luminaries as Nicholas le Prevost and Cherie Lunghi.

I then turned my attention to the Gulbenkian Studio theatre and my first full scale production as a resident theatre director. The play was *Owners*, by Caryl Churchill and after the opening night I was gratified to read my first reviews. One of them contained the memorable plaudit: '*A production which at times reaches outstanding heights.*' So far, so good.

It wasn't all plain sailing, though. At one unforgettable preview, we had an almost supernatural happening on stage - one of those freak accidents that cannot be averted and most certainly cannot be explained.

I had persuaded one of the actresses from *Chalk Circle*, Miranda Forbes, to play the highly unrewarding part of Alec's Mum. Not only was Miranda far too young for it, but it meant that she was required to spend most of the evening on stage, fast asleep in an armchair, with nothing to say, as I recall.

She did sterling work in looking the part and we had a lot of fun with it in rehearsal. Then, as I watched in performance, and as it appeared in slow motion before my eyes, the shade from a large standard lamp moved from its moorings one night, as one of the actors passed in front of it. Not only did it shift, but inexplicably it managed to lift itself and drop with razor like precision over the sleeping head of Alec's Mum. Only her shoulders were left visible. Those, too, began - almost imperceptibly, at first - to move and then to shake.

Astonishingly, most of the audience seemed to regard it as a clever and intriguing element in this black comedy and were on tenterhooks to see which route the shade would take next. For the actors on stage, however, the dilemma was excruciating. The offending item needed to be replaced on its stand - probably exposing a shaking, sleeping Miranda, tears coursing uncontrollably down her face. Would she come out of character? You must ask Cherie Lunghi, who was about to embark on a bizarre little adventure with me.

*   *   *   *   *

Come forward just for a moment to the new millennium. It was a hot day, in 2002. I was looking out of an open window, across the gardens of Sussex Square to the sea. The Kemptown flat in Brighton was on the market, and I had just got off the phone to a very excited estate agent. His pulse clearly racing, he had announced a viewing for the next day. The prospective buyer he told me breathlessly was none other than Cherie Lunghi.

Now, as I felt a sea breeze on my face and heard the gulls overhead, I was going back in time. Come with me back to the North Sea winds and screeching gulls of Northumberland, and a bitterly cold December in 1973.

Everyone seemed young and raw in those days, but Cherie Lunghi at 21 seemed particularly fresh and wide eyed. In the intervening years, she has acquired a sophistication that was lacking back then, and a vocal delivery that is now much more attractive.

In the company with her was a young South African actor, called Ralph Lawson and, within a couple of years, he and Cherie were to marry. It was a marriage of convenience and allowed Ralph to remain in the UK.

I loved Cherie's vitality and ebullience. Having tackled Caryl Churchill together and later Noël Coward, I always found her a pleasure to work with. But there was one production in particular with which I shall always associate her name.

By the end of 1973, it was my turn to do a stint with Stagecoach, the Theatre-in-Education arm of the Tyneside Theatre Company. Furthermore, I was expected to come up with something original. I was given three actors, a designer and a stage manager and, believe me, they were all about to earn their money. Anyone who has not been involved with a primary schools tour in the northeast of England in the winter time will be hard pushed to imagine what it can be like.

My three actors were: Allan Corduner, Martin Fisk and Cherie - so often, in those days, written as Sherie.

Since Allan was a consummate pianist, and since the actors would be performing in front of really young children, I went back to something that I had enjoyed as a child: *Sparky's Magic Piano*. Rachmaninov, however, didn't seem appropriate for a schools pre-Christmas tour, and so I updated it for a much livelier musical format. The end result was *Boogie Woogie*.

The actors and stage manager (and I was often there, as well) would start early in the morning, loading up the Stagecoach van with costumes, props and special effects. We would then drive, often some considerable distance, to arrive at our first school of the day in time to set up, check the piano and sound, and let the actors get into costume. Then, round about 9.30-10.00, the children would troop into the hall and sit, usually cross-legged, on the floor, in a circle or semicircle before the cast burst in. In a blaze of hastily manufactured energy and rip roaring bonhomie, Cherie, Martin and Allan then bounced their way through *Boogie Woogie*.

When it was over, and after thanks from the teachers and clapping from the children before filing back to their classrooms, the actors would change, clear everything up, load it back into the van, and set off for the second show of the day.

Thanks to our dear Prime Minister (fish hand), we had a petrol crisis at the time, and for a while it seemed that we might have to travel all over Northumberland by bus or train, cutting down considerably on our already minimal requirements.

Thank goodness things never reached that point, and thank goodness the show worked. We even took it to hospitals. And, all the while as I recall, the weather just got colder.

I was tempted, on that hot afternoon in 2002, to hang around the next day and remind Cherie of it all. She has done some amazing work over the years; Allan Corduner has become a heavy weight actor, with a mountain of film, television and stage credits to his name; and Martin Fisk later earned legions of adoring fans as the Yorkie Bar Man, in the memorable 70s TV commercial.

But, as I thought of them together - Cherie, in tiara and flowing costume; Martin, in black and white harlequin mode; and Allan, in his long striped socks and dungarees, I doubt if any of them have ever really forgotten those weeks of boogie woogie-ing around the northeast. Did Cherie have this in mind when she stumbled into *Strictly Come Dancing*, I wonder?

Anyhow, I decided to let her look around the flat in peace. But she didn't buy it. Maybe she spotted one of the posters on the wall.

Back at Newcastle, I was having a tremendous time. I was finally being paid to do the job I had long dreamt of doing; I was working with some top notch people, on a wide variety of scripts; and I was beginning to learn about some of the unexpected perks and temptations that go with being a director. I was also having to cope with a new language – Geordie.

When I arrived in Newcastle, the northeast felt like a foreign country. In fact, I could hardly understand the natives at all. It was such a problem that for reasons to do with self preservation I determined to get to grips with the language. Otherwise, since I genuinely could not follow what people were saying to me, I was gathering a reputation, common to many arrivals from "doon sooth", as 'stuck up'. Unfortunately, I didn't simply familiarise myself with elements of the vocabulary, I stupidly went on to try to use them in conversation myself. I'm ashamed to give an example.

The word 'hinny' is used as a term of endearment rather like 'love' or 'dear' further south. I was anxious to demonstrate my newfound knowledge and throw this one around. Sadly, other words had also invaded my subconscious and, as I tried to show my fondness for a poor, unsuspecting front-of-house staff member one morning, the word that came out was 'netty'. That one evidently means 'an outside loo'.

In time, however, I began to feel very much at home. This became especially so after an introduction to a strong set of individuals to whom I applied the affectionate label, Geordie Mafia. These included James Bolam, Alan Hockey, Neil Daglish and Ronald Herdman.

James Bolam will always be a 'likely lad', though I associate him much more with another television series, *When the Boat Comes In*. I also have memories of him draining the odd bottle of gin and crashing out on a sofa bed at the flat I shared at the time.

Ronald Herdman was startling in the way that he could metamorphose from his gentle, giggly and effeminate self (he was a dab hand with the crochet needle and provided many cardies for his friends), into a powerful and utterly masculine force on stage.

Alan Hockey was diabetic and, if he came to stay, you'd better be quite sure that you had the correct carbohydrate to hand. As soon as he uttered the words, "I'm going for my injection," there had to be food on the table within 20 minutes "or else". He made outrageous dramatic play out of the fact that he'd be "dead on the floor" if it wasn't.

Lizzie McKenzie and her husband, Mike, became particular favourites of mine. Mike was no Geordie, but adorable, a quite legendary jazz pianist and singer, who had played for the greats. These included Charles Aznavour, Liza Minnelli, Ella Fitzgerald, Shirley Bassey, José Feliciano and a host of others and, of course, he had many tales to tell. When I knew him, he was resident at the prestigious White Elephant Clubs in Berkeley Square and On The River and, once he found out that my favourite song is a particular Gershwin classic… well, I only had to walk into one of those establishments for Mike to stop mid bar whatever he was playing and break into a quick phrase of my personal leitmotif.

Having suffered polio, and walking always with crutches, he was a wonderful down to earth feller to his sensitive black fingertips. And he never got carried away by his success.

His wife was at the furthest end of the spectrum, if you headed off in the opposite direction. Brash, loud and with a Geordie touch of vulgarity, Lizzie was one of the campest ladies I have ever met.

Lizzie McKenzie

That mouth of hers could get you into the most extreme of tricky situations.

Imagine travelling in a car with her, there were four of us, with Lizzie at the wheel and all having had far too much to drink. It's 2am and we are pulled in by a young policeman, about to get a great deal more than he has bargained for. Extraordinarily pretty and, in Lizzie's eyes, still of college age the poor bobby is totally out of his depth as he tries to question this particular lady driver at least 20 years his senior.

She winds down her window and leans across me, as I try to look like a sober and respectable director. "Now just tell me," she says, "and I'm not bothered either way, but do you fuck men or women?"

I am hoping I'm invisible, as the policeman blushes and wriggles but determines to push ahead with his own legitimate line of questioning. It's no good. "You see, I need to know, hinny, 'cos whatever the answer," as she looks around at the rest of us, "there'll be one person here for you."

Young Mr Policeman takes a deep breath, as his authority melts away. He glances at each of us. Is he really about to choose? We are moved on, very quickly.

*   *   *   *   *

I am often asked, as people gaze at the rolling credits on a screen, "What does a Best Boy do?" It's an easier question to answer than, "What does a Casting Director do?" since a good part of a director's job is to do the casting. You may already realise that I have a bias here.

From the moment that I first read a script, a process of interpretive evolution begins. Ideas are already forming as to how the finished production will look and sound. All kinds of subtle elements and images gradually weave together into a particular DNA, which I then try to match. At the precise moment that I come to assemble the right cast, how on earth can I siphon off that process to a non-artistic third party?

But this is precisely what casting directors are expected to do. Unfortunately, they tend to work from a lexicon of largely irrelevant guidelines, age group, general appearance, character background or worst of all an identikit format: "Are we looking for a Helena Bonham-Carter type?" for example. No. What I am looking to do is to match the DNA of the character that is already formed in my head. I can offer clues, but these will only lead a casting director to actors they have seen playing something similar.

There is, of course, an argument in film and television for casting directors providing backup and logistical support. But that is all it should be, and I can find no such argument that stands up in the Theatre.

The point of all this is that Gareth Morgan was probably the first to employ a casting director for a regional repertory company, and I no more understand the reasons now than I did then. Maybe the argument revolved around the fact that we were 300 miles from London, where the majority of actors were based. But I think, at heart, that it sprang from a self-indulgent laziness and a grandeur that we could ill afford. And those very same elements have led to the virus spreading.

Nowadays, almost every theatre in the UK - financial restraints leaving them often with only one or two actors to cast - manage to spend money which they haven't got on somebody else doing it for them.

To be blunt, this somebody else often brings no creative talent with them, but nevertheless contributes to a kind of burgeoning civil service in the profession. I number them amongst the 'peripherals.'

Furthermore, there is a tendency for these people to grow aloof and detached from the very actors for whom they are expected to provide a service.

The Queen of the casting directors for many years was a lady called Mary Selway. Her name can be seen in credits of some of the major films of her day. She and I worked together over a period of time on a stage script and, as a consequence, we became reasonably good friends.

Nevertheless, I remain shocked by her behaviour. I was in her office at Twickenham Studios, one day, when as usual the phone was constantly ringing. Each time, Mary's assistant answered with the mantra, "Sorry, we're not casting at the moment," and I eventually had to say, "But Mary, you are casting!"

"Yes," she said, "but we only deal with a handful of agents - maybe four or five. The rest we don't bother with."

I was taken aback. We all develop our group of favourite agents, but I have never cast on the basis of an actor's representation. I know that Mary did do the rounds of the drama schools and fringe theatre productions, and I know that casting for film is a very different proposition to handling a stage play, but I nevertheless found it patronising. Her assistant was doing nothing for much of the time, time that could have been spent widening the net and giving chances to actors who, through no fault of their own, happened to be with an agent with whom Mary Selway didn't bother.

And what does a Best Boy do? Though he sounds like a young apprentice lad, he is actually a kind of foreman for the department – either electrics or camera – and the term stems from the days when one head would say to another head, "Lend me your best boy for a couple of days, would you?"

But I hope to be telling a story and not giving a lecture, so let's go back to 1974, to climb the stairs of an old building in Little Newport Street, just around the corner from the Play Room, in Soho.

Here was the office of another casting director, Marilyn Johnson, and she and I developed an early rapport. She was a fanatical Geminian, with a birthday the day before my own. A birthday party for her would continue on after midnight so as to begin the celebrations for mine. I was welcomed into her circle of Geminians very readily, though I'm not sure what valuable contribution she made to the casting process that could not have been provided, a great deal cheaper, by a very competent secretary.

But she had been chosen by Gareth, as the company's casting director. Once a year, we would all troop down from Newcastle, to spend endless hours and days in Marilyn's offices combing through lists, auditioning, comparing notes, recommending our own group of actors but, ultimately, rubber stamping Gareth's own choice of who should form the season's nucleus.

However, on one occasion in 1974, I was allowed out on my own.

Whilst others were grappling with *Hamlet* with Jack Shepherd, or Chekhov, I was presented with a new play, written especially for the Tyneside Theatre Company. The writer was Peter Terson and he had a huge standing in the northeast, in particular responsible for *Zigger Zagger, Geordie's March,* as well as a long list of TV credits.

His new piece, *Lost Yer Tongue?* was going to form a major part of that spring season and would be, as the brochure announced, no exception to the success record. So, hardly any pressure on me, then! To make the production even more challenging, this was very much a Geordie play, written in the language I was still trying to get to grips with.

Of course I was eager to meet with Terson and establish a rapport. He lived in the southeast at that time and, since I also had to cast the play with Geordie actors, I was dispatched to London to slaughter all these birds with one stone.

I organised a full day of auditions, and the theatre, in its generous wisdom, booked a hotel for me. For one night. Oddly, funds did not extend to hiring an audition space, and so I had to conduct all these meetings in the hotel lobby.

Come the day, I caught a ridiculously early train to London, checked in at the Bonnington Hotel in Holborn, and positioned myself near to the reception desk. This meant that, as soon as I heard the words, "I'm here to see Tony Craven," I could leap from my seat, step forward and take control of the situation.

It's difficult enough to hold an interview in such circumstances, but to audition an actor or have them simply read is awkward. There is little opportunity for them to look at the script in advance and, if they want to raise their voice or move around, forget it.

Nevertheless, I had a good day. Everyone who was expected turned up. Most were on time. And I felt at the end of it all that there was a good selection from which to choose. The end of it all, however, was a long time coming.

The final interview coincided with a lot of activity in the lobby, and we decided to move upstairs to my room, where it would be quieter.

There is, as I write, a big name Artistic Director of a major London theatre, who regularly adjourns an audition with a young actor to his flat. Then, he pounces. I hope this doesn't shock. There are many examples. There was, for instance, a gay casting director who used to conduct a bizarre kind of foreplay, screening hard core heterosexual pornography before making his move.

That same casting director, invited with Marilyn Johnson to a Halloween party of mine, petulantly refused to bob for apples. Each to his own.

At the Bonnington Hotel, I'm not sure that either of us expected the audition to continue until 7.00am the following day, but that was when we both emerged and left the hotel together. And, in my case, all happened by mutual consent, leading to a long term relationship.

Did it matter? It was difficult for me to keep my eyes open on the train to Peter Terson's, where I was expected to discuss the play in detail. I'm not sure that we didn't also have to settle on a title for it - ultimately, *Lost Yer Tongue?* It's worth remembering that for a little while longer.

I am certainly not the only director to have gone to a meeting still trying to scramble his head together, but this was a major deal for me and I am well aware that I should have handled the preceding 24 hours more responsibly.

But, please, give a 26 year old a break.

Peter Terson himself made very little impression on me, and I don't think he was around very much in rehearsals. That probably suited everyone very well at the time. Given later experiences, I'm sure that it did, but it definitely cranked up a level of suspense at his final reaction. In the event, I remember a broad grin and happy expression on his face on opening night, so we couldn't have done too badly.

All went smoothly through the first week, and audiences loved the play. On the Saturday night, Mike McKenzie travelled from London to join a full house and to watch his wife's performance.

Did I mention that Lizzie was not in the best of health? For all her craziness, she was also a serious minded actress with a great deal of talent, but she had a chronically bad chest, with a regular wheeze.

Like me at the time, she was a fanatical card player and we often played, in a foursome, late into the night. One time, after she had left and I was getting ready for bed around 4.00am, the phone rang. I've commented on the power of the phone before but, like most people, I get pretty alarmed if it goes in the middle of the night.

So, I answered with a degree of trepidation, only made worse by sounds of deep distress at the other end. It took a couple of heart stopping moments and the start of a cold sweat before I realised that what I was hearing was a wheezy Lizzie McKenzie, trying to stop laughing. Some loopy thought had come into her head on the way home and she had to communicate it whilst it was still fresh. It was fortunate for Mike that he, too, worked late.

Back in Newcastle, I settled into my seat in the theatre no longer apprehensive, but ready to sit back and enjoy the show. Fifteen minutes into the performance, Lizzie made her entrance. She was carrying a tea tray laden with cups, saucers, teapot, sugar bowl, etc. and she walked with it to centre stage.

It was there - most dramatically, as always - that she passed out and crashed to the floor all the tea things bouncing and smashing around her. The chest, it seemed, had finally let her down. As the audience gasped, I fled the auditorium. Mike gathered his crutches together and made slow progress after me. One actor (he admitted afterwards that he had always longed to do it) made his way to the front of the stage and spoke the line: "Ladies and gentlemen, is there a doctor in the house?"

I arrived in the wings expecting the worst. Hot on my heels was the only doctor in the house that night. It has to be said that he was something of a hunk and, as Lizzie came to and looked straight into this young doctor's face, she was heard to quietly wheeze: "My goodness, pet, if you promise you'll give me mouth to mouth, I'll pass out again!" Pause "Or have you lost yer tongue?"

A smile broke out on Mike's face, as he arrived in the wings behind us.

The actor who called for the doctor that night was Ed Wilson, one of the stars of *When The Boat Comes In*, and a regular stalwart of the Geordie Mafia. He ultimately stopped acting to become a highly successful replacement to Michael Croft, as director of the National Youth Theatre. But, whilst developing a similar platform for young actors in Los Angeles, he died tragically of cancer. Only just 60, he was too ill to fly back to the UK for his own father's funeral, one of the few times I ever heard him despondent. Characteristically, he always refused to complain about his own prognosis, and remained good-humoured to the end. There are many people who would want me to pay tribute to him, and I am happy to do so.

*   *   *   *   *

Watching television commercials is not something that most people choose to do, surely. These days and especially on ITV it makes far better sense to record the programme you want to watch and then fast forward at each break. The majority of people I know do just that. It's remarkable how a 90 minute drama will suddenly take little more than an hour to watch, and it all becomes a decidedly more enjoyable experience.

There was something of a golden age when commercials were witty and original and, furthermore, featured trained and well polished actors who knew their craft. Today, most of the output is so much dross. So pity me, please, for a moment, as this story continues through 1975.

I sat in front of the television, unable to fast forward through the drama, but anxious to get to the commercial breaks. Believe me, this was not something that I wanted to do, but there was one character that had been highly recommended. So, TV watching was all in the line of duty.

I was about to join forces again with the Geordie Mafia. Dave Walker, a South Shields man then working for the BBC, had written a crazy new musical, together with the composer, Iwan Williams. It was called *Geordie's Court*, and it was arranged that I should direct it.

Even at that time, I would have had difficulty in describing the piece. It wasn't a revue, and it certainly wasn't pantomime, but it had something in common with *1066 & All That*. As somebody deftly articulated it at the time, if you dethroned King Arthur and put Andy Capp in his place, you would arrive at *Geordie's Court*.

It took nothing seriously, except the joke of being Geordie. And the locals LOVED it. Show after show, around 450 people seemed to laugh continuously, and uproariously, for two and a half hours. The actors almost without exception caught the irreverent spirit of it exactly. Fred Pearson, who had only recently come from the world of amateur theatre, played King Geord the Umpteenth. Ed Wilson, Kathleen Moffatt and George Irving were all brilliant and Geordie-ism became a contagious infection that the rest of us caught.

Nevertheless, rehearsals brought the first example of another situation that a director might have to deal with. And it has been my misfortune to encounter it more than once. A particular actor, who shall remain nameless, always arrived with a briefcase, in which I am sure he carried his script and his newspaper, and his cigarettes and an apple.

Within the first hour, he almost always visited the loo. It's a place where actors can often be found, sometimes for long periods, as a first night approaches. It is a wise man or woman who refuses a dressing room alongside a backstage loo, as it is a brave actor who shares with a highly strung or nervous colleague.

However, on this particular occasion, there were no such obvious excuses. Every time the loo visit occurred, the briefcase went along for the ride. As the morning progressed, visits became more frequent; the actor became more muddled; and suggestions were whispered to me that there was a smell of vodka on his breath. He had to be tackled.

A customary pattern was followed. Firstly, came the outraged denial. Then there were distraught tears and a blubbed confession; hastily concocted reasons for such a lapse were put forward; and, finally, the absolute promise that it wouldn't happen again.

I had to decide what to do, and make that decision quickly. He was a popular figure within the company and did not have a huge amount to contribute to the show, and I believed his word as he dried his eyes and asked me to trust him. I gave him another chance, happily so, as it turned out. Besides, I had a much more important personality to deal with.

When I cast *Geordie's Court*, I had to find a rather special individual to play the one non-Geordie part. This particular grotesque was a character called Scraggie Aggie, and she clearly had to be extraordinary. She would have to fit in with the cartoon-esque style of the show, play comedy in a madcap way, as well as taking part in the musical numbers and dance routines. For a while, I saw nobody remotely suitable. And then one day I was given a nudge.

The person I was looking for, I was told, could be found making huge waves in a television commercial. Hence, I watched the screen... and waited. When I finally got to see this 30 second wonder and after a subsequent two or three viewings I decided that here was, indeed, an actress who might just possibly fit the bill. Might.

But was she free? Would she travel to Newcastle? On enquiry, the answer to both questions was a resounding, "Yes!"

This actress's name was Liz Smith, and I was about to discover what she could do. Within the first hour, of the first rehearsal, she asked me if she could take her teeth out.

This was an unusual request, although I could see the reasoning behind it. After all, if somebody removes all of their teeth, then their face kind of collapses. Immediately: FUNNY. In the same way that, if somebody farts, everyone giggles. However, this was a musical, and it concerned me very much that Scraggie Aggie's numbers might suffer if Scraggie Aggie had no teeth.

As it turned out, it made no difference at all, since this particular Scraggie Aggie's numbers remained very far from being musical. But Liz Smith's request was granted. The result, naturally, would be hysterical. Yet was it?

I have to confess that it never was for me. As rehearsals raced along, and all the usual processes of rewriting, reshaping and re-staging of a new musical were gone through, it became very clear that Liz lacked more than her teeth.

For everyone who has taken Liz Smith to their bosom as a "national treasure" please forgive me. I am well aware that to suggest even the remotest hint of criticism of a "national treasure" is to court unpopularity. There will be a few more of these "national treasures" along the way, in this tale, and I can only record my own personal insights and experiences with them.

In Liz's case, she certainly soaked up a good deal of rehearsal time. But when that happens, and when it's all about trivial issues, the whole process can become very tedious. When it detracts from what other actors are trying to do, then it can verge on the selfish. But also Liz Smith seemed so humourless. I began to wonder whether she actually got it and whether she would ever truly understand what we were all trying to do. Others would say that, as the director, it was my fault. Yet

Sue Nicholls, with Alan Hockey, Ed Wilson and some of the cast of Geordie's Court

the style and the fun were all around her. It began to seem possible that she didn't even have a sense of humour.

In general terms, I think there are comedy actors who DO lack a sense of humour, but who happen upon a format that works. And what follows is a catalogue of variations on the same theme. And nothing more. In my opinion, (and please remember that every opinion I put forward within these pages is a purely personal one) the character that Liz brought to Scraggie Aggie is the character that she continues to present - with or without teeth. And for the vast majority of the public it works.

It has to be said, however, that all in all *Geordie's Court* was a riot, and was revived at the start of 1978 with many of the same actors enthusiastically recreating their original roles. But I found another Scraggie Aggie this time. She performed the part magnificently, and garnered many more laughs than her predecessor. And, strangely enough, she has also become a "national treasure", and I am devoted to her.

That devotion goes back to the time around which I was strolling across the Malvern Hills humming Elgar. Through a season that included *Not Now, Darling* and *The Boyfriend*, there was a very camp lady on hand to keep us all in stitches.

Daughter of Sir Harmar Nicholls and, paradoxically, a veteran of *Crossroads* and *Coronation Street,* Sue is one very funny personality. We got quite pally whilst at the Alex Theatre, in Birmingham and I was one of the many honoured guests who crowded in to the opening of her spa and health farm not far away, at the family home.

There is, however, an imponderable set of rules that applies to the business of comedy. It is an acknowledged truism within the rehearsal room that if the company is still laughing at a joke, a performance, or a piece of business towards the final run-through, then the public will, more than likely, not see the funny side.

Sue Nicholls sometimes left her laughs in the rehearsal room, to the constant bewilderment of her colleagues. The public did not always get her. Maybe she was too camp, too outrageous, too insecure. I do not know the reason. Her Hortense in *The Boyfriend* was the funniest I have seen, and we all expected a riot out front. Yet it didn't happen.

On the other hand, I am happy to report that her Scraggie Aggie was a resounding success and many people simply wept with laughter at what she did. She is a hard-working, professional, warm-hearted and generous colleague and deserves to be a "national..."

The last time I saw her we had lunch together in Buxton, with Mark Eden, her husband, and Edward Arthur, the stars of that year's pantomime and she was as bubbly and down to earth as ever.

By the time of *Geordie's Court*, I had notched up six years of un-interrupted employment and climbed a few rungs of the ladder. I had watched and learned from a number of directors and had begun to develop my own style. Through working on an eclectic mix of plays, on different stages, I was walking that steep curve - coming to grips with the fact that the only way to do it is to do it.

My dear friend, Rayner Bourton, built on his association with *The Rocky Horror Show*, and accepted the job of directing Gary Glitter in a production of it. He then called me up basically to ask: "Tony, how do I direct?"

Despite all the sympathy I felt for him at the time (and who wouldn't, given the casting?) I had to throw up my hands and refuse an answer. For me, the job is impossible to define. Every moment, of every pro-duction, spent with each individual actor, on every style of script is unique. Every person involved requires something a little different from their director. My instinct and my approach will not necessarily work for you or you or you. I just DO it. And when I do it right, it seems to work. And when I do it wrong, I am the first to know.

Whatever it takes to get onto the stage or screen the bulk of what you see and hear in your head, is what you have to do despite the egos, the personalities, the financial restraints, the technical hazards, the accidents, the time restrictions, the arguments, the disagreements, the stubborn stupidity of managements, and so on, and so on, and so on.

All of this was erupting as fresh discovery in 1975, and I found myself impatiently wanting to break out into the world and throw my naïve and raw talent around, wherever it might be required. Oh, vanity...

It's time to return to the seedy haunts of Soho, to walk along Old Compton Street, past the Swiss Tavern or whatever it's called now, and round the corner back to Little Newport Street. It's time to re-enter that suite of offices there, and to open another door.

I had enjoyed so much of my time in Newcastle, but was becoming increasingly aware of a geographical isolation. I felt frustration that whatever I was achieving there none of it was being seen or noticed where it mattered: in the south of England. However elitist that now seems, it was a fact. I was already 27 years old. How old can up and coming be? And I needed to be up and coming. So, I made the decision to leave Tyneside and start investigating the dangerous world of the freelancer.

For this, I needed an AGENT.

The very concept was a magical one, in those far off days of innocence. The sensation that, within days of signing, I would jet from one prestigious engagement to another whilst turning down a multitude of offers elsewhere was one that was easily transmitted from agents, and still is.

Their seductive siren voices whisper and flatter, as you tiptoe forward into range of their nets and, before you know it, you're in there: you've got REPRESENTATION. And you become a slave to the telephone, chained to it, waiting for it to ring. Nowadays, I see them as 'peripherals' but back in 1975 I was only too eager for their advances.

In the very same Soho den in which I had teamed up with a casting director, I was now courted by the Bill Horne Agency. Open sesame to that door, let barriers lift and let me be welcomed to the inner echelons of a chosen few. I was on my way.

I was on a bus headed for Swiss Cottage. Just as Margaret Thatcher was elbowing 'fish hand' out of the way, I was starting work at the Central School of Speech & Drama. I was directing a play by Pirandello about the merging of illusion with reality (laugh on, Prof Tolkien!) *Right You Are! (If You Think So)* was its rather laborious title.

Actually, apart from the fact that most of the drama school staff there - from George Hall, the Principal, down - were an uninspiring bunch of rusty, out of touch pussycats, I enjoyed the rehearsal period hugely. I worked with students such as Simon Chandler and Selina Cadell.

And there was one lad there that I would not have tipped for stardom

- not because of any lack of talent, but because he seemed so colourless and half-hearted, with very little charisma. How wrong I was. His name was Kevin Whateley and he now seems well on his way to becoming a "national…"

The show fared reasonably well at the Embassy Theatre, but this was not what The Agent was supposed to come up with. I rushed back to his office (no doubt, on the bus) to see "whither now for the treats you have in store?"

Aberystwyth was not what I had expected. If Newcastle had seemed like a distant planet, then this was a far flung outpost indeed. Having finally mastered the Geordie language, I was going to work for a company called, Cwmni Theatr y Werin. I was at least encouraged to learn that this would be the opening production of the theatre's professional summer season, albeit for children. Would this be another Boogie Woogie?

No. But the title of the piece, by Tony Connor, seemed to sum up in a nutshell the kind of entertainment that I had been booked to direct: *Dr. Crankenheim's Mixed-Up Monster.* It had none of the wit or the camp decadence of *Rocky*, however. After all, Dr. Crankenheim was intended for schoolchildren, Welsh schoolchildren. This was a bilingual company, with a remit to provide a theatre-in-education service for Dyfed schools, and the actors were also referred to as teachers. To this day, I am not sure what education was provided by our efforts at the Theatr y Werin.

I loathed Aberystwyth from the start. Even once I had got used to the mice that scurried around my landlady's living room, and the unwelcoming odours that seemed to cling to every wall, I could not fathom how anyone could live in the town. The architecture was dreary and the people even more so. I thanked my stars every day that I was there in July, when the weather was good, and that the theatre was outside the town, on the university campus. Once I had climbed the hill and got away from Aberystwyth itself, life was bearable.

The students had gone down for the summer and all the sports facilities were ours to use when we wanted, and that was a perk we welcomed very readily. Possibly the combination of that and the good weather, taken with a genuine shared relief that nobody was going to take the play too seriously, allowed all of us to bond pretty well, and when I left, soon after the first performance, I was able to feel good about what we achieved.

According to a local critic, *The spectators were enthralled and let forth the requisite jeers and cheers with relish.* It was a mixed blessing that no paper mentioned my name at all. The only quote I could take back to London with me for my beloved agent, of course was from Mr Patrick O'Brien: *Visually this is a splendid production. Props and costumes are very good indeed and the lighting is mind-spinning (!).* Thank you, Mr O'Brien. This could all be cut and pasted, I suppose, to read: "… a splendid production… very good indeed… mind spinning…"

Little did I know that Patrick (may I call you 'Patrick', Mr O'Brien?) would be waiting for my return and would not be disappointed.

I stormed back to London. Bill Horne and I would soon be at the parting of the ways, if things didn't look up. Barely consummated, I was ready to annul our relationship. As far as I was concerned, he had single handedly stalled my career. His reaction was at once gloomy and complacent. It seemed that beyond Central School and Aberystwyth he had no more ideas.

Like so many in my position, I waited for the phone to ring, and blamed my agent when it didn't. He was the problem not me.

Maybe that sounds like arrogance but, so many years later - wiser and more mature - I still believe I was right.

The phone DID ring, but not with a job offer. Nevertheless, the result was that my whole life suddenly took the turn I was hoping for and lifted me right up onto the next level. After all, every good story, even a true one, has to have its ups and downs. But before the page turner and the career changer let us stay depressed and retread the road to Aberystwyth. I had been contracted to return at the end of the year.

The road to Aberystwyth is a dark and lonely one, and second time around seemed even more diabolical. In those days, it was the most difficult place to reach; it was well nigh impossible to get out of; and, on Sundays, we had to travel some distance just to get a drink. Furthermore, if you wanted to eat out after 7.00pm, the choice was limited to fish and chips or Chinese. One night, I made the dreaded mistake of heading for the Chinese. It was a scary experience.

Perhaps to avoid scaring the kids, I had been spared another instalment of Dr. Crankenheim and his horrors to direct. Instead, the chosen piece that Christmas was *Beowulf*, from the old English poem I had laboured over at university and which had been adapted for the stage by Christopher Sandford.

Condemned to these darkest reaches, at the darkest time of the year, I decided to drag with me a group of actors that I already knew. After all, who better to play the blonde hero who arrives to save 'Hrothgar's' kingdom than the blonde Rocky from the Royal Court, Rayner Bourton? He was joined by Stephen Hatton, David George and Brian Attree, all of whom deserve my lifelong gratitude and I did eventually employ them all again, in more glamorous surroundings.

Maybe to return the favour, Stephen suggested taking me out for a meal. All nocturnal or even late evening activity in Aberystwyth was confined to eating or watching television, and so I was more than happy to take up this invitation.

And so it was that, one dark and decidedly sulky night, we strode out into the welcoming arms of downtown Aberystwyth and made for the promenade. Having watched the shutters come down on the town's only fish and chip bar, we continued through the darkness in search of the Chinese restaurant. The only sound that echoed around us all the while was the tramp of our boots and the screech from an odd owl. Maybe the owl was a seagull, but the former suited the night more accurately.

December waves spilled onto the shore and dark clouds lowered above us, as we spied the distant glow of the sign that marked our destination. It probably read "The Cantonese Duck" or "The Great Wall of China" I forget, and it's immaterial but, as we trod the long road towards it, my colleague and I passed the time bemoaning our fate and imagining ourselves under the bright lights of Shaftesbury Avenue.

Once inside the restaurant, we began to warm through and check out our surroundings. Alongside the peeling wallpaper, another three or four customers murmured gently, as though discussing state secrets and I guess our more theatrical tones rang out in stark contrast. However, the patron soon arrived with well thumbed, faded menus and we became aware of lively appetites. I didn't want my fellow diner to be too generous on my account, but he was insistent that we didn't want for anything.

So, things in batter and bowls of rice, accompanied by hot plates and chopsticks arrived in their time, and we tucked in.

It was a pleasant enough evening and there was plenty to talk about helped along by a couple of bottles of wine and so it was quite late when we sat back and suggested that maybe it was time to leave. The streets were unlikely to be much quieter than they were when we left our digs - perhaps just a bit colder.

My friend reached for his wallet. Embarrassment heightened his already flushed cheeks as he confessed that his money was still resting on the bedside table of his room. How could he have forgotten it, I thought? My own money and cards were securely locked in my case. He would have to go back, and quickly.

It was a strange sensation sitting alone, at an empty table, toying with the remains of a 2-ply paper napkin. I realised that the other diners had long since left, and I noticed that two waiters had now joined the patron all of whom looked remarkably similar. The restaurant was gloomy, but they were lined up along the bar, fixed smiles clinging to their faces. Suddenly, one of them stepped forward and began to clear everything from the table. The patron suggested the bill to me. I nodded and smiled and asked if I could smoke. He sighed and, within minutes, the third member of this Chinese family arrived with a small, scratched ashtray.

As I smoked, and tried to look relaxed, I remembered the time it had taken to walk from where we were staying. Even then it had seemed interminable. I hoped Stephen would hurry.

The bill had arrived; my cigar stub lay in the ashtray - proof that I had finished; chairs were being stacked on tables. I decided to confess.

Almost as soon as I had admitted not being able to pay the bill, not just yet, I regretted it. Smiles were replaced by sinister and menacing glares. My friend, I said, would only be a few minutes more. Could I use the loo? I disappeared, but I knew that a waiter was posted at the door.

When I emerged, the kitchen was disgorging at least a dozen Chinese thugs - or so they appeared to me. Why were so many sited in Aberystwyth, for God's sake? Would I be found washed up on the beach, the following morning, a victim of The Cantonese Duck Mafia? Had they been sent by Mr Patrick O'Brien himself? And why are actors so often late for their entrance?

He made it back, of course. He wasn't blonde, but it felt as though he had arrived to save 'Hrothgar's' Kingdom. He paid the bill and we fled.

The show opened and I rehearsed my lines to Mr Bill Horne. "This relationship is going nowhere. Let me go! Release me!"

The actors gave their all. But what would Mr O'Brien have to say?

He nearly let me down. My heart sank when I saw the headline: *Gripping school show gets grim response* or some such, which surprised me, since it had gone extremely well on the opening day. The usual ploy would not work. Cut and paste *"gripping show gets response?"* Hardly.

It turned out that the review was in fact lamenting that once the schools had broken up for Christmas, and despite extensive telephoning from the theatre to head teachers the week before, the later performances were often played before rows of empty seats. Ultimately, Patrick was actually thrilled by what he saw *full of exciting entertainment, nicely offset by gentle humour.* Well, you could have fooled me.

The most I recall from that particular show was the understanding and realisation that I had suddenly completed my directing apprenticeship in the Theatre. I knew so because for the first time ever I didn't feel a deep involvement in the rehearsal process, only a permanent frustration that I might be starting to slip backwards. I yearned for the step up, for the rush of excitement to return and, as it happened, I didn't have to wait long.

PART THREE

Orbiting the Stars

I recall a bizarre dinner party in London. The occasion in itself was unusual, but the dénouement surpassed everything that went before. I barely knew the host, and nobody who arrived to spend the evening seemed to be acquainted with anybody else.

We were gathered together as individuals: one actor, one director, one architect, one writer, one sculptor, and so on, about ten in all. The dining table was shaped in a perfect circle and the idea was that, like King Arthur's knights, we would bring to it stimulation, wisdom, wit and maybe even a crossing of swords.

As the director, I found myself sitting next to the South African actress, Janet Suzman. From the outset, we weren't fired with any enthusiasm for one another. Having set her feminist credentials firmly down with the entrée, she then seemed intent on emasculating any male whose name was mentioned. I found it tedious, and looked for stimulation elsewhere.

We were aware of the persistent dull thud of party music upstairs, and conversation around the table was invaded, from time to time, by a raised drunken voice from above. Our looks were drawn to the ceiling, our eyebrows raised in each other's direction. It was unfortunate, I thought, that our host's enjoyment of his own evening of more erudite entertainment was being threatened in this way.

Raring to go·

At that moment, I saw the wall behind his head crack open. At first, a mere hairline fracture, but soon the entire room appeared to be in danger of splitting wide open. Having alerted the rest of the party, I noticed a restrained sense of panic wash over the other guests.

Our host rushed to his front door, and opened it to reveal a crush of party guests queuing on the stairs to swell further the already dangerous numbers gyrating in the flat above.

The police were called. Windows were thrown open, only to disclose more cars of party goers arriving below. Communal panic turned to individual self preservation. Ms Suzman was the first to seek a backstairs way out. If the police arrived and drugs were seized, then surely the Press would be involved and reputations might be destroyed. Thus seemed to go the logic.

A seventh storey flat did seem suddenly to represent a dangerous environment. We found our coats; one or two of us found time to drain our glasses; we swam and fought against the stream. There was no time for "Thanks for a lovely evening" style pleasantries. We were off.

I allowed a feminist arm to hold onto mine, as we made our way out of the building and round past the dustbins, at the back. We may have arrived as distinguished individuals, but we left in hurried pairs, as though racing to Noah's Ark.

And why am I relating this story? I hope as a neat bookend for the recall of another bizarre party, also with a South Africa connection. In fact, I was in Johannesburg standing on a balcony, helplessly watching my dinner guests as they dodged sniper fire...

But how did I get there? And why wasn't I in London with Ava Gardner, watching the First Night of my own show? We have to head for Baker Street. Elementary, my dear Watson, a dastardly act of savage ruthlessness was being perpetrated. I throw my hands up in surrender. But to bowdlerise the lyrics of the song, there are fewer than 50 ways to leave your agent, believe me. Little Newport Street was dumped, and a phone call summoned me to Baker Street.

I left the bland Mr. Horne and went to someone who most definitely divided opinion. But I was with him for the next four years. And, as with all good characters entering a story for the first time, this one needs some introduction and description. May I, therefore, present the inimitable John Mahoney.

John insisted on the Mahoney being pronounced Marny, and he could pour a vodka and tonic like nobody else I know. In fact, if you had positioned yourself outside Chalfont Court in Baker Street, where John lived and had his office, you would have had little difficulty in spotting his clients as they came out. They would look just a little the worse for wear.

Whether intentional or not, his vodka based hospitality was a great method of deflecting any criticism or complaint. You might arrive determined to get a few things sorted out and rid yourself of a bit of pent up frustration over the job situation, but within half an hour you would be giggling at John's outrageous anecdotes, however many times you'd heard them and exonerating him of all blame for your lengthy lack of employment. Even at 11.00 in the morning.

Everything was on a grand scale. One of the first things he did when I joined the agency was to hire a London theatre, The Greenwood Theatre, to showcase my talents. For the occasion, he put at my disposal his full list of clients, those that were available, and these included: Wendy Richard, Peter Davison, Jeff Rawle, Robin Nedwell, Dinah Sheridan and Jenny Hanly. We would all meet regularly, as we passed through the office, invariably making plans to work together on some project or other. Most of them never came to anything - probably forgotten once the vodka wore off, but it was all stimulating and great fun.

Lavish generosity was John Mahoney's hallmark and, for those clients adopted into the inner circle, usually young men and we all knew the score, life could take on a very pleasurable aspect. He was part of a long line of agents who surround themselves with pretty boys, starlets, television names or up and coming young talents. For their part, they invest the agent with power, the power to advance their careers and their fortunes for them.

John provided glamour and a quirky eccentricity, in a form that has probably disappeared for all time from our business. He wanted his clients to believe that he knew everybody; that he could secure a table at short notice at some choice restaurants; that he could get tickets for a sell out performance; and that he could throw a party to rate with the very best. From my own experience, much of this was true.

Ironically, he rarely went to the theatre to see a play, even if one of his own clients was in the cast. He would much rather be out front for Shirley MacLaine or Lena Horne, and I was often there with him. But he did NOT appreciate the generosity returned.

More than once, I insisted on treating him to a meal, but he would then spend the evening bitching the food, or the waiters, or the general décor - anything to demonstrate that he wasn't enjoying himself. It was hurtful, of course, but John had a sharp, visceral tongue, and couldn't help himself. It was better all round to allow him the vanity of spreading his own hospitality since he was so hopeless at accepting anyone else's.

He called me up on a Thursday evening once, to ask what I was doing for dinner that Saturday. Gradually, his plan was revealed. The new ferry crossing between Harwich and Vlissingen (Flushing) had just opened. We would have dinner in Holland.

Despite that fact that I'm not happy on water and dread any kind of sea crossing, I found myself agreeing to go with him. In the event, he brought plenty of vodka and only had to order a string of tonic waters to accompany them. That together with a calm sea made the experience palatable. In Vlissingen, we found a hotel, and arranged to meet within the hour to set out for a grand Dutch or Indonesian meal.

Unluckily for John and like so many provincial towns in Holland by 9.00pm, even on a Saturday night, the place was deserted. I might have been in Aberystwyth again and yes we ended up with a regular bog standard Chinese. It was surely not the glamorous outing that John had hoped for, but we both enjoyed the trip.

Deep down there was a sadness about him. He was a failed actor, overweight and balding, he wore a very unconvincing toupee and, once his coterie of clients and young men had vanished into the night after a lavish dinner, or show, or party, I suspect he was also a very lonely man. In later years, he bought a cottage in Brighton and spent increasing amounts of time there - no doubt wowing, and sometimes impressing, the locals. And it was there that he died prematurely, alone in his bed, leaving behind the image of a sad and pathetic figure, who was never as great as he thought he was.

So… The Agency designed with The Industry in Mind as the John Mahoney organisation presented itself, took over the Greenwood Theatre near London Bridge for one night only on February 14th so that their newest directing talent could present an anthology of theatrical excerpts to celebrate St. Valentine's Day. It seemed like an audacious gamble; I was terrified; it was an extraordinarily exciting occasion; and shortly afterwards I trotted off to Leatherhead.

I was invited to direct Restoration comedy at the respected Thorndike Theatre there. It was run by a formidable lady, called Hazel Vincent Wallace.

Some people referred to her as Hazel Bader Meinhof. Others knew her as Heavy Goods Vehicle, following an incident where the driver of one such juggernaut had mistakenly parked outside the theatre in the bay marked HVW.

Hazel was also famous for a call she made to one distinguished and experienced actor, to check his availability. When told that, alas, he was not available, her response was, "Well, if you think of anyone who could play it, please let me know. We're scraping the bottom of the barrel, as it is."

HVW and I tangled early on.

I'd gone to Leatherhead to direct *The Provok'd Wife*, by John Vanbrugh, and Hazel and I met to discuss casting. At the very top of my list of favourites to play Lady Brute was Nyree Dawn Porter. Hazel's reaction was a dismissive shake of the head.

It's impossible to exaggerate the iconic status that Nyree enjoyed in those days. Ever since Irene, in *The Forsyte Saga*, the very mention of her name usually brought an awestruck glow to people's faces, especially the men. Hazel's response amazed me, particularly since she had given Nyree her first job in 1958, after arriving in the country from New Zealand.

"Unreliable," "too risky," and "we can't afford understudies," these were some of the remarks thrown at me. Nevertheless, I was determined, at the very least, to check out her availability.

In 1970, Nyree had been awarded the O.B.E., but had been out of the limelight for a couple of years. She'd got married and taken off on a 12 month honeymoon in a ménage à trois, it seemed. Soon after, she had a baby girl - Natalya Francesca, 'Tassie' - and was only now considering work again. She invited me to her house to meet. I confess to being a little nervous as I rang the bell, but as soon as the door opened and I came face to face with this beautiful woman with a flashing smile, I relaxed entirely.

Within a few years, we would be skinny dipping in the Aegean Sea together and later I would have to kick her out of the bathroom. But, for now, as I looked at her standing there in baggy sweater and slacks before inviting me in, I was just hoping that we could work together.

Nyree was prepared to audition, there and then, but I said, "No. Just come to Leatherhead and be my Lady Brute." If everything else was agreed, I was ready to give HVW my assurance that I would take full responsibility for any complications.

And there were none. Nyree was a dream to work with on that show. There is an apocryphal story that persists to this day that Noël Coward referred to Nyree Dawn Porter as "the three worst actresses," but her own version was always that The Master had asked to see her, because he wanted her to be in one of his plays. As she walked into the room, he greeted her with, "Ah, my three favourite actresses!"

My own opinion remains that Nyree could be a fine actress. And she certainly made a great success of *The Provok'd Wife*, though the fatuous remark from the critic Sheridan Morley opening his review that, "All you need, to play Restoration comedy, is a long neck. Nyree

Dawn Porter has a long neck..." probably said more about him than anything that we achieved at Leatherhead.

HVW had neatly taken to her bed with shingles throughout the rehearsal period, and so there was no more interference from that quarter. And, personally, the show was a triumph:

Sir John Vanbrugh's Provok'd Wife is Tony Craven's first production at the Thorndike. After seeing the first night of this Restoration comedy on Tuesday, I certainly hope it is not his last. And again: *The first night of Sir John Vanbrugh's Provok'd Wife at the Thorndike on Tuesday was one of the best I have seen there for some time... Tony Craven's production is glittering, vital, hilarious and piercing in its social comment...*

Not bad. And, furthermore, Nyree and I became firm friends.

The summer of 1976 was going to be long and hot in the UK, and I didn't leave it until the first drops of autumn rain started finally to fall. In the meantime, a good deal had happened - most of it good.

*　　　*　　　*　　　*　　　*

At Leatherhead, I was asked to adjudicate for a one act play festival. Three plays a night and, at the end of the week, I had to be locked in a room, so as not to be harassed, lobbied or seduced by any group wanting to influence my decision. I doubt I needed the protection. I was already being harassed and lobbied (though thankfully not seduced) by a Canadian producer called Mark Furness.

Scratch my back and I'll scratch yours. Mark was on to my agent in a flash, and purred down the phone. He was mounting a provincial tour of *Anastasia* and had been desperately - as yet, without success - trying to secure Nyree Dawn Porter for the lead. "If Tony can persuade Nyree to do it, then I'd be delighted for Tony to direct it." Subtle.

But I was happy to scratch. And Nyree agreed immediately. Suddenly, a black edged envelope was delivered to my house. I have never found out who sent it, and I was only mildly perturbed at the time. It simply read: *I hear you're working with NDP and PW - RIP.*

Since Nyree was now regularly calling me 'TC', I had taken to calling her 'NDP' and I already knew who the 'PW' referred to. Let us fast forward briefly to the late 80s and a busy roundabout in the south of

England. It was one of those bizarre moments in my life. Over the sound of the rush hour traffic, I was yelling to this particular actor: "If you promise to behave, I'll work with you! But you have to promise me here and now!" Scratch my back, and I'll scratch yours. By then, we knew the form. It had taken a little while, but it started when I walked into Mark Furness's office in Long Acre fresh from my triumph at having wrapped up the casting of the title role in *Anastasia*.

Elsie Winegum. That was our pet name for Peter Wyngarde. I've heard others - affectionate or not, depending on the experience. I had no preconceptions about Peter before we met. As far as I was concerned, he was the star of a couple of TV series, *Department S* and *Jason King*, but my first impressions when I came across him in Mark's office were of vanity and stupidity. As I arrived, I found producer and star locked in a bitter argument about billing.

It was as clear as day that Nyree playing the title role should have top billing, but Peter was trying to achieve parity. It was an unedifying spectacle, to say the least, to watch Peter Wyngarde take out a ruler and attempt to coerce Mark Furness into a formula that would never work.

It went something like this: If Nyree's name was at the top, with Peter's underneath but, if his was to the left and hers to the right, would his name seem more important? But maybe both names should gravitate to the centre, in which case, at what point should the names overlap? Should the 'N' of Nyree come over the 'W' of Wyngarde... and so on.

The initial outcome of all this nonsense, strictly worked out on the basis of inches with that ruler clutched in Peter's hand, was a farce. The problem lay in the length of Nyree's name, and the first draft that I saw of the poster subsequently had half of 'Dawn Porter' snaking in a kind of column up one side of the page.

Yet, on that first day, Peter was utterly charming toward me, politely suggesting a few one-to-one meetings prior to rehearsal. He wanted to go through the script with me. I sensed that I was about to be tested.

Before long, I was making regular trips to Earls Terrace, where Peter was living. The truth was that the script did need sorting out. An adaptation of a French novel, turned into a stage play and then amalgamated with scenes from the film version of 1956 with Ingrid Bergman and Yul Brynner resulted in all kinds of anomalies. We were dealing with a sequence of chapters and scenes through which characters and theories had constantly evolved, and in ways not always compatible. I had to arrive at a workable version of the piece, and Peter was anxious to achieve the same.

Our sessions together were curious and, ultimately, I had to put a stop to them. Young as I was, and relatively inexperienced in the commercial world of stars and egos, I was nevertheless mature enough to see that, as Peter's character was being fleshed out and rewritten, some of the other roles were being weakened, or side lined altogether.

It was soon clear where the vanity and flamboyance was taking us. Without a doubt, my leading actor was trying to ascertain just how far his director could be pushed. Like so many actors through time, his determination was to dominate the stage. My determination equally strong lay in keeping the play in balance and in telling the story of *Anastasia*.

Most mornings, Peter greeted me in his dressing-gown - sometimes in lively, skittish mood, sometimes like a bear with a sore head. But always the childlike fantasist. Tales of how the very name, Jason King, could instil awe and terror into gangs of potential muggers were relayed to me in all seriousness.

His nocturnal escapades were regular and sometimes dangerous. However, once he turned to confront the thugs who threatened him and uttered the awe inspiring words, "I'm Jason King!" Peter apparently became invisible.

For all his belief in the macho image of his television character, however, Peter the man still needed to wear lifts on stage to make him look taller, and the extra hairpiece to add youth and swashbuckling reality to the role.

Anastasia was due to set out on a lengthy provincial tour. The casting was coming together nicely. I had David Griffin, later to come to prominence in *Hi-De-Hi* and *Keeping Up Appearances*, and Gareth Forwood.

However, I was having a real problem with the third lead, The Dowager Empress of Russia and, even though plenty of names were being put forward, none of them felt right. Then, one day, Mark's assistant Lindsay Granger charmingly suggested her mother for the role.

Lindsay was the daughter of the screen actor, Stewart Granger originally called James Stewart, but who by Equity rules again had to change his name, for obvious reasons. Ironically, he had met his first wife Lindsay's mother at the old Birmingham Rep. I hope that's all clear?

And so it was that I arranged to meet Elspeth March. Her first words, as I shook her hand, were "No, Fucker!" as it seemed at the time. In fact, as I walked into the room to greet her, I felt a small dog, a Shih-Tzu, nip my ankle, and realised that the "No!" was meant for the dog.

"What an unusual name for a dog," I said as I regained my composure.

"Yes. We used to have another called Bib."

I looked down. "Ah. Hello, TUCKER."

I have rarely fallen for an actress so quickly, and Elspeth was very soon offered the part. Her character appears regularly in this story, and I hope she'll become familiar. She was a large, formidable and commanding presence, but with one of the sweetest smiles that I can recall. And she knew everybody.

It meant that Lindsay grew up in Hollywood, in a household regularly visited by major stars, such as Elizabeth Taylor, Richard Burton, Vivian Leigh, and where Noël Coward would take to a grand piano at parties, whilst Judy Garland sang through a few standards.

Years later, when Judy Garland arrived in London to make *I Could Go On Singing*, Elspeth offered to move out and put her house at her old friend's disposal. It was Dirk Bogarde, Judy's co-star in the film who strongly advised against it: "Elspeth, darling, don't be mad! She'll wreck the place within days, and your phone bill will be astronomical calling round the world, 24:7 just take my word!" Fortunately probably Elspeth heeded Bogarde's advice.

Dirk Bogarde, who got just a little bit too close to me at a urinal at Heathrow one day; who lived with Tony Forwood; who had separated from Glynis Johns; with whom he had fathered Gareth; who was now playing Prince Paul in *Anastasia*, and en route to the Grand Theatre, Wolverhampton, where the production would start its tour.

I had to be on my toes throughout rehearsals. Nyree had developed a little bit of steel since Leatherhead days. She and Peter had worked together before, and she understood his manipulative tricks. She thought she wasn't bothering me with her problems, except that she would call her agent at night who would then call me, so that I would call Peter and sort things out before starting rehearsals again the following day.

Perhaps there was manipulation on both sides. But, at the centre of it all, was Elspeth the mother hen, clucking her mediation and delivering her professional, down-to-earth theatrical wisdom. And she rested on me, like a ROCK. Too much so, from time to time.

We'd been in Wolverhampton for less than 24 hours, and I was ready to begin a full day of technical rehearsals. Our hotel was very handy for the theatre and so I was still in my room when the in house phone rang. It was Elspeth.

"Darling, can you believe it? The reception staff have refused to deliver a Daily Mail to my room!"

I admired their taste, but remained silent. I was sure there was more to come.

"It's not as though they don't have one. So, I just wanted to let you know that I've checked us out."

"Us?"

"Well, of course! I said that my director would agree with me. But never mind. I've found us a much better hotel further out."

And so we left. We went to the much better hotel further out and, next day, Nyree and Peter joined us.

Indeed, Elspeth March was very much my Dowager Empress and I loved her performance and came to adore her as a person.

Many months later, John Mahoney received a phone call from Anna Neagle's representative. He asked how I would feel about doing *Anastasia* again, since his client wanted to play it in Australia and very much wanted me to go over and direct it. She was a big name at the time but was never going to be in Elspeth's league. However, it was a chance to work in Australia, and so I told my agent not to reject it out of hand.

After some weeks had passed, I asked if there was any further news. John confided that everyone had been very excited until they became aware that Anna Neagle was expecting to play the title role.

The heat of that summer was intense. How the cast of that Russian melodrama in their heavy costumes and furs managed the tour with so little fuss, I shall never quite understand. In Hull, the streets smelled of fish and, on the south coast, well…

… It sometimes happens that where there are two shows in town the cast of one invites the other company to join them for a party. I went along to one of those with the *Anastasia* crowd, especially having worked with Ronnie Barker, to meet Ronnie Corbett. The place was pretty crowded and noisy, but I managed to call out to the group I was with at one point, "I thought Ronnie Corbett was going to be here."

Fingers were pointed. Downwards. I'd made the clichéd faux-pas. He was standing beside me, but I just hadn't seen him. Shrunk in the heat? Fortunately, the man appeared to be deep in conversation with somebody else and looking away from me and upwards. We never got to discuss his screen partner.

Maybe the heat also helped in my separating Peter Wyngarde from his extra hair for a while, but he clung tenaciously to the lifts.

For now, all was going well. Almost. There were regular calls for my intervention - usually from other members of the cast and, almost always, to do with Peter's theatrical egotism. He could make life miserable for some of his junior colleagues, and their cries reached me in London.

Consequently, every two weeks or so, I would be found after the performance in a regional town or city somewhere, sitting down for dinner with my leading man, in some expensive restaurant, bringing him back to heel. He sometimes left with one of the waiters. As Jason King, he boasted, he could pull anyone he wanted. What I wanted, however, was discipline on stage.

To go to his dressing room and offer congratulations in all honesty on a particular performance (and he could be mesmerising) was to greet a beaming sponge. "Just keep it like that," would invariably result, the next night, in a grotesque over the top parody.

On one occasion, he took it upon himself to launch into his dialogue in French. His reasoning was that, as a member of the Russian aristocracy, that was the language he would have used at court. In making his fellow actors uncomfortable, however, he was also making a fool of himself. These were early signs that the man was losing his grip and further down the line I think he let loose altogether.

Nevertheless, as the tour progressed, there was increasing talk of

West End interest in the production. In Brighton, there were rumoured to be at least 3 managements with their eyes on the show. By the last night, one team even arrived to measure the set and make detailed notes.

The company manager gave me the nod. The cast sensed excitement. Nyree and Peter put in increasing numbers of calls to their agents. At the age of just 28, I was about to have my first West End production.

And then came a deafening silence.

*   *   *   *   *

When I was growing up, various people always seemed to come into our house on a Sunday afternoon, Robin Hood and his Merrie Men, William Tell and Landburger Gessler, Sir Francis Drake and his Good Queen Bess… bear with me, relevance will make her entrance very shortly.

It took a deal of bravery and confidence for Helen Montagu the leading producer at HM Tennent to be so cavalier with one of the 20th century's great theatrical figures. Ben Travers, a master of farce and comedy for so many years, took his latest play to her for production. She liked it, but had an important stipulation to make before agreeing to produce it.

Helen thought that there was one person superbly placed to create the leading role - Joan Plowright. Unfortunately, she wasn't available and was unlikely to be so for some time. If Travers was prepared to wait, then Tennent's would do it. However, Helen would quite understand if he decided to take the play to other producers.

By this time, Ben Travers was in his late 80s and could have been forgiven if he'd been a little impatient. But he agreed to wait. Two years later, *The Bed Before Yesterday* was in production with Joan Plowright, John Moffatt and Jonathon Cecil, and with the towering presence of Lindsay Anderson as director.

It has to be said, and I'm a huge fan of Lindsay Anderson's film work and stage drama, that he was not at his best with comedy. As previews came and went, and the First Night approached, audience reaction was far from favourable. In other words, there was very little laughter.

Lindsay panicked and delivered a single note backstage night after night: "Faster! Just play it faster!"

On the opening night, and for the first time, the play worked. The show was a great success and ran for many months. When Plowright's contract expired, she was replaced by Sheila Hancock. At the same time, there were requests for the play to be released for production elsewhere.

This is where these events dovetail with my own story.

For the first production outside the West End, Helen Montagu came to me. I was thrilled to be asked (Tennents was one of London's most powerful and prestigious theatrical producers), and to work with Ben Travers was a significant bonus. Furthermore, the casting was going to bring me into direct contact with one of those Sunday afternoon visitors. It wasn't Richard Greene from *Robin Hood*, and it certainly wasn't Willoughby Goddard's 'Gessler'. The leading lady was going to be Sir Francis Drake's Queen Elizabeth, the film star, Jean Kent.

I was dispatched to meet her. She and her husband lived mainly in Malta at that time, but they had a pied-à-terre in London, in Marylebone High Street and, as I climbed the stairs to their flat, I was remembering what an avid fan I had been of her Elizabeth.

I stood outside the door and thought of my first encounter with Nyree Dawn Porter. As I waited for it to open, I also thought briefly about Elspeth March's reaction to the name Jean Kent. She had very quickly altered one of the vowels to show exactly what she thought. I dismissed the implication, as the door swung open.

The image I had of the TV character was of an imposing, handsome, and imperious woman with a twinkle in the eye. The person I came face to face with now was also handsome and imposing, and the twinkle was immediately apparent.

Once inside, I was quickly put at my ease. Please remember that I was only 28. At that time, I had no inkling of just how big a star Jean had been in films. I didn't know about Gainsborough Girls, and I couldn't name any of those pictures that she had starred in. I certainly never imagined that a large part of the West End had had to be closed for her wedding, because the crowds who wanted to see her had been so big that hordes of mounted police were called in to control them.

So, it must have seemed fatuous and naïve in the extreme for her director to natter on about Elizabeth I. Imperious re-entered the equation. Just for a few moments. After that, we seemed to gel.

As exciting as all these developments were for me, it was equally amazing that the first production outside the West End would be in South Africa and Zimbabwe, or Rhodesia, as it then was.

I checked my passport and signed the contract. And, almost immediately, came the bombshell.

Scratch my back, and I'll scratch yours. Unfortunately, some scratches are more painful than others. And they can leave scars, often, for years to come. Betrayal comes later in this story. For now, let us just say that what happened next was no more than bad luck.

Mark Furness had finally and without warning signed his own contract. *Anastasia* was heading for the West End, for the Cambridge Theatre, and now I was no longer available to direct it. It was my production that had been sold; my work that had paid off; but I had missed out on the rewards at the last moment.

I joined Ben Travers in a private box at the theatre. Night after night, I sat with him to watch the play and talk about it. Having seen Joan Plowright's performance, I now took in Sheila Hancock's. For me, Plowright had been perfect. Hancock, on the other hand, was over the top and disturbed the balance with John Moffatt's more contained delivery. The play was sailing closer to becoming distasteful.

Surprisingly, Ben Travers told me that he preferred Sheila Hancock in the role of Alma. We had to agree to differ. Thankfully, we differed on very little else and I found his comments totally stimulating. But he was also very aware of the play's failings, and asked for suggestions from me to improve it. A couple of these he leapt on with delight.

One evening just before the interval, we were joined in the box by Lindsay Anderson. He said some nice things; we chatted a little; and, when the curtain came down, he suggested that the three of us have a drink in the bar.

As I stood there with these 2 great men of the theatre I suppose I grew in stature a little. Especially when Ben gushed that I had had some really good and useful ideas.

The following day, I had a call from Helen Montagu.

"What have you done to upset Lindsay?"

"What do you mean?"

"Well, he talked about you by name, until this morning. Now, it's 'your friend.' I think he's jealous."

I think she was right. Lindsay Anderson had translated really good and useful ideas as an attack on his production. Sensitivities and egos hem us in all around in this business.

I had preferred the company of the first Lindsay, daughter of Elspeth March, who (I couldn't stop thinking about it) would soon be rehearsing *Anastasia* with a new director, in readiness for the West End.

Another intriguing surprise came across from Helen Montagu. It's strange to think that Franco Zeffirelli's first choice for his 1968 award winning film version of *Romeo and Juliet* was Paul McCartney. Strange, because Leonard Whiting's picture and his casting together with Olivia Hussey became iconic, and it is now impossible to imagine anyone else in that version. Leonard Whiting it seemed was now joining the cast of *The Bed Before Yesterday*, and would travel with me to Johannesburg.

My abiding impressions of Leonard from that film were certainly of his extraordinary beauty, but also of his appalling attempts to speak Shakespeare. He was definitely street wise, but those flat London vowels did nothing for Romeo's language. Now he had been cast in the role played by Jonathon Cecil in London. Why?

Whilst I tried to figure that one out, I heard that Mark Furness had done the smart thing and gone to Nyree's favourite director, and one she'd travelled the world with - Frank Hauser - to take over *Anastasia*. I was depressed.

Meanwhile, the television news was full of violent unrest taking place in the townships of South Africa, and I began to wonder whether that production, too, might be taken away from me. Depression set in further.

Equity now called for a boycott on its members working in South Africa. For the time being, it stopped at advising us not to go there but although I despised apartheid as much as anyone I felt my views would be better informed by going ahead. Equally, there were voices arguing for people to visit and not to heed a boycott. I sought assurances that *The Bed Before Yesterday* would not play to segregated audiences, and they were given. On the other hand, the idea of dozens of black South

Nyree Dawn Porter & Edward Arthur, in Anastasia

*Photograph by Michael I. Barrett

Africans queuing round the block for tickets for an English boulevard comedy was in itself pretty laughable.

These were turbulent times for me. But, suddenly, everything came right.

Frank Hauser had refused to work with Peter Wyngarde. Nyree was refusing to work with any other director unless it was me. The word went out from her agent to Mark Furness: "Unless you find a way to secure Tony Craven's services as director, and bring him back to *Anastasia*, there will be no West End transfer".

I sat back and waited. John Mahoney licked his lips in anticipation of the battle to come. His claws were sharpened, and he was ready to use them to scratch deep into Mark Furness's back. As it turned out, I don't think he needed to. Mark was already squealing.

A deal was done. I would carry out any recasting that I felt was necessary, and rehearse the new people in, until the moment I left for Johannesburg. There would be a week's try out in Edinburgh and, for that and the move into the Cambridge Theatre, a caretaker director - to be approved by me - would deal with the technical transfer and look after the production until my return.

Soweto exploded onto our screens. How unimportant everything else seemed.

I returned to my *Anastasia* family with one or two exceptions. Gareth Forwood had proved a disappointment as Prince Paul and a couple of other cast members, as I had been, now found themselves unavailable. Prince Paul was the most difficult to replace, as it was the fourth lead, but Edward Arthur fitted the bill and, though he was too good looking for Peter's liking, he provided the glamour that Gareth had lacked and as far as I was concerned Peter would have to deal with the competition as best he could.

I turned my attentions to Pieter Toerien, the South African producer. He must have been the one to have asked for Leonard Whiting - on the face of it, so wrong for the part of Aubrey. Having waited so long to get the right actor for the lead in the West End, Helen Montagu seemed unlikely to be responsible. And Ben Travers? Ben was something of a lecherous old devil and was only interested in the girls, the taller and more curvaceous the better. Was Leonard Whiting a sop for Toerien?

All would be revealed.

Timing, as they say, is everything. I went to Berlin in my early teens, just after the Wall had gone UP. It was incredibly exciting. The sense of danger, the lust for Life, for treating every day as though it were the last, these were tangible. If timing was everything, then this was the time to visit South Africa.

Too many opinions were being brayed around dinner tables in London, without firsthand experience with which to back them up. I was ready to cross the Equator, to swap early autumn for the early spring and to set out on my first professional adventure abroad. The play, I was sure, would be fun to direct, but the taste of Africa and the raw political encounter - these I was looking forward to with relish.

Even I, however, could not be prepared for the events that were about to unfold. Or the dangers and seductions that awaited me.

*   *   *   *   *

I left the *Anastasia* rehearsal room with mixed feelings. The cast were on the threshold of a West End opening, and I was proud of them. We'd been through a great deal together and I wanted to be there at the moment of their triumph. But the production was in good shape; we had good new people; and there was, hopefully, a safe pair of hands to guide them through in the shape of the director Hugh Goldie.

The long, hot summer was coming to an end. As I climbed into the taxi that would take me to Heathrow, I felt the first few drops of rain to fall in months. I sat back and smiled. Our overnight stop would be in Paris. Though, on this occasion, I didn't know just how difficult it was going to be to leave.

At the airport, I met up with Jean Kent and Leonard Whiting. The other actor under contract for the play was already in Johannesburg. He was Graham Armitage, who had fallen in love in South Africa and decided to make it his home. Loyalties had been swiftly and abruptly transferred from London. Graham now maintained that Notting Hill, particularly during Carnival time, was far more dangerous than anything that was happening in Soweto.

I was intrigued to meet Leonard Whiting. Just eight years after

Romeo, he had altered noticeably. He still had his looks, but they were harder to find. He was now overweight and rounded.

By contrast, Paris seemed more beautiful than ever to me. We three travellers booked into our hotel and I got the chance to swiftly reacquaint myself with pockets of the city.

Next morning, after a leisurely breakfast of mouth watering croissants and coffee, we took a cab back to Le Bourget airport. How I cursed the conjuror. How tiny the differences between Mary Miller and Mary Millar and the Harry Corbetts and Harry H Corbett. How brutal the complexities of Thornton and Thawnton of Chapman and Lindsay Anderson and Granger.

My airline ticket was in the name of Tony Craven, but my passport bore a different identity, and the formidable madame at the check-in desk was having none of it. She was adamant that I was going nowhere with that ticket. Disaster loomed.

But nobody, it seemed, had reckoned on Jean Kent. As I charmed and cajoled, Jean marched forward. Queen Elizabeth was on the rampage again. If her director was not leaving the airport, then neither was she and did they know, by the way, who she was?

It seemed as though we were on the verge of an international incident of major proportions, as other passengers stopped to listen in. They watched a performance from Jean Kent that was astonishing, forceful, utterly courteous, and as it turned out thoroughly persuasive. Madame crumpled. A boarding pass miraculously appeared and we were on our way. To this day, I don't know how, or why. But... did I care?

Our next stop was Nice. On the flight, I set about getting to know Leonard Whiting. Jean had clearly already decided he had nothing going for him, and her opinion was going to harden considerably before we even touched down in Johannesburg.

For my part, I discovered a sensitive and gentle person, desperate that he'd been unable to handle his status, bitter that he'd been picked up and then dropped by Zeffirelli (who had kept Olivia Hussey's career going, but seemed to turn his back on Leonard), and genuinely terrified of the task before him, of making a success of this Ben Travers comedy.

Could he produce that upper class drawl that was, possibly, the only way to get away with Aubrey? I sensed it would be as difficult an adjustment as it had been to make any sense of Shakespeare. I was now convinced that this casting was a ruse. Somebody wanted the golden boy from the silver screen in the company and, if he wasn't up to the part then so be it.

From Nice, the journey was a long one. The sheer size of Africa was numbing. As the Sahara Desert came into our sights, the in flight movie began. It was still stretched out below us through the closing credits.

Eventually, and behind schedule, we landed in the Congo where we were not allowed to disembark. This was a war torn country at the time. All we could do, as the plane sat on the tarmac, and the minutes ticked by, was to look out. It was dark. Shadowy figures armed and uniformed roamed outside, rifles and guns at the ready.

It was a nerve wracking 60 minutes. Images from the television of violence and bloodletting in Soweto flashed through my head. The cosy pub room rehearsal space that I had left behind in Covent Garden, and all the friendly faces inside it, seemed suddenly very, very far away.

Meanwhile, Leonard had been enjoying the on board hospitality. By now he was sleeping, and anxious looks from Jean Kent were occasionally thrown in his direction. Partly, I am sure, this came from a sense of foreboding as to what his state presaged for the production, but it was also because she had entrusted him, as we boarded in Paris, with the safe-keeping of a fur coat.

We finally landed at Johannesburg at 2.00am, local time. Jean was off the plane first, and I followed closely behind. Bringing up the rear - somewhat inebriated and dragging a fur coat behind him - was Leonard. It was a moment or two before I realised that, though the coat he had with him was similar, it was not the same as the one that Jean was now wearing around her shoulders.

There was now another woman in hot pursuit of our Romeo, and I left him to explain his reasons for walking off with her own no doubt valuable fur coat.

Ahead of us was our welcoming committee - or rather, Pieter Toerien and his assistant, Lindy King. Two limousines waited to take us downtown. Pieter would travel with Jean and Leonard, whilst I would follow in the second car, with Lindy.

Beams of delight greeted Jean and, for me, there were warm, welcoming smiles. Heads craned to catch the first sight of Leonard. It wasn't the best of arrivals.

The son of Montague was not newly arrived from Verona, as perhaps was expected. Instead, it was a bloated and crimson faced actor staggering slightly, and looking travel weary and dishevelled who finally caught up with us. The look of disbelief and horror on Pieter Toerien's face spoke volumes. My earlier suspicions were proving to be spot on.

Suddenly, I was upgraded to the first limo, with Jean and Pieter whilst Leonard was bundled into the car with Lindy King.

It had been a long and tiring day. It seemed an age since we breakfasted on those croissants in Paris. I was ready for my bed, but as I closed the door on the apartment that would be my home for the next few weeks it was already clear that I wouldn't be getting much sleep. Auditions were scheduled for 10.00am, and a car would pick me up soon after 9.00.

How is that we can travel to other parts of the globe and still come across familiar faces? 14 years after we worked together in Newcastle, I bumped into the actress, Pamela Buchner, in a hotel lobby in San Francisco. Now, as I settled into the audition room in downtown Johannesburg, and ran through the list of people waiting to see me, I came across the name of… Pamela Buchner.

It was good to see an erstwhile colleague again and, although there was no part in the play suitable for her, Pamela and I spent time together in South Africa. She had drifted down from Kenya as so many ex-pat actors did and no doubt has her own tales of Africa wrapped up in a personal memory box.

And now this story has to get serious and political for a brief while, and I hope it is no less compelling for that. But the change of season was not the only culture shock that reverberated through those early days in South Africa.

Almost immediately, and as a reflection of the apartheid system itself, my life became a series of conflicting and contrasting elements, running in tandem with each other. Their boundaries were determined by the simple fact of who I was, and by the colour of my skin.

As a visiting director from London, of course, I was treated well. Cocooned in a very pleasant apartment block, and ferried to and from the audition room by car, I was able to look out on the city from an advantageous viewpoint.

Johannesburg itself is an ugly place, architecturally, mostly high rise blocks of flats and office buildings, but what I witnessed in the name of apartheid was even uglier. Yet, in that rarefied, high altitude atmosphere, judgements seemed to become clouded, and less easy to make, as each day passed.

Very soon, I was a guest at the ballet. It was a performance of *Swan Lake*, with the incomparable Natalia Makarova and Anthony Dowell, and it was an experience I shall never forget. But next morning, by contrast, vastly different images invaded my cosseted soul.

I went to the post office, to buy a stamp. There was nobody ahead of me, and I was immediately ushered to a gleaming and spacious counter where I was promptly attended to. My eye was gradually drawn to the other side of the glass, however, to a crowd of blacks, waiting in a long line, heads bowed.

The simple persuasion of that encounter chimed immediately with those sentiments brayed at length at all those Hampstead dinner parties. Were they vindicated? It was too early to tell.

All the time, I wanted to believe the best. Each morning, I walked from where I was staying along the 30 minute trail through the city to the theatre where we rehearsed. Along the way, I smiled and said, "good morning" to people, black, white and coloured as I passed. I enjoyed the sunshine and the exercise.

After a few days, at the end of one rehearsal, somebody asked if I wanted to share a cab ride back to the part of town where we were staying. My response that I preferred to walk was met with disbelief. It seemed that the route I had been using so regularly passed through one of the most dangerous parts of Johannesburg, taking in a notorious prison building. No 'white' went there and certainly not without a good reason.

I scoffed, of course, and set off at my usual stride. I'm pretty tall, and probably gave off confident vibes. But, as I walked, and as the warnings echoed in my head, I felt intimidated for the first time. For fifteen minutes, I was aware that I passed no other white. I saw no other European.

Starkly, and abruptly, as I looked into the eyes of those I would normally call a greeting to, I saw hatred and I saw fear. There was a sense all around of potential violence. Blacks would step off the pavements and into the gutter, if I seemed to be in their way. Waves of antipathy broke over me.

I am ashamed to admit the sorry fact that my experience that evening marked the last time that I ever walked to or from work in Johannesburg.

Back on the other side of this disturbing conundrum, there was a compelling and seductive lifestyle on offer for a visiting British director. And it would have been all too easy to take full advantage of each and every invitation.

Those invitations would take me out of the city into glorious countryside to vast estates, of gigantic spreading oak trees and lush green lawns, where tennis courts and swimming pools were provided as backdrops to yet more indulgence. There in grand, colonial-style settings lunches were rolled out in decadent and obscene proportions for our delectation and delight.

I learned to say, "No".

But there were times when it was well nigh impossible to refuse, without causing a major incident. On those occasions, it seemed the world had stopped in an Edwardian age. A banquet for two dozen people would be attended at table by as many black employees.

I heard it boasted that these were acquired from Rhodesia. In such cases it was earnestly asserted they had been saved from a life of misery by their wealthy South African masters.

Silently, and always in their starched white gloves, these people carried out their duties around us ignored by everyone, until one of them made a mistake, or dropped something, or worse. Many times, I tried to engage one of two of them in conversation, but it was difficult. And, ultimately, it was pointless.

And so, I took the reassurance that I was seeing for myself - that, in the future, I would be able to speak from the standpoint of firsthand knowledge.

But was it really all so clear cut? Seismic shifts were never going to happen in the way I thought about the situation. But sympathies would before long start to spring up in unlikely places.

I now have to push into the spotlight for as long as she allows herself to stay, the maid who was allocated to my apartment. How frustrating it was and how inconvenient that she came to complicate and unravel my deep seated views on South Africa. How straightforward everything had seemed around the dinner tables of Kensington and Hampstead Garden Suburb.

Following Soweto, women from the township were having a hard time. They lived in abject fear of their own men folk. Each day, simply in order to provide for their families, these women travelled into the city to work for the whites. Each night when they returned to their homes, their reward was intimidation and violence.

One of the first shocks to come with firsthand experience is the need to face reality. Yes, these women were treated as little more than slaves, especially if we look at them through Home Counties eyes, but they were often looked after and protected by their employers, for whom I sensed they held a genuine and unshakeable loyalty.

My maid lived under incredible strains. She was uncomfortable at her work place helping a white person to live in some style and there was a constant fear in her eyes. She feared for herself and, when she went home at the end of each day, she was in fear of her life.

I tried to establish a different, more civilized relationship with her, but the walls behind which she had retreated were much too dense and complex to scale. I could never get her to call me anything but Boss, however much I encouraged it. Tony was out of the question for her, and Mr. Craven quickly reverted to Boss.

She worked quietly and efficiently, and I grew very fond of her, but eventually I became resigned to keeping the status quo. Nevertheless, I admired her courage. Each working day she left Soweto, to succumb to the affluent white centre of Johannesburg. And she went home each evening, never sure whether she would be returning the following day. I'm happy to report that, during my time there at least, she always did.

Meanwhile, and as an antidote to those colonial-style lunches, I decided to have an intimate little dinner party of my own, for some friends and company members. The market produce looked good, especially the avocados and pineapples, and kirsch was cheap, and I thought it would be an ideal opportunity for everyone to relax and chill out. Little did I know how much they would need to.

Come the evening, and whilst I was getting things ready, I heard the sound of gunfire. It wasn't an especially unusual event, I had discovered, but always in the distance some way away. This time, however, it all seemed very close and right in the neighbourhood. I went to the balcony and looked out.

Sure enough, the shooting was going on in the street below, and at regular intervals and, although I couldn't see anybody, the odd shout and scream were distinctly audible. Furthermore, the flash of ammunition delivered was clearly visible. Initially, it seemed exciting and I scanned the street for any obvious sign of activity.

It wasn't long before I found it - an actor, clasping a bottle of wine and hovering, anxiously, in a doorway. I wonder why actors always stand out so much.

This was one of my dinner guests but, not wanting to draw attention to myself on the balcony, I watched in silent anticipation to see what would happen. In the event, all that occurred was anticlimax. The actor crossed the street as though walking the red carpet and, before long I was at the entry phone speaker to let the poor man in.

Then, as I stood by the open door and waited for the lift to arrive at my floor, I heard another, more prolonged burst of sniper fire from the street. Back on my balcony, I was aghast to see another guest running, weaving, waving a bottle, and shouting up at me: "Let me in!" She didn't need to ask twice.

I never discovered the cause of such mayhem, and everybody finally arrived unscathed, but we were all reminded yet again of how far from home we had strayed.

And what of rehearsals? Not for the first time and certainly not for the last, I found it necessary to establish, early on, the golden rule: that each production only has one director.

I had already started to get on well with Jean Kent, and I liked what she was doing with the part. However, she could not resist a degree of meddling with scenes and characters that were not her concern. Sitting behind me, watching proceedings, she suddenly would break in with her own opinions. It was all done charmingly, and she was obviously used to doing it, but it was nevertheless very irritating and confusing for the other actors.

Everything came to a head on the third day, when Jean's intervention came at a particularly crass moment, and I shut her up very quickly. For the rest of the day, I didn't speak one word to her. I didn't give her a note, I didn't give her any direction, and I didn't answer any of her questions. It became a battle of wills. At the end of the rehearsal, I thanked everybody... and left. It was a high risk strategy.

A couple of days earlier, Jean's husband Jusuf had arrived in Johannesburg. I found him delightful and utterly charming, but wondered whether he would now interfere on her behalf. We were all staying at the same apartment block and, for most of the evening, the impasse appeared to have become entrenched.

So, I was relieved when the internal phone rang and I heard Jusuf's voice: "Jean was wondering whether you would like to join us for a drink."

I replied that I would be delighted, and made my way up the few floors to their apartment. Both were sweet and charming and we spent a very relaxed evening together. Never again were there any interruptions in rehearsal from Jean, and she and I went on to become firm friends, a friendship that existed to the day she died. In fact, whilst Jusuf was alive, they always referred to me as an adopted son.

Leonard Whiting, of course, was hopelessly miscast, and was never truly accepted by either of the two leading actors. Nevertheless, I developed a respect and liking for him, based on an intuitive sensitivity that he carried with him and a genuine determination to do his best. And I honestly think he didn't make a bad job of Aubrey.

He had a strong interest in music, which we discussed, and I learned much more from him about *Romeo and Juliet*, his relationship with Zeffirelli, and why he was left feeling so bitter from the experience.

I think our producer had long since lost interest in him. But he had taken a bit of a shine to me. Compliments abounded and his advances became more and more persistent as he tried to persuade me to stay on and direct the next production. I was hotly pursued. To the fringes of the Indian Ocean.

Pieter Toerien was reputedly one of the wealthiest men in the country, with enormous influence, and it was gratifying for me that he liked my work. It was surely a mark of his respect that he wanted me to direct a new play that he was presenting at a second theatre that he owned in Johannesburg.

Believe me, I had not forgotten that my first West End production was about to open at the Cambridge Theatre. My agent would attend the first night, and he promised to keep me informed. Staying on in South Africa was not an option. Pieter Toerien thought otherwise.

He applied pressure. He called on other people to try to persuade me. Finally, he invited me to Cape Town. He had a house on the coast, and would arrange a flight for Friday afternoon. He had a long weekend in mind. He would show me the sights.

This was an opportunity that I was not prepared to miss. Along with a flight to the Victoria Falls, it was one of the must do trips on my agenda. Just to make the situation clear, however, I reminded Pieter yet again that staying on for another production was out the question (just in case the Cape Town trip was intended to twist my arm).

The flight was arranged. Pieter went ahead. I packed a bag and took it to rehearsal. Then came a dramatic phone call.

Rioting had flared up in Cape Town, and to travel the road from the airport after dark was now dangerous. Pieter Toerien was on the phone, advising me to postpone my flight until Saturday morning.

Of course, I scoffed at the idea. I was too British to let such a little local difficulty force a change of plan. But Pieter was in deadly earnest. Rocks were being hurled indiscriminately from the bridges onto cars travelling into the city.

I looked around at the faces in the office. Everyone agreed with Pieter's advice. I had no option but to comply. One night fewer in Cape Town but a safer trip, it seemed.

The flight from Johannesburg the following morning took about 2 hours, during which the full beauty of the country was rolled out below me. It's a stunning landscape and it made me reflect, once again, on the tragedy that seemed to be engulfing its people.

The trademark limousine was waiting for me on my arrival and, on the road into the city, I saw destruction everywhere along the route. Postponement had been a good idea. It would have been very dangerous to travel down during the hours of darkness.

How quickly those images disappeared, as I caught my first sight of Table Mountain and the Indian Ocean. It is impossible to describe just how magical and romantic everything seemed to me from then on, especially after the monotony of Johannesburg.

Pieter's house was built, literally, on the water, in an exclusive coastal area on the far side of town. The terrace almost floated on the surface of the sea, which lapped gently underneath, and it was easy to understand why he was so proud of this getaway home. Everything in the house was operated from a series of remote controls, and doors throughout Cape Town glided open as easily throughout the weekend.

I was spoiled. No doubt about it. We ate at the finest restaurants, took tours of the concert hall and opera house, drove all around and visited the mountain and the beaches. Even then, the perils of seduction were clear, as I stumbled across sights that jarred with the luxury of this lifestyle.

There were miles of beautiful golden beaches - beautiful, until I saw the signs, stabbed into the sand at regular intervals: WHITES ONLY. The stupidity of it all was underlined by the absence of any white. The coastline was deserted.

Meanwhile, my host continued with his seduction. On my first night at the house, after a heady evening in the city as the lights sparkled on the water, and the champagne bubbles danced in front of me, I was enchanted by the smooth, intoxicating voice of Lou Rawls, introduced to me on the terrace, and demonstrating that there was no 'Whites Only' law chez Pieter.

"You'll never find…" crooned that velvety voice, seeming to flow in rhythm with the waves gently lapping beneath me. I was close to dropping my guard. I almost submitted. I very nearly agreed to let my West End cast wait a few weeks more, and to extend my stay in Africa which was already seeping in under my skin to direct another play. Nearly.

The next morning, I walked into the breakfast room, to find a young man sitting with Pieter at the table. It was a beautiful Sunday morning, but it was about to take another dramatic turn.

I looked out at the ocean, poured some coffee, and sat down. Suddenly, this young Afrikaner man pulled out a heavy revolver and slammed it down in front of him. He looked me in the eyes, as I waited for an explanation. He had spent the night with friends, patrolling his property and defending it against a gang of black youths, who were threatening to torch it and hack him to death at the same time. It was happening right across the Cape. "You'll never find…"

I listened to his story. During my stay in South Africa, I'd listened to many stories, from all kinds of people. And the more I listened, the angrier I became at the echo of all those platitudes trotted out across comfortable dinner tables in London. This was a situation beyond the understanding of most people, and certainly out of reach of those simple minded solutions.

This wasn't just a whites verses blacks issue. There was distrust and hatred between every ethnic group. Blacks were suspicious of whites; Europeans didn't trust Afrikaners; the women were scared of the men; black tribes were fighting other black tribes; and everyone despised the coloureds. A black could be categorised as coloured, a white could be categorised as coloured and, frankly, it was often impossible to tell the difference or to discover the reason why. Whatever the logic, it led instantly to the status of outcast.

I flew back to Johannesburg, and waited news of my First Night in London. The time difference caused problems, but John Mahoney relished the international dimension. Late at night, I called him in his office.

The show had gone well. The early editions carried photographs of Ava Gardner, who had led the applause and who went on to lead the theatrical gossip, at the after show party, apparently. How I wished I could have been there, to enjoy the success. But I had another First Night approaching, and my own very memorable parties to attend. But, first, there were two VIPs on their way to see us.

Helen Montagu and Ben Travers arrived in Johannesburg towards the end of rehearsals. There were publicity events to attend, and they were sure to want to see how the show was progressing.

Ben was photographed with his arm around every girl who might have a reason to be photographed. Sometimes, they would perch on his lap and bring a wicked smile to the old devil's face. I think he was already 90 by this time, and after a lengthy flight from London one couldn't help admiring his irrepressible spirit.

Both he and Helen seemed pleased with what they saw at a run-through and, afterwards, Helen presented me with a large envelope. "It's Ben's new play. He wants us to do it. Let me know what you think."

This was the cherry on the cake. Were Tennent's asking me to direct the première of a new Ben Travers play? If so, then I was ecstatic. I took the envelope back to the apartment, poured a drink, and settled down for a good read.

A couple of hours later, I reached the Curtain on the last Act. Very soon, I was at the window, with another glass of wine in my hand. This script was terrible! It was sexist, vulgar and unfunny. In fact, and not to put too fine a point on it, the play was nothing more than a dirty old man's pornography.

I tried to think how it might be salvaged, of how I could present a reworking to Helen Montagu that might allow me to accept. After all, Ben had been receptive to my ideas for *The Bed Before Yesterday*.

I slept on it. Or, rather, I didn't sleep. I rehearsed lines of enthusiastic reaction for the morning. I reconstructed the play in my head. I considered my career, the kudos of the West End billing. Two commercial hits, running in tandem.

When I got out of bed, the next day, I knew I couldn't do it. It was garbage, and I had to say so.

"I'm sorry, Helen. It's not for me." It came out so easily.

"God, no, darling! It's a wet dream nothing more. It's disgusting. We wouldn't touch it. I just thought it might amuse you."

I tried to maintain my composure and laugh. To demonstrate amusement. It seemed to work.

Pieter Toerien wouldn't give up. He increased the pressure on me to stay for the next play. I was wooed in all kinds of ways, and even Lindy King (eventually to become a highly successful London agent) was put on the case and bombarded me with phone calls.

The Bed Before Yesterday went well. It opened to good reviews and everyone was happy. Before leaving for home, I went to a couple of parties.

At the first, I was approached by a lady in her 30s, with the following proposition: "I belong to a ladies' group, ladies who meet for lunch, from time to time. We take it in turns to invite along an interesting male. I wonder whether you would come along, as my guest? Next week?"

I agreed. At the same do, I got into conversation with a guy about my experiences in South Africa, and especially about the Equity move towards a boycott. It gave me an opportunity to articulate the opinions I had gathered during my time there, and to repeat the assertion that it was better to see for myself.

The ladies' group date actually coincided with my departure for the UK but, since that was an evening flight, I assumed that the lunch would cause no problems. Pieter himself offered to come and collect me, in time to get to the airport on schedule. But things were not quite as they seemed.

Lunch was fine, but afterwards I noticed a change in the mood. My gushing hostesses, with their erudite and polished interest in my work as a director, began to demonstrate more predatory skills. Subtlety left the room more quickly than wine was leaving the bottles. Body language translated into an idiom more tactile… I hope I paint a clear picture of what was developing.

Things finally got to the point where I began to make hurried farewells, thanking all those ladies for their hospitality and using, as my genuine excuse, the fact that my producer was on his way to collect me and take me to the airport. But where was my producer?

The notion struck me with alarm that this was his final tactic. He would force me to miss my flight. My luggage was already stowed in his car. And these ladies were now circling, in ever more rapacious fashion.

At the very last minute, the Mercedes arrived, and I dashed for the door.

"It's not too late to change your mind, you know," was Pieter's mantra, as we sped to the airport. He could not/would not see my point of view. I saw my return, later in the tour, the trip to Rhodesia and Victoria Falls disappearing more swiftly than we covered the last few miles to the airport.

Once there, and no doubt thanks to Pieter's huge influence, I was given full clearance and fast tracked through check-in and security and, from there, escorted across the tarmac to the waiting plane.

As we pulled away from our stand, I was forced to reflect on that other party. As I settled back in my seat, for the long journey back to Europe, my eye was caught by a newspaper headline, across the aisle from me: British Director Slams Equity. And another: Boycott Fears Confirmed.

I had been tricked, and shown to be gullible. Another lesson learned, never talk politics, with strangers however plausible, at a party, in someone else's country.

Otherwise, I had few regrets. The show had opened successfully; my opinions were now rooted in first hand experience; I had avoided sniper fire, discovered Lou Rawls, and refused all efforts to be seduced. Almost all.

Africa was now under my skin. It gets you that way, and it's difficult to shake off.

I flew away from the spring sunshine, back across the Equator and that vast swathe of desert and arrived back to a changed England. The long, hot summer was a distant memory. At Heathrow, the rain was torrential, the lifts were out of order, the ATM machines didn't work, 'fish hands' had delivered the country to its knees, and it seemed as though Wilson and Callaghan were about to finish the job. It was another dramatic culture change. But, then, timing as they say is everything.

As I dodged the rain and tried to keep out of the puddles, I looked back fondly to the sound of the ocean, the lure of the mountain, the crayfish restaurants of Cape Town, those spreading oaks and manicured lawns. I didn't know that I was soon to encounter other elements - Fire, Stone and Gas. But, for now, the production at the Cambridge Theatre needed attention and I was heading for the centre of a major police raid.

*   *   *   *   *

I don't have a yearning for membership of any exclusive grouping. It just doesn't appeal to me. Likewise, I have never seen the attraction of belonging to a club. I have been to most of them, but usually for meetings and so their names will recur through this narrative. A memorable face to face first meeting with Eartha Kitt, at Groucho's; a get together with David Soul, at the same place; a handshake with Tom Courtenay, at the Garrick Club; Michelle Collins at I don't know where; a pre-show chat with Tim Healy and Denise Welch, at 2 Brydges Place, all these venues were prearranged. But, generally speaking, I hate them.

Groucho's, for example, is hideous - filled with braying media types, part of my 'peripherals' grouping, all flapping their wings and squawking their smug satisfaction at being in the exclusive herd. They have paid through their snouts to attend a drinking house that always seems noisier and more crowded than any West End bar. It is less comfortable and decidedly less tasteful than many a Soho pub, with prices a great deal more inflated than anyone should expect.

If you simply want some caché without having to demonstrate any particular talent or gift then I guess that venue is for you.

Much more cosy, for me, was one unpretentious late night bar and restaurant, where leading actors knew they could retreat quietly and with a minimum of fuss after the curtain came down on their show. There, they could order a simple bangers and mash supper, unharassed by any unwanted intruders, and in an atmosphere that did not require yelling and screaming.

Macready's Club was popular with directors, actors, dancers and technical crew and all were welcome. Conveniently, it was situated directly opposite the stage door of the Cambridge Theatre, which is where I was headed just as soon as I returned from South Africa.

Almost immediately on resurfacing, I began to feel uncomfortable about *Anastasia*. Some of the reviews were less complimentary than I had been given to understand, but in particulars that I did not recognise. I went immediately to a matinee, to see for myself.

Hugh Goldie had changed things. In order to satisfy Peter Wyngarde's ego, alterations in blocking and interpretation had been introduced that were simply amateurish. I wriggled and winced at some of the things I saw, and lines from the reviews began to make some sense.

I was back at work very quickly. The fabric of the show had to be restored. It took a little time, but it came together eventually, to become better than ever.

Audience figures built, and we settled back to enjoy a decent run. Indeed, the show was a great success. But I, for one, had not reckoned on the back room dealings of Mark Furness and Larry Parnes, the man in charge of the Cambridge.

In order to get a cheap deal, Mark had been aware all along of a possibility of having to make way for another show. In the event that the show materialised, it would be instant curtains for *Anastasia*. Against all the Equity rules that governed such a termination of contract, we were told on Thursday, and closed on Saturday.

It was Nyree who went into battle for the cast, and helped to at least recover some of the advance monies required. I was furious with the management, of course. Fire eaters and conjurors had elbowed me aside in the past. Now it was an ice-skater.

John Curry, undoubtedly the greatest ice-skater of them all, took his show into the Cambridge Theatre. Ten years later, I employed him. And I let him know just how unpopular he was amongst all those actors that had to make way for his ice spectacular, at the end of 1976.

But as an antidote to ice, I was given Fire.

Thank goodness for Annie Ross. I was always a huge fan of that fabulous jazz artiste, originally, a soloist with Lamberts, Hendricks and Ross, whose records topped the charts in America. She went on to sing with all the top bands in the US and Europe - recording, along the way, with Tony Bennett - and I was now privileged to sit in a television studio and watch her perform.

With my old friend Mike McKenzie at the piano, Annie crooned *Tea For Two* to him in a version so slow, and so sexy. And why? Because Annie, who was by now making a successful career as an actress in films and on stage, was in a play I was directing and this was all part of the publicity. If she was going on TV to talk about the show, you couldn't blame the producers if they stipulated that she should sing as well.

I was back at a London theatre, with a new play, and a cast of four. With Annie, was Shirley-Anne Field, who had co-starred in *The Entertainer*, with Laurence Olivier and *Saturday Night and Sunday Morning*, with Albert Finney. They were two of the most important British films of the 60s and took Shirley-Anne to Hollywood, to work with actors like Yul Brynner, Steve McQueen, and then with Kenneth More and also Michael Caine in *Alfie*.

I put a relative unknown, Robert Grange, in the lead, and finally persuaded the film actor, John Justin, to complete the ensemble.

John's film career spanned more than 30 years - from *The Thief of Baghdad* with Sabu to Ken Russell excesses, such as *Savage Messiah* and *Lisztomania*. He had credits with the Royal Shakespeare Company, and had played Broadway and the West End, and for three successive years he was voted, The World's Most Handsome Man.

Something of the latter clearly had an effect on John, because it was heavily rumoured that his ex-wife - actress, Barbara Murray - would arrive at breakfast to find him wearing her clothes. He was, however, powerful and intelligent on stage, and seemed ideal casting for a charismatic film mogul in the play that I was directing.

So far, so good you might be thinking and a very impressive line up it was, too. However, this was to première at the Westminster Theatre which, in 1977, was under the control of the Moral Re-Armament people. For the Queen's Silver Jubilee, so went the advertising, "Aldersgate Productions and The Churches of Greater London offer Three plays".

I was asked to direct the first of these - *Fire*, by Hugh Steadman Williams and, it seemed, money was no object. The script was intended to be a modern parable about a successful film writer, who reads a book about Jesus of Nazareth and immediately decides to give up everything and follow Him. It then went into complicated areas of confession and guilt, through a tortuous plot, that ultimately delivered the message.

As the director, I was only interested in staging the play well and getting rid of the propaganda whenever it threatened to hit the audience in the face. However, what seemed at first to be a bonus that we could rehearse on the stage throughout turned out to be a poisoned chalice.

Artists need space. They need stimulus, and they need to let off steam. Aldersgate Productions and Moral Re-Armament had some difficulty in understanding this simple fact. Alarms should have rung earlier.

To begin with, they seriously let us know that homosexuals must be avoided at all times. Should any of us have problems detecting such individuals, there was a guide book with helpful tips. There were tell

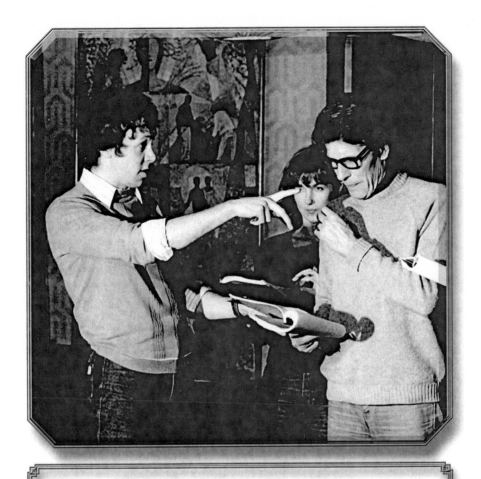

tale signs that once learned would be clear to all. These included such fascinating giveaway behaviour patterns as wearing suede shoes or guiding other men by the elbows.

We laughed, of course. We also accepted the rigorous rule that the theatre bar sold no alcohol but, instead, expected to entice the public with wine glasses of red, white or rosé grape juice.

The five of us remained forbearing over such trivial matters but considered, at the very least, that we would be left within the privacy of our rehearsals to get on with the job for which we had been employed. Not so.

Apart from the sessions attended by the writer, we also had representatives of the Moral Re-Armament tribe with us, in the form of our stage management. They were very pleasant, efficient individuals, but took great exception to the use of any language that they might consider to be profane.

As a result, we all tried for a day or two to modulate our outbursts to cries of, "Dash it!" or "Fiddle-de-de!" or even "Blow me down!"... consider this, from professional actors, struggling with some very difficult, sometimes nondescript text.

God bless Annie Ross. It was she who finally shredded the taboo. Consciously, with premeditated vigour and outrage, she suddenly let forth a string of expletives. It was uncharacteristic of her, but the immediate effect was dramatic. Our stage management team walked out and refused to return, until we had learned to behave.

As the director, I wasn't going to allow this. Having sent the cast off to the bar for a glass of grape juice, I went to the Administration Department. I told every one of them that we were trying in the face of all odds to rehearse, to rewrite and, where necessary, inject some degree of credibility into *Fire* without being constantly hamstrung by a minute by minute effort at self censorship. "Welcome to the World of Commercial Theatre!"

Faced with the threatened loss of their director and 100% of their cast, less than 3 weeks before the opening of a highly publicised and expensive season of plays "presented by the Churches of Greater London," there was no choice but to back down and allow us to continue unrestricted.

Ironically, a milder group of actors would be impossible to find. Robert Grange was sweet and gentlemanly throughout the whole production; John Justin was a pragmatist - complained, but came to heel; and Shirley-Anne managed to look permanently bewildered, whenever any question threatened to tax her intelligence too powerfully. She was happy, I think, just to be in work and to enjoy being Bill Kenwright's current girlfriend. I seem to remember that she had been educated by nuns and so was probably unfazed by the antics of Moral Re-Armament.

And Annie Ross? I adored her, and everything she brought to *Fire*. Curiously, she never seemed to rate her own talent very highly, and yet to me she stood out in that show, into which she injected style, credibility and warmth.

We opened the play on March 8th, and dashed off to Joe Allen's restaurant for our First Night celebrations. At that time, Joe Allen's was awash with actors and entertainers, at all hours. At one point, Annie was called to another table, to see her old pal Danny la Rue. After a while, he asked me to join them, which I did, and he was wonderfully kind and generous. Later in the evening, when Annie and I had rejoined our table, he sent over a case of champagne to help us celebrate.

To prove the old adage that the three most useless things in the world are a good review in The Stage and the Pope's testicles, Peter Hepple wrote that: *this was a play with merit, in theatrical as well as religious terms... to the credit of the author and his director, Tony Craven.*

The Telegraph, *The Times* and *The Evening Standard* were kind, though Bernard Levin wrote that the play was empty of dramatic verisimilitude.

Two ironies remain about that production of *Fire*. One reviewer wrote that the play does not shrink from the occasional swear word. How Annie must have laughed at that.

Finally, and many years on, having arranged to meet Michael Praed for a drink in Palace Street - another story... please, do keep reading - I was appalled to discover that the Westminster Theatre, the venue for *Fire*, was now nothing more than a burned out shell.

But from Joe Allen's, in Exeter Street, let us make the short journey to Mercer Street and to the night they raided Macready's.

It may seem from these pages that I am always tangling with the Law, and usually with embarrassing consequences, but I had no idea, as I settled down for a gossipy evening with Elspeth March one night, of what was in store.

There was no intimidating reception at Macready's, no hawk-eyed official to keep the hoi polloi in their place. Immediately inside the door behind a curtain was a small desk where your membership was checked, together with your reservation for the dining room. If you didn't want to eat, you simply went downstairs to a dimly lit bar, where you could stay until the early hours.

Somebody would usually be vamping at the restaurant piano - maybe Robert Mackintosh, Cameron's brother - and, nearly always, there would be a friend or colleague to be found, and a fair sprinkling of recognisable faces of well known actors.

At some point in the late 70s (I forget when) the club licensing laws were subtly changed, and restrictions were placed on after hours drinking, unless food was being served. I admit that I wasn't aware that the law was also applied to membership clubs.

Elspeth liked a drink. She liked to enjoy herself hugely. On the night in question, your Honour, the restaurant was in full swing. Elspeth and I occupied a small table in one corner, and were... well, she was in the process of getting mildly drunk. I had brought the car, and parked it across the road, so was determined to keep my alcohol intake low, fairly low.

Elspeth not labouring under similar restrictions herself was happily throwing back the wine and regaling me with a store of showbiz gossip and eye popping stories from her past. Every inch of the place seemed to be occupied and some people, including the actress, Moira Lister, had gone below to wait for a table to come free.

All of a sudden, there was a commotion at the entrance. The door burst open, the curtain was flung back, and at least 20 uniformed police-men entered the restaurant. For me, the following scene developed along surreal lines.

Elspeth insisted that these were all West End actors in police costumes. "I'm sure that's so and so," she declared, "It's all an enormous hoax!" As each table was now assigned a policeman, her theory was about to be tested.

She got quite giggly; she tried to blow our officer's cover; she poured him a glass of wine; and she tried to 'corpse' him with some outlandish theatrical camp. His reaction did not chime with the script she was expecting, and she gradually reined in her jokes and began to play ball.

Once our grilling was over, and we were left to finish our food, we decided it might be unwise to get straight into the car, with half of the West End constabulary milling around outside. I agreed to walk out, pretend to check the car for something, and return.

All that was missing from the street, I discovered, were the arc lights and loud hailers. We decided to stay for coffee.

The next night, Moira Lister was back again propping up the bar.

This time, she told everyone who would listen, and in irate tones, that her house in Cadogan Square had been burgled the night before whilst Macready's was swarming with the boys in blue, and whilst she had been propping up the bar. "Where are the police when you need them?" she complained, "Why the fuck were they waiting at tables, when they should have been patrolling the streets?"

I couldn't have agreed with her more. And speaking of crime...

I have watched Agatha Christie's, *The Mousetrap* one and a half times. For years, I refused to see it, and then twice in succession actors begged me to cover their performance. Fortunately, on the second occasion, the character involved was killed off in the first act, so I spent the time after the interval in her dressing room.

Dressing rooms can be fun to enter after a show. They can also be uncomfortable, even depressing. They can definitely be dangerous and electrifying places. But, sometimes, they should simply be avoided. Even if you've been invited. To explain fully what I mean, we have to pass through Macready's Club again via Harlow, a cold and depressing place.

I was directing another new play, another four hander but, this time, on a commercial tour. The play was called *Natural Gas*, and starred Jack Smethurst, Katy Manning, John Junkin and Judy Wilson. There were four actors, but two writers - Mike Sharland and Phillipe le Bars, whose wife, Tessa, was Frankie Howard's agent, at the time.

On the first day of rehearsal, these two arrived with a horde of pencils, a pencil sharpener, a stack of paper and an overwhelming dose of eau-de-cologne. They sat at two tables, side by side and, by the time the actors arrived, their installation at the front of the room had taken on a determined and permanent appearance of fixture and fitting.

Natural Gas was a comedy, dark in many ways but sufficiently worthy of everyone's best efforts and, within the first few days, it began to take shape. Jack Smethurst was well known and highly popular from such series as *Love Thy Neighbour*; Katy Manning was another great favourite, as a one time Dr Who assistant Jo, for example; and Judy Wilson was a talented and serious stage actress. So, they combined a great deal of experience.

John Junkin's claim to fame as an actor was never clear (how I longed for the 'Justin' instead), but he did have a career as a writer of television sketches and comedy shows.

I need here to put forward a view of a new play and the role of writer. However well refined the script appears to be when it goes into rehearsal, the structure will come under a degree of strain, once the director and actors begin their objective and feverish assault on it.

They get into every corner, test every line for relevance and consistency of plot or character, and batter it about daily until they can make it their own and feel comfortable with it. As some areas crack under the strain, they need to be rewritten and restructured until, eventually, the actors are ready to take possession and invite an audience in to show off their home together with the furnishings and décor they have brought to it.

Whilst the writer stands guard at the door, however, it becomes difficult for anyone to do more than admire the exterior and make some observations through the window. The writer has to be sent on a short holiday.

With Mike and Phillipe, that point was reached quickly. From the start, every suggestion was debated endlessly before a highly sharpened pencil could be lifted, to cut or replace a single line. The actors began to seize up without oxygen, unable to breathe air into the script.

The two figures, at the two tables, became the elephants in the room, and had to be prised away.

Once the edifice was secure, we moved to the Playhouse Theatre, in Harlow for the first of an 8 week tour. Within a short while, 50% of the cast was hospitalised. Katy had anorexia problems, but her role in the play was not too difficult to cover. Things were a little different, however, when John Junkin was off.

In a flurry, he was replaced by a well known actor at that time, Simon Oates. I was recalled and set about rehearsing him into the part - a kind of crash course of "here are the moves, those are the other actors, this is what it's all about, try to learn the lines by this time tomorrow!"

Morale was plummeting and the audiences were not getting their money's worth. Added to all this, our management - Jansen Productions in the shape of a man called James Verner - disappeared, and a lot of people went unpaid for much of the tour. James, under whatever pseudonym, has somehow got away with this on more than one occasion.

True to some mythical theatrical tradition, to do with the show must go on, the company pulled together. Jack Smethurst was brilliant (we worked together again and had great fun) and, somehow, *Natural Gas* was not cut off. It merely fizzled out and died with the last show. With Katy and Jack and Judy, I remained in touch.

Simon Oates never seemed like a soul mate, and I didn't expect to see him again. I didn't enjoy the brief time I worked with him any more than I had with John Junkin and I didn't think he liked me very much. So, I was surprised when I called in at Macready's one lunchtime to be greeted as a long lost friend.

He was with his girlfriend and she, too, seemed warm and spontaneous: "I've heard SO much about you from Simon!" I was dragged into having a drink with them both. "What fun it was, working together," gushed Simon, as he chatted fondly about his time on *Natural Gas*.

Attention turned to the girlfriend. She was a choreographer, and was working on a one woman show, at the Duke of York's Theatre. The show was called, *A Singular Sensation*, and the one woman was Anita Harris.

Before I knew it, I was being press ganged into agreeing to see the show, as guests of them both. Furthermore, "Please go backstage afterwards and tell Anita how much you enjoyed it. She would be so thrilled. We'll tell her you're coming. You'll just LOVE her!"

There were other ways to spend an evening, as far as I was concerned. I knew Anita Harris only as a singer of a couple of minor hits and, although I had heard that she was a kind and warm person, did I really want to spend 2 hours watching her strut her stuff?

But I'd agreed. The next problem to overcome was: Who should I ask to share this evening of glamour and entertainment with me?

When I got home that evening, the phone was ringing. It was Jean Kent. I suddenly heard myself saying, "Would you like to go with me to see Anita Harris? In her one woman show?"

Jean's spontaneous enthusiasm amazed me: "Absolutely! I'd love to! Thank you!" And thus it was that we arrived at the Duke of York's - me, reluctantly; Jean, keenly and excitedly.

The show was a disaster.

The lights dim. Three musicians appear at the side of the stage. A subdued overture begins. The audience settles back and waits. In self conscious tones, each musician enunciates "Ladies-and... Gentle–men, Miss... Ani–ta HARRIS!"

Two overweight and effeminate dancers step from the wings. I feel Jean Kent begin to tense up beside me. A beaming figure flies over the stage. Shades of *Peter Pan* and Kirby's Flying Ballet.

The dancers move, to flank their star. She lands centre stage. Or... does she? Ms Harris has not quite hit the tarmac. She remains dangling, a tantalizing inch or so from the stage. Jean bridles.

A routine begins, vocal and choreographed. The stretched smile of our singular sensation rivets our attention. The two male roly polys adapt their dance steps, whilst attempting a rescue mission. Can they unhook the grinning, singing star in time?

I sink back in my seat, already sensing Jean's astonished abhorrence at what she is witnessing. Even if she is the greatest of closet fans, I cannot feel anything from her but a shared embarrassment. Things do not truly improve.

The lights come up for the interval. I turn to see Jean's face. Urgently, I whisper, "I think we'll leave, don't you? Unless you'd rather stay?" I'm answered with a grimace. We make our way through the auditorium.

I can just hear her muttered comment through gritted teeth: "I thought we were coming to see Julie Harris!"

We laughed about it, once outside, and I'm quite sure that I was not missed in her dressing room at the end by the other Miss Harris. Quite probably, she was not even expecting me. And I learned, a few years later, arriving after a performance to see Judi Dench and Michael Williams in their shared dressing room, that when you're NOT expected it can be desperately embarrassing. The play was *A Pack of Lies*, and the venue was the Lyric Theatre, in Shaftesbury Avenue. The cast, along with Mr and Mrs Dench/Williams, included Barbara Leigh-Hunt and Richard Vernon, and I'd heard wonderful reports about both play and performances.

There were two of us on this particular Saturday night, and for reasons long since forgotten we were given to understand that Judi Dench would be pleased to see us after the performance. And so, having enjoyed the show, we dutifully presented ourselves afterwards at the stage door.

Very often, a call is first put through to the dressing room, so as to forewarn, forearm and check that a visit is expected or acceptable. On this occasion, however, we were simply pointed in the right direction and left to wander the recesses of the theatre.

We arrived outside the Dench/Williams room at the same time as Angela Lansbury, and awkwardly introduced ourselves. A sense of foreboding came over me, even as I knocked on the door. Michael Williams appeared. I'd loved his performance and was anxious to tell him so but, assuming we were friends of his wife, he quickly retreated inside and for many minutes, or so it seemed, the door stood tantalisingly ajar.

When Judi Dench finally appeared, in a state of post performance undress, it was immediately clear from the scowl on her face that we were about to be deeply embarrassed. Not only did she not know who we were, or why we were knocking on her dressing room door, but she was unable to summon up a due graciousness at our mumbled apologies that this was a simple misunderstanding.

Some people can handle these situations, and others don't even try. With a flea in our ears, we exchanged awkward gesticulations with Angela Lansbury, who slumped further against the wall, and made our way upstairs. Fortunately, Elizabeth Bell, another member of that cast, was happy to see me.

Back in 1977, the work continued to roll in and I continued my very eclectic run of directing engagements. A tenacious triumvirate of ladies asked me for the première of a new play about Beethoven. I accepted, on the basis that it would open at the Cottesloe Theatre, at the National, and that Timothy West had expressed an interest in the title role.

I attended a meeting at the National, to discover that all expectations had been built on maybes and possiblys and mayhaps and that there was no firm commitment from Timothy West. The triumvirate which included Sara Coward - or Caroline from The Archers - frog-marched me to the Round House Theatre and an unknown actor, called Colin Kaye.

We shared that summer's listings with *Let My People Come*, an evening of erotica, and a Tennessee Williams play, *The Red Devil Battery Sign* with my old friend Keith Baxter.

Our show was good, but disappeared under an avalanche of Silver Jubilee celebrations. I couldn't blame Her Majesty but, though I didn't realise it immediately, I did have reason later to regret Elvis Presley's death.

I switched Beethoven's symphonies from my Walkman to the music of the Rolling Stones. It was the start of a process that would take me back to the West End, for the third time in 2 years. Things were going well.

*   *   *   *   *

Professional partnerships, long lasting, and with substance, are not formed easily, but when there is a ready rapport, goals in common, mutual respect and, especially, a shared sense of humour, well, this is a joy.

In 1977, I was introduced to an educated, softly spoken Scot, called Alasdair Steven, with a very nice house in Holland Park and an outlook on life that appealed to me straightaway. He had an infectious sense of humour, a love of the opera and ballet and a passion for the theatre that attracted me.

Together as producer and director, but also as co-producers we took two shows to the Edinburgh Festival, one to the West End, via Newcastle; the première of a new play to Holland; and set up a modern revue format for the Royalty Theatre, in Kingsway.

Having long since parked *Beggar My Neighbour*, from the Play Room, in an out tray, I was surprised to discover that one of the cast, David George had been promoting the play in Rotterdam. He came back from there with a deal to mount a Dutch tour, with backing from the Toneelraad Organisation. This was fine by me but, fully aware of the play's shortcomings, I wanted it rewritten, and by somebody who knew what they were doing.

Alasdair Steven became the producer, and we enlisted the writer, Geoffrey Case, to pull the script together. He worked enthusiastically on the Genet adaptation and to the end product he gave the title, *Roads*.

We opened at the de Lantaren Theatre in Rotterdam billed as *Opus 73 met Roads*, on the 5th October and played there a full week. It seemed to work, and I stayed with it for its performances in Amsterdam. There, it yielded without a fight to its decadent origins, as I discovered at a performance at the Melkweg, the last time I saw the production.

The Melkweg - literally, Milky Way - Theatre was legendary in the 70s, and I was anxious that we should play there. Entered by means of a drawbridge over the canal, the auditorium resembled a kind of Turkish opium den. The audience settled on huge cushions and, already stoned, proceeded to chant or snore their way through the performance occasionally sounding a "yeah, man" exhortation, before reaching for more of the same.

Our production, which again included a degree of nudity and simulated sexual activity, caused barely a ripple across so many slumbering bodies, though outbreaks of unsimulated activity occurred that night in some corners of the auditorium and even, I am told, on stage.

Before leaving the Netherlands, and unaware of how strong the Dutch connection would ultimately become for me, Geoff Case and I made an excursion to Antwerp, a city that I love and stood before all the temptations of the railway station, its destinations board: Venice, Moscow, Budapest, Vienna, Nice... and, exercising all our restraint, turned away to Amsterdam, to pack our bags and head home.

We left poor Alasdair as producer, stage manager, and lighting designer, an area in which he didn't have an ounce of experience, as he would be the first to admit.

A few months later, we took a French play *Étrange Paleur*, by Jean Bois to the Edinburgh Festival. In a translation by Joy Merrick, it was renamed *Pallor Game*, and I booked John Justin to play one of the leading parts. Margaret Courtenay and Shelagh Fraser wanted to play the two mad sisters, but both withdrew when they heard that John was going to be in it. I scrambled together Eirene Beck and Pat Parr-Burman, who joined Michelle Newell and John Horwood.

Although the play only got the critics in to one of the last performances, and played to very small houses, it nevertheless refused to lie down, as we shall see.

But how much should we welcome the critics in early? Here is a cautionary tale.

Let us go back a year, and to the circumstances that brought Alasdair Steven and me into our professional partnership. Rayner Bourton, who had suffered Aberystwyth with me, and was already exploiting the glamour rock association of being the original Rocky, had written a stage play about the life of the Rolling Stones.

What is now called the Jukebox Musical was a relatively new genre in 1977, and so Rayner's idea presented something of a curiosity. He brought the show to me, to ask if I would be interested in directing it at Edinburgh.

The script itself was little more than the skeleton outline for a show and didn't, initially, appeal. Furthermore, Rayner clearly wanted to play Brian Jones, and it all seemed little more than a pretext for getting up on stage and emulating a Stones concert. Nevertheless, I agreed to meet with the man who was going to finance this madness, expecting to find a middle aged hippie, with delusions of grandeur and an obsession with all things rock'n'roll.

Instead, I was introduced to Alasdair Steven, who had absolutely no interest whatsoever in the Rolling Stones. He did, however, sense a commercial potential, he knew the Edinburgh scene, and was sensibly not intending to credit himself as Producer. I was won over and agreed to join the ride.

Together, we set about trying to cast the other members of the band. The biggest problem, of course, was to find a Mick Jagger and, after advertising in the trade papers, we took over an office above Macready's to trawl through the responses.

Much of it was dross, and we were subjected to some pretty painful screams, both vocal and instrumental. Our tenacity was finally rewarded, however, and luck brought us the best prize of all. We met Peter Osborn - a sensitive actor, brilliant musician, and with an astonishing ability to metamorphose into Mick Jagger, before our very eyes. I started to think we might be on to something.

Another find was Paul Felber, as Bill Wyman, who played excellent guitar and bass and had a good strong singing voice. Sara Coward a.k.a. Caroline, from *The Archers* was recruited as the one female cast member playing just about everyone, from Marianne Faithfull to Bianca

Jagger, and the lovely Steve Dawson, who had been in *Roads,* came in as Charlie Watts.

Keith was a problem, and I eventually agreed reluctantly to casting Darryl Read. He certainly had something of the weird about him, but couldn't really act and his singing used to leave me sobbing.

The Edinburgh International Festival attracts hundreds of Fringe shows every year, and the one imperative is to get yourself separated and distinguished, away from the herd. Otherwise, your product will be lost, buried beneath an avalanche of one man shows, political polemic, gay and lesbian pride, sex, drugs and nudity all squeezed into that city's space.

We were booked in to St. Ann's Centre, Cowgate just off the Royal Mile, for Three Wonderful Weeks as our poster proclaimed. Yes, we were present for the full 3 weeks of the Festival - unusual, and deathly, if you are consigned to an audience of no more than 3 or 4 Morningside drunks, at each performance. Edinburgh is the only city, anywhere in the world, where I have been accosted by middle aged female drunks, at 9.00am.

I have to confess here a loathing for Edinburgh. I apologise, because I know that I represent a tiny, tiny minority in my view that it is an ugly place, cold and unwelcoming. I see no beauty whatsoever in all that grey, forbidding granite. In fact, I get a headache within 50 miles of the place. Given that it has rained incessantly, almost every time I have visited, I can't change my original assessment. Standing outside the venue, on a cold, wet day in August, handing out leaflets to tired and pole-axed visitors, is not my idea of Heaven.

At the start of the Festival, a massive Press junket took place, at which every producer in town was trying to seduce every broadcaster or critic in town, and to stun the assembled media horde with whatever aspect of their particular offering was unique. I am happy to remember a long conversation with Joan Bakewell, that Sunday. She was well informed, witty and on the ball, and… seemed to admire my work. How could I not have loved the lady?

I watched the Dress Rehearsal in a deep depression. The script was meant to tell the story of the band, with regular renditions of all the favourites from their repertoire. But, at this last performance prior to opening, I wondered in what way this could truly appeal. I already saw the newspaper headlines in my head: NO SATISFACTION.

On August 22nd, *Let the Good Stones Roll* had its première. It was witnessed by just three people, one of whom wandered in 20 minutes late.

The second show brought a similar number through the doors, but we recognized one of them straightaway. He was Robbie Dinwoodie, the critic from the all important *Scotsman* newspaper. Alasdair and myself, together with Rodney Taylor who had provided the wigs, grouped ourselves behind Mr. Dinwoodie, and proceeded to whoop and scream and applaud, whenever any moment appeared to warrant it. I don't believe we were very convincing.

The next morning, however, Robbie Dinwoodie gave us a rave. It was just what everyone hopes for - an early, favourable review and this one we could have written ourselves: *The all round excellence is such that it is difficult to pinpoint single facets... Peter Osborn's resemblance to Mick Jagger is stunning... there are no weak links in the cast... and outstanding... is the music, a brilliant compromise of mainly taped backing music and live vocals, bringing with every Stones hit atmosphere to a criminally empty hall. THIS SHOULD NOT BE MISSED.*

The headline? Satisfaction.

I have often wondered since whether I should be grateful to Mr. Dinwoodie, or whether it would have been better, ultimately, if he had never attended. Nevertheless, his review worked. The show never again played to a criminally empty hall; it went from strength to strength, and we were the hit of the Festival.

News of the show's success filtered through to producers' offices in London, and it was not long before one of them, Charles Ross, appeared at St. Ann's Centre, in Cowgate. As if to underscore the show's appeal, another review said it all much more simply: *It's only rock and roll, but I like it! These lyrics sum up my feelings after seeing this show, though they fail to do justice to the depth of the production. The play is a must for every Rolling Stones fan... It's not all over now for this production and, when the 1977 Fringe is finished, they'll certainly not fade away.*

And so said all of us. From then on, the momentum would not be stopped. The over exuberant reviews, the packed houses for three wonderful weeks, and the naivety and bloated optimism of Charles Ross made sure of it.

I became part of the management, and Steven Craven Productions were credited on the bills along with Charles Ross and Bowcourt Productions, as the show with a new cast, tried out at Newcastle immediately following the revival of *Geordie's Court*. We all pretended that the loss of our perfect leading man, Peter Osborn, was not a problem.

I attempted to persuade Peter to stay. He was disappointed, but showed extraordinary loyalty to another play that he had just signed a contract for. He was replaced by Louis Selwyn. Sara Coward remained. David Gretton took over as Brian, and Rayner had to be banned from the theatre, after storming drunkenly through the auditorium on Opening Night.

We had the brilliant Eleanor Fazan, as choreographer; we had sensational musicians, like Pete Brewis and Keith Strachan working with us, and in the recording studio; but we were lumbered with the worst choice of West End theatre and a script that was never going to stand up in front of London audiences.

Furthermore, we had competition. Elvis Presley tributes were dominating the new Jukebox Musical genre and, although we had huge pre-publicity for the show, they were simply doing it better. On top of everything, as we approached our West End opening, some of the actors developed diva tendencies, and made all kinds of demands. Sara Coward a.k.a. Caroline, from *The Archers* was the major culprit, sadly.

But, ultimately, I believe the biggest mistake was to take that raw, loud, pulsating and unassuming show into the elegance and intimacy of the Ambassador's Theatre. It is a theatre that has come back to haunt me since.

Let the Good Stones Roll had its first preview on March 22nd 1978, and I remember having supper with Sue Nicholls, to steady my nerves.

We finally opened on March 29th. I was back in the West End. I should have felt thrilled, but I felt only despondency. As expected, we bombed. And, for the first time in my career, I tasted the bile of the critics.

The show closed on April 22nd. And the end was acrimonious.

PART FOUR

Captain of the Ship

In 1979, as Margaret Thatcher prepared to become Prime Minister, my own career was becalmed and in the doldrums. This has happened twice in my life, and it's not a pleasant experience. People who should know better tend to ask what you are doing, and then invariably follow up knowledgeably, and with a smile with: "Or are you resting?"

I'm here to tell them that, in more than 40 years, I don't recall hearing that expression very often, not in the professional theatre, at least. And anyway it makes you sound lazy and indulgent. Believe me, and I continue to hope that you will, it's not like that.

First of all, Alasdair and I were working hard at creating a future for *Pallor Game*. The producer, Thelma Holt, said that she was interested in the play, and there was a good deal of talk that we might take it into the Roundhouse in August. I got to know a very different and unattractive side to Thelma later in my career but, at this time, she did seem ready to help.

My general feelings were not helped by the abysmal weather we were having that January, and the fact that the country was riven by strikes. I walked through streets piled high with rubbish, to get to Peter O'Toole's agent in Jermyn Street. Bill Fournier agreed to read *Pallor Game* on his behalf. Six days later, he reported back that he was enthusiastic about the script and was passing it to O'Toole for his reaction, together with his recommendation. We sat back and waited.

Elspeth invited me to lunch. "Darling, Jimmy's on his way back. I've told him all about you, and he's bound to want to call in and say, 'Hello'. Darling, would you mind?" How could I? Jimmy, of course, referred to her ex-husband, Stewart Granger. Whenever he was in Town, he usually took over the top flat above Elspeth's, and where Lindsey called home. It seemed that Jimmy and Elspeth, though not able to live together any more, found it hard to stay apart for long.

Stewart Granger, of course, was a huge Hollywood star, and I was intrigued to meet him. Not because of his status - I'd never rated him much as an actor - but because I'd heard so much about him from his ex-wife.

There are very few names who for me, at any rate, have genuine stardust to scatter, and anyway we are all rubbing shoulders for so much of the time that it seems crazy to be intimidated or over-awed by yet another professional. There are exceptions, of course.

I was once asked in an interview if there was anyone that I longed to work with. My answer was based in truth. I said that there were two, and that they were both called Hepburn – Audrey and Katherine. Obviously there are more - hence, based in truth, but those two encapsulate the rarity of superstar, icon and legend. Only a handful of times have I felt the thrill of being in such a presence, and it remains that much more powerful for being such a rare event.

Stewart Granger arrived that afternoon and proceeded to highjack most of the remaining daylight hours (this was January). Having said his 'Hello', he installed himself in a chair in Elspeth's drawing room and turned the full wattage of his charm onto me.

Initially, of course, I was flattered and responded by engaging in a lengthy conversation with him about the business; about what I had been doing, and what he was doing. There was a preponderance of the latter, of course. He was handsome, certainly, and masculine. But he was also a chauvinist to his fingertips. If Elspeth spoke, or ventured an opinion, he told her to, "shut up," that she didn't know what she was talking about, and that it was all, "silly woman's talk."

He then proudly boasted that he was earning 100,000 pounds for 6 weeks work - and this was 1979, remember. The smugness and self satisfaction was overwhelming and, eventually, appalled by his arrogance and disgusted by his treatment of his ex-wife, I excused myself and left.

When I got home that evening, there was a call from Elspeth from somewhere on the motorway. She told me that after I'd left she had castigated Jimmy over the way he'd bulldozed his way in and then monopolised her guest. A huge row had followed; the two of them had ended up throwing empty champagne bottles at one another (why are they always empty?), and then she'd stormed out. She would not return to London until he was gone. Meantime, she was 'staying with the Culvers'.

I laughed. And I cried. And, the next day, I was stuck in a lift for 90 minutes. It all seemed fair comment on what was happening to me.

Furthermore, Peter O'Toole turned down *Pallor Game*. After 2 weeks of dithering, he had decided to save himself for a production of *Macbeth* that he was doing in 1980. He shouldn't have bothered. It arrived one year later, when my career was flourishing again, and his was flat lining and we met over a pair of damp underpants.

But back to my resting period. Alasdair and I pushed on with *Pallor Game*, refusing to believe that we were pedalling down a cul-de-sac. We took the script to Trevor Howard, to Margaret Tyzack and began the waiting game all over again.

Then, almost 11 months to the day from entering that period, I started rehearsals once more. This was for a new musical, at the Jeanetta Cochrane Theatre, in London. The title was, *The Last Trial of Mrs. M*, and it was a fascinating story. Set in the 20s, it concerned the historically accurate figure of Mrs Kate Meyrick. Branded at the time as the wickedest woman in London, and proprietress of some high society West End nightclubs, she was frequently in court for violating the drinking laws. All very exciting, I thought.

The list of backers for this show included such luminaries as: Brenda Blethyn, David Suchet, Leonard Rossiter, Brian Rix, Denis Quilley, Lord Olivier, Keith Michell, Ben Kingsley, Celia Johnson, Barbara Jefford, etc., etc., …and many others, including the casts of then current West End shows - amongst them, *Bodies, Oliver, Oh! Calcutta*, and *Once A Catholic*.

I was meant to be impressed, and I should have been... and you will have guessed, by now, that there is a 'But' on the way. Two of them, in fact. So...

'But' Nº 1: Despite this mind boggling list of high profile names to donate their money for the show, there seemed to be very little of that money to spend on the production. Or, perhaps, the whip round had not resulted in very much?

'But' Nº 2: More importantly, as it turned out and maybe in that list of well meaning angels something of a clue lurked, all proceeds were going to disabled actors. And this, in a nutshell, was my brief: to direct a new musical, with a cast of eight, 50% of whom were paraplegics or severely disabled actors, the remaining four, being able bodied. Furthermore, no disability should be apparent to members of the audience as though to demonstrate their fitness for the stage. This I had to do, with a tiny budget and a rehearsal period of just 2 weeks.

Was I going to refuse? Certainly not. Open up the nightclub. Strike up the band. Spotlight on the dance floor and roll on those wheelchairs!

Looking back, I was very lucky to get the team together that I did. The company manager, John Grant, was a rock solid tower of strength; our musical director, Barry Wilmore, did an amazing job also taking to the stage as Club Pianist; and for my choreographer? I'd hoped to enlist Eleanor Fazan again, as I thought she couldn't be bettered, but less than five days before we started rehearsals she became unavailable for the second week. We met at Macready's, on June 26th, and she broke the news. By the 29th, I had engaged Sheila O'Neil. She was the icing on the cake.

Diminutive in stature, Sheila was a giant of the musical stage. As a dancer, she had starred in virtually everything of note, including *Paint Your Wagon*, *Applause* and *Sweet Charity* (possibly her favourite part); she had appeared in 4 Royal Command Performances; and had made dozens of TV appearances. As a choreographer, she had already made waves, with shows for Sadler's Wells, at the Coliseum, and *The King and I*, and it was clear that she would give *Mrs. M* real class.

We struck up a rapport immediately, and have worked together several times since, and Sheila remains a close and valued friend to this day.

It was important to get a solid and talented cast, and I decided to use people that I knew. Judy Wilson came in as Mrs. Meyrick, and joined Gillian Bevan, David Killick and David Meyer. On July 2nd, these four met with the paraplegic actors - Rosamund Browne, Paul Bura, David Williams, and poor Mary Jane almost totally disabled, and for whom this represented her first professional engagement.

The first couple of days rehearsal were tense. Half the group seemed to be walking on eggshells determined to be politically correct, and not offend. Everything we said appeared as double entendre or in bad taste, until the other four broke the ice. There was a big company discussion, and they spelled it out.

Known to each other as the 'raspberry ripples' - cripples - they were quite happy to joke about their disabilities and for us to be relaxed about it. As we entered the second week, and the weather turned hot, we learned more of the history of our four ripples. It would have been impossible not to be moved by their courage.

David Williams, for example, who whilst we were rehearsing reached the 6th anniversary of his car accident. The tragedy was that his back was only broken when he was dragged from the vehicle by people who should have known better. His career was shattered at the same moment yet his lack of bitterness was astonishing.

Mary Jane had to be carried, virtually every time she needed to move. Indeed, there was a mobility problem with all the ripples, a problem that had to be solved, quite often with hysterical results. Bentwood chairs were fitted with castors on the back legs, so that in a blackout they could quickly be moved by the able bodied actors from one side of the stage to the other, or into the wings.

It required immense concentration from the actors and, at the technical rehearsal, each blackout seemed to bring cries of, "No, not the wings!" or "Get off! I'm staying ON" or "Not me, stupid, it's Paul!" as able bodied actors dived for the nearest chair and pushed it frenziedly in any direction that seemed right - usually off stage.

Somehow or other, we got the show on. We opened on July 16th, with no more than a couple of technical errors, and the performances were remarkably good. The Press were in a tricky position, given the particular circumstances, but they mostly chose to damn with faint praise. Nicholas de Jongh, my coming nemesis, wrote of an appealing and socially conscious little play, and went on typically to get the name of the leading actress wrong: *Trudy (sic) Wilson... misguidedly plays the part of the martyred and vehement tragedy queen well.* Furthermore, there was not a single mention from him of any of the other actors. And that is what they wanted and needed most.

* * * * *

Sex as a commodity has been available as hard currency since time immemorial, I suppose.

Derek Nimmo always used to tell the story of an actress, working in the Middle East. One evening, she got into the elevator with a very large, middle aged Arab. By the time they reached her floor, the price he was offering for her services had reached a few thousand pounds. Indignantly, she flounced out of the lift, locked herself in her room, and called her boyfriend in the UK. She did not expect his incredulous response: "What! You refused? We could have paid off a big chunk of the mortgage."

Closer to home, I imagine that in the public's subconscious mind there lingers a solid and unchallengeable certainty that a life in show business is rife with bed hopping and favours for favours; that the casting couch features in every producer's/director's/casting director's office, and remains forever warm from the continual pounding that it receives. So they would like to think. I don't believe it exists any longer, certainly not in that extreme and commonplace sense. But there are still some juicy truths in the old popular adage.

When jobs are scarce as they usually are, promises can be made through a process of seduction, promises that are sometimes taken up, and occasionally delivered. We all deal with these situations in our own ways, and I have certainly experienced my fair share of them. I have learned to detect the early signs from the actor, producer, dancer, whoever, and deal with it in its own way. After that, it's not really talked about.

Just occasionally, however, when the overture is played in a particularly extreme and overt fashion, I think it warrants a mention.

At the end of August, 1979, I was at the National Theatre, to see *For Services Rendered*, and afterwards went backstage for a drink with a couple of friends I knew in the show. There, in the Green Room Bar, I met with the producer, Peter Bridge. A couple of weeks later, I was invited to be his guest at the Queen's Theatre, to see the première of Richard Harris's play, *Outside Edge*. But, first, I went to Peter's office for drinks.

Once there and without explanation, he slipped me a couple of scripts to read, and said that he could help with my career.

During *Outside Edge*, Peter managed to fall asleep, but I enjoyed the play enormously, especially performances from Maureen Lipman and Julia Mackenzie. Afterwards with Peter now awake, I met the producer Eddie Kulukundis, the designer Carl Toms, and Maureen Lipman together with her husband, the writer Jack Rosenthal.

We ended up at the Garrick Club - a fascinating place, from another age and I was given the Grand Tour. It turned out to be a stylish and much needed morale boosting evening. At dinner, on one side, was Tom Courtenay and I was then introduced to the politician, Norman St John Stevas (camp, but warm and interesting). I was anticipating good times returning to my career.

Acting on the premise that it's best to strike whilst the iron is hot, I returned to Peter Bridge's office a week later, with a copy of *Pallor Game* in the hope that he might be able to move it forward. He was about to embark on the QE2 for America, and promised to read it somewhere in the Atlantic. Wickedly, he raised my expectations by suggesting that John Gielgud might be right for the lead and, if so, he would make contact. In order to emphasise his influence, he scribbled down the theatrical knight's address for me in Wotton Underwood, near Aylesbury.

Furthermore, I was invited to a party the following evening, again at the Garrick Club, to launch Peter's new production company. I accepted but, as I was leaving his office, I was stopped in my tracks by what he said next.

The Garrick Club party turned out to be very exciting, and there was genuine warmth and affection towards Peter Bridge from everyone there including Donald Sinden, Michael Denison, and old friends,

Helen Montagu, Jeff Rawle and his brother, Graham. Afterwards, as I drove Peter and his wife home, I had time to reflect on what he'd said to me at the end of my visit, the previous evening.

He'd offered to buy me a new car, and then... a blatant suggestion that, if I went to bed with him, he would arrange work for me in New York. I laughed, and left.

One of the scripts that had been given to me to read was a version of *Old Heads, Young Hearts,* by Boucicault, and I loved it. Consequently, I was excited to hear from Peter Bridge that Peter Sallis (most famous from *Last of the Summer Wine*) might be interested. Already a hugely respected classical and film actor, this was somebody that I wanted to work with. I arranged to go to his home, the following week.

The Sallis residence was in Richmond and, once again, I stood outside the front door of an actor for whom I had great admiration. It was opened by Peter's wife, Elaine, who beamed at me and apologised for us having to use the study. After introducing us, she then left Peter and me alone, and we spent a little over an hour trying to unravel the plot of the Boucicault play, as it appeared in this adaptation. We seemed to click, and I knew for certain that this was my kind of actor - great fun, highly sensitive, and theatrically very astute.

Everything was swept aside, however, after I went to the Horseshoe Theatre Company, at the Haymarket Theatre in Basingstoke, in mid-October to direct Alan Ayckbourn's, *Bedroom Farce.* Within months, I was that company's Artistic Director and Chief Executive and over the next 3 years directed more than 30 productions for them.

*   *   *   *   *

We are on our way down the M3 motorway. It is a road I travelled almost every day, until 1982, and it leads to a house in Mary Ann's Garden, in Cliddesden Road, Basingstoke. That house which was called The Shrubbery became my working home. When it was demolished, 10 years after I left, I was asked to write a piece about my time there for a book dedicated to the memory of the place. I can't resist quoting:

"Unique and special are overused words, but they both applied unconditionally to The Shrubbery. It was a magical place, which seemed

*rather than to have just moved progressively through Time, to have act-
ually accumulated all its decades of existence within itself. This strange
chameleon like quality goes some way to explaining why inspiration and
creativity were often easy to find there despite its less-than-ideal amenities
of rehearsal room and office space. To this day, I am proud of much of
the work that came out of my time at The Shrubbery, and it seems crystal
clear that the bulldozers have taken away more than bricks and timber.*

*You couldn't call the daily routine that I followed anything so mundane
as driving to work. Leaving the fumes and noise of the M3 behind me..."*

Here we must pause on the motorway, and follow it to Crete. Or to
be more accurate we must first break down and call the rescue services.

It is 1981, and I am growing impatient. I have a dress rehearsal and
first night of my own production of *Much Ado About Nothing* to attend.
Beside me, my star lies asleep on the passenger seat totally untroubled
by events. And yet, as I watch her, and think back to the previous summer, then I, too, start to relax.

The summer of 1980, when under the hot sky of a Greek island a
scooter rattled past. The blond hair riding pillion was instantly recognisable, as Nyree Dawn Porter. She was with Robin her husband, at the
time, and their 5 year old daughter, Tassie and since I was on holiday
with Edward Arthur (who had worked with Nyree in *St. Joan* at Oxford
and also, of course, in *Anastasia*), we all teamed up.

They came to our villa, overlooking the sea, one evening. After dinner
on the terrace, little Tassie suddenly jumped up and accompanied only
by the sounds of the sea, and lit by the most dazzling array of stars she
danced her spontaneous dance. Beginning slowly, and with an ethereal
grace, a sense of fun and vitality quickly took over, until we were all
clapping in rhythm and urging her on. It was a magical performance.

As it was my birthday the next day, Nyree decided to take us for
dinner at her favourite restaurant. Unfortunately, when we arrived, the
place was closed for a private christening. Once the family saw Nyree,
however, we were invited to join the party, an honour, indeed, and to
sample the joys of that traditional Cretan occasion.

Nyree had never looked so radiant, and four of us later went skinny
dipping, a moonlit swim together, in the gentle, shallow waters of the
Aegean, to finish off an unforgettable birthday.

Within a year, Nyree agreed to come to Basingstoke to play Beatrice, in *Much Ado*. It was the first of two Shakespeare productions I did for the company that year, the other being *The Tempest*. So, this was an important First Night and it was a relief when the mechanic finally arrived at the spot where we had broken down, on the M3.

It wasn't long, however, before he spotted the sleeping beauty in the car and, her identity confirmed, his work rate slowed drastically, as his eyes swivelled and stared. We were about to miss the all important dress rehearsal of *Much Ado About Nothing*, yet Nyree's only concern on waking was that there wouldn't be time enough for her Carmen rollers to heat up.

Rehearsals for The Glass Menagerie, with Peter Searles and Anna Lindup

The look on the mechanic's face reminded me of my father, when I took him to meet Nyree after the show, one time. Opening her dressing room door to us, in a state of near nakedness, my father's legs visibly weakened at the knees. He loved those occasions.

At the start of a Studio Season, at Basingstoke, I directed a production of Tennessee Williams's, *The Glass Menagerie* possibly one of the best things I have ever done. The four actors Nigel le Vaillant, Susan Brown, Anna Lindup and Peter Searles were brilliant; the critics raved; the theatre was packed to the rafters, night after night; and people flooded down from London to see it.

One evening, I spotted an actress I'd worked with the year before standing in front of the theatre, with a lady I didn't know. When they saw me, they came over for a chat. I was with my parents at the time, and made introductions to the actress I knew. We, in turn, were introduced to her friend, Kate O'Mara.

I confess the name meant nothing to me. She seemed glamorous, but self-contained and after about five minutes we all moved on. My mother couldn't wait to get me on one side, however, and whispered in my ear, "Look what you've done to your father! He's mad about her!"

How does one describe Kate O'Mara? Ageing beauty? Gutsy actress? Fading soap star? National treasure? Theatrical joke? I've heard all manner of descriptions but, despite a number of encounters with her since, and a host of anecdotes from those with first hand experience of working with her, the jury is out as to which fits her best.

She certainly doesn't like working with directors - she considers them unnecessary for the rehearsal process - but, as always, they discard them quickly those that need them most. With me, she has blown hot and cold.

She was playing Titania, in the Regent's Park Open Air Theatre production of *A Midsummer Night's Dream*. It's a magical play, and invariably suits an open air staging. At Regent's Park, however, the season always plays Russian roulette with the weather. Tradition has it there that, if it is not raining 10 minutes before the start time, then the performance goes ahead.

On this occasion, the weather was not good, and there was a chill in the air. At around 12 minutes before curtain up, however, the rain stopped and on time we all trooped in and sat on some very damp seats. It wasn't comfortable for us, but for the actors it must have been miserable.

Everywhere was damp, chilly and extremely slippery. It was easy for anyone to lose their footing and one or two of them nearly did. My greatest sympathy was for Kate. For two reasons. Firstly, she was very skimpily clad (but when is she not?) and had to spend a considerable amount of time sleeping in a bower. On cold, wet leaves, in other words. I wanted to throw a blanket over her. But she was a true pro and barely flinched.

Secondly, she had to work with a very camp and effeminate Oberon, and I would have liked to thrown something over him, as well. When I met Kate for a drink afterwards, I made the mistake of telling her, expecting a sigh and a nod of agreement. Instead, a further chill set in. Kate and Christopher Cazanove (Oberon) were, at that point, an item. Well, how was I to know?

My third encounter with Miss O'Mara was by telephone. She called me to ask if I could give a job to her son. This was Dickon, and he wanted some experience in stage management or anything backstage. Kate was very seductive, yes, even over the phone and I agreed to see her son, though my quota of Equity membership cards at that point in the season was low. Dickon came to see me, and we had a decent chat about things. In the event, however, it was impossible for me to bend the rules to help him get his foot on the ladder. Did my failure to do so cause resentment?

Some years later, I had a stage adaptation of Fielding's, *Joseph Andrews*, which had had a very successful try out production and which boasted the ideal part for Kate O'Mara. I wrote to her, asking if she would look at it. I called her agent, to get her to pass the message on. I never got the courtesy of a reply. A snub for not employing Dickon? Her distrust of directors generally? Or simple rudeness? I will never know.

"My day usually started early and finished late and so I rarely had a problem parking the car though others were not always so lucky. However long the journey might have seemed, and however much frustration and impatience had been vented en route, I never remember arriving with anything other than a keen anticipation and eagerness to start work and,

as I closed the car door behind me each morning, The Shrubbery could always be relied upon to beam down a radiant welcome."

It was certainly a welcome sight for one particular arrival.

I've never been quite sure of the definition of a born again Christian. I read somewhere that not only do they believe that they are right, and that they are the only ones to be right, it goes without saying that, if you're not one of them, then you are WRONG. Those I've come across do seem to have that kind of confidence, and so it would make sense.

None of this was on my mind on a beautiful summer's day, in late August 1980. I was in my first year at Basingstoke, and had just completed a mammoth week of auditions in London. I dashed back to Hampshire for the traditional Supporters' Club Summer Fayre.

The club was dominated by a feisty Welsh firecracker called Hannah Williams, and it was at her house that a lunch was given for whichever celebrity had been press ganged into opening this annual fund raising extravaganza. Hannah is one of those people that hold the jelly of regional theatre in its mould, and stop it from dribbling away. Unfortunately, and because there is little regional theatre left to speak of, those people are also reducing in numbers.

Back in 1980, however, jelly was in abundance, and the tables set out on Hannah's lawn were creaking under the weight of a vast spread, to welcome that particular year's guest Wendy Craig, hugely popular from the BBC TV series, *Butterflies.*

The sun shone brilliantly that August day as the guests spilled out into Hannah's garden, in eager anticipation of Ms Craig's arrival. She looked pretty, I have to say, but gave the impression that it was all something of a duty, rather than a pleasure, however it might be faked.

Afterwards, and to transport our guest of honour to the Main Event, a horse drawn carriage had been laid on. On this occasion, it was in fact a French wagonette, dating from 1896, and drawn by two Welsh cobs. Sharing the carriage with Wendy Craig in my capacity as the new Artistic Director was Yours Truly.

It took about 20 minutes to make the ride from the lunch to The Shrubbery, and Wendy held my hand rather tightly for much of the time. We didn't speak much, since the streets seemed to be lined with hundreds of fans, calling out and cheering as we went past, and she

needed to acknowledge them. Nevertheless, the grip on my hand grew tighter.

I couldn't believe that Wendy Craig could be nervous of a provincial event such as this, and so it turned out. Apparently nothing to do with fans, or speeches, or public appearance, the reason for this sudden dependence on me was down to something of a fear of horses. Welsh cobs made it all possible, but she visibly relaxed when we finally dismounted at the end of that journey. And she was quick to resume her earlier hauteur.

I don't remember any thanks to me, or any further contact that afternoon, and I have often mused on her detached quality, her slightly veiled eyes. Our paths have crossed since, and I briefly met her husband, but the friendliness was ring fenced and held at arms' length. She did a lengthy tour of a play with Frank Finlay, and it was interesting that those two were known, cynically, within the company, as Wank and Friendly.

I heard somewhere that Wendy is a born again Christian. I'll never understand them. But there are other beliefs far more loopy that remain impenetrable...

"*Inside, the world of Horseshoe was coming to life and every room was like a vital organ in sustaining the quality of that life. To the left, inside the front door, was the large, airy sitting room or green room. Here was an assortment of chairs to bring comfort to any body, whatever its size or shape. This was where I had been interviewed for the job; this was where...*"

But hang on... how did I get this job, so suddenly?

The production of *Bedroom Farce*, by Alan Ayckbourn, had come along like any other freelance job, and I thoroughly enjoyed directing it. There were good people in it, some of whom have remained friends, and I was in good form. From what I could see, the standard at Basingstoke was not generally very high, and so this was well received, and I got a return invitation.

By the time I went back, this time to direct William Douglas-Home's dreary comedy, *Lloyd George Knew My Father* the top job had become vacant, and it was heavily hinted that I should apply.

I'd thought about an AD residency for some time, and I felt at the age of 31 that I was ready for it. There was very much a sense, encouraged by the Arts Council that it takes 3 years to achieve anything - the first to put one's ideas in place; the second, to see them turn the theatre around; and, in the third year, to harvest the fruits of all one's hard work.

3 years was the kind of length of stay that I was prepared to consider and, in January 1980, enclosed with my signed contract for *Lloyd George* at Basingstoke, I sent a note, implying interest. Within days, I was sounded out further by the theatre's administrator, Stephen Lawrence.

However, I began to have severe misgivings. Would there be too many heavyweight applicants for it to be worth my while even trying? The response to my note helped to dispel those worries. The job was wide open. Furthermore, any approach from me would be studied, and looked at very, very seriously.

And then I got the flu, and took to my bed. There I lay, and watched *Goodbye, Mr. Chips.*

On the 6th February, I learned that I had made the shortlist, and would be called for an interview. Of course, I was ecstatic. Then I discovered that the shortlist included nine other names all strong contenders. My spirits went up and down, and it all coincided with auditions for the Douglas-Home play.

We must now go back, briefly, to that summer of Agatha Christie and Sue Nicholls's Hortense, in *The Boyfriend*. Here, the rehearsal pianist proved a little too ga-ga to get to grips with the music. Yet again came the plea: "You play the piano, don't you?" How could I refuse?

To my mind, Sue was the star of that production, yet Noel Finch could not be ignored. Noel was the poor, unfortunate actress whose undignified dash around the stage in Sunderland before finally breaking out through the French windows caused such mirth backstage. In *The Boyfriend*, she managed to demonstrate a gift for attracting even greater merriment amongst the audience, as she screeched her way through the performances as Madame Dubonnet. She always paused for applause as she entered, before launching her assault on the material. Though she believed that it was her character that got the subsequent laughs, for us, it was her inability to sing or deliver the role in any way.

In the London revival of the show, Marion Grimaldi had achieved enormous success in the same part. In 1971, Noel Finch was her girl-friend, and I guess Marion was honour bound to show solidarity and travel to Birmingham to see the show.

Marion Grimaldi was one of those auditioning for *Lloyd George*, and she occupied a very important period in my career later. Nevertheless, I could never bring myself to ask her how she had dealt with the experience of seeing Madame Dubonnet slaughtered in that way, or what words of encouragement she could possibly have brought to the dressing room afterwards.

On the morning of the 20th February, 1980, I walked across Waterloo Bridge on a beautiful day and then took the train to Basingstoke, all the while trying to relax. The weather was warm and sunny and, once off the train, I walked to The Shrubbery.

The panel was running an hour late. I paced, nervously. Since The Shrubbery had been a maternity home, at one time in its life, it seemed only appropriate that I should behave like an anxious expectant father. By the time I was called into the interview room, soon after 3.00pm, I'd almost gone off the boil. A gruelling session followed. At 4.00pm, I left and made my way home, picking up a bottle of scotch en route.

My optimism was rapidly draining away.

By the weekend, the phone retained its stubborn silence. I assumed the rejection call would be placed on Monday. One can always find reasons for news not coming, and I held onto little pockets of optimism returning throughout the Monday but, by the evening of the 26th, I finally accepted my failure.

That same day, we'd had another casting session for *Lloyd George*, and I had been introduced to an actress by the name of Sammie Winmill. She seemed slightly stupid, and I started to lose interest even in this forthcoming production.

When we were finally in rehearsal, and with only a week to go before our Opening Night, Sammie shocked me.

"At the back of the house was the rehearsal room quite impossibly shaped for what was required. Yet, like so much else at The Shrubbery, one soon forgot the disadvantages and relished all it had to offer. Artists and writers have garrets, it seems, and actors and directors find their inspiration in the most unlikely environments. In that run-down shabby, fusty, ramshackled and creaky old room, the creative temperature rarely cooled more than a few degrees.

I remember Steve Lawrence, our Administrator, telling me that, although he would often peep through the small window in the door, to enter that room would be a kind of sacrilege, unthinkable whilst rehearsals were in progress. After all..."

Would that Sammie Winmill had had a similar respect.

The concentration was intense, one afternoon, as we studied the profundity of William Douglas-Home's dialogue, and the actors reached for the inner meanings and metaphorical allegories clued by the title, *Lloyd George Knew My Father*.

You may consider that there is the merest hint of sarcasm in that last paragraph, and indeed there may be some merit in what you detect. But, nevertheless, the rehearsal was in full flow with any thought of a coffee break some way away. The door to the room opened, and Sammie Winmill entered almost silently, but with purpose.

She hovered behind me for a moment or two, before stepping forward. To my astonishment, she then began in sombre tones, "I'm sorry to interrupt..."

"Then don't." I responded. "Please."

"But it's very important that I talk to you."

"Now?"

"Now."

All eyes were on me, as my imagination sought a possible explanation for this dramatic interruption. I guess I sighed. "Take Five, everyone." I turned to Sammie. "In my office," as I went quickly from the rehearsal room. "Please."

Once we were in that office and seated, I waited for some indication of what it was all about: tears, indignation, nerves, a letter from home...? I couldn't guess.

"The world will end in three weeks, and I have to join my brothers and sisters. Today."

As my eyebrows rose, and I bit my lip, a monologue was calmly delivered. There was no question the world was about to finish and even though, as I calculated, we still had time to put on *Lloyd George Knew My Father,* Sammie was not going to be part of it, because her brothers and sisters were waiting for her to help them put the world's affairs in order. She was leaving immediately, but considered it only polite to tell me, so that I could find a replacement if, as she put it, I was foolhardy enough not to join her in her mission...

And so it went on. As her monotone showed no sign of modulating, and as I looked into her eyes, I knew for sure that any attempt on my part to dissuade her, to make her see sense, would be absolutely futile. The best I could do was dismiss her and get back to the rehearsal, and decide later how to handle the practicalities.

"Well, don't keep them waiting on our account. Three weeks is barely enough time to rehearse a boulevard comedy, let alone a coming apocalypse. Break a leg." And I showed her the door.

One other time that the inner sanctum was dramatically and suddenly penetrated was about a year later.

Annie Milner was an ASM with the company, and an extremely popular one at that. I suspect she was raised a Roman Catholic, though that was not on my mind when she burst into the rehearsal room, in such a distraught state that we all immediately assumed that there must be some crisis or personal tragedy to report.

Proceedings ground to a halt, as everyone paled at what might be coming.

"Somebody's shot the Pope!" she cried, "Somebody's shot the Pope!"

Indeed they had. But what could we do about it?

To return to the February of 1980, and my application, interview and long wait. On the 27th, the day was dark and gloomy. I was beginning to succumb to all kinds of feelings that chimed with the conditions, and in the evening - full of sombre thoughts - I sank into a hot bath and allowed myself to become self indulgent. Through this forlorn fog of hopelessness, the sound of a telephone gradually filtered in, its ring abruptly halted, as it was answered.

There was a message from Mrs. Joy Harris, Chairman of the Board. Would I call her back, around 10.00? My nerves, of course, were in shreds all evening. Could it be... ? Yes. I was now the next Artistic Director and Chief Executive of the Horseshoe Theatre Company.

And the world did not end.

*   *   *   *   *

I set about planning my first season. But I still had two more pre-arranged obligations to fulfil, two more productions, for which I was already contracted. One was *The Constant Wife,* by Somerset Maugham - possibly the most boring play written by him, and *I Have Been Here Before*, by J.B. Priestley, which excited me for one reason only.

The production would play at the Oxford Festival, for a couple of weeks at the Playhouse, before transferring to the famous Old Vic Theatre, in London, for a 4 week run.

Casting had been difficult from the start. Peter Cushing had been lined up, but then dropped out. Robert Hardy and Eric Porter were both approached, and both declined. But, finally, we had a strong and distinguished cast: 3 actors from Granada TV's long running saga, *A Family at War* - Colin Douglas, George Pravda and Keith Drinkel - Jennifer Hilary, Sally Sanders and, in the lead, the wonderful John Castle, who brought real style and class to the whole thing.

We began rehearsals in London, on June 23rd, and moved to Oxford two weeks later. It was a curious period, because the play itself was so dated in language and style and the time theories so hackneyed. Consequently, there was a lot of giggling throughout rehearsal.

John and Colin were terrific; George struggled; Sally was good and fun; Jennifer, as always, radiated talent; and Keith? Well, Keith was tricky. He always had a good deal to say for himself, and could be very challenging, probably stemming from a degree of vanity that, maybe, he should have left behind.

We finally opened on the 15th July, and the production was well received. By the 30th, we had transferred to the Old Vic.

It was an exciting moment to be at that theatre, with all its history. For me, *I Have Been Here Before* could not have rung more true. As a boy, I had sat in the balcony, enthralled by everything I saw on stage despite the incredibly uncomfortable bench seats. In 1980, however, I didn't have long to relish the experience. Our visit was about to be foreshortened.

This had nothing to do with the notices, and everything to do with Peter O'Toole. The critics, in fact, were divided in their assessment of what we had done. Nicholas de Jongh had his usual bitch: *the production communicates as much atmosphere of foreboding as that mythical vicarage tea party*, but others, including Irving Wardle of *The Times*, acknowledged the pluses. There was a distinct feeling of impatience in the press, as they waited for the production that followed. This was *Macbeth*, and it was not going to be a happy occasion.

The company led by Peter O'Toole was already moving in, and individuals were already staking their claims. Theatres can throw up strange worlds in the afternoons, and encourage weird permutations. I called by the Wardrobe department one day, to find it deserted save for the forlorn and haunted figure of Peter O'Toole himself.

He was hanging up some underwear, having just finished ironing a shirt. We chatted. He seemed depressed, though I avoided the temptation to ask him why he had saved himself the previous year for this. Rumours abounded that the production was going badly. Extra previews might be necessary.

Everyone, it seemed, needed more time. Time would have to be called on Priestley's Time Play. We would have to make way for Peter O'Toole's Macbeth.

Our production lost 6 performances, as a result and, although we didn't mind too much, it made no difference to O'Toole's fate. The critics had used their own time to sharpen their knives, and they used them mercilessly - slashing, in a vicious way. Our own mild notices were quickly forgotten. But I couldn't forget the ghastly look of anticipation on O'Toole's face, as we exchanged words that day.

It's strange how we can so often pre-guess the mood of the critics. Perhaps they are just too predictable in their behaviour patterns. Like so many others, I can bear testimony first hand to the tribal attack squad, with their premeditated opinions. As we shall see...

For now, however, and following three bland play choices inherited (not made by me, I hasten to add) by Somerset Maughan, J.B.Priestley and William Douglas-Home, I was determined to spice up the company's reputation - make it more exciting and relevant, for actors and audiences alike. I wanted to attract the best from the profession, and provide stimulation for theatre goers. And I wanted to hit the ground running. This would take all my energies and my time.

I announced my first season of plays: *Godspell, One Flew over the Cuckoo's Nest, Legend* and *The Lion in Winter* something for everyone.

The Green Room. *"... this was where an entire company of actors and staff would regularly assemble to meet and read through the play to be rehearsed; this was where Board members argued for hours, expressed anxiety or relief; this was where people fell asleep at the end of a night's work; this was where tea parties and cocktail parties welcomed groups of visitors; this was where actors rehearsed whilst waiting to rehearse and where choreographers went over and over a complicated dance step; this was where there was always somebody who wanted somebody to talk to; this was where the light bulbs glared down harshly during particularly difficult committee meetings; and this was where, as it seems to me now, the sun always streamed through the windows."*

Godspell opened to great acclaim thanks to a wonderful cast led by John Christie, great design and lighting, and some exciting choreography and first class musicians. The first night buzzed with youth and vigour, reflected in the party that was held afterwards. There, Elaine Page who I'd known when she was a chorus girl in Leicester and Dave Clark from the famous singing group of the 60s, joined a multitude of others, to celebrate the start of a new era. It felt good.

The only sting in the tail of that production came towards the end of its run, when I threatened to fire one actor for punching another one. I put it down to over exuberance… or fatigue.

Meeting with local teachers

There was no let up. I had worked for months to get the rights for *Cuckoo's Nest*, and we became just about the first company to stage the play in the UK. I was proud of that, and proud of the production. Actors included, Nick Brimble, Martin Fisk and Keith Bartlett and they gave the audience a powerful and moving experience.

Once we'd opened, it was straight on to the première of David Butler's play, *Legend* about the death of Marilyn Monroe. David had done his research, over many months, in America, and written an absorbing account of his version of what had happened. All I had to do was to cast the Legend.

I shall remember those auditions for a long time. I sat in the Spotlight offices and watched through the window, as those girls walked the gauntlet of Leicester Square. They teetered in their high heels, they tossed back their peroxide blonde hair, and they carried their bolstered breasts before them with determined abandon.

One of them, unfortunately, had collided with a shower of pigeon droppings, as she made her way from the station. They had fallen across her front and left her with crimson cheeks on arrival in the audition room, and with no choice but to giggle about it as she shook my hand. But, at least, her makeup was less than the two inches that some had applied to their face, and had lips less glossy, glutinous and smeared than the majority.

Some were actresses; some were models; and some were amateurs, who'd been told, since the age of 10 of their uncanny resemblance to Marilyn Monroe. All of them were hopefuls, and very few of them made the shortlist.

The obvious choice, initially, was Sandra Dickinson whom I met a couple of times, together with Peter Davison before they were married, and who often looked and sounded as though she was auditioning for the part. David Butler and I arranged a meeting and discussed the play with her, but we weren't totally convinced.

Incidentally, I always found Peter Davison very personable, though not with a particularly vibrant personality. I did wonder at the time whether he had the determination and ambition to scale the heights that John Mahoney had in mind for him.

We got on well enough, however, for me to feel able to ask a favour of him, and to provide a birthday treat for my young nephew. Peter had already become well known on television, in *Love for Lydia* and *All Creatures Great & Small* and in 1981 he took over from Tom Baker as the Doctor, in *Doctor Who* where he spent the next 3 years.

For my nephew's seventh birthday, I asked Peter if we could come along to the studios, to watch some rehearsals and maybe for him to provide an autograph for the birthday boy. Even though it must have been a burden for the Doctor, it never showed. He was generous with his time; he was charming and friendly; and it turned out to be a memorable afternoon for the wide eyed young 7 year old. But I digress.

Back to Legend, and finally I chose Linda Regan, who was just brilliant. Linda has never achieved her sister, Carol Drinkwater's, fame, but I have never regretted asking her to play Marilyn Monroe. Not so, another piece of casting.

At the end of my first season in Basingstoke, I went back to the 12th century, and the trip almost gave me a nervous breakdown. It was the end of a heavy time at the Haymarket Theatre; the company of actors were generally exhausted; the budgets were shrinking; and the audiences were coming to expect big things. I opted for *The Lion in Winter*, and the casting filled me with high hopes.

The Peter O'Toole film part of Henry II was played by John Justin. His sons Richard, Geoffrey and John by Martin Fisk, Keith Bartlett and Nofel Nawras, respectively. Sara Coward a.k.a. Caroline, in *The Archers* played Alais.

Eleanor of Aquitaine, played in the film version by Katherine Hepburn, was now to be brought to life on stage by June Brown. Fans of Dot Cotton might find that odd, but for me even with my sparse knowledge and appreciation of *EastEnders* it was a very strong choice.

The rehearsal period turned out to be monumentally difficult from the start. Sara Coward had been brought into the season in a moment of weakness. She was badly out of work, I felt sorry for her and consequently allowed a snake to slither into the grass. She tried - unsuccessfully, I think - to undermine all that I was doing.

I was wary of John Justin's continuing penchant for slipping into ladies' outfits, but didn't expect him on Day One to start making wholly implausible arguments as to why Henry should be seen wearing Alais's clothes. Despite the fact that it was utterly inconceivable that Sara's costumes would fit, I was now thoroughly bored with this predilection of John's and treated his ideas with barely concealed contempt. Sadly, however, he had another major problem.

Although he was only in his early 60s when he took on Henry, it was quickly apparent that he was losing the faculty for learning a script. Furthermore, he refused to admit the problem and, as actors in that situation usually do, he made every excuse in the book. He blamed the script, the blocking, the design, and even his own colleagues. Many of those were already tired, and their nerves were brittle, to say the least.

To top it all, any rapport that may have existed between John and

June Brown evaporated almost from the start.

I enjoyed working with June, and I think she was on the verge of an exceptional performance. Unfortunately, there wasn't time with all of the other headaches and restraints for her to pull it off completely. Not used to having an unhappy cast, I tried to keep company morale afloat. However, when we moved into the theatre for the final production week, tensions increased.

I've always maintained that there are two people in particular who, in a difficult technical rehearsal, should keep their cool throughout. They are the stage manager and the director. I was usually able to adhere to that principle, but *The Lion in Winter* proved the exception. And the catalyst was June Brown.

A chain smoker like no other, June reminded me of an Andy Capp character, in that whatever her mood or circumstance she would invariably be attached to a cigarette. In the early 80s, there were not the restrictions on smoking that there are today, and June saw no problem in indulging her habit at every opportunity. Even, it seemed, whilst portraying the 12th century Queen of Aquitaine and in the middle of a technical rehearsal.

My temper has a lengthy fuse to it but, when it blows, I'm told that the pyrotechnics can be intimidating. When it happened on this occasion, the person directly in my sights was June Brown.

At the nadir of the technical session as gremlins crawled from every corner of the theatre; as blood boiled all around; and as John Justin appeared to descend finally into a thick fog of hopeless incomprehension as to what was being said or by whom, June Brown reached for the 200th cigarette of the day.

I looked at the stage, from my place in the auditorium, and I snapped. Seated on a majestic throne, in the middle of the Haymarket stage, and wearing the full regalia of this charismatic monarch, Queen Eleanor of Aquitaine was struggling to hold a fag in her mouth whilst she reached for her lighter.

Neither I and surely not she could possibly now remember what I barked from the auditorium to the stage but, whatever it was, it brought Eleanor, Dot Cotton and June Brown to floods of tears, and the rehearsal ground to a halt.

There was a deafening silence, but there was one line from the play that should surely have rung out at that moment: "Shall we hang the holly, or each other?"

The reviews were glowing. *The Horseshoe Theatre Company has given the town a timely gift... this moving and funny production will not disappoint. In spite of illness, John Justin's performance was excellent... June Brown is terrific... the cast must all be congratulated. Tony Craven's production is a highly entertaining experience, glowing with some fine acting performances... June Brown gives a fine performance, projecting beautifully the dignity, the heartache and the humour of the part.*

Well, something must have worked on the night. But whatever heartache she felt, I think June has forgiven me. I've met her a couple of times since and she has been very warm and friendly. Perhaps she retained a slightly apprehensive twinkle in her eye and, of course, a cigarette in her mouth.

At the end of that season, everyone was tired. The box office was robust, however, and word was spreading outside of Basingstoke, of just what we were doing. But nobody had told me, when I took over the job of Artistic Director, that the company was virtually bankrupt.

*　　　　*　　　　*　　　　*　　　　*

The recession began to bite; the lady at the top was not for turning; and the funding bodies sought out their victims either to cut their grant aid or to withdraw it completely.

The Arts Council and Southern Arts were prepared to give me time. I threw myself wholeheartedly to the challenge. With no spare money to pay guest directors, I woke up after every opening night to start rehearsals for the next production.

In addition to the regular scheduling, I introduced Sunday night shows. Emlyn Williams, a regular dinner guest at our house, agreed to give his one man Dickens performance, a hugely powerful and memorable tour de force, and an enormous success. I even dusted off my piano playing skills once more, and gave concerts, called *Something in the Air* with special guests, to bolster box office interest.

The studio season, after *The Glass Menagerie* smash hit, included

Poliakoff's *Hitting Town*, and Genet's *The Maids*. More auditions followed, one actor every 15 minutes, from 10.00-6.00, 5 days a week.

"Further along, to the left, was where sat the sentinel at the gate, the lady who kept the traffic moving in that community – whether in the rush hour or at off peak times who guided everyone in the right direction, spotted problems at a distance, and solved them before they even came into other people's view. She also knew exactly when to show the green light for those who wanted to come into my office, and when to flash the red light, or a filter light that would take them in another, more appropriate direction."

This was my invaluable and indispensable secretary, Jean Luffrum. She helped me to make sure that every actor who wrote to the company received a reply. And I signed each one. To me, it's the very least that an actor should expect especially when they've already enclosed a stamped addressed envelope. Yet, it's amazing how often they are ignored.

In the office, with my secretary, Jean Luffrum.

*Copyright: Basingstoke Gazette

I got a letter during my time at Basingstoke, from the Writer's Guild, introducing me to their 'white list'. The company now featured on that list, because of my record of responding to scripts within 3 months. That seemed way too long anyway, but I have since discovered that a writer can wait up to 6, even 9, months for an acknowledgment that his manuscript has even been received. I was evidently to be congratulated, but I am nevertheless ashamed of us ALL for our shocking and desultory attitude.

Early in 1981, I was auditioning but also doing the rounds of the drama schools, in search of talent. One afternoon, I came face to face with it. On the stage at RADA, a particular actor gave a performance that, not only demanded work, but would fit into my upcoming season perfectly.

His name was Paul McGann, and I arranged to meet with him the following week. I went back to RADA to Room 7. Paul and I talked about the upcoming season; that I would need him for a minimum of two plays; and that he would have to finish his training early. He was very excited. There was no question, he said, of not coming to Basingstoke especially since it would mean provisional Equity membership. RADA finally agreed.

For some reason, Paul's subsequent biographies suggest that he made his stage début that same year, but in a production of *Godspell* at Nottingham. It's a curious error and Paul has always acknowledged, certainly in private, that I gave him his first break at Basingstoke. In fact he met his future wife there Annie Milner, the girl who so dramatically told us that someone had shot the Pope.

Paul McGann subsequently burst with equally dramatic effect onto the Haymarket stage, as George Harrison, in the Willy Russell show, *John, Paul, George, Ringo... and Bert.* I'd now covered the Rolling Stones AND The Beatles. He stayed on to join Nyree Dawn Porter and Kenneth Farrington, in *Much Ado About Nothing* and, strangely, later in his career, Paul took part in a studio recording of a concept musical based on the Shakespeare play, and called *Much Ado.*

Of course, he went on to make his name on television in *The Monocled Mutineer* and on film in *Withnail & I.*

By now, I needed a break, and dashed off to Malta to spend a week with Jean Kent and her husband, at their splendid villa in Kalkara. There, Jean and Jusuf made me feel at home, and I easily chilled out in the guest house in the grounds which I shared with a host of geckos. I shuttled between their pool and the villa of Dawn Addams, and tried to forget the schedule I had left behind.

I must have been very relaxed, one day, as I strolled through Valletta and along a deserted street in the suburbs. Suddenly, a door opened, and a woman ran out and threw her arms around me in a passionate embrace. Flattered, embarrassed and uncomfortable, I extricated myself and walked on. It didn't take too long for me to realise what had happened. My back pocket was empty.

In a fury, I went back to the house and banged on the door. After a few moments, a man appeared, a big man. Nevertheless, I pushed past him and made my way inside, demanding the return of my money. I have mentioned before that I have a long fuse, but anger now took over. After all, I had walked unharmed through the notorious back streets of Johannesburg. What could I fear from a Maltezer?

After a good deal of shouting from me, the notes were handed back. I thanked them (sic) and left. Half way back to Jean's, my legs buckled. Only then did I realise that I should have been frightened.

By contrast, I went back to the idyll of that year's Country Fayre - special guest, Jenny Hanley from *Magpie*, to be photographed several times with the company's mascot, a very fine goat which grazed at the back of The Shrubbery. Over the next few weeks, however, I came to see that goat as less of a mascot and more of a bête noire.

As I manoeuvred my way through the minefield of box office receipts v shrinking grants; balancing a soaring professional reputation with a sceptical local audience that needed seducing every step of the way, one single banana skin got in the way. I should have seen it coming. Instead, I skidded on it. It was a painful fall and I was left with the scars.

My attention was everywhere except on that approaching hazard. I started a new young people's drama group Bootlace and inaugurated Summer Schools, for anyone who wanted to come along. They were dear to my heart, and proved to be popular.

As I planned the next season, I took stock. Even though we were now generating greater box office income, and a 100% increase in activity and involvement in the community, it wasn't happening fast enough. Obligations to our funding bodies, inherited by me as new AD and

Chief Executive, together with continuing day to day overheads, in a period of national austerity, meant that profits were haemorrhaging, as we were tied to the company's past losses.

Costs now had to be cut further, even though our staffing levels were at a minimum and our production budgets modest. Faith in my appointment seemed to be many people's only insurance policy. I decided to play a little safer for a while.

Jean Kent agreed to come for the Emlyn Williams play, *Night Must Fall* together with the TV actor, Daniel Hill. *Same Time, Next Year,* a wonderfully romantic American piece, would surely put plenty of bums on seats. Christmas would be filled with the première of a musical adaptation of Nisbet's *The Railway Children*, with universal appeal, I thought.

However, for months I had been working with a writer called Peter Fieldson, on a new black farce about the murder of Joe Orton, called *Black and Blue*. It was clever stuff, and I had high hopes for it. But I had not reckoned on the provincial, buttoned up attitude of some of the local supporters.

Ironically, after I'd picked myself up and dusted myself down, and as though to underline the burgeoning reputation that the company was achieving away from the narrow confines of Basingstoke, I was asked whether we might contribute to an All Star Benefit Concert, at London's Riverside Studios, that November.

Alongside a glittering all star line up, that included Lynn Seymour, Robin Cousins, Rula Lenska, Julie Covington, Christopher Gable, Fenella Fielding, Bill Drysdale, Mark Ryan, The Dance Theatre of London, and The Famous Mothers Band, were members of the cast of the new musical, *The Railway Children*. This, according to the advance publicity, would be a show to end all shows. We duly headed for Hammersmith and stardom.

As anyone who has ever taken part in one of these events will recognise, chaos can lurk in the shadows throughout, only needing a nod, and thus an excuse, to jump out and spoil the proceedings. Usually, everyone converges on the day - individually prepared, but in total ignorance of what will comprise the rest of the entertainment, or in what order, or how much time has been allotted to each individual slot.

Some poor soul is around to direct the show, and somebody else has the more unenviable task of acting as link person, compère, or host. Either way, he or she should be prepared for anything and everything that might be thrown at them.

As I travelled into London that morning, I was reminded of an evening of unforgettable disaster that I had witnessed at the new Birmingham Rep. Let us briefly reacquaint ourselves with that period in my life. Come back with me to the early 70s... and a charity event that will cheer the soul.

The idea was to raise funds for the British Heart Foundation and, although I was brought in to oversee rehearsals and to handle the show itself, I had no involvement in its content.

Things didn't go too well throughout the day, as we suddenly seemed to have a theatre full of egos - surprisingly, you may think, for a charity function. Topping the bill was a certain Moira Anderson, one of those glutinous Scots singers, but who were very popular at the time. She deigned to fly down from north of the border but, unfortunately, left it nail bitingly late to arrive.

The band call was due to finish within half an hour of her walking through the stage door, but she spent so much time fussing in the dressing room that she arrived on stage with only about 3 minutes left of rehearsal time. True to tradition, and on the dot, the musicians put down their instruments and left the pit, before Ms Anderson had even completed one number. Since each of those tunes sounded exactly the same, I didn't see how it could be a problem.

At that time, there was a popular TV show called *The Golden Shot*, which recorded at studios directly across the road from the theatre. The time it took to walk from one to the other was literally the time it took to get across the street. However, appearing on the Heart Foundation bill that evening was a comedian virtually at the top of his brief career, and who was then host of *The Golden Shot*.

His name was Norman Vaughan, and he had a memorable catch phrase or two, which I have forgotten but which at the time endeared him to the general public. He did not have the same effect on us, since he insisted on taking a car from the studios to the theatre, and then failed to contribute very much of anything to the show.

To close the first half of the evening, the featured singer was the legendary Jimmy Young. Sadly, the longevity of his spot matched that of the old man's career. There seemed to be dozens of songs beginning with an irritating little number called, "Orff We Jolly Well Go" which was one of his catchy catchphrases. The band skipped most of the others during the limited afternoon session, for which we all breathed a sigh of relief.

Of course, somebody had to be the one to introduce all this from the stage, and to keep things bubbling along. When I heard the name Anne Aston for this role, my heart sank a little southwards on track for my boots. She had a blonde bimbo, brainless image as the Hostess of *The Golden Shot*, and we expected at the very least a series of cue cards to be mounted for her.

In the event, she was the most coordinated and the least egotistical presence in the show.

Having opened with an excruciatingly sugary version of *You've Got to Have Heart* (British Heart Foundation - get it?) delivered by some under rehearsed hoofers brought in from… somewhere, I assumed the show could only pick up from that point. As it turned out, the nadir was to be saved for the end of the first half.

As Anne Aston gave the build up that finished with the announcement: "Ladies and Gentlemen Mr. —— Jimmy ——— YOUNG!" the button was pressed backstage to raise the curtain. The new Rep had vast and heavy tabs, which were operated by hydraulics rather than a team of muscled stage crew. The speed of their rise and descent could thus be determined in advance, and with extreme accuracy.

Somehow, the arrival of Jimmy Young sent the wrong signal to the inner workings of those tabs. On cue, they started to lift but once they had exposed the feet and ankles of the second billed star they ground to a halt. The audience were held in suspense, as they gazed in awe at the great man's shoes.

As technicians rushed to deal with the problem, Anne Aston dispelled her image. With the ease of a consummate professional, she improvised and chatted whilst behind her the curtain clunked back into place. Nobody, least of all the technicians, knew whether the fault had been corrected unless, and until, the button was pressed again.

A whispered cue was delivered from the wings, and Ms Aston returned to her script. Sadly, once again, the words "Jimmy —— YOUNG!" only brought a muted reaction from the curtain, which rose sufficiently this time to reveal the singer's knees. As we held our breath; as the band struggled to slow their musical introduction; and as Anne Aston prepared to leave the stage to 'JY', the hem of the curtain hovered enticingly before clunking back to the stage once more.

When this slow inverted tease was finally over, and the curtain shot up to reveal a full, red faced Jimmy Young, we could all sing along with relief to "Orff We Jolly Well Go". 30 minutes later, when he was still singing, we were ready to shout, "Jolly Well Get ORFF!"

For whatever reason, Jimmy Young left the theatre during the interval. It was said that his anger manifested itself through an altercation with the stage door keeper, who it was rumoured received a blow to the face. There was some mention of alcohol, but at such moments there always is.

The only truths that I am prepared to verify are that the evening stretched to four hours, and that Jimmy Young had vacated the building long before Moira Anderson had reached her climax but, then, so had some of the audience.

We can also now vacate that theatre and travel again the ten years to the Riverside Studios concert, where we were a good deal luckier. Backstage, of course, resembled a busy pedestrian street, as everyone walked in all directions each awaiting our turn. Confusion lay only in the fact that none of us knew when our turn might be, or when we needed to be ready.

As a consequence, there were a few gaps and false starts here and there, but it was all held together with remarkable skill by our compère, who yet again belied a reputation for dizzy eccentricity.

Around that same time, I found myself living near Fenella Fielding, and we often passed each other in my street - she, quite literally, walking down the middle of it. She usually carried a couple of large containers, which gave her a definite bag lady appearance.

One Sunday morning, I was in the tobacconist/newspaper shop in Bedford Park run by a very cheerful and helpful Pakistani couple when Fenella called in. She dumped an enormous carrier bag on the counter, looked myopically at the person on the other side, and loudly inquired in that instantly recognisable voice of hers "Do you do dry-cleaning?"

At the Riverside Studios, I am happy to report, she was absolutely on the ball and able to shield the audience from most of the backstage chaos. Furthermore, the Railway Children performed well, were received enthusiastically, and I was very proud of them all.

So, back at the ranch what had gone so badly wrong?

Those members of the Board who had rubber stamped the choice of *Black and Blue,* about the death of Joe Orton, were clearly unaware of the manner of that death, or probably the highly irreverent style of the playwright's work. And it was savagely received.

Joe Orton was battered to death with nine hammer blows to his head by his lover, Halliwell, who then went on to commit suicide. Peter Fieldson's play cleverly retold the event in the style of one of Orton's own plays. It ended with a naked Halliwell, courageously and wittily played by John D. Collins, taking his own life, to a horrified reaction from many of the Haymarket theatregoers.

In fact, it was not the Press who received the production badly. It was our core audience, and this turned out to be a push too far, in an alien direction, for some of them.

In retrospect, it was a mistake, though I was encouraged and still am by the eloquent comments made at the time, in the newspapers: *Tony Craven, director, must be congratulated on his courage and perception in presenting this play. Whether Basingstoke is the right town for its first staging is questionable, but a longsighted young director must needs use the only platform he has – his own theatre. He must not be daunted by the opposition he will probably encounter from the stuffy-minded moralists who won't understand the play anyway. And this is a play that must be seen – admittedly not by children, but by every thinking theatre goer.*

I wasn't daunted. That production served to cement the company's reputation for being in the vanguard of breaking down outdated and fossilized thinking in the provinces. That may sound arrogant now, but as I survey the barren wilderness that is the legacy of British repertory theatre, particularly in the southeast of England, I wonder how wrong my diagnosis was, back in 1981.

What I was not prepared for was a kind of communal sulk. The production that followed - *Same Time, Next Year* - was a delight. It was moving, funny, romantic and a joy to watch - in normal times, the perfect recipe for a middle aged, middle class, theatre going public. But they refused to go. The audiences were sparse, and the recently risen ghost of *Black and Blue* stalked the empty rows. Word did gradually get around that this was not to be missed. Pointedly, one of the local reviews was headed 'Suitable For Everyone' but it was a tragedy that it was not able to play to full houses.

I began to wonder whether I would be able to fix this leaking, and poorly funded, sinking hulk. "All the King's horses, and all the King's men..." I dashed off to the Shaw Theatre, in London, to direct my first pantomime *Humpty Dumpty*.

The show starred George Layton, Jan Waters and Brian Oulton. George was our Dame, Mother Hubbard, who took to the drag with gusto. Unfortunately, his smug belief in himself as stand up entertainer was foolishly misplaced, and his oft repeated, and overly confident catch phrase "Don't laugh; don't laugh!" was greeted more than once by an anguished cry from the auditorium "We're not; we're NOT!"

Jan, as Fairy Blackheart, just dominated the stage and I, for one, relished every minute she was on it. But Brian Oulton's behaviour shocked me. After one performance, I got a message that he wanted a word. For anyone else holding the views that he did as, for instance, his wife Peggy Thorpe-Bates did, it might, perhaps, have been difficult to express them in a communal dressing room after a show. For Brian, there were no such inhibitions.

As always in Panto, a handful of children are brought onto the stage towards the end of the show, to chat, have a sing song, and take away a gift bag of some kind. Most audiences look forward to those endearing little people - often tongue-tied and overcome with shyness - to display their individual personalities. They get a big hand when they leave the stage. Brian's complaint to me, however, was that there were too many coloured children. In fact, one black boy or girl would be too many for him. He asked that they be seated at the back of the auditorium, so as to be unlikely to make it to the stage. I should have kicked him out, there and then, but he just looked pathetic. This was the London Borough of Camden, no less, and the proportion of ethnic minorities that made up the audience was significant.

Back in Basingstoke, it was becoming clear that I might not be able to put things back together again. The winter weather was bitter, with heavy snow and freezing temperatures. Corners of the Board room had iced over, as well. The Studio Season of Shakespeare, *Rudkin* and *Duet For One* went reasonably well, and then I played my final hand.

The audiences stormed back for *A Man for All Seasons,* and I tempted them further with Agatha Christie. This was my first and last production of any of her plays, and it became a litmus paper test for me. In the event, *The Unexpected Guest* packed the theatre. And now I knew it. I couldn't stay on. After more than 30 productions, and a soaring reputation in the business; after the heady excitement of so many fine performances and, I think, classy productions; after nearly three years and a million miles of commute, the Basingstoke audience finally showed their age, and slipped into their old colours.

I announced my departure. A Touch of Spring heralded the Falklands War and, as I blew the rest of the budget on the next and my final show, audiences stayed at home to watch the nightly news bulletins. Only when Goose Green seeped into the nation's consciousness, and jingoism lit up the streets, was the triumph of that last production acknowledged.

Margaret Thatcher, even as she exhorted us all to "Just Rejoice!" would have been proud. That last show was *Oh! What A Lovely War,* and I felt great about it.

Before leaving The Shrubbery, however, I had another series of Summer Schools to oversee. I added it gratefully to my legacy. A card followed me, signed by those who took part that summer: Thank you very much for your most instructive, interesting and skilled daytime acting course which was given with much love. We enjoyed every minute of it. Horseshoe – The Shrubbery 19-23 July '82.

I was ready to move on - exhausted, thrilled with what I had done, proud of my achievements and ready to take on even greater challenges. And I wouldn't have to wait long.

But the house in Mary Ann's Garden, where so many people started their lives, was razed to the ground in 1992, at the grand old age of 162. The house that became a home, where the goat grazed, as the end of the world was nigh and somebody shot the Pope could not be lost completely, however. The memory lingers on.

10 years after I drove away from the place for the last time, I could still look back with huge emotion at The Shrubbery years and write with heartfelt honesty:

"And so, beyond this point, to a walk in closet, affectionately known as the Artistic Director's office. This was the only room in the whole building where I could ever feel lonely. Despite the noise and bustle outside, this was where the inner walls would so often resound only to the cacophony of thinking, of formulating policy, of anguishing over difficult decisions of play choice, finance, casting or personnel; where the steady stream of coffee cups was, sometimes, interrupted by a stiffer type of drink; where actors cried on my shoulder; where colleagues and members of staff thanked me or criticised me; where people were hired and where people were fired; where actors read to me and where others merely handed me their CVs; where letters were dictated and signed; where phone calls were made and received; where disappointments were privately suffered and where elation and pride were privately restrained; where there was often laughter; where there was often cigarette and cigar smoke; where there never seemed to be enough time; where I would often nervously pace before starting rehearsal or attending a difficult meeting or making a particularly important speech; and where when exhausted and drained and elated and fulfilled I put the light out at the end of a long day, with sometimes only 10 hours to go before returning, I somehow always felt reluctant to admit that everything would have to wait until the NEXT day."

It was great.

The Classic Hollywood Studio Shot

Photographed by: Mike Laye/image-access.net

PART FIVE

Towards the Stratosphere

Allow yourself to be beamed up to a low-flying UFO, on a recon-naissance mission over London. Indulge me, for a moment. It is the eve of the New Year. 1983 is moving stealthily towards you from the east, but you have time to hover just for a few moments in the Islington area. Look down, and you will witness a bizarre sight.

Backwards and forwards they stagger - chaps in their tennis whites, and flappers in their tap shoes clambering, rather inelegantly, across the roof of a pub. But how can this be? And why?

It's time to leave those first 13 tumultuous years behind, to change the set and replace almost the entire cast. My story is gathering momentum again.

After Basingstoke, I only needed a short break, and then for the pace to quicken further to scale greater heights and to roam further afield. I'd been in the West End a few times, I'd run my own theatre company, and I'd travelled more than 5,000 miles to Johannesburg to work. I wanted more of the same... but even better.

The omens didn't look good, but unbeknownst to me the blue touch paper was already lit and racing toward the point of impact. But, first, I decided to go Intergalactic.

Buoyed by the success of the Summer Schools at Basingstoke, I set up my own series of workshops based at Intergalactic Arts, in London.

It was wonderful therapy, and I met up with some talented young actors that I hoped to work with in the future. For a while, I was held in a bubble set free from the demands and daily onslaughts of the politics of running a regional theatre company. And then I went to someone else's – The Connaught Theatre, in Worthing, run (at that time) by David Turner.

I'd wrestled with Agatha Christie earlier in the year, and now I was called upon to mess with Janet Green. Her play was called *Murder Mistaken*, and I started rehearsals on November 15th. There are just two reasons for noting the date.

The first of those involves the cast. This was my introduction to a certain Hazel Douglas - a great actress and, to this day, one of my closest friends. Others also remained friends long afterwards: Sally Sanders, Venetia Barrett (the first Mrs Edward Woodward, and mother to Peter and Tim), Mark Caven and Beth Ellis.

But the second reason for noting the date of starting those rehearsals was that it coincided with some other, ongoing, casting.

I had been asked to go to the King's Head Theatre, in Islington, to direct *Mr. Cinders*. The King's Head, at that time, was run by Dan Crawford, who hailed from the other side of the Pond. He was passionate about the Theatre in general, and his own theatre in particular. Consequently, it was very much a place where people wanted to work.

Dan was always surrounded by chaos, noisy activity and general pandemonium, but out of it all came order and, surprisingly, considerable theatrical success. He and I had our disagreements, but I never doubted his sincerity and feverish commitment to everything that happened under the roof of the King's Head.

Even in the last weeks of his life, in 2005, Dan called me at home from Vienna, between intense sessions of treatment at a clinic there, to ask for ideas for his forthcoming season. Nobody who has followed him at the King's Head since his death has shown anything like his level of theatrical knowledge, understanding and sheer determination to get things done. As a result, the theatre is today merely a nondescript dilution of what he put into it.

Dan Crawford had a certain irritating approach to the whole business of casting. "Keep wheeling them in," was his oft repeated mantra, which quite honestly seemed to show scant respect for the queue of professional actors waiting outside the door.

It was as a direct result of this that we found ourselves starting rehearsals of *Mr. Cinders* alarmingly without a male lead. This was a revival of a 20s musical and, in the original production, the all important title role had been taken by comedian/actor/singer/variety star, Bobby Howes. It had been inspired casting. *Mr. Cinders* called upon all of his talents, and he proved an enormous success in the part. Indeed, Sally Ann Howes, his daughter, was due to attend the opening night at the King's Head in January.

In December, however, I had seen dozens of potential Jims, but nobody who seemed ideal. In the final week before we were due to start work, Denis Lawson was suggested.

I knew of Denis from the remarkable performance he had given in *Pal Joey*, in the West End, and decided he could be just what we were looking for. Unfortunately, he was out of the country not due back for several days and there was no chance for us to meet.

Informed that Denis would do what his agent told him to do, and aware that his agent was hugely enthusiastic about the project, I together with Dan took a leap of faith and cast him. We held our breath and crossed our fingers. Needlessly, as it turned out. From the moment he joined the show, we didn't look back.

But return, if you will, behind the plate glass windows of that UFO and look down again. It is New Year's Eve, and *Mr. Cinders* is having its first preview. With a cast of 18, plus 2 musicians, dressing room accommodation at the theatre is a major headache. There is one communal space - unisex and cramped - located directly behind the stage. It is enough, just, to house the principals.

Uncomfortable as that may be, however, they have the best deal. The rest of the cast are garrisoned in any available office at the front, or in Dan Crawford's personal living quarters. To access the stage from there, the only route is upwards into the chilly December night air, and over the icy roof. Come inside, before that roof is lifted as it will be, literally, on the first night.

Mr. Cinders came with various writing credits attached, Clifford Grey, Greatrex Newman, Leo Roberts, Richard Myers but the chief composer was Vivian Ellis, and he was still very much around for this production. In fact, I commissioned him to pen a brand new number for this revival.

As I tried to get the production to a state of readiness, I was constantly subjected to Vivian's interminable chats. Sting had recently enjoyed a huge success with the show's hit number, *Spread A Little Happiness*. The composer's consequent renaissance had given the old codger a sprightly demeanour that he probably hadn't worn in many a year.

Through the closing days of the rehearsal process, Vivian was still trying to entice Binnie Hale, Bobby Howes's original co-star, out of her reclusive existence, to be a guest of honour on the first night. When she was in her prime, he had found the lady's legs to be objects of wonder, and clearly expected them to have changed very little in the intervening 60 odd years. Vivian Ellis easily put me in mind of Ben Travers on that score.

After the final preview, played in front of a small and stony-faced group of punters, Denis Lawson and I dashed over to the BBC for an interview with Brian Mathew on Around Midnight. At that time, it was one of the programmes that you needed to be on as part of any decent publicity schedule.

Brian sat in the bowels of Broadcasting House, night after night, greeting an unending stream of stars from stage, screen, television and recording studio and was expected to master the brief on each and every one of them. Denis and I took our turn, shook the man's hand, donned our headphones, sipped from our polystyrene cups of BBC coffee, and waited for the previous piece of music to finish.

We were given a very impressive introduction before Brian turned his head to me. "So, Denis, I understand that you are on stage for..." I waited, certain that he would realise his mistake, but it took a while for the penny to drop. In fact, it didn't.

Denis answered the question, whilst Brian consulted a sheaf of notes in front of him. He then looked at our star for the first time: "Now, Tony, let me bring you in here..." It became quite embarrassing, but we had to correct him, on air. Even then, I'm not sure that he quite understood.

Binnie Hale did not succumb to Vivian Ellis's charms, and the first night went ahead without her. Nevertheless, Sally Ann Howes, Jean Kent, and others joined a steady procession of bemused theatre goers through the seedy bar that formed the gateway to the King's Head Theatre. Here, where prices were still given in old money, regular drinkers must have been equally perplexed, as they watched them go by.

The place buzzed with expectation. Already, there was a sense of a West End opening night.

Inside, once all the seats were taken, people occupied any available ledge or radiator. The place was packed to the rafters - those same rafters, above which the chorus would soon slip and slide, as they made their way across the roof. One didn't dare think of a fire.

The band comprised two pianos stacked on top of one another, and it was a surreal sight to watch the musicians take their places. So dedicated was Musical Supervisor Mike Reed to the show, that he MD'd this one performance, taking time off from his stewardship of *Barnum* at the Palladium, with Michael Crawford.

The show got off to a nervous and shaky start. Outside, the weather added its own accompaniment, as the wind blew in regular, huge gusts. Suddenly, with one pull, it tore open the skylight above us. My heart stopped, for a second. But, at that moment, it seemed that all the tension inside the theatre escaped into the turbulent night air.

From then on, everything worked perfectly, and we knew that we were destined for a triumph. Denis was superb and, at the end of the evening, the audience roared its approval. Members of the Press dashed for the door desperate to make their deadlines, and to leave us all with anxious hours of waiting for their verdict.

I awoke the following morning to three raves, and much excited talk of transfer. There was pandemonium at the box office and my own phone rang incessantly. Everyone wanted to offer their congratulations, everyone wanted a ticket. Few people involved get carried away on these occasions and I certainly wasn't taking things too seriously but it was a satisfying feeling, nevertheless.

Two days later, I took a deep breath and dusted off my passport. I was heading for an exotic location, with a prestigious cast, on a never to be forgotten adventure.

On the 7ᵗʰ January, I arrived for the read through of *The Unvarnished Truth*, by Royce Ryton for the actor/producer, Derek Nimmo. Derek had a monopoly on the dinner theatre circuit throughout the Far East and Middle East and it was a hugely successful enterprise. He mounted around four productions a year, for audiences largely made up of ex pats, and there were few actors or directors who would easily turn down an offer to climb aboard this first-class merry-go-round.

For one thing, the perks were extremely enjoyable. With British Airways and Intercontinental Hotels as chief sponsors, everything was 5 star with food and drink mostly provided free of charge.

One perk I did not need, however, having just shaken myself free of Vivian Ellis was to be dumped straight into the arms of another vociferous and meddlesome writer. Worse still, not only was he the author of the play, but he was also in the cast. Along with his wife.

Outrageous, flamboyant and totally over the top, Royce Ryton was a difficult personality to harness. One dose of verbal incontinence followed another, though I decided initially to put all that down to stark terror at the prospect of being on stage for so much of the time, in his own extremely quirky play.

For those who don't know it, *The Unvarnished Truth* is a clever and well written farce, in which the four male characters dominate proceedings. I needed four extraordinarily good actors and, alongside Royce, I was lucky to have John Fortune, Frank Windsor and one of our biggest "national treasures", David Jason fresh from playing Del Boy, in *Only Fools and Horses*.

There are also four ladies in the cast, but they are barely given a chance to register before either dying or being killed off. Each is then little more than a corpse for the rest of the play to be dragged around, discussed, and bundled unceremoniously into, and out of, cupboards. This unhappy lot fell to Jo Kendall, Barbara Bolton, Gabrielle Hamilton and Morar Kennedy, Royce's wife and, incidentally, sister to Ludovic.

They must have been attracted by something else, maybe the trip? It certainly promised to be an exciting one. We were due to open in Dubai at the end of the month. At this stage, however, I had no idea just how eventful it was all going to be.

Meanwhile, within days of its opening, *Mr. Cinders* was suddenly going through a period of uncertainty. My developing nemesis, 'Nicky' de Jongh, had sounded a sour note in his review and we had to wait until the Sunday papers for another set of raves. More importantly, Denis Lawson was unwell.

Performances were being cancelled and the production's momentum appeared to be slipping away. Just a week after our triumphant first night, I was headed straight from rehearsals of *The Unvarnished Truth* to take understudy rehearsals at the King's Head.

It was mega frustrating. There was no doubt that *Mr. Cinders* was the talk of the town and, on a personal level, the staging of the show, with 18 people seeming to move effortlessly around a tiny area, was gathering a string of plaudits. Suddenly, after more than thirteen years of a busy career already notched up, I was being talked of as 'up and coming'.

Thankfully, Denis returned to good health, and I was able to focus all my attention on Adventures in Nimmoland. Royce Ryton was no nearer to suffering verbal constipation, and had to be sat on regularly. David Jason called me at home one evening to discuss the play, and generously offered his support for any tactic I chose to deploy.

But something bizarre was about to happen.

I was in the midst of a working session with David and John Fortune, when a figure sitting behind me, waiting for her scene, suddenly got up and walked to the middle of the rehearsal floor, where she proceeded to lay down and fall asleep.

Bodies on the floor we were getting used to through the action of the play, but this was altogether unexpected. When she was finally dislodged, I decided to send Jo Kendall home for the rest of the day. Once more, it seemed, I was faced with an actor's drink problem.

Other concerns floated on the horizon and emanated from an unlikely source.

David Jason and I were developing a healthy rapport through rehearsals, and we had many chats about truth. Did he regard himself as an actor who plays comedy, or a comic who happens to act? It's an interesting choice but, for me, it's essential to play above all else the unvarnished truth of a script.

David placed himself firmly in the first category, and discussions followed about possibly playing some of the Shakespearean clowns - Feste, for instance. He seemed genuinely enthusiastic about such opportunities coming his way. Unfortunately, as it turned out, there were other issues that he needed to address more urgently.

I resolved matters with Jo, who seemed almost relieved that the problem was out in the open. She gave her word that she would behave, and stay good for the duration of the tour. Derek stood by her and then rubbed her nose in it. For example, he instructed the Company Manager, in front of everybody, to clear out her hotel mini bar on arrival in Dubai.

My worries were now increasingly centred on David Jason. The first concern was a bout of flu, which left him feeling listless. But worse was his apparent inability to learn the lines.

On Wednesday, January 26th, we all met up in the First Class Departure Lounge at Heathrow, before boarding the 10.15 flight to Dubai via Kuwait. I was clocking up another 3,500 air miles. Once on the plane, we trooped upstairs to virtually monopolise the Tristar Club Class section, and settled down for what promised to be a very comfortable flight.

Encouragingly, I watched David move to the back, where he spent an hour or so concentrating on his lines. We had a 40 minute stopover in Kuwait, and were met in Dubai by a sleek looking Mercedes, shades of Pieter Toerien, you might think. Unfortunately on this occasion, there was only one such limo. It had limited space. Most of us travelled with the luggage in a mini bus.

At a leisurely dinner that evening, I sat next to David Jason - determined to give him confidence, and to make sure that he wasn't giving up on his study.

The next day, we began to put the show in place. An entire stage with side dressing rooms and full set had been constructed in the Intercontinental Hotel ballroom. Derek's production manager was an Australian, called Stan Davies, and it was his job to arrive at each venue ahead of the cast, and make sure that everything was prepared and delivered to a high standard.

Stan kept himself to himself a good deal of the time, but was popular and highly respected despite a mock disdain for everything that came out of Blighty.

After a walk into town, and a magical view of the sun setting behind a ground row of minarets, I came back to watch the first run of Act One. David's performance was getting worse, and I spent an anxious night. On Saturday, having donned a dinner suit and said my good lucks, I met up with Derek Nimmo, front of house. We were there to watch the first performance.

Once the show started, it was clear that our Number One star was ill. Furthermore and contrary to normal practice, he made no attempt to disguise the fact, switching off totally in Act 2. But, mysteriously, the audience response was fantastic. I was bemused. But Derek was happy and, for many, it was the best first night ever.

Afterwards, we all received an impromptu invitation to join the Minister of Culture at his table for drinks. It seemed a kind gesture... at first.

His wife was English, and it wasn't long before it was suggested that we have lunch on board their yacht the following day. Unfortunately, the alcohol or, maybe, a suddenly remembered pride intervened. As everyone around the table relaxed and enjoyed the hospitality that was lavished on us, the atmosphere suddenly changed dramatically.

Before we knew it, His Excellency was on his hind legs, shouting at the four actresses. They had demeaned themselves; they had insulted all women, allowing themselves to be dragged around a stage as corpses; and, as for the rest of us - Royce, in particular - we should be ashamed of ourselves for encouraging such disgrace.

One by one, we extricated ourselves and met up elsewhere for a late supper. We never did sample the lunch on that yacht.

At the next performance, I began to see David Jason, Mark 2. Whilst thinking of all those discussions with him in rehearsal about truth, about him being a serious actor who happens to play comedy, I watched the effects of the drug that is the public's response.

At some performances, truth disappeared altogether. He could turn the show into a cabaret act, introducing funny walks and pulling funny faces. Had we employed Norman Wisdom, by mistake? No. David needed the laughter by whatever means. The audiences loved it, of course, but the rest of the cast were shocked - not least, because he never really did learn the script.

Nevertheless, I responded very well to Dubai. I've been back many times since, and I'm delighted that I got to experience it whilst it was still a place, and not just a destination; whilst it still smelled of the East, with a mystery and beauty unique to itself, rather than as an international theme park, reconstructed and artificially recreated as a playground for the nouveau riche.

At the start of the second week, there was suddenly a knock on my door. There stood Derek Nimmo. I had a very soft spot for Derek. He could be pompous and patronising towards people at times, but it seemed that - once he was an Englishman abroad - he dropped all pretentiousness. He absolutely loved exploration, and was a joy to have as guide. That day, he asked if I had 10 minutes free for a walk. We were out for two hours.

We took an abra across the Creek, to the old souk, to the old town and fort, with a stop for 7 Ups and formosas, in what one always hoped and expected an Arab bazaar would be like. Intrepid and nosey, Derek would explore wherever took his fancy. We went into people's gardens, and peered into their sheds and animal enclosures, and followed any path that looked as though it might lead to something interesting. He was proud to be my guide that day, and I shall remember that outing for a long time.

In truth, I've been very lucky to work with some wonderful characters, and some delightful, talented people. Over the following 18 months, I was going to travel to the other far end of the spectrum and meet with the exceptions. But in Dubai, that late January and early February, I was able to enjoy the heady mix of fascinating sights, wonderful hotel experience, and to work with great colleagues.

Amongst many unforgettable moments, one evening remains in the memory when John Fortune, Frank Windsor and myself separated ourselves from the rest of the company and had dinner 20 floors up at the Villa Veduta (was it called that?) with the most fabulous night time views over the city. John and Frank were the perfect twosome to get away and relax with. Both were entertaining and John – in particular – had a sense of humour that is both off-the-wall and deep black at the same time. It was all very welcome that evening.

I was also lucky to have a friend on contract in Dubai at the time. He and his wife had a house there, and he insisted that we go to the top of the Trade Centre one evening. The building was still under construction - very open and unoccupied - and, as the scattering of mosques became illuminated, one by one, the sun sank over the desert, bathing it in glorious colours and an even more mystical, almost hallucinatory, shimmer. Accompanied by the call of the mullahs, this all amounted to a staggering beauty such as one is rarely able to see.

Privately (or so I thought), I accepted a challenge from the General Manager of the hotel for a tennis match on their splendid floodlit court. The man was quite a bit older than me, and I considered that at the very least I would hold my own.

As the appointed hour approached, two of the hotel waiters emerged, in full livery. One carried a tray with two glasses, the other followed with a cool box. It was a sensible precaution in the heat and I was pleased to see it. What I was not prepared to see, however, was the appearance of the cast and stage management preparing to watch or gloat.

Of course, I was thrashed and left exhausted but the spectators were entertained, and lemonade has never tasted better.

At the end of my trip, we all took a bus across the desert - travelling through mountains reflecting a kaleidoscope of different colours past camels along the way, until we reached Dibba. I remember it as a glorious place, peaceful and picturesque, with goats on the beach and a pretty harbour where fishermen were working on their nets. Then, it was on down the Gulf of Oman to Korfa Khann, where we marched our Intercontinental lunch boxes onto the shore, before being driven off by a sand storm.

On my last evening, Derek invited me to his room for a farewell drink. He was a great raconteur, and kept me mightily entertained. I was sure I would work with him again.

Soon came the time to leave. I was looking forward to my luxury return flight to the UK, and settled back to enjoy it. On our stopover in Kuwait, however, a stewardess came to tell me that I needed to move back to the Tourist Class section. Affronted, I let her know that I was very happy where I was, thank you. She retorted, gently, that as a member of the British Airways Playhouse Company, I was technically on a staff ticket, and was obliged to give way to paying customers.

I'm ashamed to say that I was in something of a sulk, as I collected my belongings and moved to the back of the plane. But, as I gazed on the retreating deserts below, the deserts of the East that had so beguiled me, I soon forgot all about it.

It was cold in London, and it snowed on my first day back. Two days later, I was back in rehearsals - this time, in Bristol with *Epsom Downs*, by Howard Brenton. The sense of having hit the earth again with a bump was profound. After Dubai, the air felt bitter, there was thick snow by the end of the week, and even the rehearsal room was cold. But progress was made, and we opened the play quite agreeably, in mid March, at the Little Theatre.

Meanwhile, transfer plans for *Mr. Cinders* having stalled a couple of times appeared more certain. There was talk of The Lyric, and I set about recasting some of the roles. There was a good deal of inexperience in the King's Head cast, and there were elements of the grotesque creeping in, particularly, I thought, with Angela Vale's performance.

Philip Bird, who had met his future wife, Andrea, during the production, did not want to commit to a West End run and, though I was sad to lose him, I felt we had a good replacement in Steven Pacey.

Come late February, however, it seemed that Dan Crawford had not even secured the rights for a West End production, and there were several anxious days of waiting whilst attempts were made to resolve matters. Dan blamed Samuel French's, but some of us preferred to reflect on his legendary chaotic organisational skills.

Finally, we got the go ahead for the Fortune Theatre in April, and we moved into top gear. The New York Herald Tribune picked *Mr. Cinders*, as one of "the best three shows in London" and coincidentally tensions increased in the audition room.

Dan was proving awkward. He wanted to make all the decisions, whereas I had to insist on final approval. This put him in a bad temper, and there followed some uncomfortable auditions, at which it has to be said actors were treated appallingly. Some of them complained to their agents, who in turn complained to the management, and Yours Truly had to make a number of calls to smooth things over. It was all so unnecessary.

Fortunately, I was about to get away for a couple of days.

On the afternoon of March 25th, I was back at Heathrow - this time, with a return ticket to Vienna in my hand, another 750 miles. I also had instructions, on arrival, to make my way to the Hilton Hotel, where a room was reserved in my name. There, I was to wait for someone to make contact.

This may all sound as though I was going to join a remake of *The Third Man*, but the reality was that I had been asked to direct a major production at the English Speaking Theatre in the Austrian capital. Originally sounded out about Graham Greene's *The Complaisant Lover*, which didn't appeal very much, we had finally settled on Noël Coward's *Tonight at 8.30*.

It was a smooth flight and, once installed in a magnificent room at The Hilton with wonderful views of the city, I ordered room service and sat back to await the call. Unfortunately, none came.

Meanwhile, as this was my first visit to Vienna, I was anxious to get outside and explore. Come 9.00pm, I did just that, but next morning - after breakfast, a walk in the park, and a perfect strudel in the hotel coffee shop (I recommend them), I was still waiting. At 11.00, the phone rang. Dr. Schafranek and Miss Brinkmann were waiting in the lobby.

As I took the lift to the ground floor, I reflected on what I knew of this couple. Franz Schafranek had set up the English Speaking Theatre 20 years before, to provide a vehicle for his American actress wife, Ruth Brinkmann. Since that time, it had become by the mid 80s a prestigious, must be seen at venue for the cream of Viennese society.

Ruth presented herself as the clichéd Hollywood star. Wrapped in furs, and sporting huge dark glasses, she shook my hand and said, "Mr. Craven, I am so pleased to meet you." Franz gave a slight bow (I'm not sure whether he clicked his heels or not) and, in similar vein, embarrassed me with, "We are honoured to have you here, Mr. Craven."

As we rode the limousine to the theatre, in Josefsgasse, I managed to persuade them both to call me Tony, and the atmosphere gradually became more informal, as I met key members of the theatre staff. After that, the rest of the day was busy discussing designs, auditioning and getting to know the theatre itself.

In the evening, I went to the closing performance of *Arsenic and Old Lace*. There were a few mediocre performances, but I was impressed by the two leading ladies and, after the show on a tour backstage I struck up an instant rapport with both of them. They were opposites, in every way.

Jean Sincere was an American, who had been on stage for most of her life appearing, for instance, in the original *Brigadoon*, on Broadway. She wouldn't allow a puff of cigarette or cigar smoke within 20 miles though I got away with it, briefly. Her husband, Charles Zambello, one of the most delightful men I have ever met, had been an actor himself, but now worked for TWA, the airline, as Head of Operations in Europe. Based in Vienna, Paris and later in London, this couple had magnificent apartments wherever they were.

Mary Martlew, on the other hand, was English through and through. She had taken a lengthy break from acting, latterly assuming the role of doyenne of Vienna, her husband having been the British ambassador. She knew everybody and glided effortlessly through the upper echelons of Austrian society. Smoke never bothered her though a lack of champagne did. When her husband died, she had returned to the stage and was masterful on it.

At the after show party,

The playbill for Mr. Cinders

I immediately invited Mary to join the cast of *Tonight at 8.30,* and both she and Jean became close friends of mine over the months that followed.

But for me, it was back to London to begin rehearsals for the transfer of *Mr. Cinders* to The Fortune. We'd arrived at a good cast. Christina Matthews had a sublime lyric soprano voice quite unsuitable for *Les Miz* or Lloyd Webber, but perfect for us and she became Denis Lawson's new co-star.

It was a busy period, combined with flights back and forth to Vienna, to finalise the casting there, but on April 19th we started previews. There was a danger of Denis's performance hardening, and losing some of the innocence and disingenuous quality that he captured so cleverly at the King's Head, but I think he managed to avoid that.

He was extraordinarily ambitious then, and desperate for an American film career - really, I think, he would like to have been Dustin Hoffman. We had tea together one day in Hampstead, and were joined by his good friend Jonathan Pryce. Immediately, I got the sense that Denis was envious of the direction in which Jonathan's career was going. *Local Hero* was current, of course, but it was on stage - Pal Joey and now Cinders - that Denis was finding success.

Opening night. Bill Kenwright sat next to me and filched my programme but, then, he's not one of nature's givers. The show went well, and the audience was peppered with celebs and personalities. Most of them stuck around for the after show party, and I chatted with a good many of them, but strangely enough it was Judith Chalmers who made the strongest impression. Perhaps I was more exhausted than I thought.

I was not too exhausted, however, to stay up half the night and collect the early editions from King's Cross Station and check out the notices. By and large, they made good reading. But now it was straight into rehearsals for the Coward triple bill for Vienna, and I was starting to learn a little more about Miss Brinkmann.

*   *   *   *   *

We spent the first two weeks in London, which allowed me to get over to the Fortune regularly. I'd got a strong, experienced cast together well used to playing Noël Coward. Ruth Brinkmann had elected to play the Gertrude Lawrence part in each of the three plays. For an American actress, of modest talent, this represented an obvious delusion of haute grandeur and, from the first day, the lady struggled to match the ease of delivery that the others brought to these sparkling Coward scripts.

Within a week, she buckled and on the pretext that somebody else should be given a chance she relinquished her part in the opening play of the trilogy, *We Were Dancing*. Mary Martlew (Heaven sent, as far as I was concerned) could not suppress an audible sigh of relief at the news. Rehearsals were starting to be fun.

Meanwhile, back at the Fortune, business was brisk, but there was a particular buzz in the air, one afternoon. A private booking had been made by Princess Alexandra, to celebrate the birthday of her husband, Sir Angus Ogilvy. Their children James and Marina were due to attend with them, and instructions were given that this was to be a strictly private affair.

Their seats were in the circle, along with other members of an un-suspecting audience, and the only concession to security was for them to spend the interval in the comparative privacy of a box. It was also made clear that they would not be going backstage, and the cast would not know of their presence until just before the curtain rose.

In the interval, I dutifully joined the royal party in their box, chiefly to answer any questions they might have. What I encountered was an immense enthusiasm for the show, together with a longing to meet everyone afterwards and to congratulate them. It was flattering, of course, and I retreated backstage to spread the word and organise a reception line at the end.

Anyone who has ever waited in line for presentation to some VIP or other will recognise the inexplicable lunacy that sets in on these occasions. Despite constant reassurances that this was a private visit; that the arrival on stage would not amount to a presentation; and that this was no more than an opportunity for a quick, "Hello" and "Well done", the nerves spread, and cast and stage management obstinately, and resolutely, formed a line standing, their hands behind their backs, with eyes right towards the wings.

In the event, the Royals cut through this stiff formality immediately, and quickly imposed an atmosphere of relaxed and friendly chattiness. I think everyone enjoyed the 10-15 minutes spent in their company, but on a personal level the meeting brought a strange and fascinating twist later in the year.

Soon, I was back on a plane to Vienna. In those days, the actors followed over land and arrived hung over and exhausted a couple of days later. Alright for some, you might think, but the director needed time to prepare the stage and lighting for the technical rehearsals that would follow.

I was installed in a very pleasant apartment, and the show moved forward to a smooth and straightforward opening. Stuffed with Viennese glitterati, the audience must have struggled to understand the English, but their reaction was encouraging, and we were all taken off to a grand hotel afterwards, for a sumptuous black-tie champagne reception. I was proud of my cast, and pleased to share their relish at such an introduction to the city.

Throughout my time there, I was treated to every delight that the management and Mary Martlew, in particular, could find, to make me more intoxicated with Vienna and all it has to offer.

Apart from all the sight seeing, there was lunch in the Vienna Woods, trips to Baden-Baden, invitations to a schloss or two, receptions with a bunch of princesses including a Bourbon-Parma (could anyone really believe that we were in a socialist country?), seats at the opera and reservations at some splendid restaurants.

Fascination and an intrigued curiosity wrapped themselves around me. After all, Vienna had been The Mecca of the musical world through the 18th & 19th centuries, and the city still preserves those buildings where Mozart, Beethoven and Strauss lived and worked.

Even I needed a rest from it all, occasionally. One Sunday morning, as I was enjoying a well deserved lie in, Mary called to invite me to a lunchtime concert. I was less than enthusiastic about exchanging my bed for a draughty concert hall, but she persisted and I'm glad that she did.

I found myself at a subscription concert in the world famous Musikverein, listening to the legendary Vienna Philharmonic, conducted by maestro Claudio Abbado, in a mouth watering programme of music that left me walking on air.

The next day, I had to return to earth, as I was booked to give a talk at the Max Rheinhardt Academy, an honour, indeed. It went well and, during the ride back in the car with Franz, he broached the subject of my return. "This year, we celebrate our 20th Anniversary here at the theatre, and will mark it with a special landmark production, and there will be a Grand Gala Performance." I turned nonchalantly to watch the buildings as we passed, whilst my driver held this deliberate and suitably dramatic pause.

"Ruth and I would very much like you to direct it!"

I don't know whether I was expected to beam and cry, "Yes, Yes, YES!" but I didn't. My first thought quickly spoken was: "Well, what's the play?" By now, we were back in the city centre.

"Ruth, of course, must play a significant role. And we have decided on *Pygmalion*."

At least we were not back to *The Complaisant Lover* and, as we sat at traffic lights stubbornly stuck on red, I turned the idea over in my mind. It seemed to me that, as Mrs. Higgins, Ruth would not damage the play too much. I was relaxed, as I turned back. "As 'Mrs Higgins', I suppose?"

"No-oooo!..." Franz suddenly seemed exasperated, as he crunched the gears and moved away from the lights, "... as Eliza!"

I was dumbfounded, but managed to open my mouth to speak. Franz, however, was ready with his defence: "Ruth is exactly the same age now as Mrs. Patrick Campbell was, when she played the role, originally. You know."

But I wanted to say, "Yes, Franz, but that was then, and now is now, and Mrs. Pat Cam had the talent to possibly get away with it... in 1913." But I didn't. They had been too good to me. Instead, I thanked him and said I would think it over when I got back to the UK.

On the flight back to England, there was a grin on my face. Anna Neagle and *Anastasia*, all over again. It was decided. I would write to Franz, and point out that, in my opinion, Ruth Brinkmann was far too old to play Eliza. And too American. Once I had posted the letter, I forgot all about it.

I was happy to be back at the Fortune, and to enjoy the continuing success of *Mr. Cinders*. There was usually a sprinkling of friends out front, or other interesting people to entertain. In particular, I remember an introduction to Joanna Lumley in the stalls bar, one evening. She was good company, and we found ourselves chatting like old friends until the bells were rung for the start of the show.

In the interval, we picked up on our conversation and had a drink together. What strikes me so clearly now is not just that she was enjoying the show, or even that she was so articulate and amusing and able to talk such sense but that, as with all true professionals in this business, she and I responded to each other as colleagues. It was so easy, because we shared a common vocation. I'm sure it happens in every walk of life, time and again, but some people who acquire a celebrity status tend to seal themselves off hermetically from everyone but their own inner coterie. It's only ignorance, I guess, but I do feel sad for them.

Very soon, an envelope arrived bearing a Viennese postmark. I braced myself for a backlash. But on the contrary this was a conciliatory Dr. Schafranek. He and Ruth had thought over what I had written and had come to the conclusion that I was right. Would I consider *Candida*, another Shaw play... and more money?

Candida herself is not central to the action of the play, much of that is down to the interplay between young Marchbanks and Morell. It fascinated me, and I agreed. Within a year, I was to work with a very famous ex-Marchbanks, and I knew how important the casting of this part was. Anyone who follows Shaw's own directions for playing Marchbanks nowadays would be committing theatrical suicide but, nevertheless, as with Mozart in Shaffer's *Amadeus* the actor has to be brave and dangerous.

I found the perfect actor for this production - James Telfer. Here was a young talent that blazed, and once I had found a Morell, in John Golightly I was excited about the job.

We spent the first couple of weeks in London again and, no doubt under pressure to deliver in this high profile 20th Anniversary production, together with a growing sense that she might be outshone, Ruth Brinkmann involved me in one of the most extraordinary exchanges that I think I have ever had with any actress.

During somebody else's script, she suddenly interrupted:

"Tony, I need your help. You see, I find I don't know what to do whilst other people are talking."

The room went very quiet. After all, this is one of the most fundamental and basic understandings for any professional actor (amateurs, I know, have - for very good reasons - a regular problem with it). It was difficult for me not to show a degree of disbelief. Nevertheless, the words came out instinctively:

"Ruth... try listening."

"Oh. Okay. Right."

All directors have to be very aware of the fragility of an actor's self confidence, good or bad. With the rest of the cast hanging on every word, you can get into a painful and desperate blind alley from which there is no easy exit. Unless, of course, cruelty is your thing.

There is a very famous story of a director, who seven days from an important opening night, stopped the rehearsal and called a particular actor to the centre. "Now, listen," he said in front of the entire cast, "I know you're not very good. You must know you're not very good. Our job between now and opening night is to make sure that the audience don't find out." Cruel.

Back to the *Candida* rehearsals, where an hour later Ms. Brinkmann stopped proceedings once again.

"Tony. I've tried listening. And it helps. It really does. But now I don't know what to do with my hands."

It was not the place to begin basic acting lessons for my leading lady and co-producer and, in my light hearted reply, Ruth may have detected an element of disdain, but there was nothing I could say or do that would rescue her from the way she would now be seen by her colleagues. And I did try my best.

For my first stay in Vienna, I'd been loaned a very nice apartment though a little way from the theatre. Now I was to share a vast place, a few paces from the theatre foyer, with James Telfer and Graham Pountney. I wasn't sure how this would work. Actors need to be able to get away from their director at the end of the day and vice-versa.

Graham, meanwhile, began to show maddening and childish tendencies. His sense of machismo, for example, gave him a big problem with actors linking hands for the curtain call, even though this is a common and well recognised practice. As it turned out, however, it was not Graham and it was not James either that was to be the problem.

Firstly, though, I got the shattering news that Mary Martlew, still in Vienna, had been diagnosed with breast cancer. I went straight from the airport to the private clinic where she was waiting for an exploratory operation. Even though this was scheduled for the next day, and Mary had no idea whether she would even survive it she insisted on serving champagne.

She had had her hair done that afternoon, "I can't tolerate the idea of my anaesthetist seeing me looking a mess!" and although she was clearly frightened, we had a fun couple of hours together before I made my exit. At the door to the street, at the end of a long corridor, a member of staff leapt out to make sure that Mary was not on her way to another social occasion, he was right to be suspicious. Aware of how emotional the whole scene was likely to become, I gave Mary a quick kiss and hurried away to locate my new apartment.

This comprised a very large set of rooms, requiring a loudhailer if you wanted to speak to anyone in the far reaches. It was plenty big enough for three. Or was it four? A couple of days after James and Graham arrived, we got the answer.

Firstly, one of us would come back after rehearsals to discover the lights on and there were a lot of lights. Next, whilst we were in the apartment, individual lights went on and off by themselves - one by one, or all together. Then, a door would suddenly slam shut, without any obvious draft or wind to cause it.

Within days, doors were opening from a closed position and then slamming shut again. It was unsettling for us all, but James in particular was alarmed, and refused to be in the place on his own. Or rather, with something else.

Sleepless nights are not good at any time. To suffer them immediately before an important opening night can be positively destructive. But that is what was happening.

Desperate to call a halt, the three of us agreed to move our beds and jam the doors between our rooms tightly open. Then if anything untoward should happen at least we would all be within earshot. We lay awake, isolated in our rooms, and waited.

Need I remind you that this is a true story?

It was the wardrobe in Graham's room that first moved. Then I heard knocking on the wall behind my bed. Something swept through James's room, disturbing his clothes. Realisation dawned. This was a mischievous poltergeist, but not a malevolent one. And I don't think it stayed in residence for very long after that night. Maybe it got bored when we weren't entirely freaked, and moved on elsewhere.

Candida opened successfully, and I had to get back to London. In Vienna, the Grand Royal Gala Performance took place the following week, in the presence of HRH Princess Alexandra. I was sad to miss it, but on the following day I got a message that the lady had asked after

At the First Night reception of Candida, in Vienna, with Christina Schofield ('Prossy')·

*Phto: Victor Mory, Vienna

me, remembered *Mr. Cinders*, and sent her congratulations on "another delightful production". I seemed to have a royal fan.

It was the end of my association with the English Speaking Theatre, though I returned to Vienna some years later. Today, the theatre is a pale shadow of its former self. Franz and Ruth both died tragically, within a very short time of each other.

But, after I'd returned to England, James Telfer somehow got above himself. He spoke his mind to Ruth, and refused to apologise when asked to. He became persona non grata, and since I was responsible for casting him it was my fate, too. An angry letter came from Franz, but I was unable to make good his wife's wounded honour. I stood by my actor - magnificent as Marchbanks - and I remembered the bows: "We are honoured to have you here, Mr. Craven."

At home, I was straight into production at the Young Vic Studio of a new play, by Benjamin Kuras. It was probably baffling for the audience but the cast - especially Jonathan Oliver, who played the lead - remained stoical throughout.

*   *   *   *   *

Echoes of Mary Selway are suddenly all around.

The undisputed Queen of Casting Directors used to share with me a particular frustration with American film executives. She could put forward the name of a truly distinguished British actor for a given role and the suggestion would be greeted with unbridled enthusiasm. Then, the very next day, it often happened that she was sent back to the drawing board.

According to Mary, what had happened would be that the executive producer had consulted with some American friends over dinner. If the actor concerned was not known instantly to these anonymous socialites, then his or her name was struck from the list within 24 hours.

We had our own American producer, with a similarly misguided approach to recasting *Mr. Cinders*. By January 1984, Denis Lawson, on the verge of receiving a SWET Award for his performance in the show, was reaching the end of a 12 month contract, and we needed a replacement.

Joel Spector the show's co-producer had brought a deal of finance to the show and this gave him grounds, he believed, for determining its future.

He had a head of hair that gave him a look of Liberace and whether he'd been born with it or purchased it somewhere it never moved from its fixed position. Unfortunately, the man beneath it had the same tendency.

Having watched the flair and style that Denis brought to the show, and acutely aware of the ease with which Bobby Howes had slipped into the same role, it was hard to understand how Joel Spector could get it so badly wrong.

As the director, I was looking to actors such as Nicky Henson to step in, but also felt we had a number of lesser known but highly qualified people standing in line. I felt that, even if we couldn't persuade a name to take over, the show itself had acquired sufficient popularity to give somebody that name providing they had the correct qualities: vulnerability, charm, comedy timing… and youth.

But someone had told Joel that we needed Lonnie Donegan. His friends had assured him that this was the big star we were looking for. Even though the skiffle king sported an MBE, and had notched up more than 20 UK Top 30 hits, I was quite sure that he would be swamped, if he tried to step into Denis's shoes.

Initially, the whole production team reacted with a mixture of horror and amusement. It was clear that the man was not an actor and had no feel for the part. Furthermore, and in addition to everything else, he was too OLD. But I agreed to meet him. It would have been churlish not to, especially with our leading co-producer hell bent on the idea.

Everything I encountered at that meeting with Lonnie merely served to confirm my first instincts. This would be absurd casting, which I doubted would even provide a box office boost. Ominously, however, as we continued to see other contenders in a string of auditions, the rest of the producers lined up behind Joel Spector.

Dan Crawford surprised me the most, and I had a number of passionate conversations with him in private, urging him to intervene. Time was getting short, and I was being heavily and overtly pressured. It was suggested that I spend some time with Lonnie and his wife at their home so as to get to know him, as though this would impact in any way on his stage abilities. Reluctantly, I travelled over to Brentford one evening, for an evening with the Donegans, in the rather kitsch surroundings of their riverside home.

In retrospect, it was a fatal mistake. We could find little in common either socially or professionally and any potential working relationship was now soured by a distinct lack of rapport on a personal level. My only hope was that the man would see things in the same negative way and withdraw.

The following day, I was besieged by other members of the team wanting to know how far my opposition would take me. Many of them offered to follow my lead, if I decided to leave the production altogether. I certainly hoped that it wouldn't come to that but, by the evening, it was clear that the producers would not budge. I had 24 hours to decide what to do.

I'd seen some good people, and I'd seen some stinkers. An endless stream of performers, variously described as names - many of them long since clapped out - had trooped into the Fortune Theatre, where I greeted them, auditioned them, and dismissed each one with a kindly platitude.

In retrospect, one of the most sensible suggestions was Mathew Kelly. Unfortunately, way back in the early 80s, he was known only as that weird being, the television personality and a silly one, at that. He traded on his height and his goofy looks and, quite honestly, if he registered in my consciousness at that time at all, it would have been as a game show host or kiddies entertainer. It was only later that he began to prove his considerable credentials as a straight actor.

When we met, I discovered a delightful character incredibly enthusiastic. I couldn't fault his professional approach, and he showed a truly serious intent. He'd seen the show a few times, and it was clear that he was longing to play the part.

Mathew's charm won many people over, but I dismissed him at the time for the simple reason that he was much too tall. Denis is pretty small, and although Mathew might have captured some of the comedy, I felt he would be goofy rather than endearing; clumsy rather than charming; and laughable, instead of being lovable. But he might also have brought something a little special with him and, if we met again now, I would apologise for not pursuing him more strongly as a contender.

In the event, we moved on and, one afternoon, an entourage appeared at the centre of which was Davy Jones, of *The Monkees*. In essence, this was also a suggestion that I took seriously. Physically, he was right.

Vocally, we assumed, he was also right. And it seemed likely that he would have oodles of charm. *The Monkees* still had their followers, and Davy was the only British member of that very American group. I began to warm to the idea.

Unfortunately, all the boxes I thought were ticked turned out to be blank. There was no hint of charm. His speaking voice grated. His acting was as wooden as Sherwood Forest. And his singing voice had all but disappeared.

I turned to the producers, expecting a sympathetic wince. Instead, I saw the dazzle of excitement in their eyes. It seemed that they were bewitched by the legendary past that this little man had inhabited, instead of seeing and hearing the present reality.

I said goodbye to Davy Jones, and left the building.

Denis Lawson was due to give his last performance at the end of January, and he remained solid and committed to the end. Even though as I understood it, he was offered a film part with Woody Allen. It could have been the perfect breakthrough, but there was no question of him reneging on his contract with *Mr. Cinders*. He turned the job down.

As I weighed up my own options, I got hold of one piece of information that made my decision easier. The management had agreed to put Lonnie Donegan on a short term, 3 month contract. For tax reasons, evidently, it was important that he didn't stay in the country beyond that time. I backed down, and agreed to rehearse him into the show.

Almost immediately, I regretted it.

Working days were lost. Over and over, Mr. Donegan was not able to rehearse due to a mystery illness, we suspected heart trouble. Anyone who saw *Mr. Cinders* will know how much energy was required for the piece. Denis always gave it his all. In Pal Joey, suffering extreme exhaustion, he was put on a diet of Mars Bars and Guinness to get him through some performances. But Lonnie was regularly, even early in rehearsal, giving way to metal fatigue.

As the weather turned colder, and replacement rehearsals finally got into full swing, my depression got deeper. To watch an inept performer by day, and then to contrast him with the consummate star of the evening performances was bad enough. But, to make matters worse, Lonnie was rapidly earning the title of Most Unpleasant Man I'd ever worked with.

He was sour, ungracious, arrogant and lazy. I wasn't sure whether to laugh or cry, but clung to the hope that we could last the 3 months and get the show back on course in the spring.

I have always taken the view that awards ceremonies represent little more than self indulgent navel gazing, and so with no wish to be hypocritical I didn't take up my invitation to that year's SWET Awards (since renamed the Laurence Olivier Awards). Nevertheless, I was thrilled that Denis Lawson won Best Actor in a Musical for his performance in *Mr. Cinders*. Without any doubt, he deserved the accolade, and every one of his last performances was sold out.

Denis Lawson with his SWET Award, alongside Barbara Dickson

We gave him a great send off party that week, and he emerged from the show with the respect and affection of everyone involved.

On January 30th, we witnessed the performance of no more than an adequate understudy, and tried to come to terms with the fact that we would have to put up with it for 3 months. Showing taste and clever timing, Binnie Hale chose the same month to bow out, and the theatre's front of house lights were dimmed in a mark of respect.

Unsurprisingly, the producers cheered Lonnie's début to the hilt. More of a surprise was the enthusiastic reception given by the audience that night. Even the *Financial Times* waxed lyrical. The reality, however, was that the box office immediately slumped, and the producers were soon asking me to waive some of my royalties.

To cap it all, Lonnie called me into his dressing room, some 10 days after his first night.

"So, tell me. In this acting lark, how soon before I can get a holiday? A few days off?" I think my nostrils must have flared in such positive disdain that he immediately turned back to the mirror: "Well, I was only askin' that's all."

It was clear that we would never be bosom buddies, and I was never again invited for an 'at home' with the Lonegans.

A final word on Denis Lawson. He has endured much in his personal life since *Mr. Cinders*, and has watched his nephew Ewan McGregor scale the heights that Denis himself dreamed of. But he has gone on to establish himself as a force to be reckoned with, and I will always be proud to have worked with him.

Incidentally, someone revived *Mr. Cinders* for the King's Head some years later, a different director, and a different leading man. It failed. The production that began rehearsals without a Jim in 1982 and ran until 1984 represented one of the highest of those many, many peaks that I had reached up until that time.

But all stories need contrasts, a betrayal, perhaps, or an assassination, or an attempted murder. Which of those might describe what follows I leave to you. And you might also be able to identify some of the perpetrators.

*   *   *   *   *

Mike Reed, a mega successful musical director and who had become a great friend working with me on Mr. Cinders, was talking about a new show that he had written, together with the librettist, Warner Brown. They wanted me to direct it, and they wanted to try it out at the King's Head. Could I cope with the disorganised chaos of that theatre yet again? The answer came to me very quickly.

I was being pursued by a writer called Peter Mahon. He'd become a great fan, and wanted me to direct all of his plays. He sent me a script called *I'll See You Again* and, since both Susannah York and Julia Foster were in the frame, I was happy to take it a step further.

Both ladies were full blooded professionals and persuasive performers and whereas one was off the wall, and the other by contrast demonstrated a rapier like intelligence, it seemed to me it could have been a fascinating experience.

Unfortunately, the production was to be overseen by a producer called Richard Jackson who also happened to be the agent for both. I had a meeting with him in early February and decided on the spot that I had developed a soft spot for Dan Crawford, and that I would prefer to put my faith in him. What an error of judgment was that. But there was worse to come. Another musical fell into my lap, and I was about to experience the dirty side of the business from all sides.

The Theatre seems to be a particularly attractive recreation area for wealthy amateurs - individuals who don't need to demonstrate, or get by on, any talent. Their cheque book dispenses with such formalities, and it's amazing just how susceptible otherwise intelligent theatrical minds can be when it is brought out.

I was about to get involved with just such a person, whilst being ruthlessly manipulated by one of the West End's most powerful organisations. In fact, developments elsewhere and bad timing on my part all joined forces that summer to trigger the perfect storm. As a consequence, my instinctive trust of people was badly shaken, and it took a long while to return.

Rumbling along in the background, of course, was Lonnie Donegan who continued to tarnish and weaken the spirit and charm of *Mr. Cinders*. Nevertheless, musicals were now coming my way, and I was focusing on two in particular. Each of them involved a huge amount of work, before even being confirmed for production.

As early as January 1984, I had been approached by a man called Sean O'Mahoney (one of his many pseudonyms), who had come up with a musical version of *The Importance of Being Earnest*. It had a working title of *Borne in a Handbag*, and he boasted that this would do for Oscar Wilde's play what Lerner and Loewe had done for Shaw's *Pygmalion*. In other words, Sean was going to startle the world with another *My Fair Lady*.

He was one of those wealthy amateurs that I've already introduced - in his case, making his money through publishing. He also had a very high regard for himself as a composer.

At the far opposite end of the spectrum was Mike Reed/Warner

Brown, still trying to persuade me to direct *Painted Faces* at the King's Head. This was a fascinating but ambitious concept, fraught with problems - six one act plays with music, loosely connected and spread over two consecutive evenings in the theatre.

There was no commitment or date from the King's Head for this, and there was no positive plan for *Borne in a Handbag*. Yet I found myself getting involved with both. In early February, I was meeting with Warner to help him shape, rewrite, and sharpen up the book for "PF". At the same time, I was under instructions to follow up on casting ideas for "BIAH".

It was essential to try out Sean's piece on a provincial tour before there was any talk of the West End, and he had to find a producer able to put the right tour together. Unfortunately, he came up with a man called Vincent Shaw, legendary in the theatre for being unimaginative and third rate. His plan was to open at the Wimbledon Theatre in May, at least giving us plenty of time to get things sorted out. And there was a lot to get sorted.

I met with Sean at his office in Ealing, and he assured me he was on the case. One week later, he told me that the tour was confirmed, and that no expense would be spared (he was capitalising the entire show himself). I reckoned I needed a short break, and accepted an invitation to stay with Jean Sincere and her husband, Charles Zambello, in Paris. They had a very beautiful apartment close to the Arc de Triomphe at that time but, whilst I walked through the snow by the Seine, I got word that the tour had collapsed. My immediate future was suddenly wide open.

To help make this bitter pill a little sweeter, I got to hear Mike Reed's music for *Painted Faces* for the first time and it was very exciting. I immediately agreed to work with Mike and Newton, as a King's Head production was confirmed. And then came a bolt from the blue.

As the clocks went forward to introduce British Summer Time, I was spending a weekend in Bournemouth, enjoying the typical start to a British summer. It poured with rain, and I drove back to London early. As soon as I was back, the phone rang. It was Ray Cooney, and he was speaking for the Theatre of Comedy Company. They had got hold of *Borne in a Handbag* and wanted it at the Ambassador's Theatre, with no pre-London tour.

When a leading West End producer calls you at home on a Sunday with the offer of a job, you do well to give the idea due consideration. But my instincts were already telling me that this particular plan would be a mistake. The Ambassador's was too small - as I'd discovered with the Stones show. This was intended to emulate *My Fair Lady*, and I knew that Sean O'Mahoney had a big orchestra in mind. I expressed my reservations to Ray, but said that I would think about it.

Sometime later, he called again. This time, he hit me with some pretty heavy emotional blackmail "You're the only director who can do this. If you don't direct it, I won't do the piece at all. You will have the full resources of the Theatre of Comedy and SWET behind you." Finally: "Don't you trust me?"

By midweek, I was in Thelma Holt's office to start planning the show and, by the evening, I was discussing costume designs with Linda Matheson. Now I had to replace Lonnie Donegan, and get *Mr. Cinders* back on course.

As before, the producers moved as one. Someone, anyone, would do it, as long as they had sufficient profile to give confidence to the hapless, bewigged Joel Spector. I would not have been surprised to see Ken Dodd walk through the doors.

Elsewhere, casting gathered momentum. I sent of a script of *Painted Faces* to Stanley Baxter; through the Theatre of Comedy, I approached Elaine Page and Georgina Hale; and I met with Mark Wynter at The Shaftesbury Theatre.

Eventually, both shows were cast, and a date fixed for each opening. *Borne in a Handbag* was re-titled *The Importance* and boasted a high level cast: Judy Campbell, Patrick Ryecart, Robert Dorning, David Firth and Sheila Bernette. The cast wore Wilde's comedy well. How would the music fare? Sean O'Mahoney was now John Hugh Dean. We had until the 21st May, the first preview.

Painted Faces was re-titled *Six for Gold* and, with Rosemary Leach, Susie Blake, Peter Land and Peter Reeves, the show looked on course to be equally stylish. We had until Press Night, on the 27th June.

My schedule for the year was now almost complete and, with just 4 clear weeks assured, I booked a holiday in America.

Lonnie Donegan was ultimately replaced with Lionel Blair. I tried to direct the schmaltz out of his performance, but it was a hopeless task.

Events moved swiftly though they didn't appear to do so at the time. Sean, still largely financing *The Importance,* was trying to interfere in every aspect of the production. I had to walk a very slender tightrope, having him believe that his influence was greater than it actually was, just to avoid absurd and terrifying bouts of paranoia.

The cast tackled Oscar Wilde's lines with aplomb. I was grateful for Judy Campbell. We developed a rapport the moment we met fortunately, since I had to talk her into accepting the role of Lady Bracknell. My only worry through rehearsal was whether she was vocally strong enough. Despite radiating authority and a sure touch all round, her speaking voice had become frailer than I would have liked.

Patrick Ryecart, who had blazed onto the scene with a performance of Marchbanks, was christened Darling by me since he used the word interminably. Sheila and Robert as Chasuble and Prism were ideal together. In fact, the entire cast were doing the play proud. And therein lay the problem.

We should have stuck with the play. The dialogue had been crunched into lyrics which, in turn, were carried by some uninspired music.

But there was much that was heartening, and one or two elements that made everything else seem trivial by comparison. My assistant at The Ambassador's was a fabulous guy called Robert Lawrence. Young, handsome, educated and articulate he had been badly wounded on service in the Falklands conflict. It had left him with a damaged body and a withered arm that was of almost no use to him. It all just seemed such a waste.

As I attempted to manufacture a silken purse from a drooping sow's ear and knock *The Importance* into some shape, we took time off after one rehearsal to accept an invitation from Judy Campbell and her daughter, Jane Birkin, to Pimm's and champagne cocktails at her home. Back at the theatre, problems mounted, however.

John Hugh Dean (Sean) refused to alter his orchestral arrangements, in order to accommodate a realistic number of musicians. Given the dimensions of The Ambassador's stage, it was difficult to find anywhere to put them.

Initially, the plan was to use the area below the stage - until, too late, the technical team discovered that that was an unworkable solution. The designer rushed to find an alternative. Meanwhile, the ever cheerful Sheila O'Neil whom I had insisted on as choreographer fought to give life to some of the numbers.

By early May, I was being bombarded on a daily basis with letters from Sean, who was giving a decent impression of a man who was unbalanced. But everyone else seemed pleased with the way things were going. Thelma Holt watched a run-through and was extremely encouraging. Sean, however, was disgruntled and called a meeting for the following week.

At 6.00pm on Monday, Thelma and I listened, as he gave us notes. We listened politely, and then privately agreed to ignore them. It was full steam ahead to the first preview. How did it go?

It was a case of stylish performances from an experienced cast, interrupted by dreary music, which was much enlivened by Sheila's choreography. The set and costumes looked good, but the solution as to where to position the band was causing all kinds of problems.

Two towers had been constructed on either side of the set and, within these, stacked above one another, and looking for all the world like participants in a game show, sat the musicians. Each was sealed in his own little box, accessed by steps from the wings. It was a mightily precarious and risky endeavour.

Both Ray Cooney and Thelma Holt, however, bristled with enthusiasm at what we had achieved.

On the following day, Sean struck again. He demanded the sacking of Sheila O'Neil, together with a whole catalogue of cuts. The music, naturally, was spared. Yet again in rather less courteous terms I had to tell him to butt out. Throughout the week, as we continued to hone and improve the show during the daytime, the evening performances played to good and responsive houses.

Nevertheless, as the weather turned cold and miserable, and we inched towards the Press night, I knew in my heart that this show would be slammed. By now, we were in rehearsal for *Six for Gold*, and I was soothed by Mike Reed's glorious music and Warner Brown's witty and original lyrics. I braced myself for the last day of May and the official opening at The Ambassador's.

It was Judy Campbell's birthday, but she must have hoped for a better present. Things could not possibly have been worse. The house was dead from the moment the curtain rose, and every kind of technical error was heaped on the show. There were foul ups in the flys; there were microphone problems; and one musician mercilessly seated at the pinnacle of the stack dropped his drumsticks.

The sound of their noisy and interminable descent through each stage of that tower's construction was listened to in silence, and in rapt astonishment by the audience. The melody of their fall reverberated throughout the theatre - more cacophonous even than John Hugh Dean's music and, when they finally reached the deck, that last clunk sounded the positive death knell for all that had come before and that came after.

Sheila and I, sitting together in one of the boxes, sank lower into our seats, stifling our pained laughter and wishing for the cast's sake that the show would come to an end.

The reviewers bayed and crucified it. On a personal level, I escaped reasonably lightly, but for John Hugh Dean, in particular the notices were horrific. I felt immune, and calmly tried to give notes of encouragement to the actors and crew the following day. But the newspapers scented blood, Mr. Dean's blood.

On the Sunday, individual newspaper columnists and critics were calling my home, at regular intervals. They were kind, some of them positively cooed and sympathetic, but what they really wanted from me was a contact number or address for our producer/composer/lyricist/adapter. He was unknown to them, and so their files didn't have that information.

Maybe I should have complied and given it, and let the man have what I believed he deserved. But I was responsible to the show, to all the actors and musicians and the creative team, and I felt that I should remain loyal to the Theatre of Comedy, to Ray Cooney and Thelma Holt. I truly tried to retain some dignity for all, and to get us through what might remain of the run of the show. I hedged, and gave nothing away. But there was a knife already headed for my back.

If I was hoping for some respite and calm within the *Six for Gold* rehearsals, then I was quickly put right. After less than a week, Mike and Warner decided that this was such a mammoth project that they needed more time to refine their work. They wanted to put back the opening night.

All writers have jitters early on, but should not expect to change the schedule every time their nerves need a little calming. It was surely out of the question. Dan Crawford would not countenance the loss of revenue involved, and everyone would be affected.

At The Ambassador's, a relatively cheerful cast were getting on with the job, in front of a good sized audience evidently enjoying the show. On the following day, I learned that Mike and Warner had been quietly but forcefully working on Rosemary Leach. She now refused to open on the 27th, as agreed. Having booked a flight to the US on July 3rd, I had no intention of cancelling it. I bided my time and waited to hear from Dan Crawford.

Another day, another shock. Sean O'Mahoney announced that he would redirect *The Importance* or, he would take the show off. It was true to form and nobody was impressed. He would find himself up against a fully professional, and powerful, West End producing management. Or so I thought.

I looked to my allies Ray Cooney and Thelma Holt for their support. And they simply disappeared. It turned out that their object had been achieved. The theatre had filled a vacant slot, and it hadn't cost them a penny. I discovered that they had known all along that this was a probable turkey. They thought with a decent director it could just possibly scrape by. If not, they would wash their hands of it.

And that is what happened. Thelma Holt's u-turn seemed the most treacherous. Ray Cooney was just a coward, "Don't you trust me?" It meant that I had to face down Mr. O'Mahoney on my own.

But 2 days later, the notice inexplicably went up, and the show played its final performances.

It would be 20 years before I would experience such brutality again. But, by then, both the profession and I had changed considerably.

To help out Dan Crawford, who pleaded for my help, I agreed to postpone *Six For Gold* until July 2nd the day before I was due to fly to America. Everything seemed settled. I was enjoying rehearsals, and the show felt good. By the time I was back, it would have run itself in and Dan would no doubt be talking about a transfer. But the writers had yet another surprise to spring on me.

The opening was shifted again. This time, the date set was July 5th, and I had no doubt that such indulgence could be repeated time and again. It was the writers' baby, and they were prepared to make any number of sacrifices for it. But, for me, I had put in hours and hours of my own time, working with them unpaid to get the score and the book into best shape. I had more work coming up and had already agreed to one postponement, even though both Dan and I thought it unnecessary.

Ultimately, I had given Mike and Warner a first class production, a fact they were only too ready to acknowledge, but there was nothing more I could give, or was prepared to give.

On July 2nd, after watching a very successful preview, I was given an emotional farewell. Most sad to see me go, it seemed, was Rosemary Leach. Rosemary is a decent actress, and that goodbye represented a decent performance. Certainly, I was convinced by it at the time. But haven't you noticed? the villain who is only unmasked at the very last moment is always played by the Star.

When I flew to America the following day with *The Importance* closed; *Mr. Cinders* on the point of closing, drenched in Lionel Blair saccharine; and *Six for Gold* ready to open without me it felt less like the start of a holiday and more like an escape. Little did I know...

PART SIX

Riding the Shuttle

Time for an interlude. Above the clouds, the sky was blue, the wine was a comforting red and I was looking forward to spending a little time away from the Theatre. We were on our way to Oakland, California.

You may remember that, four years previously, I was introduced to Marion Grimaldi and subsequently cast her in *Lloyd George Knew My Father*. Her mischievous wink had landed on me and stayed with me, and when she moved to San Jose, of Silicon Valley fame an invitation to visit had quickly winged its way in my direction. Now that I had a 3 week break it was time to take it up. Our port of entry to the US was Baltimore.

These pages are naturally peppered with the First Person Singular but, as we stand in line for the lengthy wait at Immigration, let the First Person Plural reveal itself.

You need to check an earlier episode, from 1976, and my first West End show. As we transferred *Anastasia* from the touring circuit to the Cambridge Theatre, the role of Prince Paul was likewise moved from Gareth Forwood to Edward Arthur. In 1978, at a house party in Bath, my relationship with Edward transferred from the professional to the personal and that is how it remains to this day.

Fast forward to 2008, and you will find us on a train from New

York to Newhaven, Connecticut on a sentimental and very poignant journey. But to join us there, the intervening years have to… intervene.

For now, we have passed through Immigration and entered America for the first time.

This was a period of excitement. Even the coffee at Baltimore tasted good, but we were soon racing down the runway again, this time, en route for Kansas City. Though it was a long route to take, the adrenalin barely stopped pumping. We tumbled out and felt the dry, landlocked waste of the mid West.

Back on board, we stretched our bodies out to sleep, as the third leg of this journey took us within sight of San Francisco. The now defunct World Airways had delivered us in style though not in record time. Marion and her partner, Mel, whisked us away in the Buick to our final stop - the suburbs of San Jose.

The next day was Independence Day July 4th. As I recall, this was an excuse for a gigantic belt loosening breakfast at Denny's. Stacks of pancakes with maple syrup occupied just a small portion of that groaning plate. The weather was hot and, after pina colladas at Macy's, jetlag brought siestas by the pool, before the barbecue was lit and we all dressed for dinner.

Lest you think that I had forgotten all about my show at the King's Head, believe you me I waited anxiously for news from London. But none came. Instead, it was time for an introduction to San Francisco.

When you have 3 theatricals together, there is always a show to be drawn to, and we had tickets for the Golden Gate Theatre on Friday night. Edward crooned, "there must be opium in the air," as we got our first taste of the city. Lunch on the terrace of the Hyatt Hotel; Fisherman's Wharf; blueberry cheese cake; and cocktails at the Top of the Mark, these were the magical treats awaiting us, before the evening show: *La Cage aux Folles*.

For anyone who experiences for the first time a big American musical, with a genuine American musical theatre orchestra and cast the excitement and exhilaration that it pumps into your being is hard to shake off. July 6th 1984 was just such an occasion and I remember almost every minute of it. It began a 48 hour joy ride that, in retrospect, began to shift the course of my career for the next two or three years.

For, on Saturday, we were back in San Francisco to watch British actress, Lynn Redgrave, in a matinee of *Sister Ignatius Tells All*. Since Lynn was an old friend of Marion's, we were invited to join her for tea and cakes after the performance. She was great in the show, and adorable to be with. Did I really expect to leave the Theatre behind?

At this distance in time, it seems hard to believe... BUT, the next day, I was driving the sleek white Buick to Monterey, as Edward and I took off for Los Angeles, and a meeting with two very classy television producers. But first, it was lunch at the River Inn, Big Sur, sitting in the sun and tapping our feet to the sounds of the resident jazz band.

The sun shone all the way to Morro Bay, where we booked in for the night at a very comfortable motel. A great friend of mine, American, always used to say that whenever he visited California he wondered why the whole world didn't live there. Then after a while, and in the Second Degree of Visitation he would always remember why.

In July 1984, I'm happy to say, we were still quaffing the joys of introduction.

Meantime, in and out of the fog we drove, through big country and in hot, hot sun. And then before Malibu, we stopped to make a call.

I had been given an introduction to Jonathan Estrin and his wife, Shelley List. In the 80s, they were the supervising producers on the hugely successful American TV series, *Cagney & Lacey*. Shelley was also a writer, and was adapting her books for the television network, HBO, for co-productions with Canadian TV. So... they were high flyers.

I called them at their home in Venice, and we were immediately invited to a barbecue there that evening. There was just time to stop off in Santa Monica, to book into a motel and freshen up, before heading over to L.A. and the canals at Venice.

Jonathan and Shelley had an amazing home as befitted their status, and we were given an effusive welcome, before being led through to the garden at the back, where an enormous barbecue was underway. It was good to be the first guests to arrive, because it gave us the chance to get to know our hosts a little, as Jonathan tossed a mass of oversized steaks and chicken hunks onto the barbecue.

In time, we were taken back inside, where a table was set... for four. That mountain of food, it seemed, had been roasted up just for us. Despite our appetites failing to do full justice to the meal, however, it was a fun evening and the conversation was lively and entertaining. When the subject of *Soap* came up, a favourite TV sitcom at the time, Shelley instantly offered to introduce us to a member of the cast, Sal Viscuso. Before we left, it was arranged that we all meet for breakfast at The Rose, two days later.

Tuesday gave us a chance to explore Los Angeles a little, after an hour's tennis in hot sunshine. The itinerary may have been predictable, but no less exciting for that: the Freeway, Downtown, Hollywood, Sunset Boulevard, the Chinese Theatre, Beverley Hills, and a romantic evening on the terrace at Gladstone's, overlooking the Pacific Ocean.

I confess that I am not at my best first thing in the morning so, to get ourselves over to The Rose for our 9.00am breakfast meeting was something of an ordeal. I longed for the coffee, so that I could open my eyes.

We did not expect an encounter with Arnold Schwarzenegger - looking like an upturned coffin in a suit - and it was humbling to see Shelley jogging her way into the place, having already completed one business meeting on just one glass of freshly squeezed orange juice. Welcome to LA.

Sal Viscuso was already there. Had I anticipated his manner, I might have made sure I was wide awake. But neither of us was prepared for the full on, hyper active speed at which his entire CV tumbled out of him. A complete range of gesticulation marked every twist and turn of this swanky and detailed sell. We half expected him to launch into a full-scale audition.

I drained my coffee and ordered another. Welcome to Hollywood.

We bid our farewells to Jonathan and Shelley. There were one or two further meetings in London over the next few years, but Shelley's life was tragically cut short by cancer, in 1996.

Understandably, we were now anxious to return north, a slow re-treading of our route: to Pismo Beach; more tennis along the way; on, through fabulous light and countryside where I could finally shake off the spectre of Lonnie Donegan, to San Simeon where we spent the night; another stop at the River Inn; further sun-drenched beaches where, at last, I could wash Joel Spector right out of his Liberace style hair; Carmel and Monterey; and back to San Jose.

All the while, and however hard I tried, I couldn't quite shake off the lingering suspicions over what might be happening back in Islington. I couldn't even make contact with my agent.

This interlude, however, allowed for very few pauses. The next day, we drove past rolling cornfields, plains and mountains to Mariposa, before a spectacular drive into Yosemite National Park, where we were booked in for a couple of nights.

As the weather got hotter, and we chilled out back at San Jose, there was still no word from the King's Head. Little did I know that there were four hands already wielding the blade that was poised above my back, but I was aware that all was not well even as we drove to Freemont, where we caught BART (Bay Area Rapid Transit) into San Francisco.

For the first and last time in my life, I ate a 12oz hamburger, at Original Joe's. We then walked to the cable car, and took a tour of the Bay, Golden Gate Bridge, Alcatraz, and back for more cocktails at the Top of The Mark. There were so many other delights to come, including a breathtaking drive to the observatory at Mount Hamilton, and stunning views of the Sierra Nevada.

Our whistle stop introduction to California came to an end on July 26th, and I peered across the cloud tops from the plane windows, to watch for what might be approaching. Two ladies from *Six for Gold* - one cast member, and one the wife of a cast member - had been man-oeuvring, in my absence, to have me removed from the show. Perhaps they were not getting the success they felt they deserved; perhaps if they had had more time...? It was left to my old friend Dan Crawford to compose an explanation – even though, as he later confessed to me – it was done under pressure.

His letter was waiting for me on my return. I had apparently not given the production enough of my attention. Those ladies' behaviour left me wounded and scarred, but couldn't tear through my new sense of determination. And my conscience was clear. I had been amazingly flexible, within an extraordinarily tight schedule. I had given the production "enough of my attention" for months. I had other contracts. Three days after hitting Heathrow, I was back in rehearsal for Derek Nimmo.

But leap frog this, for a moment. And join me in a radio interview for Radio Sussex in early November. I'd returned to the Connaught Theatre, in Worthing to direct *The Long & The Short & The Tall* - a play that was first staged by 'my friend', Lindsay Anderson, in 1959. I was proud of the production, but have good reason to remember it for two other reasons. Firstly, I don't often put on the television at the start of a rehearsal day, but I was drawn to it on the morning of October 12th 1984. The scenes that I watched were shocking and compulsive, and I will long remember the image of Norman Tebbit being dragged out of the Grand Hotel down the road from me, in Brighton, on a stretcher, and still wearing his pyjamas. The IRA had struck.

Secondly, I was summoned to Radio Sussex to discuss on air *The Long & The Short & The Tall.*

I was invited for a lot of interviews at the time, but this one had significance. For an hour, I sat with the astrologist Russell Grant, my fellow guest. In between bursts of music, we talked in turn about ourselves and what we were doing and, whilst the records spun and our interviewer busied himself with whatever interviewers do, Russell 'misbehaved'.

The atmosphere grew a little tense, over 60 minutes, and so when a question came towards the end: "Tony, is there anything you would like to ask Russell?" I couldn't resist a swift challenge.

"Yes. What star sign am I?"

I was equally swiftly put in my place.

"You're a Gemini." (True) "And, next year, you will be going a long way away, for a long time." (This may be your dearest wish at this moment, Russell, but I think it unlikely.)

After all, I'd recently returned from Hong Kong - another 6000 miles, please note.

Terence Frisby's play, *There's A Girl In My Soup* might not have been my ideal choice of play, but I wanted to work for Derek Nimmo again and I'm glad I did. For a number of reasons. For instance, Hong Kong has become one of my favourite locations, even though my first few hours of experience were a bit scary.

Arrival at the international airport there in 1984 was an exhilarating way to meet the city, together with many of its inhabitants along the way. A sudden descent brought the wings of the aircraft alarmingly close to residential apartment blocks on either side. As the plane headed for the runway, it was possible to peer through their windows and watch their TVs for a few seconds or anything else people might be up to. An unexpected gust of wind, and you could get entangled with somebody's washing line, it seemed.

And wind was what we had. As we got out of the car that had whisked us from the airport, and staggered into the lobby of the Hilton Hotel, we were helped on our way by the first stirrings of an unusually strong tailwind. Once inside, and having been escorted to our rooms, we were advised to stay there and keep our eyes on the television screens. A major hurricane was on its way, and was due to make landfall slap bang in the middle of Hong Kong.

This was the production that I had started on as soon as my interlude in California was over. It starred Gerald Harper, Bill Maynard and Gary Raymond and had repercussions long afterwards. Gary was delightful, if a touch lazy; Gerald was very pleasant, in a slightly condescending sort of way and I always reckoned that his head was somewhat out of proportion to the rest of his body. And Bill Maynard presented a gushing, blubbery kind of sycophancy that quickly unravelled into an insincerity of sinister proportions.

There were others in the cast, of course, but these may be sufficient to absorb for the time being. Currently, I am unpacking, whilst keeping a weather eye on the TV screen. Also, on a very choppy looking swimming pool, at ground floor level. We are on red alert, and the boulevard comedy that we have travelled so far to present has acquired a surreal insignificance, as you can imagine.

I have survived two earthquakes, but they were both over very quickly. Sitting on a high floor, waiting to be struck by a hurricane, does not equate in the same way. But maybe when it hits, I am thinking, I can finally jettison all the tacky narcissism of *Six for Gold*. It was a good show, but ultimately fell victim to the public's dislike of one-act plays spread over two nights with no real star to carry it. It had nothing to do with a very healthy preparation and rehearsal period.

At the last minute, the threat is downgraded to a tropical storm, as it turns away and heads northeast. However, we have caught the edge of it and when I finally get outside to look around there is plenty of shattered window pane glass, showered from high rise buildings and strewn across the streets.

Hong Kong remains one of my favourite cities. Not only is the location so perfect, but the islands are idyllic, and there are stunning views from the Peak. If you can also cope with a few million Chinese, whose sole business is to make money, then nobody could fail to be impressed with the place.

I'm always fascinated by the way people deal in their different ways with foreign travel. For instance, a lovely actor called Martin Stone was in the company. He had barely been outside the UK during his 20 something years yet, on arrival in Hong Kong, he didn't leave the hotel for several days. Maybe he was an accidental tourist, because there was one experience that even he couldn't miss.

During our stay, we were invited by the Royal Navy to spend the day aboard one of their frigates, HMS Monkton. We were given the full VIP treatment, and it came to an end too quickly. However, before we disembarked, a couple of the officers who were clearly enjoying this break from routine asked if we would be interested in visiting an authentic Chinese restaurant, later that evening. "The best in town,"

In Hong Kong, aboard HMS Monkton - Gerald Harper, Gary Raymond, Bill Maynard, with some of the Royal Navy crew

they said. How could we refuse?

I was expecting an elaborate and elegant business - perhaps on the water - frequented by the great and good of Hong Kong society. But this was not Vienna. We climbed the stairs of a large old building, aware of an almighty din above us. Was this emanating from the restaurant?

When we arrived at the first floor, and the doors opened, we saw what could only be described as a vast aircraft hangar, stuffed with tables and crowded with diners, all of whom were intent on throwing as much rice and other food down their throats and onto the floor and tabletops as quickly as possible, before rushing back to their businesses and getting on with the job of making money. We joined in. The food was absolutely delicious, and it was a thoroughly good evening.

The art of the kitchen also features in *There's A Girl In My Soup*. Every night, in front of the audience, an omelette is prepared and cooked on stage and brought to perfection by the leading actor, at just the right moment in the dialogue. Gerald Harper proved to be supremely good at that. But he was presented with a major problem one night.

The hotel kitchen from where the eggs were provided for each performance misunderstood their instructions on this occasion. During the show, as Gerald picked up the eggs to crack them and begin the routine, he quickly realised that they had been hard boiled.

Hard boiled I had to be, to deal with my next experience. Bill Maynard was having trouble with his genitals, and retired to his room. The hotel doctor was called, and we feared having to cancel one of the performances. I admit there were suspicions within the company that it might be a case of lazy malingering and, eventually, the muttering reached Bill himself. He asked if I would go and visit him, and I readily agreed. I needed to know exactly how matters stood and there is no pun intended.

He lay in a semi darkened room, emitting all kinds of poorly noises, and insisted to me that he was genuinely in a bad state, though able to go on stage that night. I was about to leave, when he suddenly switched on a light, threw back the covers and exposed the full display of genitalia to me.

Even his huge fan base would find little attraction surely in the idea of having to peer at Bill Maynard's swollen particulars. For me, a swift glimpse was sufficient. I offered my sympathy and hopes that we would indeed see him (clothed) on stage that night, before beating a hasty retreat to my own room, to concentrate on writing postcards.

An excruciating hour at the Chinese Opera, the following evening, completed a jarring 24 hours. Nevertheless, I was sorry to leave the company in the early part of September. I'd made one or two good friends, and had the pleasure yet again of working with Derek's then company manager, James Gill. James was wonderful with all the actors on those tours, and provided constant support to his director, and we remain in regular contact to this day.

*   *   *   *   *

Crowd scenes are notoriously difficult to manage, and I have tried not to introduce them into this story for fear of clogging up the pages. Nevertheless, one of the many extraordinary aspects of working in this industry is the speed at which the dramatis personae list increases. Hundreds of characters pass through briefly before moving on.

Bear with me, therefore, whilst I throw the spotlight on two more central to this narrative, and both writers. One is a young English actor when we first meet him, Gregory Day. The other is an American, Jeffrey Beatty, who was spending time in Europe. Their paths will cross, in time.

The first entered my life through a chance remark that I made to a member of the stage crew, during the production week of that ill fated musical at The Ambassador's, *The Importance*. I was thinking seriously about adapting Joe Orton's novel, *Head To Toe*, for the stage, and it came up in conversation.

"I know a guy who's trying to do the same thing. You should meet."

And so it was that Gregory Day came to the King's Head Theatre, whilst I was in the early stages of *Six For Gold*. Greg's acting career *Grange Hill*, for example was fizzling out, and he was turning his hand to writing. In time, he would become a major force in television, as a PR and Publicity Man, Channel 4, and then Channel 5 and he is very good at his job.

Back in 1984, he already had a gift for selling, and he persuaded me to work with him on the Orton project. Although it quickly became clear that the novel was a non starter for adaptation, Greg took the same themes and set about developing them into a play, *Bust*. We organised a series of intensive workshops, in order to move it forward. Matt Frewer was one of the actors to take part, and that's where we can leave it for now.

Jeffrey Beatty, on the other hand, had trained as a lawyer in the States, but was already feverishly writing plays when we met. He was born in Boston, but loved Europe. His wife was English, but loved America. Although they had decided to make Massachusetts their home, whilst they brought up their two daughters, Jeffrey took every opportunity to travel to Europe and soak up the culture.

During one of his extended stays, he submitted a play to the Tabard Theatre, in Chiswick, which was accepted. My name was suggested to direct it and, since I was living in Bedford Park at the time, we met to discuss it.

But it's a while since the name of Elspeth March has graced these pages. She had three very close friends - Maggie Smith, Joan Collins and Diana Rigg - and they were often at her parties in Quarrendon Street. There'll be more of them later, but round about this time, I had a magical and memorable encounter at one of those do's.

To help Elspeth out, I often took it upon myself to refill glasses - mingling, with a bottle or two in my hand. In fact, Joan Collins once mistook me for a waiter, how dare she. On this particular occasion, I managed to extricate myself from one very luvvy kind of group and headed for the stairs to see who might be above.

Half way up, I came across a figure, sitting all alone and holding on tightly to a very empty glass. I offered a choice: wine or champagne and sat down to pour it. Thus it was that I found myself having a warm heart to heart with Jean Simmons, the second Mrs. Stewart Granger. Already a huge fan, I was nevertheless struck by her natural warmth and vulnerability. And astonishing beauty. I tingled for weeks.

I certainly did not tingle when I happened to escort Elspeth into Jill Bennett's dressing room (remember her?). This was a production of *Separate Tables* and Elspeth of course knew everyone, and we had to do the rounds of the entire cast afterwards. We left a very courteous

John Mills and arrived to greet Miss Bennett, who clearly thought I was some kind of servant. As she and Elspeth chatted about the play, I was ordered around to pour drinks and deliver chairs, until Elspeth introduced me with a deft touch: "This is my dear friend, Tony Craven. He directed me, in *Anastasia*!" The effect on Miss Bennett was instant and remarkable.

Meanwhile, workshops with Greg were continuing, and we arrived at a final draft of *Bust* at the end of March. I then went into rehearsals for a new play by Peter Mahon, at the same time rehearsing a one man version of *Murder in the Cathedral* for Brian Barnes, which was scheduled to open in Bogota, Columbia. I was also taking classes at the Actors' Centre.

But my short term future was suddenly thrown wide open by a call from Marion Grimaldi, in San Jose. She was proposing that Edward and I might like to go to California for a few months, to start a new theatre company. And wouldn't it be exciting if we all wrote the first play? Dr. Mel Marshak was prepared to finance the venture. Hats off to Russell Grant. It seemed that his eerie prediction was about to come true.

I celebrated with a trip to Glyndebourne and a production of *Arabella*, starring a very old friend of mine.

It's a strange thing, but my professional involvements musically have tended to neatly mirror my private tastes. This particular opera at Glyndebourne, however, has to be traced back to my university days.

Dame Felicity Lott, known throughout the business as 'Flott', was a contemporary, and she is now, I am proud to boast, one of the country's finest and best loved sopranos. She sang for Prince Andrew and Sarah Ferguson at their wedding and got scant thanks for it, apparently.

Back at Royal Holloway, however, we were close. We were intimate. And many people expected us to marry. Our history together has remained a tangled one, but we continue to be friends and to crack open a bottle of wine together when we can manage to be in the same country, at the same time.

She was delicious in *Arabella* and I retain a huge admiration for the girl whom I accompanied on the piano, for the audition that took her into the Royal Academy of Music and to the threshold of her career (even though I was buried in the pit and couldn't see her).

But my musical tastes only stretch so far, as is about to become clear.

One of the cast members of *Girl in my Soup* that I haven't yet mentioned was a lady called Annette Lynton or 'Netty'. She was glamorous and stimulating, slightly reminiscent of Joanna Lumley and, when she returned from Hong Kong, we resumed our friendship. One evening, we met for dinner in London, together with her boyfriend.

Netty and I chatted and reminisced about the show for some time, whilst the boyfriend sat quietly listening. From his appearance, I assumed he was a bank manager or accountant, but having decided that he must be bored with our conversation I set about drawing him out.

It turned out to be one of the more embarrassing introductions of my life.

I guess the dialogue went something like this:

"So. Are you in this daft business as well?"

"In a way."

"But you're not an actor?"

"No."

The replies were brief and unhelpful. I persisted. "So. What do you do then?"

"I'm a musician."

This was good. I felt I could relate to this. "Ah. Do you play an instrument?"

"Yes."

I was getting in deeper, and beginning to get the impression of being ever so slightly teased. Netty kept sipping her drink and smiling. "What do you play?"

"Drums."

There's an old adage that you should stop digging a hole for yourself if it appears to be getting deeper. But I was on a roll.

"Are you in a group?"

"I'm in a band, yes."

And, if this sounds like an edition of *What's My Line?*, then that's certainly how it felt at the time. My sense of exasperation led me to sound patronising. "Do you make recordings?"

"Yes."

"And would I have heard of this... band?" Knowing it was unlikely.

"I don't know."

I knew I was about to make a fool of myself. "So. What are they called?"

"Pink Floyd."

He grinned. I had just met Nick Mason and, over the months that followed, he and Netty introduced me to the fascinating world of one of the biggest bands on the planet. Watch this space.

For now my immediate future was decided. I had an offer of another production with Derek Nimmo, this time in Singapore. I would then travel halfway round the world, for an extended stay in California. I would need a work permit from the American Embassy first, but then I can never resist the lure of an exciting opportunity.

Squeezed in before that, however, there was *A Change in the Moon*.

*　　　*　　　*　　　*　　　*

Jeffrey Beatty and I became instant friends. His sense of verbal humour chimed with my own and his educated East Coast American style translated directly into his writing. It may seem banal, but here was a writer who knew how to use words.

So, even though The Tabard Theatre was little more than a room above a pub, it was in every sense my local and I couldn't wait to get stuck in to Jeffrey's play. The theatre was run by a harem scarem Irish writer, called Sam Dowling, whose heart was in the right place, but who became lost in the world of practicality. Nevertheless, he ran The Tabard for the benefit of writers and I could only applaud that.

Jeffrey's play was called *A Change in the Moon*, and drew on his background as a lawyer in Boston. It was romantic, moving and filled with musical reference. Since his wife, Annabel, had been a ballet dancer and bore obvious similarities to the leading female character, it was pretty clear that this was in many ways autobiographical. Her part was played in this première production by the Canadian actress, Shelley Thompson.

In retrospect it may have worked to the play's advantage that Shelley didn't get on with her leading man, Stephen Hoye. She regularly complained that, in their romantic scenes on stage, she couldn't get his tongue out of her mouth, and was always asking for me to intervene. Not easy. But the electricity between them gave a lustre to their performances and, for me, the whole production period was a joy.

Here's a cautionary tale for theatre critics. Stephen had arrived in England to make a career as an English actor, and had been very successful at it. Nobody knew that he was born and brought up in Boston, but it made him ideal to play the autobiographical Jeffrey.

At the second performance of *A Change in the Moon*, we welcomed *The Times* critic, Martin Cropper. Although his review was not unfavourable, he swankily criticised Stephen's Boston accent as not authentic. What a blunder. The writer, also a Bostonian, thought the accent was spot on.

All in all, Jeffrey was delighted with the show, and wrote a touching letter to my agent afterwards. It contained an offer. He wanted to give me first refusal on directing all of his subsequent plays anywhere in the world. And he was always true to that undertaking.

I have a number of books in my possession, with signed dedications from the author. One such is a children's book, called *Gumphlumph*. Gumphlumph has two voices and twenty hands, and was created by the author for tales to tell to his own children. In May 1964, he told one of the stories on the BBC and the success of the programme encouraged him to put Gumphlumph alive and kicking, as he put it, into a book.

It seems incongruous that such a character should be dreamed up by Stratford Johns more readily known as the tough, unapproachable Inspector Barlow, of the BBC TV series, *Z Cars*.

My copy is signed: 'With Love Seasons Greetings 20.10.85'. The Ayckbourn play was my next assignment for Derek Nimmo, and starred alongside Stratford my old chum Jack Smethurst. But the whole cast was terrific, and I could not have been more happy with the production.

Meanwhile, I was setting about getting a work permit for the USA and I had to prove that no American national was more qualified than I was to do the job as Director/Writer/Producer. The process involved acquiring letters from various luminaries to support this claim, and I am forever grateful to Michael Attenborough and Derek Nimmo, amongst others, for writing such glowing tributes to my talents, so as to ensure prompt receipt of that visa.

The Seasons Greetings cast and stage management arrived at Heathrow on October 16th. This distinguished group included our very camp Australian company manager, Rob Swann. Rob had an outrageous and anarchic sense of humour and, as we approached the security section of the airport, he suddenly stopped and screamed out, in mock horror: "My God! What did I do with the GUN?" There is a gun required, as a prop in the play.

Within seconds, the area was swamped by uniformed officials carrying the real thing, and Rob was hauled off for questioning. The rest of us, used to this kind of behaviour, chuckled and laughed, and then made our way in the opposite direction to the First Class Lounge.

We were heading off to Singapore, and luxury that this time surpassed even Derek Nimmo's usual standard. We would be staying at the Shangri-La Hotel, regularly voted one of the best five hotels in the world. But would Rob be coming with us?

When he failed to reappear after half an hour, I thought I should go and look for him. Stratford came with me. If you have ever doubted the power of television, or the persuasiveness of a long running series, you would have been as amazed as I was to watch what happened next. To all the security guards and plain clothed police officers, Stratford Johns was part and parcel of Inspector Barlow. One word from him, and the situation was instantly defused.

We had our company manager back, and we were on our way.

Stratford and Jack were joined by their wives, and the atmosphere was cheerful and relaxed for the whole production period. We visited Raffles Hotel, before its refurbishment and modernisation, and in a grand gesture I ordered the famous Singapore Slings for everyone.

Rightly so, perhaps considering they had a performance to give later in the day, some of the cast declined. I couldn't let them go to waste, so I was forced to have more than my quota. They were delicious, but the rest of the day disappeared in a kind of haze.

The show went extremely well except that some members of the audience were disappointed in the manner in which the play darkens towards the end. It has to be remembered that, for most ex pats, this was a rare occasion to see a West End show, with a known cast and to make it a thoroughly memorable night out they drew heavily on the hotel's bar stocks. They wanted the laughter to continue for as long as possible.

On my last night in Singapore, on the 25th October, I joined some of the cast in the hotel hot tub Jacuzzi for a few farewell/congratulations/good luck drinks of my own. I was able to reflect on a job well done and, as I looked up at the night sky, to look forward to the 12,000 miles I was about to travel, and the start of yet another new adventure.

I was back in London for just two days - time for a send off party from our friends before climbing back onto a plane, this time for San Francisco.

Earlier that summer, I had been flying with my brother, who used to pilot a Cessna 4 seater light aircraft. Once in the air, the up draught from the copses and woods below gave a distinct shudder and turbulence to the plane, and I began to wonder whether some of the rubber bands that were surely holding the whole contraption together might not snap, separating the tail from the nose and us from each other.

All was well, however, but as we lined up for landing and began our shaking, swerving descent I crossed my fingers anxiously, waiting for a violent thump as we hit the runway. In the event, this was a gentle touch down, and I began to emit a sigh of relief. We immediately speeded up once more and, before I knew it, we were in the air again. My brother turned to me, with a grin. "That's called a touch and take-off," he shouted, over the roar of the engine.

So, as our flight to California soared above the earth, I already had my title for the play we had yet to write. It would be called: *Touch & Take-Off*, and it would take the West Coast by storm. But for one small moment of disaster.

*   *   *   *   *

"You will be going a long way away – for a long time." Full marks to Russell. With a break for a show at the Pitlochry Festival Theatre, I was in America for almost 9 months. I got my social security number and my American driving licence; we made a lot of friends and got to know a lot of people; and after the triumph of *Mr. Cinders*, the failure of *The Importance* and the innovative halfway success of *Six For Gold* I audaciously got to direct an American musical, with an American cast, on American soil.

But, first, let us look down on the Golden Gate Bridge, as we begin our descent into San Francisco. For me, it's like coming home. The whole of the Bay area where we will be staying is spread out in dazzling sunshine below us. As the wing dips, the full display takes our breath away.

A clean canvas is set before us. It is for us to colour it. Three artists join hands. But where to begin?

I recall a particular lunch at Bob White Place, in San Jose - our head-quarters. The weather was idyllic, as usual, and the feeling around the table was as warm as the sunshine that was bathing the pool in light. Everything was calm and flojo, as the Spanish say.

Suddenly, I felt ill.

A sense of rising nausea hit me, and the room appeared to swim before my eyes. I became aware of the light fitting above me swinging like a pendulum and, as I tried to focus on the horizon, on the blue sky outside the window, I was struck by the movement of the water in the swimming pool, undulating and sloshing against the sides.

There was an earthquake taking place, and all that one had heard about San Francisco, about the Bay area, about the San Andreas Fault all came into my head, and I knew that we should get outside.

"Nonsense," said Mel, as she reached for more salad. "This is okay." Within seconds, everything was still again. "More bread?" I heard Marion ask with a mischievous look.

The day continued. But was this an omen?

Mel, Dr. Mel Marshak was a psychiatrist/counsellor, who charged a great deal of money to listen to people talking about their emotional worries and turbulent lives, very Californian. We learned from one such patient that she spent most of her expensive hour listening to Mel talking about her problems.

Mel was a highly intelligent, combative, generous, neurotic, stimulating and volatile lady, a chain smoker, who liked nothing better at the end of the day than a stiff drink. Estranged from her son, she flirted with men but distrusted them, and had settled into a feisty relationship with Marion who, in turn, had developed a tougher, slightly more masculine edge than I remembered from Basingstoke.

Nevertheless, both were never less than fascinating to be with and, once Mel was packed off to the office for the day, Marion resumed her theatrical twinkle and mischievous sense of fun.

After a couple of days spent recuperating from our flight, Edward and I sat down with Marion to begin work. We had decided to call ourselves the Dolphins Theater Company, and the thrill of what might await ran through each of us. However, as we cleared the table, deposited our pads of paper and pens, and pulled up our chairs, it dawned on us that we had never really discussed the kind of show we intended to première.

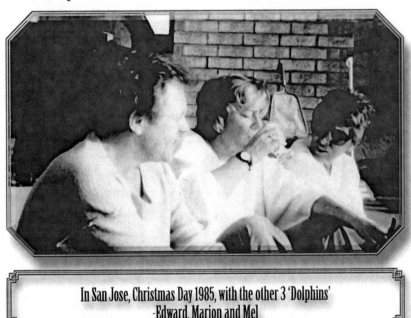

In San Jose, Christmas Day 1985, with the other 3 'Dolphins' -Edward, Marion and Mel

It soon became clear that music would be involved. Edward and Marion, of course, would introduce a song from time to time, and I would play the piano. In order to keep to a realistic budget, it was also taken for granted that I would be on stage as one of the actors, for the first time since my triumph as an aged Colonel Redfarn, in a production of *Look Back in Anger* that I directed at university. On that occasion, I did tend to overdo the talcum powder on my hair in the interests of ageing so that, every time I shook my head, a cloud of grey seemed to envelop the stage. How wise to forgo any ambitions to become an actor.

Sitting with us at that table was a large and shapeless writer's block. We stared at each other; we drew meaningless doodles; we considered the temptations of sunshine and swimming pool outside the window.

Improvisation was something that we all understood, however, and it soon came to our aid. We brought a tape recorder to the table and adopted any character that appeared from our imaginations.

Within a short while, our days acquired a regular routine. We spent many hours on the artistic side, creating sketches and episodes that slowly gained form and shape. We then shared out the business chores. We needed contacts, rehearsal space, advertising, try out venues, sponsorship, business cards, company registration, sheet music, costume, the list was endless, and we were starting from scratch.

At the end of each day, I would retire to an office to transcribe all that we had recorded during the creative sessions, so that a printed version of what we would come to rehearse could be edited, rewritten and committed to memory. In other words, a script emerged.

We had breaks, of course, and we swam and played tennis. We had slimming lunches and fattening dinners à quatre, with Mel, and Edward usually took it upon himself to walk the dog. He was regarded as an eccentric lunatic by the local population, as he traversed the streets of suburban San Jose. Nobody walked. The car was de rigeur.

Halloween came around, and an enormous jar of treats was set up in the hall. It was new to us, but it was fun - despite feeling like characters from *Meet Me in St. Louis*.

Thanksgiving came and went. We had guests for that enormous turkey, and I was introduced to sweet potatoes, pumpkin pie and blueberry pie. We were generally being absorbed into Californian society, and living the life style.

Every day, we woke to blue skies and sunshine and the temperatures, without humidity, seemed ideal. There were regular trips into San Francisco, cinemas, restaurants and theatres. In particular, I remember an awe inspiring production of David Mamet's play, *Glengarry Glen Ross* with Peter Falk. (Back in the UK, I had a brief, eccentric correspondence with Mamet, when I was pursuing the rights for one of his plays.)

Edward and I were invited to San Jose State University to give some classes and workshops to the drama department and, in order to earn our keep, we began to pursue the idea of the Dolphins running their own acting workshops for anyone from the Bay Area that might be interested. And they responded.

There was not a day that wasn't crammed with activity, and all the people that we met and came into contact with were enthusiastic, helpful, friendly, and upbeat. Whereas, in the UK, we might have expected a negative reaction to what we had set out to do here, in California, it seemed that anything was possible.

We struggled to find news from home. In the papers, National News meant Californian, and World News meant American. Margaret Thatcher was on the brink of being toppled by the Westland crisis, but the media ignored it. Britain was only mentioned when Charles and Diana came to town, to New York.

By Christmas, the show was coming together well, and we decided that everyone deserved a short break for the holiday. Mel had now been roped in - with mock reluctance, on her part - as a character in the show that would only be heard in God-like form, but not seen. She was The Voice. We were now, in all senses, a company.

I had been offered a production at the Pitlochry Festival Theatre, in Scotland, to start rehearsals in early April so, I had a deadline... of sorts. The play was called *The Happiest Days of Your Life* and, had I made a connection towards the end of December, 1985, it would have seemed fair comment.

Christmas brought very happy days. We'd had a festive trip into San Francisco to see the lights, to shake hands with the Santas, and to do our shopping and many presents were exchanged between the four of us. On the day itself, we drank champagne by the pool, with our feet in the water, before a pig out lunch and a lazy afternoon in front of the television.

The plan was to spend a few days in San Diego, and to relax until New Year. Mel and Marion decided to fly down, whilst Edward and I took the car. Affectionate, warm and excited goodbyes were said, and we set off towards Los Angeles retracing our steps from the previous year.

This time, once on the main highway through the city, we kept going - due south - to reach San Diego by the evening. It was a thrilling trip, and we managed to get down into Mexico, to Tijuana, where the contrast with the US resort couldn't have been more marked. Across the border, affluence was left behind, replaced by poverty in the town, and stench on the beach.

No wonder, we thought, as we crossed back into California and saw would-be emigrants literally hurling themselves at the barriers. They were determined to get across at any cost, but were dragged back by border guards instead. It was unpleasant to watch and we were glad to reach our motel again in San Diego.

But somewhere between Sans Jose and Diego a fracture had appeared between we two and the ladies. There was an atmosphere that was difficult to penetrate or to fathom.

Marion and Mel flew back to the Bay, and we drove to LA, to stay with my friend, Jean Sincere and her husband, Charles Zambello. Another new set of experiences presented themselves but, soon, we were on our way back on New Year's Eve to Bob White Place.

En route, we celebrated the English New Year and arrived back to welcome 1986 to the US with music, and fireworks, and sparkling toasts. But, for the Dolphins, something had shifted.

Now, however, the pace quickened. Rehearsals started again on the 6th. We moved to the Elks Hall - complete with elk heads - at their Lodge. Sinister and weird. We took on a stage manager, Della Falcon, and we booked our tryout theatres: one at the Northside Theatre on February 21st; one at the State University Theatre on the 23rd; and one at Eulipia on the 26th.

Meantime, I had accepted an offer to direct *Fiddler on the Roof*, in San Francisco, in the summer, and was meeting with MDs and choreographers and producers. This was a hectic time. But a huge explosion was primed to go off just around the corner, and the timer was already set.

*   *   *   *   *

Touch & Take-Off was a show that we were all proud of. It took each of us into areas that we'd never arrived at previously. It presented musical challenges and acting hurdles, together with breathtakingly complex monologues to deliver. It contained elements of the absurd, and episodes of pathos and sentiment. There were moments of farce and quick fire banter that taxed our powers of memory.

It was Peter Cook and Dudley More in *Huis Clos*; it was musical revue; it was theatre; it was stand-up; it was all that and more, and it worked.

But it had taken it out of all of us. We had lived under the same roof for four months and our friendships had been tried to the limits.

One evening, as we were gearing ourselves up, a few days before we were due to give the first performance, storm clouds gathered. As with all major tempests, however, this one was ushered in by a chilling stillness. We gathered at the end of the day. Only Mel was absent. Upstairs in her room. Was she sulking? Was she jealous of what the rest of us had to do? Having financed most of the preproduction period, was she expecting greater returns?

Marion took the pin from the grenade and tossed it towards Edward and myself. "Why don't you find out for yourselves what's wrong?" We reluctantly picked up the device and went upstairs.

We never discovered the cause of it all, but we were blown apart by the impact. Within minutes, screams splintered the air; violence, both verbal and physical, rocked the foundations. As Marion baited her from below, Mel attacked us like a wild thing, before locking herself into her room and barricading the door. Emotions of such epic proportions flew from us all, and things were said and yelled with such vehemence that we never thought possible.

And a few days later, we all took to the real stage to deliver the fruits of all our work. The show must go on. The storm clouds must pass. The sun had to shine again. We pulled it off. The show was a success. There was talk of a full run and transfer to San Francisco. In effect, mission accomplished.

And, with one day in between to pack, Edward and I flew to New York, on the last day of February. From 80° to 30°. We left the blood, sweat and tears behind, and headed for Broadway. But I was already booked in to Bob White Place again, from where I was due to commute to the city for *Fiddler* rehearsals.

But, for now, I stood in the Port Authority Building, in New York, freshly arrived from California surrounded by luggage and anxiously scanning those that came near. For ten minutes, I was on my own. I was approached for money; I was accosted by drunks; I was offered drugs and sexual favours; in short, I felt like an extra in a Robert de Niro movie.

Once out of there, and a watch was slipped from Edward's wrist. The grill that separated us from the yellow taxi cab driver felt ominous. We trundled past Broadway.

One of the few ambitions of my career that I haven't achieved is to have a show that would play in New York. It almost happened, many years later, but I've only been a visitor. My lodgings, however, have been of the very best. In 1986, we were staying with a friend of mine, and her film producer husband. The cab dropped us outside their block on Central Park West. Arriving at our floor, and stepping inside the apartment, we were confronted with a huge window that ran the full length of one room. Facing us and lit up was one of the most photographed views in the world: the Manhattan Skyline. We just had to laugh.

"If you arrive in New York for the first time, and have only a few days to see it which are the must see places to visit?"

We'd established that the young couple seated next to us in the restaurant were both from New Jersey. They were having a quick meal before going to the cinema, but had clocked our British accents, and we got into conversation. They seemed the right people to put the question to. They conferred.

"Tell you what. We can change our plans and give you a tour… if you like?"

Would we be kidnapped, or murdered or were these two genuinely being hospitable? The thought occurred, as we climbed into their car.

For the next two hours, we were driven across the bridges, through the districts, past the sights, upper side, lower side, west side, east side, Wall Street, Brooklyn, Harlem - the full panoply of New York City by night. It was the most amazing introduction to the place and, when we were finally deposited outside our apartment block, at 2.00am, we were on a skyscraper high.

The next morning, we felt we could explore at leisure. And on Sunday with our hosts, we strolled through Central Park, had brunch à la NY, and felt the city at our feet. To cap it all, Jeffrey Beatty whose play I had directed in Chiswick flew down from Boston to join us for dinner. The Dolphins at play, we leapt with excitement and, then, we were back over the Atlantic and touching down in London.

The canvas changed rapidly. The sparkling wintry glow of New York became the bleak grey ice of London, and soon altered again to the damp unwelcoming heath lands of Scotland, and the jumping salmon of Pitlochry. *The Happiest Days of Your Life* was now the interlude. As the Americans sent their war planes to Libya, and the government faced another crisis, I was singing *L'chaim* to myself and studying *Fiddler on the Roof.*

I wasn't crazy about Pitlochry itself, a claustrophobic kind of place, with a sinisterly alien feel to it but the play was fun, and quite unlike anything I'd ever done and, when we opened on May 9th, the audience appeared to enjoy the proceedings immensely.

It's less than 400 miles from Pitlochry to London. I drove back two days later and, on the 15th, flew back to San Francisco, a journey of more than 5,000 miles. This time, I was alone, but had hardly time to enjoy a single night's sleep before starting auditions for *Fiddler on the Roof.*

The Cappuchino Community Theatre was based in the city, and so there was a lot of commuting to come. For fun, I took the driving test.

The theory part of the exam, the written element, consisted of 100 questions, with a set of multiple choice answers. Mel had an old one for me to look at and, whilst much of it was sensible and useful, there were some crazy bits in there, too. For example:

"You are driving along the freeway and start to feel tired. Do you: a) Turn the radio up real loud; b) Put your head out of the window and breathe the fresh air; or c) Pull over and take a rest."

I got the answer pretty quickly to that one.

Imagine my amazement when I arrived at the test centre to be handed a paper with the identical set of questions. The girl at the desk was dumbfounded. "Gee, you got 100%! Let's see what you do in the vehicle!"

Outside, waiting for me, was a fierce looking woman in a plain suit with a tight bun and an even tighter face. The car purred and spat, as we caught sight of each other. Like an answering dog, she barked at me. "Drive the car forward three feet!"

I spent a moment trying to calculate three feet, as I inched forward 36 times. It turned out that the distance was immaterial. The lady preferred that I drive to pick her up, rather than she should have to walk towards me. I decided to adopt my most seductive English voice. "Good after…"

I got no further. "Don't speak until you're spoken to!" she barked.

I tried again, with some allusion to the weather. "Isn't it a lovel…'

Again, "Don't speak until you're spoken to!"

It became her mantra, as we drove the 15 minutes or so of the test. Left turns and reverses, stops and three-point turns all were rasped out with a degree of nastiness that I had rarely encountered.

When we arrived back at base, and I had parked the car, she prepared to leave. "Well, have I…?"

"Don't speak until you're spoken to! And take this sheet of paper to the desk!"

I muttered thanks for her many courtesies and headed for my dumbfounded friend with the bobbed hair. She consulted the sheet of paper, then looked up. Did I detect an amused twinkle?

"Congratulations. But 'cha only got 92% this time!"

I now possessed a State of California Driving Licence. And the Dolphins Theater Company were soon to possess a Business Licence. Yes, we would soon all be reunited and ready to start rehearsals once again - this time, hopefully, for an extended run in the heart of San Francisco.

I worked hard. I held auditions for Fiddler; I gave newspaper and radio interviews; I met with choreographers and musical directors, with designers and sound technicians; I took seminars at Lincoln High; I attended production meetings; meetings of the Bay Area Theaters, in Los Altos; I was in Palo Alto, and I was in Sausalito for wardrobe meetings. And rehearsals began on the 9th June.

Nervous though I undoubtedly was at rehearsing this archetypal American Jewish musical, with a semi-professional American group of performers I was too busy for those nerves to get through. In addition,

I gave myself a crash course in Jewish tradition and ceremonies.

Towards the end of June, Edward arrived via Los Angeles and, on the 27th, the Dolphins attended a performance of a revue, called *Tune the Grand Up*, at the Zephyr Theatre, in San Francisco. The producer of that show wanted to produce *Touch & Take-Off*.

But the take-off was never going to materialise.

The four of us tried to pick up where we left off. Rehearsals began again in between my own, and we had a run-through on July 5th the day after Independence Day. It was two years since our pig out breakfast at Denny's.

Our workshop schedule increased and, on July 8th, Edward and I were invited by some of those workshop members to the Hilton Sainte Claire Hotel, in San Jose, for a cabaret performance given by artistes from around the area.

Halfway through the evening, and eager to know more about our show, various people tried to pressgang us into an impromptu preview of one of the musical numbers. Having had one or two drinks, we tried to get out of it. But there was a determination in the air; a bar stool was positioned on the stage; and I was waved towards the piano.

Thank you, Peter Skellern, for *You're A Lady*. It formed our recital - rusty and nervous - but we gathered applause at the end. It was the last time we ever performed it.

Fiddler on the Roof went into production. *Touch & Take-Off* continued in rehearsal. Marion asked to join our workshops. Things had never quite returned to the way they were between the four of us, but we had a shared goal and we were about to achieve what we had set out to do. Almost.

Marion Grimaldi, with her vast experience and expertise, chose to give members of the workshop group a demonstration of stage deportment, of how to carry themselves, in different styles. Halfway through, and as she turned at one end of the hall, she slipped and fell.

Marion had broken her hip. For several weeks, she would not be able to walk. *Tune the Grand Up* completed its run in San Francisco. Our chance to follow it into the theatre slipped away.

Fiddler on the Roof opened successfully on July 25th. On the 30th, we said our goodbyes and flew to Los Angeles where we shook hands at the airport with Jean and Charles Zambello. By this time, Charles had retired from his job as a mainstay of TWA in Europe and returned to being an actor. He had swapped his immaculate shirts and regimented ties for Bermuda shorts and garish Hawaiian shirts and the new image was quite a surprise. But a weight had clearly lifted from his broad shoulders and he was sporting a wonderfully self-satisfied grin as he bounded forward to meet us. He couldn't have been happier, back in his LA home environment and the carousel of Hollywood auditions.

I reminded him of the apartment in Paris where I'd stayed with them both, and which after they left remained with the airline company for a while. Charles invited us to take advantage of it being vacant. "Just pick up a key from the concierge downstairs", he had casually suggested. "She'll let you in." You will know by now that I cannot resist an opportunity to visit Paris but unfortunately, on our arrival, the concierge was not as obliging as her pre-publicity had suggested. She was happy to part with a key, but her heavily upholstered derrière could not be prised from the comfort of the seat she occupied at the entrance to her domain. We were left to find our way à deux.

Since it was already dark, and the timer switches in the hallway allowed the light to blaze for only a few seconds at a time, I had to find my way into the apartment from memory. Of course, in retrospect, I should have taken into account the legendary and haphazard nature of much of the wiring in these long-standing Parisian apartment blocks. Searching for the light switch in the kitchen, my fingers came into brief contact with a very live wire and, for a moment, my feet appeared to leave the ground as I was launched towards the fridge on the other side of the room. It was, shall we say, a "shock".

Another shock was felt the following morning, when Edward got up early to investigate our surroundings. Passing through the living-room, he came across a naked man on the couch, either asleep or unconscious. In case he, too, had been rendered immobile by a taser strike from the electrics, I got myself dressed and went to investigate.

By this time, the unexpected guest had disappeared, leaving only the crumpled cushions as evidence of his few hours spent on the couch. We learned afterwards that he was a legitimate visitor – a TWA employee who had hit town late and moved on early.

Since this is a true story, chronology does not always suit context, as J.R.R. Tolkien might have said so, following this brief digression, we must re-join a cheery Charles and Jean in the Departures Hall of Los Angeles Airport and continue on our way. We were headed for London, from where I went straight to Scotland, to check on *Happiest Days* which was still in repertoire. Shortly afterwards, on the 7th August to be exact, I got a phone call.

*　　　　*　　　　*　　　　*　　　　*

Disappointments are always parked round the corner in this business, ready to screech across your path when least expected. They have to be ruthlessly kicked aside, in my opinion.

The final twist of the fates in California was no exception. It had, nevertheless, been a thrilling and invigorating ride for the best part of a year, and I wouldn't have missed any part of it. Had I been expecting some quiet time for reflection, however, I was to be thwarted. There was not a dull moment, from the day I arrived back.

I was asked to do a play with Martin Wimbush, about the Duke of Wellington, and I picked up the collaboration with Greg Day on his play, *Bust*. We decided to try it out at the Tabard Theatre, at the first opportunity. In addition, the Liverpool Playhouse checked my availability for that year's pantomime. And then, Derek Nimmo was on the phone again. He sounded almost irritated.

"So, you're back. At last. I want you to pop down to Sonning and tell me what you think of the show."

I was aware that he was referring to the thriller, *Wait Until Dark*, and I knew that the director was a man who had done the play many times. In fact, in a rather austere production, he had directed it for me at Basingstoke. His name was Cyril Frankel, and he was sure to have done a professional job.

"Yes, but there's something wrong and I can't put my finger on it. Get back to me when you've seen it, will you?"

I'd been back in the UK for a week. I'd been on a flying visit to Scotland. And now I was driving to Sonning, in Berkshire. My heart sank. I recognised a very familiar name on the poster - Peter Wyngarde.

The next day, I was back on the phone to Derek. "There's an imbalance between the characters. Mainly because Peter is being characteristically indulgent. But there's nothing I can do about it."

"We open in Singapore in a little over two weeks. Cyril's in a terrible state, tears all over the place. Wyngarde's giving him a nervous breakdown. Will you take it over for me?"

I was travel weary. I love the play, but did I really want this pressure?

"I'll do it, on one condition. I'll do it if Peter gives me his word that he'll knuckle down."

And thus it was that ironically on the Glorious Twelfth day of August, I met with Peter Wyngarde, at a roundabout just outside Sonning, and over the roar of rush hour traffic shouted at him and told him to behave.

The next day, I was back in rehearsal. One week later, I stood, packed and waiting, for Derek's chauffeur driven Rolls to take me to Heathrow yet again - this time, for the 6,700 mile flight to Singapore. Another trip with incident. From the start.

I use the word chauffeur advisedly. Driver just does not suit. Derek

Nimmo's old retainer was always in full livery and never without a few bottles of champagne, primed and ready, in a cool box. He remained stubbornly in another era rather like a member of Lady Penelope's retinue in *Thunderbirds*.

Nevertheless, he also considered the streets to be open race tracks, where other vehicles merely presented irritating obstacles to the Rolls's progress. I waited in some trepidation for the first sight of that car, sleekly breezing up the street to collect me.

Once at the airport, I headed straight for check-in, anticipating a lengthy, but comfortable, Club Class flight to Singapore. It was not to be. Once more, as a representative of the British Airways Playhouse Company, I became a member of staff on a stand by ticket. The girl would not even take my luggage.

I dragged everything through the security checks and waited patiently by the gate. The flight was called; a steady stream of passengers responded; the departure lounge emptied; I rose to my feet.

With relief, I was upgraded to First Class, and took my case to the door of the aircraft, where it was handed over to a smiling stewardess. The flight was blissful, and I arrived in Singapore on time and relaxed. As I stood at the carousel, a very small Australian lady joined me.

"Excuse me, but have you been to Singapore before?" She wanted to know if I was familiar with her hotel and whether there would be a courtesy coach to take her there. We chatted.

"My greatest fear," she said, "is to lose my luggage."

"Don't worry. You won't," I replied. And she didn't. I personally helped her to load it onto a trolley, and then wished her a safe onward journey.

After a while, I began to realise that I was the only one left at the carousel which, though still turning, was devoid of any luggage. My suitcase, so confidently given for safekeeping to the flight attendant, had gone. This was a situation that was new to me and, as I scanned photographs and colour sheets at the appropriate desks in vain (nothing matched) I began to feel the fatigue that follows a long journey.

Having reported the loss, all I could do was to take a taxi to the hotel and try to get a good night's sleep. In the event, I lay awake for hours, alarmingly listing an inventory of all that the case held inside it.

When Derek arrived with the company, the following day, he was highly amused. It was 36 hours before I saw my luggage again. It had been to Melbourne, located by Singapore Airlines and returned by Quantas. BA had obviously washed their hands of it.

Peter Wyngarde had become a very loose cannon since I'd last worked with him. No wonder he'd had his previous director in tears. It was like trying to contain a highly strung and slightly rabid dog. He now claimed to be a member of the British House of Lords but one who, having inexplicably lost his Pass, was unable to take his place in the Chamber.

His birth date moved around eccentrically within an entire decade, and his vanity appeared to be the only constant. Particularly worrying for Derek and the entire cast was that he continuously made derogatory remarks about the play to the Press, whilst supposed to be promoting it.

It was with some private glee that I witnessed him separated from his hair. In *Anastasia*, I had battled with him to remove the piece that he wore. But now, as he dived with Jason King like machismo into the hotel swimming pool, it was definitely Peter Wyngarde who surfaced.

It was a strange sight that greeted me. As he shook the water from his panic stricken eyes, a mass of soggy hair floated stubbornly on the surface toward the deeper end.

Derek was so anxious to keep Peter within manageable boundaries that he asked me to stay with the production until Hong Kong, at least the second leg of the tour. Another 1500 miles across the South China Sea. I was happy to return to Hong Kong, but in doing so I inadvertently provided the stage management with a headache.

The tensions and drama of *Wait Until Dark* centre on the search for a cache of heroin, cunningly concealed in a doll, until discovered during the course of the action. Before leaving the UK, the stage management had arranged for several bags of salt to be hermetically sealed. Since looking remarkably like the real thing, these were vital props.

And the Customs Staff were similarly taken in, on our arrival at Hong Kong airport. The props were discovered and menacing looks were thrown toward our stage manager. Suddenly, we were a little troupe of travelling players - a timid pack of theatrical vagabonds.

A large knife was poised above these hermetically sealed packages.

They were about to be sliced open, the contents taken away for laboratory testing. "No!" we all called, in unison. "Please!"

The knife wielding official hesitated. He looked perplexed and unsure, but not convinced of our innocence. "What is in these bags?" he asked, threateningly.

I should have kept my mouth shut, but I was trying to help. As the stage management answered: "Salt," I insisted: "SUGAR!"

Heads turned. I raised my hands in surrender. And buttoned my lip.

It was sorted out, and the heroin remained intact. I enjoyed the delights of Hong Kong, once more, and Peter learned finally to behave. The daft thing was he could turn in a stunning performance when he was able.

The last time we met, he appeared to have mellowed and regained some of his sense. He apologised for his behaviour in *Anastasia* and for the first time acknowledged the performances of his fellow actors as having been better than his own. Sometimes.

He may have lost his hair a few times; he may have divested himself of some of his vanity; but he seemed to me to have lost very little of his fascination and individuality. He remains in many ways unique. His kind are replicated very rarely.

John Curry, the greatest ice skater that England has produced, and certainly the most artistic and therefore replicated even more rarely, is sitting opposite me in the audition room. Having just left Peter Wyngarde behind in Hong Kong, it seems an appropriate moment to remind John of how *Anastasia* was scooped from its comfortable home at the Cambridge Theatre where it was enjoying a highly successful run in order to make room for the *John Curry Ice Spectacular.*

He seems suitably apologetic, even contrite. He is, after all, trying to make the transition from ice skating superstar to novice stage performer, and his agent at London Management has begged me to see him.

But does it really make sense to take him to the Liverpool Playhouse and cast him as Buttons, in *Cinderella*? He seems over awed, rather than demeaned, to have been waiting with all the others, at the Spotlight Building in Leicester Square, to audition.

As soon as I was back from the Far East, I was into double auditions. We needed to cast *Bust*, as well. For that, we were incredibly lucky to chance upon Otto Jarman for the lead. He was absolutely the good looking American hunk that we were looking for, and we decided to incorporate his image onto the poster.

In order to explore the concept of a man experiencing firsthand exactly what it feels like to be a woman, Greg decided to adopt a particular conceit for the play which would also give it a nightmare quality. A clean cut, athletic American boy arrives in the UK and from the moment he touches down he is seen by everyone as a woman. Initially providing some comic potential, the play gradually darkens, as the hero suffers sexual harassment and, ultimately, rape.

Otto - now, under his real name, a successful film producer - had the talent and commitment to play the role very powerfully. For the poster image, I decided to take him to Mike Laye.

One of the images for Bust·
*Photographed by Mike Laye/image-access.net

I regard Mike as one of the finest photographers of his generation, specialising particularly in theatre and music images. He had already done a couple of portrait sessions with me, and I trusted him one hundred percent to bring his imagination to bear on this project.

Otto was enthusiastic and patient. For two hours, he was photographed from every angle and with a variety of expressions and poses. Mike and I were not happy with the results, but Mike persisted. Finally, almost in desperation, he rummaged amongst some old studio props and came up with a battered and worn polystyrene plinth.

Half naked, Otto was pushed into this so that once he knelt down or crouched inside it he appeared as a sculptured bust. It was a very masculine image, maybe erotic, and once Mike had developed a tag line to accompany it, the photo became pure advertising genius.

Above the picture of Otto, the poster read: Why does this woman think she's a man?

I was once asked to direct Mandy Rice-Davies in a play. Mandy was, along with Christine Keeler, at the heart of the Profumo sex scandal, which discredited the MacMillan government in 1963. I turned the production down, because I had a cynical view of why the management had cast her.

The play was called *Dirty Linen* and, although it was a perfectly respectable piece by Tom Stoppard, Rice-Davies in combination with that title would almost certainly have brought in a different kind of theatre goer.

A friend of mine, working in the box office of the Phoenix Theatre during the run of the sex revue, Carte Blanche, told an amusing tale. The show had followed others, such as *Oh! Calcutta* and *Let My People Come* - two shows which tried unashamedly to push the limits of what could be shown on stage. Quite obviously, nudity was one of the selling points.

One day, a man immediately recognisable as representing the mackintosh brigade came to the box office. On being told that the evening show was sold out, he paused, before gushing and salivating, "Well, do you know if there are tickets for Dirty Linen?"

The poster for *Bust* brought a healthy advance to the box office at The Tabard, even before the papers had reviewed it. Quite often, a breathy caller to the theatre would first ask if there were tickets available, and then immediately ask to be "as close to the front as possible, please". "My hearing is not so good" was the most frequent excuse.

As it happened, The Tabard was small enough for every aspect of the performance to be clearly seen, even for those seated at the back.

Greg and I were proud of the show and, together with Otto Jarman, set out to find a life for it elsewhere. It was some time before we achieved it, though we did go to a meeting with Paul Raymond, for discussions about a slot at his theatre. We took it no further than the discussion stage.

John Curry won me over. His dance steps, at the very least, would provide nothing but comfort for my old friend Sheila O'Neil, as choreographer. And I was right. But John had not confessed all, at our meeting...

Running the Liverpool Playhouse at this time was a man called Ian Kelgreen. It soon became blindingly obvious that he knew nothing about pantomime.

First of all, there were no follow spots or follow spot operators allowed for in the budget and these are used as a matter of routine in pantomime; secondly, there seemed to be no expectation that we might actually need musicians; thirdly, I was expected to deliver the transformation scene that is central to the first act finale without a single pony (mind you, there were enough mice scuttling around backstage to have been turned into a whole string of white ponies); and finally a chorus is useful in a pantomime, if only to provide jolly townsfolk in the opening scene, and regally dressed dancers to fill out the ballroom scene.

After a few tantrums, arguments and threats, I got 3 out of 4, not bad but, nevertheless, as the curtain rose on the first performance 11th December it was a plucky Miranda Bell, as Dandini, who sang her heart out in the village square, devoid of villagers and completely on her own: She "defied any tear to appear in her eye."

But it was John Curry who needed the most pluck. He had agreed to appear as Buttons in the show, probably for the experience and he was brilliant in the choreographed routines. He handled the dialogue remarkably well, and was a good, all round company member. In fact, he was a really sweet guy.

Unfortunately, as it turned out, he was allergic to children. It's not a great advantage when you need them on your side, in a show aimed primarily at... children. Of course, he could expect no mercy from a Liverpool crowd. "Gerroff, yer poofter!" was sometimes heard from the raucous little darlings.

By the time he reached the song sheet, and came face to face with half a dozen or so of these audience members on stage, his exquisite performance techniques eluded him. He was reduced to spouting a bundle of nervous gibberish.

He and I had a quiet word.

The Brokers' Men stepped in and took over from a very relieved John Curry for that particular spot, and all was well.

It was a good show, with Tamara Steele, as an intriguing Cinderella; Richard Walker and Edward Arthur as a couple of Merseyside Ugly Sisters, Euthanasia and Asphyxia; and Annette 'Netty' Lynton, as Prince Charming.

New Year's Eve, 1986. People made their way to Theatre House where many of the company were billeted. One of the Brokers' Men clawed his way out of the embrace of an ageing scouser prostitute, as he ran the gauntlet of her patch outside. We were gathering for a New Year party. Nick Mason flew up in his private plane. Netty could drive back to London in her sports car, at breakneck speed, in almost the same amount of time.

Of course, we're only party animals now and again, contrary to popular belief. It was a while before I started going to Pink Floyd parties, and they were very different affairs. The first one followed a sell out concert at Wembley Stadium. I'm not a great fan of the music, but couldn't resist the temptation. Our VIP tickets took us to the Special Enclosure, and to walk into that space and join 90,000 others was a thrilling experience.

Those productions are strangely old fashioned, though with their flying pigs and big bangs, their theatricality works, and the crowd creates its own mesmerising sound track. Something in me would have to have been missing for me not to respond.

We made a quick getaway, just before the end. To get caught up in that mass exodus was not an appealing prospect. Police and security guards were everywhere, and there was bound to be a crush. And besides, we had invites to the after show party, at Chelsea Harbour. That turned out to be an altogether different gathering.

And different again was our reunion in Liverpool. I felt that everyone at the party deserved to get a little drunk, to let their hair down, to dance some un-choreographed steps, to kiss and hug at midnight, and to make merry into the early hours. The New Year seemed bright.

But John Curry did not appear. He kept his rather private and shy self away, and I understand he spent the time alone in his hotel room. It was a pity.

After I'd left Liverpool, I had a sweet letter from him expressing the wish that we might work together again. But John always suspected that the AIDS virus would catch up with him. It had ravaged many of his friends in New York, and it had played around with John so often that it was inevitably going to saunter across the Atlantic and stalk him.

They found each other in the end and, seven years after we rehearsed *Cinderella* together, John Curry died tragically aged just 44.

The winter closed in, at the start of 1987, and I was making slow progress through the snow and ice to rehearsals in London. I was lucky. I was heading back to the warmer climes of Dubai and Abu Dhabi this time, with Richard Harris's play, *Outside Edge*. Peter Bridge may have fallen asleep watching the first performance, back in 1979, but I remembered it well.

My cast was led by Peter Byrne and Ian Lavender, and Hilary Crane finally got to play the part that her husband had written for her.

Ian Lavender is the most delightful person, and a clever actor, but he was not right for the leading part in *Outside Edge*, Roger. Set around an afternoon's cricket match, Roger captains the team and oversees it

Geoffrey Davies, Hilary Crane and Ian Lavender, relaxing in Dubai

all with a pompous and humourless rigour. He's a tin pot dictator and a little Hitler. You should want to smack him.

Yet Ian still retains a kind of lovable innocence on stage, displaying many of the qualities that made him so endearing in *Dad's Army*. He's too soft to contain the steely, petty obsessions that the audience can laugh at in Harris's play, and I don't think he was totally successful in the Middle East production.

But it was a wonderful company to be with, and everyone displayed enormous fortitude at a lunch we were invited to on some Arab Sheik's yacht.

Our host kept this vessel permanently moored, because he was afraid of the water and inclined to sea sickness. He was an overfed and over watered bully, to be exact, and drank his way through a vast quantity of alcohol through this lunch.

Whilst the rest of us tried to retain a certain English sang-froid, the Sheik triggered a huge row with his wife who was on board, by ordering her to make way, that night, for his mistress. The wife was resolute in refusal, and her husband stoked the fire with more alcohol. The mistress was nowhere to be seen.

Suddenly, without warning and to our total surprise and horror, we were bundled onto a motor launch. Some of us had been trying out the jet skis and had barely time to make the transition, before we were out on the open seas travelling at full speed.

The maniac at the wheel seemed unconcerned that various pieces of furniture were being torn from the deck and decanted into the water. Whilst the wife shrieked her demands for him to stop, the rest of us clung to each other and prayed that we wouldn't follow the chairs overboard. Soaked to the skin by the spray, and fearing for our lives, we waited for sense to prevail and order to be restored.

Somehow, it all was, and we returned to our lunch and our cocktails, before thanking our hosts effusively for their kind hospitality, and making a quick getaway.

This was the last production that I did for Derek Nimmo. He did ask me to direct a new play by Bernard Slade, who wrote *Same Time, Next Year*, and I was very excited at the prospect. We got as far as the design stage, but Derek suffered a fall at his home, from which he never recovered. I do miss him, and will always be grateful to him for the fascinating introductions he gave me to the places and people on those tours.

As it happened, I had to wait another 5 years before I could submit once more to the lure of the East.

I remained friends with Richard Harris (I went on to direct his play, *The Maintenance Man*, at the Queen's Theatre, in Hornchurch), and with his wife, Hilary Crane, and with Helen Cotterill, who played Mim... and many others, too. The address book sometimes starts to groan under the weight.

And that can be a blessing. Because, through Richard Harris and Hilary Crane and Julia Mackenzie, I was put in touch with a very special person.

*   *   *   *   *

Once in a while comes a phone call that alters the whole tone and complexion of one's existence, and Life is never quite the same again. Such was the call that put me in touch with Irene Handl, a genuine "national treasure". But, oh, how cruel were the Fates for their procrastination, for there was not much time left.

There are some spirits whose orbit we pass through too fleetingly - those whom we wish we could have encountered much earlier. To this day, I consider it my very bad fortune that I wasn't led to Irene Handl's door until just a few months before she died.

Born in London, in 1902, of an Austrian father and a French mother, Irene didn't go onto the stage until she was in her late 30s, but she was an instant hit. When we met, she was already in her mid 80s, and still in sparkling form. Every day spent with her was a revelation but, in the short span that remained for her, not enough of them in which to discover the full depth and talents of that extraordinary lady.

I knew of her as a performer, naturally. As a film and television actress, too often type cast, but I was amazed to be introduced to her two books *The Sioux*, and *The Gold Tip Pfitzer*.

I was totally oblivious like so many to this phenomenal gift that Irene possessed as a writer. To this day, I have come across very few people who have read either of those two towering novels. Maybe to try to rectify that situation, she was adapting them for the 1987 Edinburgh Festival and having been asked to work with her on them, and subsequently having read them, I was only too eager to be involved.

And so it was that we met at Irene's home, near Notting Hill. I sensed an immediate rapport and we were soon at work editing the books, ready for Edinburgh. This was to be a kind of one woman show, but I know that Irene herself thought they would work well on film or adapted for television, and she encouraged me to pursue the idea. I did, in fact, later get the rights from her publishers, but was never able to move things forward.

From the start, she was full of mystery and fun. She had a wicked sense of humour, and used it to blistering effect on people she didn't like. "She's like an ancient Briton! A dehydrated prune!" was her description of one such well known colleague.

These working sessions were characterised by a good deal of laughter and I was delighted that, included in the inscription that Irene wrote for me in one of those editions, was a word of "thanks for all the fun". I think we enjoyed each other's humour, and I certainly looked forward enormously to each visit.

And, even once I'd left her, she would always call to make sure I'd got home safely. I moved house in London that year, and Irene never failed to ask, "And how's your new home, dear?" Even when she wasn't well, she showed much more interest in other people's welfare than her own. And not just towards her colleagues. She adored animals, and flowers and plants and was capable of what I would call miraculous attention.

I once arrived with a large bunch of flowers, which she immediately put in water. Generally rather than delay the start of our working session she would leave them until later to arrange but, on this occasion, one of the stems had got broken. Almost severed, the flower head hung dying.

Others might have taken that one out and thrown it in the bin, but not Irene. Upset at such a loss, she determined to nurse it back to health. Lifting the head gently by its broken neck, and talking to it soothingly, she first called the other flowers to support it. When I returned the next day, the bloom was well on the way to supporting itself and did, ultimately, make a full recovery.

A shrewd judge of people, Irene had an uncanny ability to relate to them. We discussed Prince Charles and Diana once, Irene had met them both, and she suddenly exclaimed what beautiful eyes Charles had but, "Oh, Diana! Such stormy eyes. I fear for her. I really do."

When we stopped work, there was always a good deal of chat. One name that was never far from her lips, of course, was Peter Sellers. Irene never denied that they'd been lovers. She certainly adored him. And they had written a pile of comedy scripts together, mostly just for the two of them to perform, in private. But Irene was anxious to show them. She did play Sellers's wife once, in a film - a role that she admitted came to her very naturally.

For some reason, I have always been convinced that there was an element of the supernatural to Irene Handl. Her insight to so many things was uncanny. As if to prove her powers, there was a moment after leaving her, one day, when I was standing on the platform at Notting Hill tube station.

Suddenly, the violent draught from an approaching train produced a maelstrom of dust and paper and plastic bags that tore past me down the tracks. A single page of a newspaper, however, landed at my feet and refused to advance any further. It wrapped itself around my leg and waited. I opened my eyes and looked down.

The headline stared up at me: Emlyn Williams Dies.

As someone that we both knew, Irene and I had discussed him only an hour before. Weird.

Not long after, she herself became ill, suddenly very vulnerable. I began to visit her more often, and in the evenings. Always a haven of tranquillity. On the 27th November, 1987, I saw her for the last time. She was confined to her bed, and was desperately weak but, even then, she managed a few chuckles.

Before I left, she told me she had something for me. There was an envelope on the table. Would I look after it for her? Inside, to my astonishment, was one of those scripts that she and Peter Sellers had written together, but which they had never performed in public. I was deeply touched and have kept it safe ever since as promised.

Two days later, as I walked along the canal in North London - ironically, on my way to the flower market - I learned that Irene had died. The months of our knowing each other seemed very short, yet I felt a genuine grief, as one does at the passing of a close friend.

Characteristically, there was one more revelation to come. The funeral took place on the 8th December, and I made quite sure I was there. After all, Irene had planned the event herself. As I recall now, it comprised mostly a series of music tracks played over a loud speaker and all by Elvis Presley. Only then did I discover that Irene Handl had been the Honorary President of the Elvis Presley Fan Club (UK).

The event brought a series of smiles to our faces, as we remembered the woman we had all grown to love. Smiles turned to laughter, and then suddenly to heart wrenching tears, as the coffin moved away, and the music changed to *Je ne regrette rien*, sung by Edith Piaf. It was a coup de theâtre, for sure and, as we left, imprinted on every face was a pride at having known a very special person.

For that was the most important of Irene's talents, a talent to make so many people fall in love with her.

✻   ✻   ✻   ✻   ✻

Which one is the reality? Well, right you are, Mr. Luigi Pirandello if you think so.

As I approached my 40th birthday, I didn't dare to predict the way ahead. After all, Irene Handl didn't predict the demise of Emlyn Williams before that headline swept through the tunnel below the streets of London. Maybe it was possible to predict that Margaret Thatcher would be swept to yet another election victory that year, but did anyone foresee that it would be her last? And Michael Fish is forever linked to his blunder in not predicting the Great Storm or hurricane that swept through the UK on the night of October 15th. No, 1987 was definitely not a year to put faith in predictions.

Expectation is invariably flanked by surprise or disappointment or both. Flashes of premonition come unimpaired, forcing reality to become blurred.

At the start of a quick break in Lanzarote, I was looking for the fork in the road. It was dark, we were lost, and the hire car was not responding. Traffic came towards me, as I tried to turn. The car inched towards the edge. We were on the precipice of a cliff, with the bay beneath us. This was reality, alright, and I only just managed to avert disaster.

Less than a week later, I dreamed of the house we'd left behind in London. A stranger peered out through my kitchen window. He had a sinister look on his face, but I was trapped in a dark lane at the back, helpless - incapable of doing anything. This was a reality only in my sleep, of course. Until we stepped out of the taxi in Chiswick.

I have no firsthand experience of rape. But I learned about violation, that night. The light was on, and the front door was open. Every inch of every room had been ransacked. Every mattress had been turned, and every drawer turned out. Correspondence was taken from envelopes, and books were left open and torn on the floor. Only the dreaded defecation was missing.

It turned out that if I had been, in reality, standing in the lane two nights before, then the man whose face stared at me through the window in my dream would have passed me. For it was down the lane that the intruder(s) came, before making an entrance through the back door into the kitchen. The neighbours alerted the police.

The police secured the back door, and turned a light on. They wrote a note for us to make contact when we got back. And then they departed through the front door. And left it open. Who could have predicted that?

What I didn't even guess at or recognise at the time was that my career had already entered a transitional phase. I was already at a fork in the road, though hopefully not perched on a precipice.

I met with a man called Fredie Pederson, at the Regent Palace Hotel, who invited me to work in Sweden for 6 months; and I was asked to go to Belfast to direct a play there. But I refused both offers, because I was now getting more directly involved with writers, and their writing, and I needed to stick around.

I worked with Len Richmond, on his play *Risky Kisses*, which I directed with Prunella Gee and Jeremy Gittins; with Richard Harris, of course, *The Maintenance Man*; with Greg Day, on further rewrites for *Bust*; I directed a play by David Henry Hwang, *Broken Promises* at the Soho Poly; I was approached by the *Upstairs, Downstairs* scriptwriter,

Alfred Shaugnessy, to direct a new play of his; I was working at long distance with Jeffrey Beatty, in Boston, on drafts of his latest masterpiece; and I was asked by the Guildford School of Acting if I would write an adaptation for them of Henry Fielding's novel, *Joseph Andrews*.

And then there was Leslie Frewin.

Alongside all the other books with personal inscriptions that sit on my shelves, some of which I have already mentioned, are a couple of books by Leslie. One is called, *The Importance of Being Oscar,* and is inscribed: *For Tony, with something akin to Love.* The other is *The Late Dorothy Parker*, and bears the message: *For Tony – with Luv.*

What happened in between? We got to know each other. Leslie often travelled up from his home in Devon sometimes with his wife, and sometimes not. He wrote at least one book about the Café Royal, in London, and that was where he liked to meet. I had a very exciting time, working with him on a play called *Dottie*, which was adapted from his own fascinating and absorbing biography of Dorothy Parker.

Leslie was anxious to get this play staged, and tenacious in his efforts to do so. The most likely venue for a try out production turned out to be the theatre at Bromley, and we set about attempting to cast this iconic figure of the American entertainment industry and to put her on stage.

Finally, we were led to Ali McGraw of *Love Story* fame. The introduction came from the hugely talented and experienced film costume designer, Anthony Mendleson. Anthony had a couple of Oscar Nominations and several BAFTA Awards to his credit, and I was flattered that he was such a fan of mine. Of course, he knew everyone and introduced us to Ali. Dorothy Parker would have been a perfect role for her and a huge boost for the play.

To and fro went the correspondence, and I got the impression that all was going well. Ali McGraw was interested definitely and had some shrewd comments to make. Ultimately, though, as so often happens, we couldn't quite clinch the deal. I don't know whether Leslie ever got the show on, but it certainly deserved to be seen.

As a contrast to our lunches and cocktails at the Café Royal with Leslie Frewin, I was suddenly summoned to the Britannia Hotel, to meet two Dutchmen - Joop Doderer and Guus van der Made.

These two were in London to find a British director to travel to

Holland to direct a new stage play with Dutch actors, in Dutch. It seemed a bizarre quest, but I was intrigued.

Joop (pronounced Yope) was a big name in the Netherlands, a comedy actor, who could also turn his hand to Shakespeare and the classics, but who was also something of an anarchic performer. Guus was an actor, with aspirations to becoming a writer. His father, Saco van der Made was, in turn, a well established and well known actor in his home country. You now know more than I did when I first met them.

They were charming and courteous and appeared to hold me in some respect. I eventually asked them the question that in my mind was the most pressing.

"Why a British director? I don't speak any Dutch. In fact, I've only ever been to Holland twice, once for a long weekend in Amsterdam, the details of which remain lost in a fog of debauched and hung over memory; and, secondly, for a Chinese meal in Vlissingen."

"Discipline," came the answer, "Only British directors can bring discipline to the production."

Suddenly I felt like a supply teacher who might be sent off to teach in an inner city blackboard jungle. Were the actors in Holland always stoned, or rebellious, or lazy, or drunk? Or even worse? I was about to find out.

My agent negotiated a fat fee, with expenses, and a lengthy rehearsal period. The play was called *Een Fijn Span* and was a mess.

I flew to Amsterdam for discussions. A mere 220 miles. A hop, skip and a jump. Closer than Pitlochry. And a great deal more fun.

My next introduction was to a lady called Debbie Zomerschoe, who spoke Dutch and English, both with a broad Lancashire accent on account of her mother being from Lancashire. The name was unpron-ounceable to me and I called her Gumshoe. It was easier.

Debbie was to be the production organiser for *Fijn Span* and re-presented the producers van Liempt and Jacques Senf. The latter was an overweight and camp individual, but reputedly a brilliant booker on the tangled maze that is the Dutch theatre touring circuit. He had once been kidnapped, tortured and thrown - bound and gagged - into a canal for reasons that were never made clear to me. Possibly as a result of such treatment, he had become diabetic and was arguably the most tight fisted producer in the business.

But all was calm in Amsterdam on my arrival at Schipol Airport, on June 20th, 1988 for discussions with those involved. I stayed the night, dined with Guus and Gumshoe, at a very fine Indonesian restaurant and, the next day, on the terrace at the famous American Hotel, met my designer.

I knew as he walked towards me that he was very ill. He carried with him the emaciated body of someone who is fighting disease, but whose immune system is already drained of the wherewithal to win the battle. Yet Hans was welcoming and positive and seemed to relish the idea of us working together. He had spent some time as a resident designer in the UK, and we fell into an easy relationship.

A script was sent - on one side, the Dutch, with an English translation facing it. I treated it like a piano score and learned the notes, so that the text was in my head by the time I was due to start rehearsals in late August.

Unfortunately, I'd learned the wrong notes. On the first day, as I listened to the actors' reading, I realised that the score in my head was a German one and the melody I heard was Dutch. I would have to learn the language. And the company would have to learn some discipline.

If I was at all sceptical about that side of things, it didn't take long to put me right.

During World War II, apparently, a key word that the Dutch used as a shibboleth to detect German spies was the name of the place where I was due to stay, Scheveningen. It's a seaside resort on the outskirts of The Hague, and I had a self-contained apartment in the house of a family there. Supposedly, this made my lodgings handy for rehearsals. But it caused problems, and resulted in my driving a post office van for a couple of days. But first, come with me to the blackboard jungle.

On the first morning of rehearsal, my producer was late. When he did arrive, there were speeches, I was welcomed, the company was toasted and an enormous plate of cream cakes was delivered to the table, along with bottles of champagne. The jollity and joie de vivre might well have continued seamlessly into the lunch break, if I hadn't brought proceedings to a halt. Well, they wanted discipline.

I don't believe that I am a very difficult director to work with for either producers or actors, but there are times when I have had to make demands. There was soon to be one such occasion. I was expected to rely for my commute to rehearsals on the services of one cast member, Maya Bouma, and her little car.

Maya, though a middle-aged actress with a character face, had a penchant for young lads, and became quite excitable around them. There

was a moment in the play when she had to open a door and scream for her husband offstage. Some of the younger actors and technical crew decided, at one performance, to line up in the wings and collectively moon at Maya when she opened the door.

I raced round to the auditorium to

With Maya Bouma

watch her reaction, and was disappointed to see nothing more than the usual sequence, and no noticeable effect on Maya. Admiring her stage resilience or, more likely, assuming that the guys had chickened out I went to the dressing room, in the interval.

When I asked what she had thought of all those young bums presented to her in the wings, Maya was flabbergasted. "I can't scream without closing my eyes!" she admitted. "I didn't see ANYTHING!" Her sense of being cheated was palpable. "Can they do it again?" she begged.

It was kind of her to collect me each morning, and then to wait for me at the end of each rehearsal, so that she could take me back to Scheveningen. It didn't seem right to me, however, and turned out to be far too restricting, for both of us. I told the management that I needed my own transport.

Meantime, Guus van der Made who was also an actor in the show was enlisted to work on rewrites. We spent many evenings together, trying to get the play into decent shape. I was also worrying about Barbara, an actress who was just not capable of playing the part. In fact, I was surprised that she went as a professional actress, in the first place.

I was taken, by Guus, to collect my hire car. PTT represents the Dutch postal and telecom service, and their vans are painted bright green with a corrugated roof. A retired one of these was what I was now expected to drive. Not only was it demeaning to drive a post office delivery van to work, I also got a headache from the noise on the roof, every time it rained.

I threw a temperamental tantrum, and exchanged the van for a car.

I also needed to exchange Barbara for a qualified actress, before we got much further into production. I knew that she had tickets booked for her husband and extended family for the première, and I needed to move quickly. I met with a casting director and, the following day, two potential replacements came to audition.

Mimi Kok was the first. She was so sensitive to her name being announced to an English director, that she asked Guus to introduce her as Mimi Cook. It made no difference. Every time she spoke, she was convulsed with a gin and tobacco soaked cough that sprayed her words in every direction. Each time, I looked away and then tried to return with a smile.

When it came to her reading, the problem seemed to get worse. Strangulated Dutch barked out in dry, raucous coughing was difficult for me to listen to, and I confess that my face was not held as straight as it should have been. I was soon ready to see my second auditionee.

This was Pamela Teves, who looked as though she should be wearing a nosebag and riding in the Grand National. Looks were not so important for this role, however, and at least Pamela didn't cough. She got the job.

I broke the news as gently as I knew how to Barbara. She was devastated, of course, and the tears flowed. The day before, she had invited me to dinner. I suggested we postpone it.

The next morning, Pamela arrived for work. Joop was quick with his reaction. "Look what just cantered in," he muttered. Pamela Teves, however, had set her sights on conquest and, within a few days, she had him wrapped around her hoof.

I enjoyed rehearsals and my time at Scheveningen. Walks along the promenade, and the smell of the sea; an introduction to bittenballen and poffertjes and stroopwafels; and warm hospitality from everyone around turned out to be just some of the delights.

Mr. Senf, meanwhile, was on his way toward witnessing another tantrum from me. I am told that there are very few Dutch words that begin with the letter 'C', and so when my producer saw the name 'Craven', he thought he saw 'Graven'. Posters for the play flooded towns and villages all over Holland, proclaiming the director as a graveyard, or some such. "Graven". Why should my name, so straightforward, cause problems yet again? My agent confronted Mr. Senf (now there's a name!).

A capital 'C' in the correct colour was printed out in thousands and distributed in earnest around the country for some poor minions to stick over the offending 'G'.

We had our first previews at the end of September, and I dashed back to London to hold auditions for *Risky Kisses*.

Len Richmond's play with its Ginger Rogers/Fred Astaire sequences was becoming a complex production, and the producers who brought it to The Tabard were becoming extravagant in their ambitions, and penny pinching in their financing of it. How common is that?

I got them a good cast, nevertheless. Alan Hunter joined a glamorous Jeremy Gittins, the long-suffering Vicar, in *Keeping Up Appearances* and Prunella Gee, who brought Ken Campbell and Sylvester McCoy into my social circle.

We opened towards the end of the year. It was wonderful to direct, and a great success - sadly killed, at the end of its initial run, by the politicking and manoeuvring of its author and naïve producers.

In between, in mid October, I was back in Holland at Hoorn for the première of *Een Fijn Span*. I watched the sunset over the Ijselmeer and had dinner at Joop Doderer's hotel before the show. It went well and, through a standing ovation at the end, I was called onto the stage to receive the applause of an ecstatic audience. There were flowers everywhere, it seemed, thrown from the auditorium and from the wings.

Cameras flashed and a string orchestra played, as Jacques Senf led myself and the whole company into the bar for more applause, champagne and more gifts than I was able to take to the plane the next day.

Onstage with Joop Doderer, First Night, Een Fijn Span

I now seemed to be inextricably linked to the Theater Plezier Company, and was invited back for the next production. And what of the discipline?

Things did change with my arrival, and the company did respond to this new regime that I brought to them, but there was one tradition that remained and which I never truly could get used to.

So, let me introduce you to a man called Hans Boskamp. Hans was an ex-professional footballer, who played for his country and who was therefore held in some reverential regard. He was a big man, and his wife also held a couple of splendid assets, carried before her with pride, so that she always tended naturally towards her husband.

Hans had been one of the organisers of the PR stunt that saw John Lennon and Yoko Ono in a mammoth lie abed in an Amsterdam hotel. He also was one of the team that mounted the première of the musical *Hair*, in Amsterdam. It was held in a giant marquee, just outside the city, and on the opening night it seemed that everyone was so stoned that the performance was 90 minutes late in starting. I should know - I was there.

When he retired full time from football, Hans became an entertainer, a cabaret and recording artiste. He could give a rendition of *My Yiddisher Momma* like nobody else, and I still have in my possession a signed CD that he gave me. He tried his hand at acting for a while and as a friend of Joop Doderer's (Hans was reputed to have saved Joop's life, following a heart attack), he was introduced into my company for *Een Fijn Span.*

But Hans was also a bon viveur and whatever town or city he landed in, he always knew where to find the finest restaurant and the best stocked bar. This mattered hugely to the acting company that travelled with him.

A stage actor's life in the Netherlands usually requires stamina. Every performance takes place in a different location, and so much of the daylight hours are spent travelling, and the return journey can take until well after midnight. For some reason, the itinerary can take in Maastricht to the south on one night, and then Dokkum in the far north the next.

Some actors, of course, also have to do the driving. Holland is one of the most overcrowded countries in Europe and, even at 2.00am, when road works are carried out, a traffic jam or 'fila', can take a long time to disperse. The question naturally arose: When does an actor get to eat?

With Hans Boskamp in the company, there was only one answer. Once the company had familiarised themselves with the stage and the dressing rooms, Hans would lead everyone to the best restaurant in town. Once they were all ensconced, I was astonished to witness a full 3 course meal devoured, complete with bottles of wine, and coffees and brandies to finish.

Such indulgence would never be allowed in the UK, for obvious reasons. Strangely enough, however, the evening performance was rarely affected and the drive home was usually safe. On one occasion, I was in the car with Hans, his wife Tineke and Maya Bouma. Hans was in ebullient mood and insisted that, once we arrived at his apartment in Amsterdam, we would all drink champagne before going our separate ways home.

Tineke was the first upstairs, and as the rest of us disembarked and followed her, we heard a scream. It turned out that the place had been burgled. A lot of jewellery and cash had gone, and it was a scream of horror that had come from Tineke when she discovered what had happened.

Of course, the police were called but Hans insisted, in the meantime, on going ahead with his plan to open some of his best champagne. Maya was shaking with fear (of what, nobody knew), but naturally everyone was a little disturbed by events. It certainly brought a chill to me, as I recalled our own, recent robbery.

Nevertheless, it was a surreal scene for the two policemen who arrived to find - instead of a distraught and weeping huddle of people - something akin to a party in progress, and Hans calling, "Champagne?" to them, as they reached the top of the stairs.

*   *   *   *   *   ⸰

During the first part of 1989, I was regularly on a plane backwards and forwards to Amsterdam and Rotterdam checking on the show and giving any necessary notes. Theater Plezier had decided, in their shrewd wisdom, that I was the director for them. I was invited to do their second show, *Laat Je Niet Kisten*. I agreed.

At the same time, I was working with the students at the Guildford School of Acting on my adaptation of *Joseph Andrews*, which would be premièred in Guildford before moving to the Young Vic, in London.

I had friends with money invested in a great new musical show, called *Three Guys Naked*, which had its first performance at the Donmar Warehouse on January 13th. As racy as the title might sound, it was purely a high class musical revue, and I can't understand why it didn't make it. Nevertheless, it was a good evening, and we all decamped below stairs at the Theatre Museum for the after show party.

Soon, I was at Heathrow Airport again, but this time to meet Hans Boskamp, who was on a flying visit to persuade the agent of a piece called *Rescuers Speaking* that he should be the one to produce it in The Netherlands, with me as director. He flew back to Rotterdam the same day, and the production looked assured.

In April, I was yet again in Holland - this time, for the final per-formance of *Een Fijn Span* in Groningen, where the choice of restaurant even for Hans was appropriate for our celebration of a successful show.

Time for a holiday in Crete, once more, but I was soon back and into rehearsals for *Joseph Andrews*. It was exciting to do that show, to take the novel and adapt it, and then to direct the first production. The cast were amazing, the reviews were glowing, and the box office bounded with activity at both Guildford and at the Young Vic.

But, amongst it all, I was doing something quite different.

Rumour has it that Stephen Sondheim's agent had to send legal representatives to the Shaftesbury Theatre, in London, during the run of his musical, *Follies*. Even though the British production was dull, Sondheim's interest was not caused by any lack of standard in that area. It was to do with the performance for a short while of one of its stars.

Eartha Kitt took over one of the roles - probably for the chance to perform one of the show's classic numbers, *I'm Still Here*. Unfortunately, so the story goes, the lady played a little too fast and loose with the lyrics and had to be brought to heel.

Ironically, Ms Kitt subsequently used the song's title for her own autobiography. It's a meaty and fascinating tale, of course, and out of the blue I got a call from her literary agent.

It was suggested that I could adapt the book for the stage, and thus provide a vehicle for an Eartha Kitt one woman show. My immediate reaction was: "We need to meet. I'm a huge fan, and would love to do it, but I suspect that she's something of a diva. I want to be sure that we can work together."

As it happened, this massive legend of the entertainment business was due to perform in cabaret upstairs at Groucho's. You may have gathered already that this was not my kind of club, but who could resist such an opportunity? After all, this was the person whom Orson Welles described as, "The most exciting woman in the world." It was agreed that I would see the show, and meet the star afterwards.

Thus at 9.15pm, on June 20th 1989, and halfway through the rehearsal period for *Joseph Andrews*, I crept in, at the back of Groucho's Cabaret Room, to watch Eartha Kitt in performance.

Love her or hate her, fascinated or repulsed, like Marmite, Eartha Kitt never fails to get a reaction. She was into her 60s by now, but she was still fully in command of her voice, of her material, and her audience. It was a mesmerising hour in that room, with one of the world's greats. I couldn't wait to meet her.

I was joined by Robert her literary agent towards the end of the show, and he suggested that we all gather in an anteroom, off to one side, once Eartha had had time to change.

I stood around chatting to various people, and then noticed that Robert had disappeared. It was time to head for the anteroom.

The next 10 minutes will remain in my memory for a long, long time.

As I walked through the door, and closed it behind me, a door directly opposite opened, and I came face to face with Eartha Kitt, for the first time. Robert was nowhere to be seen.

There was a feline purr, as she looked me up and down. I don't believe that her back actually arched, but I half expected it to, and I could most definitely understand how she had made such a success of Cat Woman. Her eyes narrowed, as they finally came to rest and she looked me straight in the face.

"So…" she growled. There was a pause. "Might it be that you are Mr. Tony Craven?"

I nodded, but could hardly believe my reply.

"I might very well be, but… "I paused, in similar fashion. "Who shall I say is asking?"

This was a gamble on my part, gambling on a sense of humour. Her performing talents were not in any doubt.

The mouth split wide open, and a deep throated laugh came out. As she held out her hand, the eyes twinkled, and her laugh modified to a chuckle. "I'm Miss Eartha Kitt."

Deal done. We were almost instantly joined by Robert, and got into a general discussion about Eartha's thoughts, her ideas for the show, etc… By now, it was late and we agreed to meet for a proper get together, a week later.

"Ladies and Gentlemen. This is your Captain speaking. I have both good news and bad news for you this morning. Let me start with the bad news. There is a string of thunder storms stretching right the way across the North Sea. We can't avoid them, we have to go through them. The good news is that this should only take about 10-15 minutes. Thank you for your attention."

When the pilot talks about 10-15 minutes, you have to be sure that he means longer. I was on yet another flight to Amsterdam, and it seemed like there was a good 20 minutes of severe turbulence. I spotted a number of coffees and drinks hurled involuntarily into the air.

I was in demand now in Holland. About to direct another new play for Theater Plezier, my agent was still negotiating for Wilfred Harrison's play, *Rescuers Speaking* to be mounted under Hans Boskamp's aegis. I had met with Jeffrey Beatty in London, he was specifically over to discuss the draft of a new play that he was writing.

In the meantime, I was full of the success of my own adaptation of *Joseph Andrews* and my thoughts were regularly being invaded by ideas for this show for Eartha Kitt.

As we emerged from the turbulence, I looked at my passport and smiled. "I have no idea how old I am. Believe it or not, I have no paper that says I was ever born. Maybe that's why they call me a legend, because I don't really exist."

Those are the words of Eartha Kitt, and she was still refusing to admit to her age. I have never been quite sure how she ever obtained a passport, if she had no birth certificate or document to verify her existence. But it would have been ungentlemanly to have pushed the lady too far. Especially at our second meeting.

Eartha (I never got used to calling her 'Eartha') was staying at the Mayfair Hotel as she usually did, when in London. We decamped to the bar for a further get to know you session, and ordered some water and lemonade.

"And half a lemon." The barman turned. Eartha smiled. "And I mean half a lemon." He nodded and left, and we settled down for our discussions about the show.

A little while later, the barman returned with our orders, some ice… and half a lemon.

To my astonishment, Eartha reached for the citrus and squeezed it over her face, rubbing it in with the softened peel. It might have explained her magnificent complexion? But, according to this extraordinary and truly legendary lady, the finest celebration could take place only with "a bottle of Dom Perignon champagne and a good helping of Beluga Caviar".

In Holland, and no longer in Scheveningen, I was installed in a small bedsit flat, overlooking the Vondelpark in Amsterdam. It was a glorious location, and I could often sit at the desk in the evening working on

I'm Still Here and listen to the live jazz that floated up from various groups in the park.

My floor was reached by means of a narrow, almost vertical staircase. A long rope attached to the front door was threaded along the railings by the wall, and extended to the top of the house. Visitors were given access by a hearty pull on the rope, which then cunningly released the latch on the street door. Sophisticated entry phones, with CCTV and intercom, were thereby rendered unnecessary.

My landlord occupied some hidden area close by to my own quarters and, when I caught sight of him at whatever time of morning, noon or night he was always dressed in pajamas and slippers, and shuffled hither and thither, with an air of Wee Willie Winkie minus his candle.

Joop Doderer and Pamela Teves

Once more, Guus and I worked on the script, but in other respects the atmosphere had changed. The woman who had cantered in the year before, Pamela Teves, had now completed a full dressage sequence. Joop had joined her in the saddle and seemed to idolise her.

Through this woman's influence, Joop had become estranged from his close friend Hans (who had saved his life, if you remember); had alienated much of the rest of the cast; and the dear Maya, who screamed with her eyes closed and had been my unpaid driver for a short while, was now rendered a mute and unhappy player in the company.

There were some fine actors in that show, as well, and the final product was every bit as successful as *Een Fijn Span*, but I didn't enjoy the experience as much. Mostly, this was due to the overbearing ambitions of Miss Teves. I was witnessing the first lumbering steps up the ladder to stardom, ruthless, calculating and well out of proportion to the talent that she carried with her.

Nevertheless to her credit, and having almost destroyed Joop's marriage, until he saw the light, she managed to scale enough backs to reach a certain level, and now is a regular soap opera star on Dutch television. I hope, for her sake, that it was all worth it.

The show previewed in Vlaardingen, in September, and premièred in Leiden on October 11th. I rushed back to London.

My brilliant designer - the one that I had first seen making graceful, if sickly, progress towards me at the American Hotel - had succumbed, finally, to his illness. His partner, a clever performer and writer, held out for another two years before following his lover along the same sad and painful route.

And now Mary Martlew was dead. The lady who had entertained me so courageously the evening before her exploratory operation in Vienna; the handsome and elegant doyenne of the social scene; the fun loving actress with a searing talent for the stage; the smiling, seductive and statuesque figure who in her last months had shrunk so pitifully but whose personality could, and did NOT, ever diminish; the lady had lost her battle with cancer.

Not for the first time (and most certainly not for the last), I went on the 28th November 1989, to the Actors' Church, St. Paul's in Covent Garden, for Mary's memorial service. A light had gone out, but the reflection of her presence still shimmers to this day.

*　　　　　*　　　　　*　　　　　*　　　　　*

Scripts were scattered all around, and I was torn in different directions. Greg Day had taken rewrites on *Bust* to a stage that required the play to have another tryout. I arranged for it to be a project for students at the Birmingham Drama School. The incomparable Jeffrey Beatty was concluding another play of his with strong potential, called *Convictions,* which we took to the Warehouse Theatre in Croydon.

Eartha Kitt's agent was knocking on my door for progress on *I'm Still Here*, and Wilfred Harrison was pressing for a production of *Rescuers*

Speaking in the Netherlands. It was time to learn Dutch.

I was back on the British Airways shuttle to Amsterdam, regularly keeping in touch with *Laat Je Niet Kisten*, and I was enrolled to the Assessment Panel for the London Studio Centre, becoming the Simon Cowell figure of that select few. My old friend Sheila O'Neil was chief assessor, and the formidable Hazel Bader Meinhof took her seat beside me.

In February, 1990, I got a call from Eartha Kitt's agent, for a meeting at her new house. It seems that the star had just completed on a London pad, and we were invited over. At 11.00pm, on a Sunday night. But, in these circumstances, who was refusing? Nocturnal meetings elsewhere were about to drive me to call for police protection. Eartha's, by contrast, was a benign get together in very informal surroundings.

She had clearly only just taken possession of the West London home. Robert and I sat on packing cases, whilst Eartha (sin citrus) perched at the top of a flight of stairs - centre stage, it seemed.

It was a jolly occasion, cocktails and laughter, but I don't recall very much in the way of achievement, or any particular reason for us being summoned at such an hour. She was very much still here, however, and the project was still very much an enthusiastic cause for her.

I was back in Amsterdam, at the end of March, and temporarily homeless. An apartment had been arranged for me, but the deposit had not been paid, and I wasn't going to get possession of the keys until it was. Late night panics, and a frantic drive across the city. If anyone ever lays claim to any idea that the Dutch are a well organised race, please take my word for it... and laugh at the very suggestion.

It was April Fool's Day when I moved in. Initially, it seemed an inauspicious date that might have an appropriate resonance.

So, come with me to Amsterdam. I am standing in the window of my new living quarters. I am a few minutes walk from Waterloo Plein and the Muzik Theater. It's a spacious apartment and, at the back, is a private terrace where I can work and drink coffee with my friends. I look over the stately Amstel River, and watch the tour boats go by.

Their guides seem to point to my building, as they swing round the bend. Cameras are lifted and people look to where I am standing, at that full length picture window. I should take a bow. Life here is very pleasant. By day. At night, it is very different.

I wasn't warned about the history of the place. I go to bed at the end of the day and, at 2.00am, the phone rings. It's by the bed so it's a bit alarming. When I answer it, there doesn't appear to be anyone there. Except the line is not dead.

The next night, it happens again. This time, there is a voice - a male voice - who asks, "Who is that?" in a menacing fashion. He doesn't wait for a reply. After a few anxious nights of this and I am hardly able to rest I pull out the phone and dump it in the kitchen. I can sleep again.

A couple of nights later in the dark early hours the doorbell rings. This really freaks me. When I get to the answer phone, there is the same voice with the same question: "Who is that?" I hang up and try to get back to sleep. But now somebody is banging on the door... and yelling.

Question: What would you do?

There are no multiple choice answers. I call the police, and ask them to investigate.

Who is responsible for putting me into this apartment, that it turns out was home to a maniac who has become obsessed by his ex-wife? He has seen another man enter his ex-wife's house... and is insanely jealous. What he doesn't know is that his ex-wife has also moved out. And rented the place to me.

It's sorted, but I am still nervous for a few nights. I seem to hear somebody breaking in from the terrace. I'm in a long forgotten Alfred Hitchcock movie.

Rescuers Speaking was a very worthy and informative piece put together from eyewitness accounts about all those people who put their own lives in jeopardy, in order to help the rescue of Jews in World War II. I had a good cast, including the plucky and good hearted Maya Bouma who seemed to need the work now. We premièred in Gorchem on May 3rd.

The following day, we were in Almere, coinciding with a national day of remembrance for the liberation of Holland, at the end of the war. There was a moving ceremony taking place in the town square, and I stood on the perimeters and watched. What surprised me were the numbers of young people who had turned out. I could understand the impact for their parents' generation, but these kids seemed without exception to be deeply involved.

I spoke to a couple of them. "This is a day when no German should cross the border into the Netherlands," said one. "They wouldn't dare," said another. This was not just football rivalry. These passions ran deeper than that and it gave our performance of *Rescuers Speaking* that night a greater significance for me.

A few years later, Maya Bouma threw herself off a balcony. Her life had become a mess. Nobody had noticed. Her screams were internal, but she kept her eyes open and kept smiling. I was angry for her.

Back in England, the hectic and eclectic sequence of work continued. I was working again with Jeffrey Beatty on his courtroom drama, *Convictions*, at the Croydon Warehouse. It was a hot September that year, and the theatre had no air-conditioning. I guess it was uncomfortable for actors and audiences alike, and the show did not do as well as it deserved to.

In the autumn of 1990, as the premiership of Margaret Thatcher was finally starting to crumble, so too was my low back. I staggered, painfully, between different commitments and, as the Prime Minister teetered and was then toppled, with a Major change at the top, I was in Birmingham where the students proved hopelessly inept at delivering *Bust* and all its rewrites; I was in Chichester, to see Mandy Patinkin in *Born Again* and a meeting to discuss directing *The Marriage of Figaro*; I was on a flying visit to Appeldoorn, in the Netherlands, to see a speciality show *Mini & Maxi*, who had an international following, but wanted me to direct them and tailor their show, to take the UK by storm; I was in London, for rehearsals; and then Cardiff and Eastbourne... phew!

E & B were my next employers. The 'E' was from the impresario Paul Elliott, and the 'B' from Peter Byrne the actor, who, along with the rest of us, was almost drowned in The Gulf by a drunken sheik, if you remember.

Peter was no longer directly involved in the company that was responsible for the hit musical *Buddy*, and Paul made a great deal of money from rolling out a menu of extravagant pantomimes across the country each year. He booked me for *Cinderella*, in Cardiff and *Aladdin*, in Eastbourne, and they were scheduled to open back to back.

And so it was that I travelled to the Hollington Boys' Club in London, on November 26th to start rehearsals for a truly enjoyable production of *Cinderella*. My stars were: Windsor Davies from *It Ain't Half Hot Mum*, Jonathon Morris from *Bread*, Janet Dibley who had been in the chorus of *Mr. Cinders*, and Dame Hilda Bracket without the Evadne Hinge.

We had just one week to get the show into shape, before travelling to Wales - hard work but great fun. I had never visited Cardiff before, but I thoroughly enjoyed working at the New Theatre. It's a well run place, with an attractive auditorium, a friendly stage door, and a very welcoming staff. However, I had a few problems with the city itself.

On arrival at the station, I climbed into a cab and asked for the New. "I can do that," the driver said with a grin, "but it involves a couple of illegal manoeuvres!" The traffic system must have been designed by a child.

On my first evening, I checked into my hotel, along with the lighting designer and MD. We went straight to the bar - a necessary pit stop for us all, after a hectic and tiring day in the theatre. Orders for beer posed no problem, but when I asked for a glass of red wine, the poor girl behind the bar was bemused.

"No, we don't keep any wine, sir. Can I offer you something else, perhaps?" It was a disappointment, but I was flattered on the next evening to be presented with a bottle of what I wanted, as soon as we arrived in the bar, and by the very same girl. A smile spread across my face until, that is, it became apparent that there was no corkscrew available.

Windsor Davies was cast as Baron Hard-Up in that production. Of course, he was extremely popular in Cardiff, and the audiences showed their affection every night. Having rehearsed together in London, I had already developed a soft spot for the man. Windsor always showed warmth and good humour, and he managed to be gentle and jolly at the same time. A professional to his finger tips, and ideally cast in *Cinderella,* he was one of the chief contributors to the job being such a happy one for me.

Strangely, Windsor did not make top of the bill in Cardiff. And nor did our Fairy Godmother, Dame Hilda Bracket. That place went to Jonathon Morris on £6,000 a week in 1990. He'd been almost sacked by E & B, a couple of months earlier.

Led by his agent and by his own vanity, Jonathon had refused to wear costume (he was playing Buttons) for the photo shoot, set up for publicity and poster design. He arrived off the train in a stylish and expensive suit, female agent in tow, expecting to wear it throughout the shoot. Paul Elliott, who had little respect and, I suspect, even less love for actors in general, put him on the next train back to London. It was a courageous move threatening to lose him his biggest name, but it seemed that Jonathon needed the work more. An abject apology eventually followed, and an agreement to tow the line for the rest of his contract.

Jonathon had a number of handicaps and personal problems, but his popularity with the kids - even though, unlike John Curry, he occasionally got a little too close to the ones who were invited onto the stage - appeared ultimately, to justify his salary. He did have a tendency to lose his voice very easily, which was a pity, because he was very talented. We stayed in touch for a while afterwards, and I admired his performance in a touring production of *Anything Goes*, but he subsequently disappeared from the scene and quit the profession.

And what of Dame Hilda?

In the words of the song, A house is not a home. Some people allow their persona to inhabit a number of dwellings, but are only really at home in one of them, the one where they feel genuinely comfortable. Patrick Fyffe seemed to me to be just such an individual, but most of the time he was NOT at home.

It must have been a major disappointment to all their fans when Hinge & Bracket split up and went their separate ways. Together, they had become a class act, but would they be able to pursue successful solo careers? The jury was still out on that one when I came to know Bracket. Dame Hilda, that is.

Of course, I didn't initially meet Hilda. I rehearsed with Patrick and, apart from the moments that he opened up with that extraordinary singing voice, there was nothing about him that especially set him apart from the rest of the company. In other words, he was a solid professional, who worked hard and was stimulating to be with. But in all honesty the pressure was on, and there was little time for anything but work.

As we high tailed it off to Cardiff, I was ill prepared for the surreal nature of what I was about to experience. A Press Reception had been called at lunchtime, for photographs and interviews, all the usual jamboree that goes with the publicity machine. Everyone gathered in the bar, for the regular fare that appears monotonously on these occasions, a glass of wine, a few crisps, and a curling egg sandwich.

All the leading members of the company were there, together with key production and administration personnel. I chatted with Windsor and Jonathon and others and then looked around for Patrick. Instead, I came face to face for the first time with Dame Hilda Bracket.

It was an odd sensation. Here was a totally different persona to the one I had just spent the week with. Standing in front of me - complete with wig, full makeup and a fetching little day dress - was an utterly female character, with whom everybody, including those hard-nosed Press members, was expected to communicate and interact on her level. Of course, after 5 minutes in her company it seemed the most natural thing in the world.

I was soon to discover that this dual personality was something that Patrick played to the hilt. For example, he was thrilled that he could leave the theatre at the end of each performance with such ease. The stage door was regularly besieged by fans and autograph hunters, and running the gauntlet could be quite difficult. Whereas Windsor and Janet and Jonathon were being polite, stopping to do their duty, Patrick walked past them all, in his civvies, a bloke, possibly a stagehand, and he wasn't given a second glance.

I began to think that it was there that Patrick Fyffe really felt at home. In fact, I later discovered that I was almost certainly wrong.

For now, following a hugely successful opening, I had to dash back to London and rehearsals for *Aladdin* with Rolf Harris. And, by co-incidence, Melvyn Hayes.

Melvyn had left an image of himself through *It Ain't Half Hot Mum* as an effete and camp individual, and it followed him around incessantly. In fact, the image clung ferociously. But it was so false. Because he was small and slight, and because he had cleverly created such a believable character, Melvyn seemed to have to return to it again and again. And it wasn't what he was about.

All of this led him, logically, into playing Dame in pantomime. And once more, because he threw himself into the parts with so much energy and professional talent and because the audiences so obviously adored him, Melvyn returned each year to the pantomime stage.

He's a delightful man, witty and amusing, but with an emotional depth belied by his public persona. I enjoyed the experience of working with him very much, and he responded with 120% energy and commitment. The rehearsal period with him was rewarding, but I saw at first hand the toll that this annual experience took on him.

We were due to open at the Congress Theatre in Eastbourne on December 20th (having opened *Cinderella* in Cardiff on the 8th) and on arrival, prior to the technical and dress rehearsals I naturally did a tour of the dressing rooms to see how everyone was settling in to their new environment. On entering Melvyn's room, I was shocked to find him in an overwrought and emotional state.

At first, I had to assume that he'd received some bad news, but it turned out that the problem was actually facing him in the mirror. Literally. He confided to me that every year as he returned to the wigs and the makeup and the ridiculous theatrical drag of pantomime Dame, he promised himself that he would never do it again. And yet once more he found himself surrounded by the same paraphernalia, and the same heavy makeup that now was streaked on his face with tears.

Melvyn deserved better than that. And, just occasionally, the clown's mask must slip.

Should Melvyn Hayes be part of that trove of "national treasures" that we stack up so easily and take for granted? The assumption must be that the whole country adores and treasures them. But for me and especially when, close up, the silver plating looks a bit grimy and artificial, I'm prepared to be more selective. Anyone who has followed this story closely will know that I have found some rotten apples in the box, along with some very genuine articles - but I can only report as I find.

Rolf Harris is embedded in the nation's consciousness, and appears to have enjoyed his iconic status. I worked with him twice in successive years in pantomime and he shared the bill in Eastbourne with Melvyn Hayes.

I once challenged Paul Elliott, the producer, on the subject of casting those shows. But, first, if you can bear a brief and daunting return to the miserable town of Harlow, I would like to sneak you in to the fit up and technical rehearsals of *Natural Gas,* the play that couldn't hold on to either Katy Manning nor John Junkin.

Working as a production manager at the Playhouse was a man called Brian Hewitt-Jones or, as many people knew him, Brian 'Screw-it-Up' Jones. He got under everybody's feet and seemed to contribute nothing to the proceedings except to chase his dog around the auditorium when it was running amok, as it often did. He (Brian, that is) ended up briefly in the arms of Sara Coward a.k.a. Caroline in *The Archers,* before she changed life's game plan for herself.

Brian also ended up working for Paul Elliott, and was given the job of tracking down a few names to put on the stage, some of them for the first time ever, in the deluded hope that these might excite the children who would then flock to see the pantomimes. Brian certainly dropped me in it, a couple of times. A name for him seemed to be anyone with connections, or who'd made an appearance or two on a TV talent show. Breathe a sigh of relief that we have now left Harlow – never to return!

My argument with Paul was with his casting of pantomime villains, those characters who usually take no part in the musical numbers, but need to be played by ACTORS. When we did *Aladdin,* a traditional pantomime with one of the great archetypal villains of all, Abanazar, the part was given to a mate of Rolf Harris.

According to Paul Elliott, casting such characters was difficult because "80% of actors are crap". I had to tell him that, even if his assertion were true and it's a ludicrous one, the other 20% are mostly sitting around at Christmas time waiting to be called.

We decided that Abanazar was there as genie to Rolf, an errand boy and minder. Together, they made a strangely unkempt, unwashed kind of chauvinistic pair and I know that there were one or two people around who wanted to keep a safe distance. Certainly their hands were not often in their pockets at the right moments. Especially at the bar.

Still, there is no doubt that Rolf as an entertainer, doodler and didgeridoo player consistently comes up with the professional goods. I confess that, along with many others, his performance of *Two Little*

Boys even in the rehearsal room could bring a lump to my throat.

Nevertheless, I struggled to get an acting performance from either of those two men. But then, maybe the whole point of having a "national treasure" is that the audience get exactly what they expect and hope for and nothing more.

That lesson, incidentally, was not learned by Patrick Fyffe.

During the production at Cardiff, Patrick and I became good friends and, when it was over, he kept in touch. And how! Although he was a kind and gentle man, he could nevertheless talk for HOURS on the phone, and there were occasions when I dreaded his

As seen by Rolf Harris

call, especially if it happened to come at an inconvenient moment.

Half the evening could disappear very easily and, even though Patrick was never less than fascinating in conversation with a great deal to communicate and gossip about, those calls started to wear very thin. He had some stinging words for his ex-partner, Dr. Evadne Hinge, claiming that they had never had a good relationship and were both delighted to have brought the pairing to an end. Nevertheless, they had become interdependent - successful as a double act, but increasingly lost on their own, and it came as no surprise that they were eventually reunited, if only for a brief period.

One person in Patrick's life that I never met, and chose not to, was a man with whom he shared a house (or was it a home?) and who had a tremendous hold over him. He was a medium, or spiritualist, and Patrick would do absolutely nothing without consulting him. Would it be a wise move? Would it bring bad luck? Would it be financially advantageous?

This guy could evidently see auras around people, and it was for that reason that I refused to meet him. One friend who was introduced to the great man was, so the story went, refused a handshake, because his aura showed that he would soon die of cancer. The prognosis turned out to be accurate, even though the poor man concerned didn't know at the time. I didn't want my handshake declined.

Patrick pursued his new solo career relentlessly, and wanted me to help him in that endeavour. He was a dazzling Fairy Godmother in *Cinderella* and was offered Dame, in *Jack & the Beanstalk*, the following year. I never thought that Dame Hilda, with her genteel persona and operatic voice, albeit with a risqué line in humour, would fare very well as the traditional pantomime Dame, and I was apprehensive when Patrick asked me to cover a performance and then give my assessment.

It was a disaster. Dressed in twin set and pearls, and adopting the archetypal Hilda character of the county lady, Patrick was earnest and true, honest to every sweet aspect of the lady he brought onto the stage. The brutal truth, however, was that he was utterly at odds with the traditions of the genre in which he found himself.

It was beyond redemption, unfortunately, and I had to choose some very critical words carefully, in the dressing room afterwards, for fear of destroying his confidence and leaving him with nothing to carry him through the rest of the run. He seemed too vulnerable.

This cosy home in which he was now living away from the high camp world of the Black Cap, and Hinge & Bracket; away from the faceless bloke who slipped, unnoticed, out of the stage door; away from the chattering gossip of lonely nights on the phone; and away from the shadowy environment of auras and creepy mystique; the quiet genteel life of a country spinster was, I think, where Patrick felt comfortable. It would have been cruel to evict him unnecessarily.

He tried his hand at writing, and gave me a pile of one-act plays to read. They were charming, but unlikely to set the West End stage alight and, to my knowledge, they remain un-produced.

Patrick Fyffe died tragically young. He had amazing abilities and, within his range, performed exquisitely. The talent that was God given, surely, and which can haunt me even now, was that staggering singing voice that soared so effortlessly across octaves that are out of reach for many female vocalists.

During the performances of *Cinderella* in Cardiff and in Leeds, where the show transferred for a short run, I always made a point of watching one particular scene for the unapologetic theatricality of its close. It was a simple front cloth scene between Cinderella and her Fairy Godmother, and culminated in a song from Dame Hilda. He sang it beautifully, and was never less than moving.

By the end, the Fairy Godmother stood by the proscenium arch, in a single follow-spot light, finding from somewhere a very high note on which to finish. As the last ethereal echo of his song filled the theatre, the light faded to black, and he/she was suddenly gone.

When I think of Patrick's subsequent passing, that moment in the theatre when he just seemed to vanish, magically, comes to mind as a metaphor, and I remain saddened that such a poignant and short lived talent should have left the stage so abruptly.

*　　　　*　　　　*　　　　*　　　　*

Ironically, I went on to the operatic world myself soon after, and was able to listen to Mozart all day, together with the antics of various opera singers, in a production of *The Marriage of Figaro*, which I directed and which opened in Tunbridge Wells. But what I was really excited about was a play by Beth Henley.

The Lucky Spot is one of those American pieces that I seem to have been drawn to consistently throughout my directing career, and I took it to the Wimbledon Theatre Studio, then called The Attic. Casting was critical, as far as the play was concerned, with a bunch of characters that simply cried out for the right actors to jump in and to bring them to life.

I auditioned extensively, finally getting together a brilliant ensemble, each of whom was ready to approach the piece with un-abandoned relish, though one was a member of the management team and grabbed a role for herself as part of the deal.

I was all set. The day after opening *Figaro*, I headed towards King's Cross for a day on the panel for some more London Studio Assessments. It was the 18th February 1991, and I narrowly escaped the bombs that went off at Victoria that day. It seemed ominous but, in fact, helped to pump up the adrenalin still further for rehearsals of *The Lucky Spot* that were due to begin a couple of weeks later. This was a thrilling piece, that called for all kinds of danger and commitment from the cast.

By this time, I was living away from London and my day started early. I didn't truly need the distraction, but there was a call from Nyree Dawn Porter to ask if she could stay for a week. She was on tour, revisiting her role of Irene, in a stage production of *The Forsyte Saga*. How to resist her cooing tones on the telephone?

She arrived in the style befitting a star of her fading magnitude, with several pieces of luggage that had to be ferried to the top of the house, and the room in which she would be staying. She wasn't able to do much herself. Philip Madoc, her Soames in the production, had already left her with a case of mild whiplash, apparently, following a rather passionate rendering of the rape scene. Philip was clearly a much wilder and stronger man than I had envisaged.

Our working days did not dovetail too well. And this coincided with an important second week of rehearsals for the Beth Henley play. I got up at 7.00, each morning and, after a shower and a shave and a speedy breakfast, I was out of the house before anyone was awake. Or so I thought.

Nyree had evening performances, arriving back late, but with her days free. On the Tuesday morning, and barely out of the shower, I stood in front of the bathroom mirror to have a quick shave. Through the half misted glass, I spotted Nyree's face at the door.

"Good morning, TC."

"Er... hi, Nyree. You're up early."

"I thought you might pick up some shopping for me today."

Here was a lady with the entire day at her disposal. Even taking into account her whiplash (which was no way in evidence), she had a stage management team, a dresser and a company manager to do her bidding. I'm surprised I didn't nick myself with the razor.

"No, Nyree. I'm sorry. I won't have time."

A sulky face disappeared, and I was left to finish shaving and get dressed in peace.

That night, Nyree brought back her new boyfriend, who was with her on the show. Might he have gone shopping? They unloaded bottles of wine and a late supper. I was ready for bed, but... well, I thought I should be polite.

It turned out that this was expected to be a regular late night get-together for the rest of the week. My production came first. I declined. And, even though this had a lasting effect on our friendship, there was no question that I would suffer sleep deprivation, unnecessarily, during my own rehearsal period.

The Lucky Spot was a triumph. The cast, with one notable exception (the one I didn't cast) gave passionate and fiery performances. It was thrilling to be in the same room with them, and we played to packed houses. The national Press reacted enthusiastically: "A pot of gold at the end of the District Line".

Beth Henley heard of the production in America and wrote to me. She would be delighted and honoured for me to direct any of her other plays. Praise indeed.

She was represented by the prestigious literary agents, William Morris, and I became a regular visitor to Soho Square for meetings with her personal representative, Alan. Despite the waves, we had not been able to persuade a single commercial management to get off their comfortable West End office chairs and make the short journey to Wimbledon to see the show. Alan agreed to help move things forward, but I also had another ally.

Ian Oliver, one of the cast members and now one of my closest friends, got the bit lashed between his teeth and explored a number of possibilities. The correct venue would be vital, if we were to transfer the production. The Attic had been ideal. *The Lucky Spot* was set in a dancehall, in 30s America, and the space at Wimbledon seemed to provide the right seedy, claustrophobic ambience.

Before we knew it, we were in meetings with the management of the Café de Paris in the West End. With its peeling décor and vast period staircase, this was a genuine dancehall extraordinaire. And of the period. Budgets were drawn up; Mr. Blake, at the venue was fired up; Ian and I had time for tea with a certain Lindsay Kemp; and we were chasing the investment. On the 1st August, the plug was pulled and we considered ourselves in an unlucky spot.

I continued my contacts with Alan, at William Morris, however.

There were other Beth Henley plays that attracted me. But my schedule remained busy. I whirled through that eclectic frenzy once more, with stars from *Eastenders*, with Dexter Fletcher, Dora Bryan, Eric Sykes, Spike Milligan and, once more, with Rolf Harris. I took a show into the London Palladium, and I even went back finally to the Middle East, to one of the most exotic locations on earth.

And then abruptly, it would all stop. Without warning, I would enter the second barren desert of my career and, this time, the phone call to get me out of it would be a long time coming. When it did, I took the most daring and most audacious gamble of my career. The decision I took on the spur of the moment would take me on an unstoppable journey into the unknown.

But then, anything can and does happen in this business. A few years after our happy working relationship began, Alan Radcliffe quit his job at the William Morris Agency in Soho Square. Suddenly, he needed to devote all his waking hours to his son's career. Daniel was cast as Harry Potter and the rest, as they say, is History.

PART SEVEN

Into the Unknown

It was already beginning to snow. Not the soft, white, comforting kind but dirty, persistent lumps of grimy wetness. I was trudging through Brussels. Trudging, it seems, is something you only do when conditions are hard. Or when your spirits are low. On this occasion, both were true, and I was ready to give up. The word nadir springs to mind, an anagram of drain. There seemed to be plenty of those in the vicinity of Brussels International Railway Station. It was disgusting, and I couldn't wait to get out.

Throughout the 80s and early 90s, it seemed I was forever on the move. E & B certainly had me in a tailspin at the end of 1991. I started rehearsals for *Aladdin* on November 25th, in London. Once more, Rolf Harris topped the bill and his Abanazar came too.

This time, the show would open in Aberdeen, at His Majesty's. I flew up on the morning of December 1st and stayed at the Douglas Hotel. There was no problem with supplies of red wine or corkscrews and, in fact, this was third time lucky. After disliking Edinburgh so much and feeling so uncomfortable in Pitlochry, this was one Scottish experience that I enjoyed.

Aberdeen suited me very well, though I had little time to get to explore the town. The theatre, however, was terrific in every aspect, beautifully run, welcoming and efficient, with a friendly stage door and pretty auditorium. We opened on the 6th December and, within 24 hours, I was on a plane back to London to start rehearsals for *Robinson Crusoe*.

This starred Eric Sykes and Pam St. Clement and, within a week, we had moved on to Eastbourne for another opening at the Congress Theatre, on December 19th.

Pam St. Clement is associated with *Eastenders*, and little else. I don't watch the show, and she meant nothing to me when we met. However, she struck me as a dull lump, with little sense of humour, and it's probably fair to say that there was very little sparkle in her Fairy's wand. With a limited degree of dramatic talent, I suspect the soap series happened to suit her, and she must be aware of how lucky she's been.

And what of Eric Sykes?

I am sure there will always be artistes who need to carry an entourage with them, a trusted, handpicked group, ostensibly to be of assistance but, more urgently, to stroke the ego and nourish a sense of importance.

Of course, the very notion sits uneasily with that of being an actor in a company, with other actors, and so the phenomenon tends to emerge from the wider world of entertainment. The solo performer at the top of his/her tree likes to ring fence their sense of separation from the rest of mankind.

Usually, the entourage is represented by a single individual constantly at their side, as secretary, companion, sounding board, or just a general gofer and factotum. They arrive together and generally leave together and the presence is always there in the dressing room.

With this familiar face beside them all the time, the artiste becomes further isolated from his/her colleagues. Regular interaction between them both on and off the stage is lost. Inevitably, cracks begin to appear.

With Eric Sykes, his sidekick when I worked with him was a lady called Janet. She shielded him from the outside world and fine tuned his isolation. It has to be said that Eric was very good at cutting off from people. He could do it in rehearsal; he could do it on stage; and he could do it when it suited during periods of relaxation.

Very deaf and increasingly facing blindness, Eric wore spectacles without lenses. Strange, perhaps, until you came to realise that those same spectacles carried his hearing aid. And, so in the pub at lunchtime, or in the company of his fellow actors, generally to cut himself off, he merely had to remove his glasses. All external and ambient sounds were thus removed, until he chose to reconnect once more.

This could be an endearing trait, and nobody could possibly have begrudged him the opportunity to switch off and have a moment or two of quietness. But Eric could also cut off abruptly at other, more dramatic moments, and it was not for the fainthearted to witness.

When we worked together, for the first time, on *Robinson Crusoe*, it was an apparently successful alliance. By the end of it, I had a copy of his book, *Sebastopol Terrace* in my possession, and it was inscribed by the author: *To my favourite Director.*

Eric was also about to insist that I direct a major project of his, one that was dear to his heart. It was intended to reinforce his claim to be not just a comic and a writer, or a director of classic comedy films like *The Plank*, and the star of a monumentally successful series of sitcoms, with Hattie Jacques, but an ACTOR.

But even then I have to confess that I couldn't reciprocate the sentiment he wrote in that book. And, when he died, and I heard all of those fond and glowing tributes to him, I wanted to talk about the other side of the man - the one that I encountered.

For instance, I witnessed his brutal method of cutting off in performance from the actors that he chose not to like. He simply turned his back on them. Or worse.

At one particular matinée of the pantomime, I was shocked and embarrassed to be in the audience and to watch Eric Sykes publicly humiliate a fellow professional. The colleague in question, only a little down the billing order, fluffed a line, as he walked onto the stage. It was a feed line and, as a consequence, Eric didn't get his laugh. These things happen, a momentary slip unimportant, and the show moves on. But Eric smelled blood.

Here was an opportunity to belittle a cast member that he didn't like. In front of a packed house, he ordered the man to leave the stage "and try again." Swallowing his pride, the poor fellow did so. But, once more, the entrance did not go exactly as rehearsed. Without any charm or twinkle in his eye and making abundantly clear his anger, the star repeated the procedure. Three times this happened, and I have to say the relish with which Eric Sykes pursued his prey was palpable.

Over the next twelve months, I got to know him even more closely.

In the meantime, however, I was able to get away from this cold, egotistical world, and slip into the warm embrace of high class jazz. Right in the middle of rehearsals for Eastbourne, I went to Oxford, to meet with Paul Jones and Elaine Delmar.

Paul Jones and Elaine Delmar

The jazz trumpeter and band leader, Keith Smith, had gathered together a sensational group of musicians, and was about to tour the country with a show called *Hooray for Hollywood*. His vocalists would be Paul and Elaine, and he asked me to stage the whole event.

Paul Jones, of course, will be forever associated with the 60s band, Manfred Mann. He was their lead vocalist, a great blues singer and brilliant harmonica player. He went on to achieve a notable solo career and it was something of a coup for Keith Smith to get him under contract for the show.

Elaine Delmar, on the other hand, is one of those English jazz vocalists that - were she in America - would be a huge star. But, like Annie Ross, Marion Montgomery and others, she was destined to have a more limited following - jazz aficionados and musicians with exquisite taste. Just listen to her singing Gershwin, for example.

I was ripe for doing this show and took to Paul and Elaine immediately, though with instant reservations about Keith Smith. My collaboration with Eartha Kitt had gradually disappeared into the ether, since, ultimately, nobody could guarantee her availability, at any one time, for a limited run. Too many people, it seemed, had a hand in organising her itinerary, worldwide.

Maybe *Hooray for Hollywood* was my reward for all the work I'd put in to that show. One of Eartha's mantras, after all, was, "what goes around, comes around".

Elaine Delmar drove me back to London, late that night, and in my head I had already accepted the job. We would open at the Watford Palace Theatre, before embarking on a tour that included, to my mouth watering delight, the London Palladium. I settled my contract on January 6th, and was thus swept into 1992. We began rehearsals a week later, at the Bull's Head, in Barnes and we shall leave it there for the time being.

By now, I had been introduced to a lady called Laura. Laura was in the early stages of developing a company that was very much along the lines of Derek Nimmo's stock in trade, in the Middle and Far East. Derek was fiercely protective of his ownership of the circuit, and I could see trouble ahead, if Laura infiltrated that very lucrative and exclusive club.

Nevertheless, she approached me for advice, and my brains were picked over on several occasions at dinner, at lunch, or just over drinks. The competition with Derek lessened, as she chose to go in a more alternative and risqué direction, and Laura was soon to offer me her next production. The problem was she couldn't decide on a play.

Hooray for Hollywood opened in late January, at Watford, and through February I followed it to various venues in the UK. But I was juggling other things, too. Once again, Greg Day was touting *Bust* around the place. I finally suggested to him that we needed a recognisable name attached to the play and, on St. Valentine's Day, I went to Victoria to meet with Michelle Collins.

Why a burst of *Eastenders* should hit me around this time, I do not know. In 1980, I had admired and appreciated the input of June Brown but after the non-event of Pam St. Clement I was now disappointed in Michelle Collins, even though it was a pleasant enough meeting. She struck me as one of those actresses who, though effective on television, would have very little charisma or flair on the stage. And it has to be said she had few engaging ideas to put forward on *Bust*.

Eric Sykes seemed keen to retain my interest, and called me to his office a couple of times. Our chats were regularly interrupted by phone calls from his celebrity friends or fellow golfers. I always find it very irritating and insulting to be left dangling, whilst having to listen to one half of a telephone conversation. Especially if neither participant seems in a hurry to end it. I do remember a call from Tommy Cooper, though. He was on for a long time and had Eric in fits of laughter. When Eric finally put the phone down and stopped laughing, he explained. Tommy Cooper was worried that he might have to have a leg amputated. Why did this cause such mirth? I wanted to know. "Ah, Tommy. He just makes me laugh."

I joined another series of Assessment Panels for the London Studio Centre on the 28th February and, once again, narrowly missed being blown up by a bomb at London Bridge. Somebody was obviously out to get me. Maybe it was Hazel Bader Meinhof's attempt to remove me from the panel.

In early March, Laura finally came up with a play. She asked me how I would feel about *An Evening with Gary Lineker*. Since I knew nothing about the play or the production, I got a ticket to see it at the Duchess Theatre. Without seeming blasé, I did feel that there had to be a good reason this time for doing another Middle East production. Derek Nimmo had spoiled me.

On the other hand, and being prepared to act brazenly for once in my career, I decided that it was time for Edward to savour the experience. As I arrived at the Duchess Theatre, my mind was made up. If there was a part for him, and if the play was good enough, then I would do it.

As it transpired, both boxes were ticked and I agreed, in principle, to direct *An Evening with Gary Lineker* in Dubai. Meantime, I was gearing myself up for the Palladium.

Keith Smith was a chaotic manager and could be very unpleasant with people. But he was an excellent musician and surrounded himself with some of the very best. I was happy to get involved further. He was considering building a show around the legacy of The Empress of the Blues, Bessie Smith, the legendary American singer of the 20s and 30s.

Keith claimed to have the ideal artist to portray her - Angela Brown. I went to Worthing to see her in performance, and realised immediately that he was not exaggerating. This was a stonking great talent, with huge personality and a presence to match.

I still have a private tape of Angela with Keith Smith and his band, and it lifts the soul, whenever I hear it. It truly does. Every one of those musicians shines in that exuberant jam session, and I got very excited at the prospect of working with them.

Unfortunately, it turned out that Angela Brown was based in Germany and Keith just couldn't tie her down. And it was left to me to bring some order out of the chaos that the London Palladium date was heading for.

*   *   *   *   *

I have nightmares. Like many people, of course, these are often linked to the work I do - chaotic rehearsal rooms, actors running amok, arriving without having read the play, that sort of thing. Actors are renowned for their nightmares - they're in the wrong costume, they're in the wrong play, or they just don't know their lines.

Joseph had dreams. Fat years and lean years. He had many colours of vari-lites and follow-spots. It all came together on the night of May 17th, 1992.

I proudly stood on the stage of the London Palladium. When I was a kid, I often had tickets for the hugely successful TV variety show, *Sunday Night at the London Palladium*. Then, in my 20s and 30s, I saw many a film and recording legend in performance there.

All of this went through my head, as I looked out into the auditorium. Every major singing star the world has produced; every top-of-the-bill comic; and so many stars of stage and screen, each of them had had the same view, from the same vantage point, as I did then. And now I had my own Sunday night at the London Palladium.

I went to my dressing room.

I have worked with 3 brilliant musical directors over the years. Mike Reed who supervised *Mr. Cinders* and took it through two recording sessions; Alasdair MacNeill an unsung hero and whose career, as we shall see, became entangled with my own for a while; and then there was Mike Dixon the MD on *Six For Gold*, and whose career reached the heights as musical director for Shirley Bassey.

When *Hooray for Hollywood* went into the Palladium, albeit for one night only, the resident show was *Joseph and his Amazing Technicolour Dreamcoat*. Mike Dixon was its musical director and I used his dressing room that evening. The first thing I saw when I walked in was the *Six For Gold* poster on the wall, above a welcoming note from Mike on the table. That gesture meant a great deal.

It's amazing to me how many people think that a show just happens. They don't understand that every aspect has to be co-ordinated and structured, and that everyone needs to know exactly what it is that is meant to occur and exactly when.

I'd met with Bill Smith from the theatre, and we'd had at least one production meeting to discuss our requirements and to work out a lighting plot. The *Joseph* lighting rig was vast and complicated and there would be little opportunity to reset it. Fortunately, it was all computerised, and we calculated that to formulate the dozens of states that we needed would not take too much time. Time, after all, was money.

Sunday was spent putting all of this into action, ready for the evening performance. The day also delivered my nightmare.

The Palladium crew members were brilliant and worked hard to achieve all that I wanted. Vari-lites swept across the stage. Dramatic lighting states were fed into the computer. Follow-spot angles were rehearsed. Sound checks and speaker adjustments were made. But…

Was I foolish to assume that Keith Smith had included the services of a stage manager in his contract with the theatre? And if he hadn't, who was going to cue everybody, as to when everything happened? The show was too complicated to explain.

With just a few hours to go, before curtain up, I looked around in vain. And the crew looked at me. I'm sure you've got there already. Returning to my days as stage manager, I spent the entire performance in the control room, and called the show.

There were many notables and jazz aficionados in the audience that night, including Benny Green, and my sacrifice was not in vain. Many of them congratulated me on the show afterwards. For sure, Paul, Elaine, Keith and all of the musicians had given of their very best.

After the curtain fell, my family proudly gathered in the dressing room reserved for the male chorus of *Joseph*, whilst I went round to congratulate and thank everyone. No *Six For Gold* posters on those walls, however. The photographs of skimpily clad male hunks brought the odd raised eyebrow, I gather, and an awkward moment or two.

Brussels was a more desperate nightmare, however.

But now it's time to go east. To the east end and to another Eastender.

An Evening with Gary Lineker was coming together. I learned that the tour would take in Dubai, Oman, Jordan and Bahrain, and Laura had acquired her sponsors - a cigarette company (dodgy) and the airline, Emirates (very nice, thank you). I was introduced to her two partners in the enterprise, Duncan and Carl, and I turned my attention to casting.

What did I think of Leslie Grantham? Dirty Den had apparently been sweet talked into doing the show and wanted to meet me. I admit I was in two minds about it all, but we arranged to have lunch together.

Meanwhile, I got a call from Bill Kenwright and discovered exactly why Eric Sykes had been so keen to maintain contact with me. Bristling with his own brand of sincerity and charm, Bill checked my availability for a new play by Johnny Speight. Eric would be the star, and insisted that I would be the director.

Now what did I know of Johnny Speight? I was fully aware, of course, that he had created the character of Alf Garnett in the TV series *Till Death Us Do Part*, and that he had written for a number of sitcoms and comedy talents including Eric Sykes, Spike Milligan and Hattie Jacques. I was not aware that 3 years earlier he had penned a golfing comedy for TV, called *The 19th Hole*.

It transpired that he had now turned this into a stage play, which Bill Kenwright was going produce. The production would open at Leatherhead, before heading off for a nationwide tour. So far, so good. I asked for a script.

Nine pages arrived.

"When do I get the rest?"

"That's all there is, I'm afraid."

Given that we were scheduled to be in rehearsal within a few weeks, this presented something of a challenge. I was off to Bill's office, to meet with Johnny Speight, another personality from the east side of London and, within 24 hours, I was spending the day at the Speight home, in a script conference.

Dog-eared pages were dragged from drawers. Remnants from the TV script were offered up as possibilities. There was little conference. Mr. Speight, it was clear, wasn't too bothered about the content of the play. His reckoning was that, between Eric Sykes and myself, some form of final text would magically appear and that all would be well.

I was angry, I must confess. Having spent so much of my time with other writers, and having watched them work hard refining, rewriting and honing the dialogue, for hours on end, this was laziness personified. The man was clearly very comfortably off and was resting on his laurels. I opened the conference and gave him some ideas.

Given that the entire play was set in a golf club, I suggested spending a little time at Johnny's own club, so that I could meet with some of the personalities there. As well as informing my very golf-less brain of what it was all about, I thought that it might just focus the playwright's mind and renew his enthusiasm.

It was a fascinating morning spent at the golf club and, a couple of days later, we all convened at Kenwright's office, ostensibly to report on progress. Bill, however, had other ideas. He coolly dropped his bombshell.

Suddenly, there was a spare slot at the Liverpool Playhouse, which he needed to fill. Kenwright was now supporting the theatre, and it would be convenient and helpful if we could open *The 19th Hole* there. Could we go into rehearsal in five days? Gulp!

All heads at the meeting turned, as Bill smiled and fired the question at me. "It all depends. What does our director think? Can we do it?"

There was an implication in the lines. If I was truly worth my fee, then I should be able to make it possible to produce a script and then cast it. In 5 days. I looked around at all those faces as they willed me to provide a solution, to give the green light, and make the Kenwright organisation happy.

"Why not?" I returned the smile.

Through Thursday, Friday, Saturday and Sunday, I sat with the phone and a full set of Spotlight Casting Directories. I was contacting actors not only for the Kenwright show, but also for *Gary Lineker*. In between sessions, and whilst waiting for agents to call back, I was on the phone with Eric Sykes, Bill Kenwright and Norma, Eric's manager at Orme

Place, working on the script.

And, by the way, I had to meet with the designer to finalise the set design and costume plot. We went into rehearsal on the 24ᵗʰ August, with a good cast including Bruce Montague and Derek Newark and a skeleton script that I was desperately trying to throw some flesh at, and to make it stick. During the same week, I was holding *Gary Lineker* auditions in the evenings.

And, on September 2ⁿᵈ, I travelled to the East End, to have lunch with Leslie Grantham. It was not the best of environments, a pub on his own turf, but I was very impressed with the man and the way he handled the onslaught that came his way.

As we attempted to discuss the script, and to get to know each other, he was constantly being approached by his fans and by people generally, who were filing into the pub and wanting an autograph, a chat, or to have their photograph taken with the great man.

Leslie Grantham carried everything off with charm and with patience, to his credit, and was embarrassed that our meeting was so frequently interrupted. But it seemed that everyone either knew him or felt they knew him, and that he was every Eastender's personal property.

Gradually, things settled down and we managed a very positive talk. As I came away, however, I still had niggling doubts about his ability to deliver on this particular script.

A few days later, *The 19ᵗʰ Hole* company travelled to Liverpool and we opened on the 17ᵗʰ September. As far as I was concerned, it was a miracle. Would anyone else think so?

On the Saturday evening, Kenwright came to the show with his mother. I'm sure it was convenient that he could combine the trip with a big Everton game that afternoon, but he was gracious with me, as he introduced his mother and, for the first time, acknowledged what we had achieved.

"This is Tony Craven, the director. I asked him to do the impossible. And he seems to have pulled it off."

His mother was very friendly, but she didn't seem too surprised by what he said.

And what of Eric Sykes this time around? There was no doubting his colossal talent, but I do question whether it should have been let loose in the company of professional actors. The uninterrupted experience of being the sole centre of your performing world - constantly fed, whenever you return to the dressing room, by an ego-stroking, unquestioning entourage, can lead (not always, of course) to a belief that other people might be there merely to reflect the brightness of your own talent.

When we did *The 19ᵗʰ Hole* together, the play was already constructed as an edifice to support the star. But then Eric proceeded to drain it of anything that might make an actor feel comfortable, before inflating it with the unique oxygen on which he lived and breathed. He even tried to decide which of the cast members he would like to be with him on stage, at certain points, as his audience.

I've searched hard, but in vain, to find a generous spirit in him. On Opening Night, when traditionally the leading actor is at the forefront of the distribution of Good Luck cards and gifts; an opportunity for him to demonstrate his appreciation of the talents with whom he shares the stage; perhaps acknowledging that his or her star salary and billing dwarfs that of those around him Eric questioned the need for such gestures.

He remained ring-fenced and isolated, seemingly content with the adulation that he would receive from his audience, and the indestructibility of his own talent. Best, maybe, to be left alone with just the entourage in attendance.

But at least Eric Sykes had talent.

Let me just rifle through my list of dramatis personae and unveil once more that comedy character, Mr. "Screw It Up" Jones. That year, he brought his influence to bear on my Eastbourne pantomime, and cast as *Cinderella* a Ms. Emma Steele. The sole for reason for this was the fact that she was the daughter of the entertainer, Tommy Steele.

I soon got a call from the musical director, at the E & B suite of offices in Aldwych. I shall let you eavesdrop the voice I heard at the other end of the phone, and a brief resumé of the ensuing conversation.

"Have you heard Emma Steele sing?"

"No. But I hope she can. She's got half a dozen numbers or so in the show, plus a couple of duets."

"Well, I think you should come and see for yourself."

"Okay. Let's get her in."

I was fearful. A meeting was arranged, and we asked Emma to sing. A couple of bars in, I stopped her. This was appalling.

"It's not in my key," she squealed.

This had nothing to do with keys, and everything to do with a duff voice. We spent half an hour with her, but our hands remained in an acute gesture of despair well after she had left the office. In the interim, I had reduced her contribution to just two numbers and one duet. The MD later received a call from Tommy himself, to ask if he would go to the house and teach his daughter to sing. Unless he could provide a voice box transplant, it seemed unlikely that he would be very successful.

Two weeks into the Johnny Speight play in Liverpool, my latest cast member to fall victim to the demon drink did so, and I had to find time to audition his replacement.

Otherwise, things were going well.

*　　　　*　　　　*　　　　*　　　　*

There are 5 speaking characters in *An Evening with Gary Lineker*. Along with Leslie Grantham, I now had Edward Arthur, Mark Fletcher and Felicity Goodson. The remaining actress was to be brought in by the management. But there was one part that we couldn't cast. Yet.

At the end of the play, in a fantasy sequence, the real Gary Lineker is scripted to appear on stage. Obviously, this has to be a look-alike. However, there was no way that Laura was going to pay to carry an extra cast member, with no lines to speak. My suggestion was for each venue to hold a competition (generating useful publicity) to find the most likely ex-pat contender for the part, in advance of our arrival.

But such a tiny problem paled into insignificance, following the next development in this developing saga.

Leslie Grantham pulled out. Laura managed to chirp it over the phone to me, and then: "I'm going to Majorca tomorrow on holiday. Can you sort it all out for me, please?"

I agreed to trawl through my address book to find a suitable star who might replace the decidedly replaceable Grantham. Oh, Derek, where are you? I muttered to myself. I was on the verge of calling him, and then remembered the cut-throat competition between the two impresarios.

Having spent every waking moment that I could spare, crawling over the case and lining up a couple of possibles, Laura's partner, Duncan, was suddenly on the phone.

He twittered and chirped. "We've recast the part. Another *EastEnder* so the venues will be pleased…" It's difficult to strangle somebody over the phone. I wanted to. Certainly, my voice must have sounded strangulated. The name that Duncan cooed to me meant nothing. Apologies to Chris McHallem, who apparently played a character called Rod Norman, in *EastEnders*.

Rehearsals were set to begin on October 5th. *The 19th Hole* opened at Leatherhead on the 6th. We had a Lineker read through, my opportunity to meet Chris and Helen Griffin. Having chatted to Leslie Grantham about the part, Chris McHallem presented a shock. Looking less like an actor and more like the punk rock musician he had once been, he didn't seem to fit the role at all. And he was desperately shy.

Standing next to him at the window, when I went into the rehearsal room for the first time, was more black leather, wild hair and weird makeup. My heart sank. This was Helen Griffin provided by the management and who looked as though she inhabited a completely alien universe to that of Mark, Edward and Felicity. Was this going to be a disaster?

The answer to that question revealed itself over the coming weeks - gradually, but positively - as a resounding 'No'. The company gelled magnificently and the performances grew in stature, so that the whole production began to acquire an exciting and convincing aura of success.

The weather was disgusting, and we all longed for the change in temperature, skies and ambience that the arrival in Dubai would surely bring. Everybody suffered the usual jabs and visa rigmaroles and prepared for the public dress rehearsal that the management had arranged for us all. It was a good ploy, and it became our deadline day.

Then Laura arrived with that anxious but smiling face that, in my experience, always forebodes some disturbing news. Spill the beans, please, Laura, and put us out of our misery.

"There's been a change of plan…"

Surprise, surprise. There had been a cockup and the Dubai date was now to be at the end of the tour. The bad news was that we would therefore have to spend an extra week in London, under grey skies and Lowry rain, egging the pudding and making sure that we didn't peak too soon.

The good news, as far as I was concerned, was that we would be opening in Muscat, an area that I hadn't visited before.

Agents were contacted, a little renegotiation done, and the company held its nerve. We were now due to leave on November 3rd.

Meanwhile, I'd been following *The 19th Hole* around the country. Fortunately, they were mostly southern dates but I had to restage the production for Chichester, where the layout is a permanent in the round thrust. The night before I left for the Middle East, the production opened at the Theatre Royal, in Brighton and I watched the performance.

I confess that I was never a real fan of Spike Milligan. He just didn't make me laugh. And, to compound the sacrilege, I have to admit that I never did get *The Goons*, either. I rarely found them funny. Which is what makes the following encounter so sad.

At the same time, and since I find myself momentarily sitting in the confessional, I recall an excruciating evening at the Shaw Theatre, watching Max Wall on stage. Around me, an audience of grown-ups were unable to stay on their seats, they we laughing so helplessly and their collective wail, of so much uncontrolled mirth, grew bit by tiny bit into a tidal wave that crashed over me. Painfully and incessantly.

It crashed over me because, amongst all of this hysteria, I sat totally still thinking only, "You sad, pathetic old man with your tights and your silly walks!" There was a mass audience; and then there was me. An audience of one. We must have been watching something different.

One of the fascinations of working with, or getting to be friends with any well-known people, is that you often rub shoulders with some of their friends and colleagues. This was true, to an extent, of Eric Sykes. Of course, I was far too late to meet Hattie Jacques, she died a good ten years before my association with Eric, but I am sure that that would have been fun.

On November 2nd, in Brighton, I needed to get round the dressing rooms at the end of the show, to give everyone my notes before leaving for Oman. Eric Sykes was always slow to leave the theatre, whereas other cast members tended to dash for trains back to London as soon as they could get away. So, I got used to leaving my visits to the N° 1 dressing room until last.

The Theatre Royal is a comfortable and familiar building, with a friendly stage door, and I got the nod early on that Eric had a guest in. Fortunately, there were only a few comments that I wanted to make on the evening's performance, so when I knocked on the door to his room I didn't expect to stay for more than a couple of minutes.

Once inside, however, I was introduced to Spike Milligan, who was quick to express a lively cynicism towards directors in general. The remark was meant as a put-down, but it was also assumed to be funny. Mr. Milligan laughed loudly at his own witticism, whilst I smiled politely and then turned to Eric with my notes.

As I started to leave, Eric insisted that I stay and join the two of them for a drink. It wasn't unusual for him to entertain in that way, though I would usually wriggle out of it, once the business of giving notes was done. On this particular evening, it seemed, I had no choice. Perhaps the two of them just needed an audience.

I am very well aware that thousands would have leapt at the opportunity to be in my shoes, at that point. Many people have told me since that they would have paid good money for the entertainment that followed. But for the next 40 minutes it was I who was destined to be the 'Audience with Spike Milligan and Eric Sykes'.

For 40 minutes, the banter between them was quick-fire and un-scripted. The humour crackled and sparkled without let-up, and the improvisation was sometimes turned onto me. Off-the-wall, lunatic exchanges of the highest order sped between these two friends and colleagues. They were a mutual inspiration for one another - each familiar with, and fine-tuned to, all the idiosyncrasies and manic cap-abilities of the other half of this double act.

My mind went back to the Shaw Theatre, and the spectre of Max Wall.

I realised, as the minutes ticked by and as I turned to the drink in my hand for comfort, that many would have reached for the word genius, at that stage. Or, having paid their money, would have begged for an encore.

However, if anyone thought the experience would set me on my own road to a shining Damascus, then I need refer them back a page or two. Spike Milligan did not make me laugh. I think I gave an even better performance of enjoying the performance than the two performers did and they both found it hysterically funny. But, for me, there was an acid cruelty to it all. And when the nastiness took a rest, the void was pumped full of silly voices and undergraduate lunacy.

For one of the few times in my career, I felt alien to the backstage elements, as I finally emerged from the dressing room. The ghosts of so many theatrical geniuses stalking the darkened recesses on either side seemed to smile, wanly and pityingly, at my ordeal. And, as I reached the stage door and stepped out into the chilly night air, I found myself looking forward more than ever to a flight to the East, the following day, in the company of ACTORS.

So, another 3,600 miles or so, another magical carpet ride. We flew to Dubai, changed planes, and later arrived in Muscat, Oman. Our destination was the exotic sounding Al Bustan Palace Hotel and it turned out to exceed all expectation.

This belonged to the Sultan. Folklore had it that he chose the most beautiful bay in the country as its setting. Then, unperturbed that it was already the site of an established fishing community, he simply relocated the entire village further along the coast. Once done, he built his palace complete with its own theatre/opera house, where we would be opening our production.

As we entered the lobby for the first time, we emitted a communal gasp of wonder. This was the size of a cathedral, and dripped with opulence and eastern magnificence. Furthermore, we were there for a week, with all expenses paid.

My jaw dropped for a second time when I caught sight of the poster that advertised the show. It proudly proclaimed that the cast was led by Leslie Grantham. Our producers were deliberately keeping the news of his replacement from the management, banking on his name filling the coffers from ticket sales, until the last moment. I was appalled. Chris McHallem was wreathed in embarrassment.

For the time being, however, I was delighted to see the joy with which this cast, which had worked so hard, took to the luxuries on offer. Each with a room the size of a tennis court, they ambled through each morning to take an exotic breakfast on the outside terrace before sashaying past the vast swimming pool toward the soft, white sands that fringed the Gulf of Oman.

It was a problem calling them to rehearsal. But, rehearse we must. Mark Fletcher could be found arranging his lounger on the beach; Chris was usually wandering the coastline, picking up pebbles; Felicity Goodson with her blonde hair and trim figure was often surrounded by adoring males; and so on… and so forth. I had to crack the whip once or twice.

Occasionally, one or two disgraced themselves, as they piled their plates a little too high with the cuisine provided, in a choice of restaurants, but the show came together, technically and artistically, in fine style. We found an excellent Gary Lineker, and the production had its first performance, in front of an enthusiastic crowd, on the 8th November.

There were some who took the title of the show too literally, and expected a Q&A session with the footballer himself, but that was surely inevitable.

Sadly, at the end of the week and after just two shows, we had to say our goodbyes to the Al Bustan Palace. Following the performance, we all congregated on the beach at a very lively cocktail bar, and congratulated ourselves on a memorable and successful week.

The air was balmy; the sand was still warm; and the stars twinkled overhead. The only negative, as we enjoyed the hotel's hospitality, was the way in which a group of local beauties was paraded on a stage by the bar. Each was introduced by the madam, who then gave out their room numbers. It was offensive, but out of our zone. We continued our celebrations well into the night.

As we headed for the airport, the following morning, I was aware that we were about to go our separate ways. The cast flew to Amman, in Jordan, and I went on to Dubai. I had several hours to wait there, before my flight to London, and the management had thoughtfully provided a room at the Dubai International Hotel, where I could rest. In fact, I spent much of the day lazing by the pool, alternating cool drinks, bursts of swimming and bouts of sleeping. And then quite suddenly a stab of foreboding hit me in the gut. Why should that be? It had nothing to do with the upcoming flight, though I was very aware of another wait in Dubai, when my plane was apparently stuck on the tarmac at Delhi.

We, the passengers, were taken to a convenient hotel, to pass the time. In the evening, I was contacted with the option of either waiting for my next BA flight due in the morning, or catching a Singapore Airlines flight leaving soon after midnight.

I opted for the latter, and allowed myself to be attended by those smiling, undulating stewardesses as portrayed in all the commercials. Unfortunately, when we were little more than an hour out of Heathrow, the Captain explained that England was fog bound, and that we were being diverted to Amsterdam.

The sudden change in schedule brought a rapid change in our cabin crew. Within minutes, they had morphed from fantasies out of a television commercial to characters from a disaster movie. All sense of calm disappeared, as panic set in.

If England was drenched in fog, then Holland was merely drenched. The rain teemed as we arrived. That day, at 5.00am, it was not an attractive place to be. I was almost a full 24 hours late, when we finally touched down at Heathrow. But this was different, and the apprehension and foreboding would not go away.

I lay back in the sun, closed my eyes and tried to concentrate on all the positives. I had reached a level that was no more than a fantasy when I was buying those ring binder strengtheners in Birmingham, all those years before. Maybe Tolkien was right. Maybe fantasy IS the true reality.

After all, I was doing a job that I loved; travelling the world; meeting extraordinary people; and, furthermore, being paid for it. I'd come to understand what it all entailed. Along with the obvious one, a director takes on the role of teacher, psychologist, father, friend, psychiatrist, God, disciplinarian, saviour, comforter, and shoulder to cry on. Always some of these - sometimes all. There was a myriad of temptations to avoid and a raft of perks to enjoy. Even the word 'Director' had now and then brought the unexpected.

I soothed my soul with the memory of once such occasion when I walked into a restaurant in downtown Los Angeles with an American friend of mine. As soon as we arrived at the bar, this friend mischievously announced that he'd brought a British director to have lunch with him. The ramifications of that remark were extraordinary. I can honestly say that there were more waiters and cocktail waitresses in attendance throughout that meal than I would normally expect to see around any one table anywhere. But, then, as my friend knew very well, the place abounds with out-of-work actors hoping to be 'spotted', and the very word 'Director' sparked a communal rush of anticipation. If only they had known that my influence in that city represented a big fat zero.

I swam to the bar in the centre of this pool and ordered another lemonade. The dark mood had passed.

There was just a touch of envy that the *Lineker* cast were spending time in Jordan and a visit to Petra, with only one performance of the play. But then, ultimately, I didn't envy them the way they were left stranded by the management when they tried to leave.

Whilst Laura, Duncan and Carl were topping up their tans in Bahrain, the next stop on the tour, the cast were discovering that taxes had not been paid in Amman. And they were not going to be allowed out of the country until the account was settled. Our company manager's credit card was unable to take the strain, and it was left to one of the cast members to cough up. It all led to tearful, apologetic scenes from the producers, when they were reunited in Bahrain.

I was back in the UK in sufficient time to check on *The 19th Hole*, in Croydon, before flying off to Amsterdam, for a long weekend with friends. On November 21st, as I watched on television the flames engulfing Windsor Castle, I was packing again to fly back to Dubai.

Repercussions following the delayed start to our tour meant that Felicity Goodson was unable to stay for the final week. She was already booked for pantomime in the UK. Enormously popular within the company, and fantastic in the show, she was a hard act to follow. But the management found a replacement and flew me back to Dubai to rehearse her in to the production. For the remaining two performances only. The sponsorship deal with Emirates was surely becoming strained by now.

The other sponsors were meanwhile testing my own patience. All of their regional reps had decided to descend on Dubai on a jolly and to attend the opening performance. I carried out my social/PR duties with them after our dress rehearsal and then retired to my room.

When I went back to the theatre later, to check that all was well, I was aghast. In my absence, every corner of the room and, more importantly, every available space on the set had become emblazoned with the sponsor's name. It was shouted from every corner of the stage.

In turn, I shouted for any rep in earshot. "But we're sponsoring the show!" was their logic. "Not on my set!" was my response.

After lengthy negotiations, the offending material was removed. I made just one concession. I allowed one sentence of the text to be altered for that evening's performance. Instead of, "Do you want a cigarette?" the actor now spoke the memorable line: "Would you like a Silk Cut?"

Poor Mark Fletcher. He bragged that he would get himself upgraded to First Class for the flight home. As the rest of us waited at check-in, we watched him arrive, and turned to follow his progress. He certainly looked the part. Dressed in his very best suit, he carried himself with dignity, assurance, and a well rehearsed swagger. Unfortunately, it was all in vain. Within a few feet of the First Class check-in desk, as he shot a radiant smile to the girl who would fall prey to his charms… his suitcase fell apart.

His confidence disintegrated at the same moment and, having gathered his belongings together in haste, he altered course and joined the rest of us in our queue.

Two days after my return to London, I started rehearsals for another *Cinderella* in Aberdeen. E & B had surpassed themselves. I had to open in Aberdeen on December 10th, three days after starting rehearsals for Eastbourne. Heathrow was becoming my second home. But I did manage to catch up on *The 19th Hole* in Richmond.

But now it was back to the non-singing Emma Steele. Ear muffs in position, please.

*   *   *   *   *

Three times I have been introduced to Christopher Biggins, and on each occasion he has behaved as though it were the first. I have found myself wondering whether there is a condition known as "Affected Amnesia Syndrome".

Dora Bryan and I were nudged together, gently, over a period of time - meeting at the occasional party or some other social gathering, before we worked together. Her party piece was still her ability to perform the splits on request, and so she was often to be found on the floor, legs akimbo, surrounded by an admiring and applauding group of fans no doubt wondering if she could get up again! Dora usually had a silly grin plastered across her face - the spontaneous mask of the performer, I would guess, rather than an expression of any groin pains.

At the Devonshire Park Theatre, in Eastbourne, she would prove to be a popular Fairy Godmother in my production of *Cinderella*. She was billed alongside Dexter Fletcher, who was giving his Buttons. I never really discovered where Dexter had made the name that entitled him to such billing, but I took to him readily and decided that he was an extremely talented young performer.

Like Eric Sykes, Dora had her entourage in the dressing room though, in her case, it comprised no more than her friendly little dog - who was no trouble - and her husband, Bill, who would deliver and collect the two of them each day.

Prior to the production, of course, I'd been to Dora's home in Brighton, for our pre-rehearsal chats and so I had already become well acquainted with the entourage, before we moved along the coast. *Clarges,* as the place was slightly pretentiously known, was the building where Dora Bryan and Bill lived, with I think accommodation for other members of the family. It also had a career as a kind of guest house for a while until, that is (rumour and gossip shouted loudly), the kitchens were raided by the Health & Safety people, who subsequently took away its licence. I am utterly unable to verify that rumour, but... "no smoke," etc...

She is a very funny lady, that much loved "national treasure". She made me laugh endlessly during *Cinderella* rehearsals, and she managed to decant the funny performance to the stage with ease. She knew how far to take the high camp, and when to reassert the magic of that role.

But the offstage persona is grounded in a very different kind of performance. It is studied and well polished, and is presented with considerable aplomb. Because it has been honed over such a long period of time, it's almost indistinguishable from the real Dora Bryan. I eventually came to the conclusion that it is a character that Dora can switch on like a light bulb. And, make no mistake, that 'on' switch is pressed for much of the time. But this is not precisely what Dora is, though she is, very much, what she does.

There was a moment, of course, during those madcap rehearsals that I gently asked if the Fairy Godmother might like to do the splits, at an appropriate moment should we be able to find one. That slightly nasal northern voice was quick to decline, and was only too happy to demonstrate why. She fell to the ground and adopted the familiar grin. "Now," she said, "these days, somebody has to help me up."

A couple of months later, I arrived at a party to hear, immediately, from our hostess: "Oh, Tony, Dora's here." I was led through to where the party was already chugging along. "Dora, look who's here!" and we were left together.

To my astonishment, Dora Bryan looked up from her chair and said: "I'm sorry. Do I know you?"

Was this wicked humour? I wondered, momentarily. But she held her quizzical stare just long enough for me to realise I should take the question seriously. "Dora," I said, quietly, "I should bloody well hope so since we've only recently flogged ourselves silly to provide some Christmas entertainment for the good burghers of Eastbourne!"

There was a pause. "Oh, yes," she said. "You're the director I like, aren't you? How are you?"

At that moment, I wasn't sure whether I felt the same way. But of one thing I was absolutely sure. This was another case of AAS (Affected Amnesia Syndrome), and a cure should be found at once. Until there is, however, I can truly say that, though I have no interest whatsoever in working with Christopher Biggins, I am very happy to have had that ride along to Eastbourne with Dora Bryan. Even without the splits.

And Emma? I confess that we turned her microphone down during her duet, and I hid her behind a gauze to soften her solo number. It may seem unkind, but I think the audience appreciated it, and… well, this was nothing compared with those dirty tricks reputedly played by the stage crew at the Palladium, on their least favourite performer - Emma's father - during *Singing in the Rain*.

The frenzy continued. *Cinderella* had its Press Night just before Christmas. By the end of December, I was in rehearsal for a one man show with Brian Barnes, as Charles Dickens, a production that subsequently played around the world. Then, I was straight down to The Mill at Sonning, for a production of the Francis Durbridge play, *A Touch of Danger*.

My energies were being sapped by this whirlwind. I'd directed six productions in seven months. Maybe the Gods became sympathetic. At the end of February, they lifted their arms and withdrew their breath. They stilled the winds and becalmed me in the centre of an ocean, where I was left to float helplessly adrift. All I could do was to await their pleasure and, meanwhile, hope for fresh breezes to fill my sails again.

*   *   *   *   *

There's a definite chill in the air. I realise that the fog has rolled in, but it came so quickly. There is nothing to be seen on the horizon. An actor can be called and be working the next day. For a director, a production has to be set up weeks, often months, in advance.

This dead weight is familiar. I felt it, for the first time, over a decade ago. I was young then, innocent and naïve. I allowed myself to drift, aimlessly, until the skies cleared. I didn't know it would last as long as it did and, expecting each week for it to be over, I hung on to my sanity.

Things are different this time. I have scaled certain heights. I have a reputation. I cannot allow myself to drift. Nor can I plummet. Then... I would lose my sanity.

But, first, I can rest. I can visit Twickenham Studios and work on a script with Mary Selway. I can dish out my worldly wisdom from the Assessment Panel. But the din of activity has shrunk to a distant echo. The silence is swelling to a different cacophony.

I have to do something. I must mould events, with my experience, into a grand design. March passes, and I realise I am going nowhere.

It is April. My time is given over to thoughts of creativity, of creating a future where, currently, none seems to exist. I have travelled the world. I have absorbed other cultures and other traditions. Despite the insular beliefs, it doesn't all happen in London or the UK. There are theatrical giants in other parts of the world.

A shape is emerging. May brings foul weather, but the outline of a project comes with it. It is ambitious. It is expensive. But I believe in it. I remember seasons of *World Theatre*, at the Aldwych, productions from around the world, brought to London and played in their original language. And then brought to the audience with the aid of instant translation, over headphones.

Each nation in Europe has a theatrical heritage, and these should be shared around. I shall set up the company to do it. It is called Theatre Europa. It's not a very original title, but it explains the concept. The mission is set.

It is 3 months since my last production and I am ensconced in the library doing my research. The fog around me is denser, colder, greyer. Before it envelops me entirely, I reach out to friends and ask if they would like to be on the Board of Theatre Europa. I meet with a lady called Fran. She will design a logo and develop some business cards. My Dolphins experience helps here.

June 1st, and the company launch. I am excited today, and the weather is perfect. Am I a lunatic? People's eyebrows suggest it may be so. But, I am pushing ahead, and our first Board Meeting is set for the 11th at the Charing Cross Hotel. Suddenly, the weather changes. Wales is under water.

We decide to publish a brochure, and start advertising ourselves. I have been introduced to a printer, who will do a special rate on the brochure. We have reached the end of June, and the artwork is coming together. But who will finance all of this?

Theatre Europa exists. Today July 12th 1993 is the date of our Incorporation. We are all in deep into this. Is everyone committed? We seem to be waiting for events to unfold, and I am already booked to spend a week in Spain. We fly to Malaga and soak up the sun for seven days.

August 6th. We got back yesterday, and I am feeling flat. My obsession with Theatre Europa seems to be worrying people, but we are now waiting for our letterhead paper and our brochure. Then we can start in earnest. Nothing else seems to be happening. All I have arranged is a recording of the Dickens show, on the 17th, at a studio in London. And we have another Board meeting, on the 22nd.

Suddenly, I am booked for a show in Norwich. Theatre-in-Education on the perils of AIDS. It's called *Love Bites*. It gets in the way, but I feel I must do it. There is a current pulling me into dangerous waters, and I am powerless to fight it. Individual sponsorship for Theatre Europa is helping us to move forward, but I am becoming isolated again, as the sole driving force. Things must change.

It's October 2nd. The game's over, girls and boys. This is never going to work. I can't do it on my own. I now need physio on my back. I am getting a cold. I am losing touch with reality, for sure. A year ago, I was on top of the world. This is a cruel business, when it all turns nasty. But now we have an account at the Allied Irish Bank. How very European.

It is already mid November and nobody is responding. Dear friends, I am letting you all down. I am sorry. I will give it one last shot but secretly, I am back to waiting for that telephone call; for the fog to clear; for the rhythm to return; for me to discover just how far off course I have moved. Maybe in the New Year. Maybe in 1994.

This is only the second time in my career, but… is it the end of my career? After almost 25 years, after more than 100 productions, was it all just too good to be true?

I am about to find out.

It's New Year's Eve, and I am settled into the Old Hall Hotel, in Buxton. Tomorrow, I shall watch *Aladdin*, but I am currently praying for my own genie to arrive with a magic lamp. Theatre Europa is teetering on its already rickety legs. I must be bad company. Paralysis is beginning to set in. I must relearn how to fight, and not to cower and stagnate. I owe it to myself and to everyone involved with this ill conceived venture.

I have relied on the Helen Cherry Trust to come to our aid. Today February 8th I learn, "No, sorry. We can't." The snow lies thick outside and the fog obliterates everything inside. Only at home, in the warmth and security of my private relationship can I find comfort and support. It is there that I find the strength to carry on.

I am at the airport. It is the 14th March. My final throw of the dice. The flight leaves, on time, at 2.50pm - destination, Amsterdam. Each of my appointments, over the next few days, represents a vital meeting and could determine my future.

March 15th. 11.00am. I am at the Ministry of Arts, in The Hague, to talk to John Brester. 1.00pm. I arrive at Royal Dutch/Shell, in The Hague. 3.30pm. I am greeted by Julia Ladiges, at the Netherlands Theatre Institute.

March 16th. Travel to Brussels. 11.00am. Here, at the European Commission, in Rue de Tréves, I meet Mrs. Welshe. 2.00pm. M. Viseur spares me his time, at the European Consultancy Group, at Avenue Louise. 2.30pm. I have moved to CELSA, to speak with Jean-Pierre Palante. 4.30pm. I have just left the Flemish Theatre Institute, and a meeting with Bart van der Eynde.

The weather has worsened. I am trudging through the snow and hating Brussels. I fear that I have failed in all my endeavours. My will is disintegrating. I shall call a Board Meeting. It's fixed for 5.30, on the 22nd, at an office in New Oxford Street.

More than a year. When will I emerge from all this? Edward says soon. I believe him.

Fragments of a nightmare, shattered by a phone call. The lightning hit yesterday - a blistering strike, that wrenched the fog from its anchor, and exposed a blinding whiteness from the sun. I can barely see. My limbs are shaking. Let me steady myself. I am still rocked by my conversation, still tethered to my depression.

On Sunday, I admitted defeat and lost all motivation, except to give in to failure. I could still feel the wounds from those pinching shards of grimy wetness, as I trudged through Brussels. I ached with exhaustion, and shook with the cold.

Today is different. I am in a different place and I can see the way ahead. If I dare to tread the path that has opened up. I have a few days to decide.

And so it felt.

*　　　*　　　*　　　*　　　*

Well, every story should have its share of tragic episodes, and that was my annus horribilis. I did not "look back on it with undiluted pleasure," as a more distinguished speaker put it, soon after the fire I watched at Windsor Castle. Of course, it was not all 'horribilis'. There were high points, too. But the pain was real, and the fear was tangible. I had plummeted from extraordinary heights of activity and success to the lowest point that I could ever remember. And I was about to blast off again.

And, so, what happened?

A brief rewind, to savour the dying moments of that annus. If I'd known there was only a week left, I might have savoured it more. I might have enjoyed my visit to BAFTA, or my trips to the Earls Court Road where I met with Emily Hurley and Eileen Daly, at the *Europa Times*. I certainly appreciated a drink with Clive Dunn, at the Players' Theatre. When I told him that I thought I would never work again, he smiled and dismissed the idea, "Of course you will. I'm sure you're far too good at what you do." What a nice man.

I did not enjoy a production of *Mill on the Floss*, at the Theatre Royal, Brighton. I was asked to review it for Radio Brighton & Hove. My late night review was hardly complimentary, and caused all manner of a stir but I spoke as I felt.

A visit to the Purcell Room, on the South Bank, to see Brian Barnes in my production of his one man show, failed to lift my spirits and - I remember it well - on May 23rd, at the start of another barren looking week and after more than a year without work, I registered utter defeat.

Of course, in retrospect, this was just a blip in my career, and I was soon back on top, but at that point I couldn't see 48 hours ahead. I didn't know (how could I?) what would be communicated, via the telephone, on the 25th.

When the call came, it was from my old friend Guus van der Made, he whom I'd met at the Britannia Hotel and who had been an actor/ writer on a couple of shows for Theater Plezier in Holland. But things had changed dramatically. He was now a producer for the Endemol Television Organisation, based in Alsmeer and Hilversum.

Endemol was brought about by the conjunction of two men: Joop van den Ende and John de Mol. Both were millionaires, but had very different tastes and personalities. Joop was the Theatre man, who went on to become Holland's answer to Cameron Mackintosh. He actually built theatres, in order to produce musicals, such as *Les Miserables, Cats* and *Evita*.

John, on the other hand, had rather tackier taste and an overriding enthusiasm for the Television industry. He introduced reality shows - for example, *Big Brother* and game shows and talent shows, many of which were ultimately imported into the UK.

The Drama Department, in which Guus was now working and finding his feet, was developing traffic in the other direction and adapting scripts, especially sitcoms, by UK writers, for a Dutch environment. They were only interested in the successful ones.

With Guus van der Made and Caroline ten Cate (minus parrot)

Having newly arrived in post, Guus was looking for a director that he could rely on, one that he could trust, and who shared his sense of humour and understanding of actors. He was about to produce a comedy series, originally shown in the UK under the title *Tom, Dick & Harriet*.

Was I available? And then, suddenly almost as an afterthought: "You have directed television, haven't you?"

I could not believe my response. Or how easily it came out of my mouth. "Of course. Many times."

"I'll get back to you."

I put the phone down.

For the next few minutes, I tried to explain my audacity to myself. My logic could only be based on the simple premise: If he could learn on the job, then so could I. Were we both about to fall flat on our faces?

A week later, I was on the 12.50 flight to Amsterdam, and to Alsmeer the headquarters of van den Ende's empire. I was given a whirlwind tour of the offices and began to wonder what kind of a buildup this highly experienced British television director had been given by Meneer van der Made. Everyone seemed incredibly impressed by the reputation that had gone ahead of me.

I was booked in to the Tulip Inn for three nights, and a busy itinerary had been arranged. But first I had to impress the Head of Drama, Frans Rasker. We were due to meet over dinner at the local yacht club. This being early June, we could sit at the water's edge and discuss my career.

In the event, and with Guus at my side, Frans felt that he needed to impress me with his credentials, and those of the entire organisation. I was wined and dined in style, and managed to retain a relaxed demeanour throughout the evening, even though I was braced every minute for the question or comment that would blow my cover and have me frog marched back to Schipol.

As the evening drew to a close, I looked up and searched the night sky for my lucky star. The brandy tasted warm and mellow, but my stomach was still churning. Suddenly:

"There is just one thing that I need to warn you about." Aah! Frans held me in his sights, and his face which had borne a thrilled-that-you're-here smile for most of the evening now acquired a dark and serious look. The eyes were penetrating. For one moment, I thought he must be of German stock.

"Our star is one of the biggest, and he is not always easy, I'm afraid. He has given other directors many problems. Ultimately, I have to warn you, if he can't work with you, then - well he is our star, and we must always be on his side." There was a pause. "Do you understand what I'm saying?"

By now, I was so impressed with my own qualities and qualifications as a television director, with a string of successes behind me, that I was able to discover an easy uncrossing of the legs and a confident smile, as I leant forward to answer him.

"Believe me," and I so meant this, "if your star loses confidence in me, or if he makes life too difficult, then I assure you I will be long gone, you will not need to ask me."

Frans's features relaxed once more. "Excellent. Welcome to the family!"

Personally, I had an uneasy night at the Tulip Inn, but by 9.30, the following morning I was meeting with the Head of Wardrobe; at 10.30, I was introduced to my PA; and, one hour later, I met with the female star of the series, Martine Bijl.

Then, it was off to the studios in Hilversum to meet the designer and his team. I forget all the other studio bosses and production personnel who were lined up for discussions with me, over the next couple of days. But I remember being taken to various apartments in Amsterdam, for me to choose which I preferred, and then to a recording of the Dutch version of *Man About The House*, in front of a studio audience, on the Friday night.

On Saturday morning, I was back on a plane to London with a pile of scripts and studio plans and lighting options and lists of names and a signed contract that reflected my international status as a leading British television director. I also had a headache and a longing to wind back the clock, so that I could change my mind.

I was in unknown territory, and the task ahead was staggering. But in case you are too shocked by all this chutzpah, let me distract you with a few facts and figures.

I had been contracted to direct 13 episodes of a series called *Het Zonnetje in Huis*, from the English sitcom, written by Brian Cooke and originally shown in 1982 as *Tom, Dick & Harriet*. Each episode was 25 minutes in length and starred three of Holland's most popular and well loved actors. The series would be recorded in front of a live studio audience, every Friday night, following four days of rehearsal and camera rehearsal. This was a multi-camera production, with a minimum of 3, and sometimes 4, cameras. A good portion would be shot on location then edited in time to be included at the Friday recording, in order to get an authentic reaction from the public.

Now, of course, you are fully apprised of just how much chutzpah was involved. So, it's back to the story…

Having picked a few brains in the four days I had at home in the UK, I flew back to Amsterdam ready for some hard work, and to meet my stars. I was installed in a very beautiful apartment in the centre of the city and, comfortingly, if I stood on the balcony, I got a perfect view of the famous Carré Theatre.

But, for the next four weeks, I barely registered my surroundings. My every waking moment was spent either in the studio, or at my desk studying and working.

I'd already had a chat with Martine Bijl, a very popular cabaret artiste, turned actress, writer and general intellectual. She was also the creator of a range of rather sinister dolls that went on display from time to time. She was blonde, probably in her 30s, and fun, but she appeared to be intimidated by, and overawed by, her two co-stars. These two were a father and son team, bearing the name Kraaykamp, a name adored all over the Netherlands.

John, the father, was not in evidence when I arrived at their home for a prearranged meeting, on my first day at work. But Johnny, his son, was very welcoming and eager to talk about the show. He was dashing and dark haired, with an easy grin that often camouflaged a more nervous laugh. It was plain to see that he was often caught in his father's shadow, secure there, but looking for ways to break away.

John Snr. made his entrance. This was the Star, of whom I'd been warned. Tubby, with a classic comedy face, he presented himself as a shy and gentle individual, whilst examining and assessing every word I said. I could spot the danger signals, and drew on my years of experience of dealing with the full gamut.

I had been given a very nice car to drive and, on my 46th birthday, I took it to Hilversum to start rehearsals for Episode 4 (we always recorded out of sequence). This was the part that came easily to me. Working with actors was food and drink for my soul, and the cast reacted positively. Most actors will speak of getting very little input from their director in television. Sometimes, they barely meet. And so, there was a delighted frisson in the *Zonnetje* company as we worked and rehearsed in depth, for the first three days.

Interestingly, the Dutch word for rehearsal can be translated as re-petition, and many directors take that concept seriously - anxious to disappear to their gallery, to sit behind their monitors and communicate with their actors only through the Floor Manager and a set of earphones. My group bonded together very quickly, and we got to know each other very well.

But, as the week wore on, I was badgered for my camera script. Every shot, from every camera, had to be worked out in advance. Would it be a long shot, a medium shot, a close-up, or a panning shot, etc.? And the sequence should always allow time for each cameraman to move, to adjust his shot and to refocus, before being called on again.

I procrastinated.

The Studio in Hilversum

On the evening before the script was required, finally and without fail, I sat at my desk and stared at the text. This was the moment of truth. On the following day, very nearly 50 people would be linked visually and audibly with their director and would be expecting a very nearly perfect and smooth running Camera Rehearsal, before a run-through and general rehearsal, so that everything was in the can, as a backup.

Then, at 8.00pm, in front of a packed studio audience and following a 10 minute warm-up, the show would be recorded.

After very little sleep, I walked into that vast studio and looked at the dozen or so huge and complicated sets; I checked the complex lighting rigs and set dressing with heads of department; I answered questions from Wardrobe and Makeup; I conversed with my 3 cameramen and my Floor Manager; in essence, I stood at the centre of this huge and expensive operation, as the clock ticked by, and drew on every ounce of every year of experience, and every intellectual and artistic sinew of my being, and I managed - just - to avoid physical and mental collapse. And I pulled it off.

For sure, the first few episodes were littered with mistakes, many of which were rescued in the editing suite, but I learned quickly. I had the confidence of my cast and my producer, and gradually I won over the entire crew.

These were four of the hardest weeks of my life. They included late night and early morning location shoots, offline and online editing, sound recording, casting, producer's runs, wardrobe meetings and script meetings. And, when I had a break, 3 weeks, I used it to recharge my batteries and to work, prepare and steady myself for the next 9 episodes.

I also had to meet with two men who would replace Brian Cooke as scriptwriters on the show. Their office was in Gloucester Place, in London, and I nipped over there at the first opportunity. Had anyone attempted to construct a clichéd writer's garret and litter it with an eccentric dollop of chaos, then they would have been hard put to better the premises that I entered that afternoon.

Paul Minett and Brian Leveson occupied this space with jollity and industry and, although they seemed just a little too pleased with themselves, nobody could possibly deny the enormous contribution they have made before that time, and since, to television comedy writing.

Exhausted as I was, I was also elated and, as I celebrated a quarter of a century in the biz, I felt good. I was in the mood to congratulate myself. And, furthermore, the money rolled in.

*   *   *   *   *

I'm told that any rock aficionado will recognise a mention of the *Division Bell Tour*. This gigantic undertaking took in 68 venues across the world, and required a fleet of more than 60 articulated trucks to move the sets from one country to another. It was the final such tour by Pink Floyd. On May 25th 1994 - the day I got the call from Holland - the band played Montreal, in Canada and, with an exquisite degree of timing, they reached the Netherlands in September.

Netty called me from the Barbizon Palace Hotel, in Amsterdam. I hadn't seen her or Nick for a while. We'd been to their house in Hampstead, across from Boy George, a few times for dinner. And the odd party. And we'd been out with them to a couple of favourite restaurants, I have a feeling that Nick was taking some time out to teach himself Japanese cookery. Besides that, they had invested a little in Theatre Europa but, otherwise, events had interrupted the relationship for a while.

Netty was excited. Did I feel like joining the guys for their gig in Rotterdam? I couldn't resist the lure of this experience and so, on September 5th, at the end of a day's rehearsal of Episode 10 of *Het Zonnetje in Huis*, I gave myself a break and dashed from Hilversum to join the Tour Bus, as it was about to leave the hotel. Come with me, for the ride.

The word bus does not seem particularly appropriate for this well fitted out luxury vehicle. It's very comfortable and all very relaxed on our way down to Rotterdam, until we get within a few miles of the Feyenoord Stadium. It's now obvious that the sheer numbers trying to get to the concert have caused major traffic problems, and we have ground to a halt.

A phone call is made. Within minutes, several police vehicles arrive with sirens blaring to escort us for the remaining miles to our destination. It's a relief to finally reach the venue and disembark. I don't know what to expect now, but the backstage area is incredibly informal and stress free. There are plenty of sandwiches around and things to drink, and the band members chatter animatedly with me and with other visitors, as they amble in and mooch about.

Netty is my guide, as we approach the start. I can hear a distant hum from the stadium, and hear effects and microphones warming up. It's a huge undertaking, this event, and I find myself admiring the entire crew, as they move efficiently around and check everything. The tour requires a crew of more than 150 people, and the intimidation of my television studio in Hilversum starts to feel very manageable.

Eventually, I am taken around the perimeter of the crowd to the VIP area. Situated right in the middle of the pitch of this vast football arena is a 3 storey construction, housing the lighting and sound crew and equipment. We make our way to the top layer, and walk out for me to take my seat.

I look around. I am seated in the centre of this crowd of 100,000 roaring fans - slightly above, so that I look down and across them. It's an exhilarating and unique sensation, as far as I am concerned. I am live at the highest grossing tour in rock music history. This is one of 110 performances all in all, the band will play to around 5.5 million people, and I'm glad to be one of them.

The first set begins. Is this *Shine On You Crazy Diamond?* Whatever it is, the atmosphere is electric and the special effects are amazing. Is this an airship flying over us, across the stadium? I am swept along by the raucous enthusiasm of those people around me and, before I'm aware of it, we've reached the interval.

I get to talk to a few other VIPs and get a better look around. By the middle of the second set, I'm getting just a little bit bored. Sacrilege, I'm sure. Towards the end, Netty is at my shoulder. "Quickly. Follow me." And I do, of course.

We traverse this vast arena and the crowd that fills it. This is the most exciting part of the evening for me. I am now standing in front of the stage, between the musicians behind me and that seething, cheering mass in front of me. It's an extraordinary feeling and I can't imagine what it must be like to occupy that stage and play your music to such acclaim. The show is clearly reaching its climax now.

I hear *Comfortably Numb* and the crowd are wild. The night sky is ablaze with lighting special effects. There are explosions and smoke and, suddenly, a total blackout. The arena erupts. It's a deafening sound, as the lights come back up and the musicians launch into their encores.

Had I known it, the number *Run Like Hell* is my cue. Again, the blackout but, this time, my hand is grabbed. My guide is there once more, and hustling me away. We "run like hell". The roadies and technicians and backup personnel part to let us through, as we hear a decibel explosion behind us. They are baying for more encores - yelling, screaming and going crazy. But we are already on the bus. The band are with us; we are on the road; we are heading towards Amsterdam, before the thousands left behind are even aware that we've gone.

Somebody opens champagne. Understandably so. I learn later that this tour will gross one hundred and fifty million pounds. Only the Rolling Stones will outdo it. Back in the arena, once it has emptied, the stage and all of its components will be dismantled and loaded onto dozens of pantechnicons, before heading off to the next date: Prague. Long before that, we are back at the hotel in Amsterdam, enjoying a late night drink.

Over in Hilversum, we have our wrap party for 13 episodes of *Het Zonnetje in Huis*, on September 30th. I am high on relief and, as I climb into the car to drive back to my apartment, I switch on the Angela Brown tape, full volume, to celebrate my success.

But, the following day, I get a summons to the office of the Head of Drama. First thing, Monday morning.

*   *   *   *   *

At 11.00am, on October 3rd 1994, I presented myself at Alsmeer HQ, and sat in front of Frans Rasker's desk. He had a grin on his face, and I was offered coffee and cakes. And then, almost immediately, he got to the point. A decision had been made to sack one of their directors, half way through a series that was being made at the studios in Baarn. 7 episodes had already been shot, but nobody was happy with the results. Would I direct the remaining 6?

There would be more money, of course, and my contract would be extended through to the 22nd November. I would need to start rehearsals in two days. "Another cake, perhaps?"

My first question concerned the outgoing director, and his cast. Loyalties can play a strong part in proceedings. I did not want to take over a resentful and uncooperative group of actors. No move had been made, as yet, whilst the department waited for me to become available, but I insisted that the director be told immediately. The cast should be informed of the change soon after, and it should be made clear to them that I, personally, had no role in this putsch.

It was agreed. But then I discovered that recording would take place on Saturdays.

"I'm sorry, but I can't. My father has his 80th birthday at the end of October, and a big party has been planned. I have to be there. I'm sorry, you'll have to get somebody else."

This was when I began to discover, for the first time, the full nature of the impact I had made. There was a momentary hiatus, before:

"Fine. We'll move the date of that recording, and arrange a return air ticket so that you can attend your father's celebrations."

This was a big deal to alter the plans of all those involved and re-arrange the studio schedule, just to suit me. I smiled. "Okay. Then I'll do it."

I instantly began work on my new series. The cast were apprehensive at the start, but soon relaxed and all went smoothly. On October 29th, having apologised to my father that I would have to miss his birthday, I caught the midday flight to London and sped to Buckinghamshire ready to make a surprise appearance at the family do. 48 hours later, I returned to Amsterdam.

Since this is a true story, and therefore not all loose ends are always neatly tied, I would nevertheless not want anyone to think that I had abandoned Theatre Europa entirely. On November 9th, I went back to Brussels, arriving with a much lighter heart than when I'd left.

And, this time, I drove. I went straight to the Royal Flemish Theatre, where I had an appointment with another man called Frans. We talked for a long time and I got the impression that he liked my proposals.

Having directed 19 episodes of television, I was now ready for a break. But the company wouldn't let go. Just before Christmas, Guus arrived in London and arranged a meeting. He brought with him a lady called Pam Valentine, whom I was amazed to discover was the sister of Simon Oates - you may remember that he was responsible for my tickets to the Anita/Julie Harris show.

Pam was writing a grown-up sitcom about a paraplegic. Its working title was, *Two Wheels on my Wagon* and it had been in development for some while. It had first done the rounds of British television, before being bought by the van den Ende organisation. I was now in line to direct this ground breaking series… if I was interested.

I could not dismiss the idea out of hand but, after one hell of a roller coaster year, I was ready for a lengthy holiday. After the Christmas family gatherings, I was back at Heathrow - en route to Antigua and the island of Grenada, where we went on to stay with friends at their magical retreat overlooking Smugglers Cove. Our holiday would last three weeks, and it went in a flash.

With barely time to turn around, I flew to Luxembourg, a mere 300 miles, where the company had arranged for me to edit the last series. I'd never been to Luxembourg and, quite probably, won't be returning. It seemed an odd place, populated by some very un-welcoming folk, who live wedged between banks.

However, I was relieved to have got out alive. Our dear production assistant, Caroline ten Cate, was deputed to drive me around for the three days that I was there. Caroline was devoted to her pet parrot, which had mastered the art of being a telephone impersonator. In fact, so convincing was its telephone impression that many people had tried answering it over the years. Rumour has it that the parrot was employed on the set of one series specifically to ring on cue.

This is mere background information for you to picture the scene on my second morning in Luxembourg. Caroline collected me early, and the parrot was already installed on the back seat. With one hand on the wheel, my driver started on her makeup, whilst chattering about the edit we'd done the day before. The parrot rang on the back seat, whilst Caroline took her hand off the steering wheel, in order to extricate a cigarette from her bag and light it whilst the other hand was still applying makeup.

I turned to hit the parrot as it rang again, but this time it turned out to be Caroline's own mobile. For the next 10 minutes, as we zipped through the streets of Luxembourg, I listened to one half of a Dutch conversation, whilst the parrot continued to ring unanswered in the back. At the same time, the driver juggled a mobile phone, a cigarette and an eye makeup stick with the rear view mirror turned away from the rear view, and employed as a makeup mirror instead.

I survived.

We did find two very good restaurants - one Indian, one Thai - and completed the editing job, on schedule, for me to return to the UK. I spent three more sessions on Theatre Europa with the Board, before we decided to wind it up. Nothing had come to fruition. People had lost money, to be expected in this business, but I felt the failure personally. It was a painful learning curve, which all of us rode to some extent, but which came close to causing my own wreckage.

But immediately, I was asked to direct some audio books. This was another new experience for me, and I jumped at the opportunity, especially since the job also included the abridgment and edit. The first of these was *Ironing John*, by James Leith, which was to be read by John Alderton.

John Alderton, and especially his wife, Pauline Collins, were very much in the public eye at that time, and I looked forward to the opportunity of working with this very experienced actor in the studio. I spent a good deal of time on the abridgment and was happy with the result. A date was set for recording, May 1st.

In addition, I did an adaptation of the Thomas Hardy novel, T*he Well-Beloved* and started on a book about Led Zeppelin.

What a disappointment. There was a sourness about John Alderton, from the moment he arrived in the studio. We'd already had an unsatisfactory chat on the phone about it all, but he seemed pleased at least, to be doing it. In the event, it became clear as soon as he started to go through the book that he hadn't actually read it. At least, that was the only explanation I could come up with, and which made sense, other than the possibility that he just didn't understand it. Either way, he hadn't done his homework on it and his approach was very lazy.

Time and again, we had to go back over sections. I had to explain them, and then leave him so that he could read through them again to himself. Then, once he had become familiar with the text, we would finally try to record it. One studio day turned out to be not enough, and it was finished some time later.

Ultimately, the company behind all of these audio books went bust, and I never received payment, a few thousand, for any of them. C'est la vie but it was lucky that I was busy.

I always had a strong feeling that I would hear from Alsmeer again. Guus was sent to London to negotiate a new contract, and I agreed on a new series with him. It featured a Dutch actress, with a similar status and career to Maggie Smith, and she was the chief reason behind my rapid acceptance. But it meant that yet another new challenge was waiting for me - a baptism of fire, once more.

Meantime, Pam Valentine gave every impression of being as impenetrable as her brother. She had come up with a fascinating idea, and had written at least two very promising scripts, but was unable to move with it along the lines suggested and required by the TV company, the Head of Drama, the producer and the director.

Guus and I met with Pam at Gatwick Airport on March 15th and had lengthy discussions. I flew to Amsterdam with her on the 3rd April and we even began auditioning actors for the series. But all to no avail. Her tastes just did not coincide with those of the very people who could turn her scripts into a reality. She was completely inflexible, and *Two Wheels on My Wagon* was finally abandoned.

The news that really took me by surprise and delighted me, however, came on June 6th when we learned that my first television series, the first *Zonnetje* that I did, had been nominated for the prestigious Gouden Televizier Ring award for that year. I was flabbergasted, thrilled and disbelieving. My star was rising indeed.

Before the winners were announced, however, I had to go to Majorca. I'd discovered the island a few years before, when we'd stayed at a very splendid villa owned by the agent, Irene Dawkins. That was a holiday; this was work. The new series included an episode shot entirely on location in the Balearics and so, at the height of the summer, we all boarded a plane in Amsterdam and set off for our week in Majorca, 900 miles.

This was a big challenge for me, to direct an entire 25 minute episode, on location, with one camera and with only six days in which to do it. The whole thing turned out to be equally challenging for our gutsy, trusty floor manager. He later retired, spent, worn out and suffering a nervous breakdown but, back in 1995, he was ready to throw everything at the job.

On location, on a beach in Majorca

We landed in Majorca at 5.30, in the evening, and I went straight from the airport to check on locations. I had a short while to absorb them before preparing a camera script, overnight, ready for our first heavy shoot of the next morning, in the north of the island. We had just 3 hours to get it in the can. After lunch, we went straight to the beach, NOT to sun ourselves, please! but for the next location shoot.

It was late June, and the beach was crowded with holidaymakers all of them overexcited, noisy and fascinated by what we were doing. In addition, every group appeared to have a family of 25 children and dogs with them, and the screeches and shouts and screams and barks created big problems for the sound guy.

Nick, the floor manager, took his job a touch too seriously and tried to get some quiet for every take, even shouting, "Quiet, dogs!" at the bemused holidaymakers, just before yelling "Action!" for anyone who might be listening.

We were at the airport, we were at a campsite, we were in a bar, and we were all day on a terrace outside a busy restaurant. The middle of summer… and it rained for much of the day. Our formidable technicians created sunlight and warmth out of grey and drizzle, with lights and lighting umbrellas and, ultimately, it looked as though we had shot it in the studio.

It was full on, for the week.

Our location for the final scene was a palatial villa, overlooking the sea. At one stage, I had mentioned to Irene Dawkins that her own villa might be suitable. When I saw the final script, and noted that a swimming pool was essential (which Irene's place lacked), I had to disappoint her. I'm not sure that she ever forgave me for it.

Timing is everything. The ultimate shot of the last scene was meant to take in a breathtaking sunset, as the titles rolled. The pressure was on. Everything had to be finished in time. The sun was immune to Nick's orders and would set exactly when it was due to set. We worked frantically. The final scene hove into view. And so did the clouds. The sun set early that night, as it sank into the grey. It was depressing.

When we arrived back at Schipol Airport, on Sunday evening - smiling grimly as the Dutch passengers delivered their customary applause on landing, I wondered how it would all look in the edit.

I was surprised. It looked good enough. We wrapped on August 18th, and I went straight into a recording of a *Zonnetje* Special. As I was buried in the editing suite for that one, in early September, I was interrupted by the arrival of Johnny Kraaykamp jnr. He had been given one of the biggest breaks of his career, starring in the Dutch *Only Fools & Horses* but he didn't like the way it was going.

He had travelled all the way to Hilversum to ask me, to beg me, to implore me… to stay and take over the series. I was flattered, but I had to refuse. I didn't have the time. But I understood exactly how important I had become. Within weeks, I was put under contract, with a requirement to do a minimum of just two series a year. And the choice was mine.

If we fast forward to the end of the decade, and look back: I had completed over 100 episodes of television and received 4 nominations for Dutch Emmy Awards; I was now the highest paid director of Drama

It's a wrap, with the permanent cast of Zonder Ernst

on the payroll; I had a car whenever I needed one, and a permit to park anywhere in Amsterdam at any time, and for any length of time (this was the equivalent of buckets of gold dust); I had a beautiful apartment on one of the prettiest canals in the city, the Prinsengracht, kept permanently at my disposal; I was given a Business Class return ticket to London, every weekend; I was given first refusal on new series; and I had worked with some of the biggest names in Holland asking for me as their director. And I had learned Dutch.

I could trace it all back to those two words, spoken in May 1994, when Guus asked, in passing: "You have directed television, haven't you?" and I answered: "Of course."

But where would I go from here? And what else was waiting for me in the future? I was already beginning to find out.

PART EIGHT

The Moon, Stars and under the Sun

When I heard the news of President Kennedy's assassination, I was incongruously dressed in black tie - in a car, en route to a dance. I remember it well and, furthermore, I'm almost certain that we were going to Porchester Hall in London, at the time.

It may seem that I'm off on one of those regular tangents, but I also have a strong recollection of walking past a church, on a Sunday morning, when I heard the news that Marilyn Monroe was dead.

And I was definitely arriving upstairs on a bus, when I came across a friend reading a newspaper. "Anything interesting in the news?" I asked. This was 1966.

"Alma Cogan's died, if that's of any interest," came the reply. Well, in actual fact it was. I'd been a fan of that singer, who called herself Fred and had a famous giggle in her voice. I even attended a fan club reunion one year along with Maureen Lipman, Sandra Caron, Alma's sister and others, including Joan Greenwood and Lionel Bart. The latter was rather rude, I thought.

Greg Day, a familiar character in this story, was determined to push ahead with *Bust*. He had got it put on in Germany under the slightly garish title, *Titten* and was convinced that the play had legs. In 1997, during one of my TV stints in Amsterdam, he flew over for the weekend to discuss how we could get the play produced again in London.

On Sunday morning, he was in the shower enjoying a lengthy ablution and, whilst I was awaiting my turn, I switched on the television. And that was how I heard the news of the death of Princess Diana.

Before long, a gallon of Campbell Blair soup spilled over us, "People's Princess," etc. and Greg and I left to go for a walk in the real world. Even in the centre of Amsterdam, however, there was a strange atmosphere around - especially amongst British ex-pats and tourists.

The following day, I started rehearsing an episode of a series called *Zonder Ernst*. There were one or two sick jokes already doing the rounds in the studio, and I reacted badly. The Dutch are an incredibly parochial race, and carry with them an insane jealousy of our Royal Family. They love to criticise or gloat when things go wrong.

On Saturday, September 6th, I flew to London. It was the day of Diana's funeral and the landscape was deserted. I'd fortunately missed all the gnashing of teeth and public wailing, the baying for all those gathered at Balmoral. The silence everywhere was eerie. The airport, on arrival, was stilled - people watching events on a big screen. On my way through, I saw a snatch of what seemed like vitriol from the Brother Spencer.

Bust became *Stripped*, and Greg and I decided to produce it ourselves, at the Riverside Studios in Hammersmith. It felt great to be touching base with the theatre again, after 3 years of continuous work in television. We named our production company after the Joe Orton novel that had brought us together: *Head to Toe*.

Meanwhile, Jeffrey Beatty was writing his masterpiece. We were now firm friends and in regular contact - so much so, that I asked him to write an episode of television in Holland. It turned out to be a mistake though through no fault of our own. Now we must rewind to the previous year.

I knew that something was going on. The figure of Frans Rasker hovered again. This time, he was trapped. The broadcasters of *Het Zonnetje in Huis* wanted an extra series, it was one of the most popular in the country. Additional studio time had to be found, and it would all have to be put together quickly. The stars had to agree. And they did. With one crucial condition attached. I had to direct it.

This was outside of my contract, and I needed a break from the gruelling weekly grind. So, I said 'No'. But… Mr. Joop van den Ende himself, through his Head of Drama, Frans Rasker had already said 'Yes'. There was a stalemate.

I was taken for dinner at the most exclusive Indonesian restaurant in the city. The sweat on Frans's forehead stood out at a distance. This was a crucial meeting for him, since he had to persuade me to change my mind. Guus, by now Head of Comedy, stood at his side, once more.

It was a very fine meal, and I enjoyed myself. But I was reluctant to swing into 13 more episodes, sandwiched as they would be between two other series. Frans's hand felt clammy, as I shook it and took my leave. Guus stayed behind, no doubt for post mortems and recriminations. The next day, I expected grim faces and accusations of ingratitude.

Instead, I got an invitation to spend the weekend at Guus's log cabin in the woods. Yogi Bear, eat your heart out. Guus was a good friend by now and, as we drove through the night after Friday's recording he confessed his mission. "Do whatever it takes to get him!" he'd been told. The weekend budget was unlimited, apparently. I decided to play along.

We spent a lot of money that weekend on food and wine and champagne and brandies. It was a cold February, and I could walk on water. Literally. You don't believe me? This is a true story, if you remember.

I had already been fascinated by the skaters on the Prinsengracht canal outside my apartment windows. The canal had frozen over and on a bright, moonlit night I had to test it for myself. I walked across, and I laughed. Everything was now possible.

"Alright, Guus, I'll do it." I hope he got a bonus. It was going to be hard work for everyone involved. And that was when I asked Jeffrey for a script. He was thrilled. He flew to Amsterdam. And he wrote a zany, off-the-wall comedy episode… that had absolutely nothing to do with *Het Zonnetje in Huis*. But it was funny.

It was his first trip to the city, and it poured with rain. As though on the seafront at Bognor Regis, we sat in the car looking out through the windscreen wipers at grey skies, and discussed his ideas. Another memory.

It was Elspeth March's 85th birthday that year, and a grand party was held at a London hotel. Of course, it was stuffed with her friends and colleagues and, as a close friend, I was there. Elspeth was seated in the centre of the room to receive everyone. Sadly, her sight was beginning to go and we needed occasionally to announce ourselves, as we approached.

The wonderful Simon Williams was, as always, a kind of co-host and moving force behind the party. So many people I'd met many times at Elspeth's: Hayley Mills, Maggie Smith, Diana Rigg, Joan Collins, the list went on. Elspeth was a very popular lady, and the day was uplifting.

I was used to flying. Sometimes, I began to wonder just how much of my life had been spent in an aeroplane. But Peach Air was something different. It was surely an Irish airline, perhaps a farcical prequel to Ryanair. Edward and I took a flight with them one day.

The day was cold and wet, and we both had the flu. Parked on the distant grey horizon, our plane looked to be reachable only by missionaries and explorers. No huskies were offered. We walked. Through the rain.

As we climbed the steps, a wind chased the weather around our legs and then past us, into the plane. Once installed in our seats in the back row, the wind and rain lashed at our necks incessantly. Puddles formed on the floor behind us. We brought them to the attention of our stewardess. She snatched a cover from one of the seats and then, with her foot, used it to mop up the water. She then replaced it.

Come take-off, she had difficulty closing the door. 'Bang' it went, over and over. Her colleague approached, a dead ringer for Graham Norton in drag.

"What's the problem?" she barked.

"I'm just not sure if it's closed properly," came the whining reply.

Graham walked away. "Well, we'll soon find out, won't we?"

The engines started. I imagined propellers whirling. The noise was deafening. Could we be on a World War II bombing raid to Dresden? Fortunately, not. We reached our destination, and Peach Air flew off into a golden sunset retirement.

We have entered the last chapter of this story. There should be endings and dénouements, and there will be some, but it's very far from over, I hope. Where to begin?

Head To Toe gave *Bust/Stripped* its final outing. We went into rehearsal on September 14th 1998, with a cast that had taken a long time

340

to assemble. Nevertheless, it was clear within days that the rewrites had not substantially aided the play, and the actors began to sense its weaknesses.

We had a very fine production manager on the team. On loan from the Fortune Theatre, her name was Fleur Howard, and she worked incredibly hard to pull the technical side together. She liaised with the Riverside staff; she dashed off to organise props and costumes; and she chased up the set providers for us. She always seemed to be clambering onto her bike.

Suddenly, rehearsals were interrupted. Fleur had not appeared for a production meeting, and there was no response from her mobile. After an anxious wait, the news came through. She'd been in a fatal accident, knocked off her bike and killed. Crushed by an articulated lorry. The driver had chosen to turn left, and not seen her.

A pall hung over rehearsals. It was difficult to motivate people, but… once again, the show had to go on. The box office was buzzing. The business was good. The production was not so good. Perhaps I was finally bored with the play that had been around for 15 years. Perhaps my theatre technique was rusty. Perhaps I was sick at my stomach. The show was a great success, but provided no satisfaction for me.

On the same day that Fleur was killed, I had an evening appointment at The French House. Remco Kobus, a leading figure within the company, had flown from Amsterdam for a talk. I was already in my 5th year of television, and was now starting a second series of *2.4 Children*.

The leading lady, Simone Kleinsma, was a favourite of Joop's himself. "Look after her for me," he had said on our first recording day. No pressure, then. But she needed support and encouragement. Although a big musical star in Holland, this kind of acting was new to her. I looked after her, and she grew in confidence. She started to want to do things her way, to follow a rehearsal schedule that suited her. Remco had arrived to check on my compliance.

Following the tragedy of Fleur's death, this seemed like monumental trivia. I agreed to meet Simone's suggestions halfway. But that series marked the end of my association with Endemol. And I was ready for it.

I had already moved on.

By now, we were spending a lot of time in Spain. In Almería, to be exact. Our dalliance with Peach Air was just one expedition there.

Edward was having a busy career and, though I snatched him away occasionally to do a show for me, our schedules were not allowing us to spend much time together. Nevertheless, there had been a dream lurking in our shared consciousness, ever since 1987, to buy a hideaway home in the sun. Whenever the idea surfaced, it was always pushed away by events, however. Following Elspeth's 85th birthday bash, we grasped the nettle and went on a rekky to Almería.

Seven days later, we had bought an old cortijo and set about renovating it. With its fabulous mountain views, its orange and lemon trees, and its few olives, it was the perfect retreat and became the ideal place to relax. It was there that I began to formulate ideas for the novel I'd always promised myself I would write. And, once I'd broken away from the Dutch television scene, I found I had time to do it.

But first, of course, I looked at the television landscape in the land of my birth. Now was the time to come home. Or so I thought.

I was spurred on by a visit to the studios in Utrecht by the producer, Beryl Vertue. I did a series there, and was met every morning by the smell of fresh coffee wafting out of the Douwe Egbert factory.

Back to Beryl. Ironically, she had once been the agent who represented Spike Milligan, Eric Sykes and Johnny Speight, but she was now a highly successful television producer at Hartswood Films, of programmes such as *Men Behaving Badly*.

She was a guest of the company that day, and came along to a recording. We chatted before and after and she suggested that I make an appointment to see her when I was back in the UK. It was something very much to bear in mind and, in the February, I travelled to Twickenham to see her.

Soon after that meeting, I went to the BBC to see Geoffrey Perkins, who was the Head of Comedy there. It was clear to me immediately that we wouldn't get on. Strangely, he didn't seem to have any sense of humour, and he probably thought that I didn't understand BBC comedy. He couldn't deny my artistic accomplishments to date, however. But I left feeling that, not being part of the Oxbridge set, I would not be welcome working in his department.

Undeterred, I called on my old friend Michael Simpson. Michael was married to Jane Freeman from *Last of the Summer Wine* fame and, if you have been paying attention, you will recall that I served as Best Man at their wedding.

Michael was a producer with *The Bill*, by now, and I suggested to him that there might be an opening there. We met in Wimbledon, down the hill from *The Bill* studios, and he took me for lunch at Little Italy - full of bonhomie and so-happy-to-see-you talk.

After that, I could be found in the offices of Witzend, a production company that was responsible for a large number of highly successful comedy programmes on television. Here again, I had a contact with one of their producers, Guy Slater, who had preceded me at Basingstoke and championed my appointment there. With Guy, I was offered coffee and biscuits.

Finally, I got to Alamo Productions, a similar such production company, where I was given a cup of tea and a chat with Claire Hinson responsible for *Birds of a Feather*, amongst others.

There is an old adage, of course, that it is not what you know, but who you know and, in 1997/8 I knew both. I had had formidable success working on a multi-camera setup, over 4 years, and on well over 100 comedy/drama programmes. And I had achieved considerable recognition and stature for all of that. Furthermore, my contacts in the UK were impressive. Or so I had thought.

British television is still considered by those who work in it as the very best in the world, with incomparable standards of excellence in every department. Alas, it is not true any longer to the same extent, and production values, scripts and acting talents are regularly outshone by other European television companies, French, Swedish, Danish and by the Americans.

My university was London, and all of my television achievements were gathered outside of the UK. The argument was always made to me that these two conditions disqualified me from being given access to the cameras of UK studios. I find it inexplicable and sad, not through any sense of sour grapes, as you may think, but because such an attitude demonstrates an appalling insularity and arrogance.

A speedy zap of UK television channels proves that I can rest my case with confidence.

Having amassed an impressive CV, over a quarter of a century and now with a house in Spain, I turned my attentions elsewhere.

*　　　　*　　　　*　　　　*　　　　*

The legendary cabaret singer and stage star, Elisabeth Welch, waited until everyone was in bed, before unlocking her door and descending the long wooden staircase to the ground floor. She then crept into the sitting room and curled up in front of the television, where she stayed - an enigmatic smile playing on her face - until the early hours.

Anthony Steel, the heartthrob movie star from another age, whose career had been marred by illness and tragedy, was now released for the occasional away day, whenever a bit of acting work still presented itself. When he'd delivered his lines, he slipped back to his room, a touch of pride restored to his still handsome face.

Peggy Mount, whose celebrated bark had withered to a croak, received friends and ex-colleagues who nevertheless had to reintroduce themselves before she could recognise them. She had finally succumbed to blindness in her old age.

These were scenes from Denville Hall, in 1999.

Early in the 20th century, Alfred Denville an MP, actor-manager and all-round theatrical impresario bought Northwood Hall, in Middlesex. He dedicated it to his son, Jack, who had died at the age of 26 principally as a result of an accident on stage. The building was renamed, and quickly acquired charitable status as a home for elderly actors, those over 70. In the intervening 80 years or so, it has become a revered institution in the theatrical profession, and many actors have expressed a profound wish to spend their final days there.

One of those was Elspeth March. By 1998, Stewart Granger had been dead for 5 years and Elspeth was considering her own future. She still had the flat in west London, and still held court there for a stream of distinguished colleagues. A friend for more than 20 years, I could still listen, enthralled, as she talked about her life and experiences. That rich, throaty laugh was as infectious as ever, and her memory only occasionally malfunctioned, as she scrolled down through the years to recall anecdotes and gossip concerning some of the major stars of the 20th century.

But now with her sight failing, and as it became increasingly difficult to get about, she was under no illusions that she could remain independent for much longer. Denville Hall was her preferred choice, as the day approached when she would have to move to a Home. There was pressure for her to look within her own London borough for a suitable nursing home, but there was also intense lobbying on the other side. As I understand it, it was Simon Williams who was largely responsible for clearing the hurdles that threatened to block the move to Middlesex. He was a close friend and a genuinely kind and sympathetic human being, as well as an influential figure within the Actors' Benevolent Fund.

And so, her wish granted, Elspeth finally down sized to a bed/sitting room at Denville Hall. The reality of it, however, demanded brutal choices over which of her many prized possessions, books, photographs, pictures, furniture and mementos she would be able to take, and which would be left behind. The first separation was from her darling dog, her companion and friend and the parting distressed Elspeth terribly.

All in all, when the time came for her to take permanent leave of the flat, with all its echoes of so many famous voices and effervescent laughter, the magnet for so many visitors and phone calls, sadness seemed the overriding emotion. Almost immediately, the change cast a shadow across her features.

When she finally took up residence, she was aware that an unaccustomed loneliness had moved in with her, a companion not to her taste. There were other theatrical luminaries there at the same time, but Elspeth complained that there was nobody to laugh with, or to chew over the odd piece of gossip or theatrical memory. Imagine the joy, therefore, when her old friend Betty Marsden moved in. This would finally be the company she craved.

On the very day of Betty's arrival, these two larger than life actresses hooked up immediately, and the dining-room that lunchtime was enlivened by the sound of their irrepressible laughter and wild excitement. They now had each other's company to brighten the coming days. They were in such good spirits that, as the staff began to clear the tables, Elspeth suggested an adjournment to her room. Once installed there, they could continue the party with a glass of good Scotch whisky in hand.

And so the merriment spilled over into the afternoon. The pair swapped increasingly outrageous tales from their long theatrical histories. At one point, Elspeth launched into one of her many anecdotes about her good friend, Joan Collins. It was a funny story, and it set off a prolonged reaction from Betty Marsden. She laughed and laughed… "Well, it wasn't that funny, Betty"… and continued to laugh, until… she drained her whisky, fell forward and died.

Elspeth, of course, was distraught. She blamed herself for everything. But members of Betty Marsden's immediate family were reassuring: "Can you think of a better way to go, in the company of one of your dearest friends, with a glass of whisky in your hand, and… laughing? It was the way she would have chosen herself!" I'm sure that was true but, for Elspeth, the sorrow was compounded by a renewed sense of isolation now closing in on her.

For a lot of Elspeth's intimates, to make the trip anywhere outside a 2 mile radius of Shaftesbury Avenue seemed to require a major degree of planning and courage. For them, easy though it was to pop down the road and spend a half hour or so with their friend, Elspeth when she was in London, for a cup of tea, a drink, a few laughs and some salacious tales from the past, it was not so appealing to make the trek to Northwood. Even less to what is after all an Old People's Home.

And this failure, on the part of so many, to continue to just turn up, made the contrast in daily lifestyle even bleaker for Elspeth.

And what of her three closest friends, almost always at those gatherings, and who were regularly thrilled to welcome Elspeth into their dressing rooms after a show? I always found Diana Rigg a little cold and aloof. Maggie Smith was retiring and withdrawn. And Joan Collins?

I first met Joan in 1980 at the first night party of *The Last of Mrs. Cheyney,* at the Cambridge Theatre. Elspeth and Simon Williams were also both in the cast.

This was before she hit the heights of *Dynasty* and *The Stud* and *The Bitch*, and at that stage, she was uncharismatic and lacking in glamour. Over the years and a succession of wigs, she did appear to acquire a sense of fun and excitement. It finally gave her an aura of fascination. Or so I thought. Even though she briefly mistook me for a waiter…

In those early months of 1999, as Elspeth sat alone, she had cause to quietly complain that only one member of her close trio of friends had made the journey to Northwood. Since her arrival, only one had turned up at Denville Hall and she more than once. The extra mile, it seemed, was just too much for Dames Maggie and Diana.

The last time I saw Elspeth March was a week after her 88th birthday. Edward and I went to Denville Hall, in March 1999. Even though her sight was failing, and though still uncomfortable in her new environment, Elspeth still retained a magnificent presence. She greeted us in the building's spacious drawing room - her hair beautifully coiffed, as always, and that dazzling smile spread across her face.

With Elspeth March

We had lunch together in the communal dining-room, which was disappointingly much as one might expect in any old people's home. It was quite a relief to retreat to Elspeth's room afterwards. And yet… witnessing the very compact nature of those individual bedrooms can be disturbing. They seem to press in on the personality that occupies them. Theatrical grandees with highly successful careers behind them, and lifestyles to match, visibly shrink in their new surroundings.

I felt a sadness for Elspeth in that respect, but she was on good form that afternoon - delighted to be in the company of friends and colleagues, with whom she could enjoy a good laugh and who could bring her up-to-date on the goings on outside. All that had changed, it seemed, was the set.

As we said our goodbyes, she recommended a walk around the grounds. The spring was already showing tentative signs of an imminent arrival, and the gardens were looking pretty. We suddenly found ourselves directly outside Elspeth's room. Seated in a large armchair, she stared out wistfully through the glass, toward the gentle rays of the sun. The gardens, in close proximity, provided a kaleidoscope of colours, but I don't believe that she could distinguish very much. Even though we waved to her, and even though a sad smile crept across her features, I think that we, too, were no more than unidentifiable shapes and blurs.

It was, however, an image that remains to this day imprinted on my consciousness. Within a very few weeks of that visit, Elspeth had gone.

On July 29th, I was once more at the Actors' Church, in Covent Garden. It was a predictably starry occasion, and brought together in passive reunion many members of the *Anastasia* company, from 23 years before. It was poignant to watch Nyree Dawn Porter hobbling down the aisle, aided by a stick, some accident, I believe, and then to be with Elspeth's many friends at the reception at The Ivy afterwards.

It was all a magnificent tribute to the lady's enduring popularity, and to the respect and affection in which she was held. I miss her to this day.

*   *   *   *   *

Amidst fears that, as the clock struck midnight at the start of the new millennium, planes would drop from the sky, and life as we knew it would come crashing down, I retreated to Andalucía and considered ways of getting Jeffrey Beatty's new play into production.

He and I had developed the perfect rapport over the years, both professionally and personally, and Jeffrey had come to trust my opinions and assessments of whatever script he was working on. Meantime, as a huge admirer of his talent, I was keen to encourage him to keep writing.

Throughout the months before 2000, we'd been exchanging emails and developing a script, called *The Inheritance*. It was based on the true story of an outrageous scam, perpetrated in the 20s and 30s, firstly in the US, and ultimately travelling to London. Thousands of innocent, yet gullible people lost everything they had on the back of this scam - at the same time, having to deal with the devastating effects of The Depression and the great Dust Bowl droughts of the Midwest.

It was a compelling story, and Jeffrey was weaving it into an exciting script for the stage. It would definitely represent the pinnacle of his achievements to date.

Following the box office success of *Stripped*, Greg Day and I were looking for a new project for the Head to Toe company, and it occurred to me that *The Inheritance* would be a classy and contrasting choice. I sent Greg a copy of the script and waited for his reaction. It didn't take long for him to confirm my own thoughts. But there were two problems.

Firstly, where could we find a suitable venue to produce the play independently, under the auspices of Head to Toe? The Riverside Studios was an obvious option but, despite the sellout production of *Stripped*, rehearsal conditions had been almost intolerable. Understandably, the human tragedy that hit the production halfway through that period still haunted us.

Nevertheless, choices were limited and we concluded that since we now knew what to expect, many of the pitfalls could be anticipated and avoided second time round. Finance would come from Jeffrey's own backers in the States, and we finally decided that if the sums added up we would put aside our reservations and approach the Riverside.

The second problem came from Greg himself. With his vastly experienced and astute PR hat on, he reckoned we needed a new title for the play, if we were to stand any chance of attracting an audience. The search was on.

Plans for production moved forward quickly and, at the beginning of March after weeks of stormy, wet and windy weather we felt a touch of spring, as we got confirmation of a June opening at the Riverside. We were producers again.

I flew back to Spain for a period of reflection. It was then - as I was chilling out and enjoying what I thought was a well earned break - that

I got a phone call.

It was a call that produced tiny ripples that, in time, would become waves that within 5 years would crash over me with extraordinary force. The effects would resonate, loudly and clearly, right through to the summer of 2009, when dozens of newspaper column inches and personal blogs were devoted to a piece called, *Too Close to the Sun*.

Back in 2000, however, this was nothing but a narrative for the future. All I registered, as I answered the phone that afternoon, was a man's voice, with a strong northern accent. His name was John Robinson, and he began to outline plans for a musical he was writing. I eventually took his number, a Devon number, and promised to return his call when I was back in the UK.

Little did I know it, but I had just taken my first step on a road that would involve, over time, such names as: Patti LuPone, Michael Ball, Paul Nicholas, Dave Willetts, Elaine Page, Michael Praed, Sheila Ferguson, Frazer Hines, Sarah Brightman, Mark Wynter and even Shirley Bassey. There were others, too, glimpsed along the way but, at the start of April as I disembarked the ferry from Bilbao at Portsmouth, these were still characters waiting in the wings. And there we must leave them for the moment.

My only thoughts, at the time, were of the upcoming casting sessions at the Riverside. Winter returned that month, as I held days of auditions. I managed to persuade the authorities to give me a space inside the Studios itself but, unfortunately, the space could change by the minute.

One minute, I was parked in the Cinema at the bottom of a dimly lit and steeply raked auditorium. Every time the back doors opened to reveal an actor, in silhouette I had to dash up the stairs towards them, before they lost their footing in the dark. There was always the possibility of an over enthusiastic presentational flourish, leading to an actor plunging helplessly down the stairs towards my outstretched hand.

At other times, I was located deep in the inner recesses of an upper floor, where each door had a security lock. For good reasons I am sure, the security number was changed regularly. As I went backwards and forwards to collect each actor, tapping in numbers en route, to get to them a thought occurred that a single security digit might be altered. Suddenly, and without warning. Would it mean a hastily convened corridor interview, as we became trapped in a maze of time locked zones? Would our absence be noted in time to mount a rescue before the building was locked for the night?

The most likely scenario, however, was that I would simply forget the numbers. Consequently, I took to wedging a few doors open as I went, in order to make the return journey less stressful. On Fridays, with the transmission of Chris Evans's TFI Friday show, security became even more intense.

Despite all the problems, I was buoyed by the standard of actors arriving to see me, and I was aware of a strong and impressive cast coming together. It was the kind of play that cried out for a Sam Shepard and Jessica Lange in the leading roles, and I was determined to have some good authentic American actors in the cast.

I was thrilled, finally, to get Donna King who had trained at the Actors' Studio, in New York; John Chancer who brought to the rehearsal room invaluable family reminiscences of Ohio in the 30s; Ronald Furnee and Rosalind Adler; John Capes from Florida; and English actors, Bill French, Martha Collins who had trained at my old university college, and a brilliant, charismatic presence from Adam Astill.

Jeffrey Beatty and I had agreed to follow Greg's PR instincts, and retitle *The Inheritance* as *Scam*. To this day, I am not convinced that a play's title is important to its success, but Greg convinced us that the change would give the production a blistering and seductive relevance at the start of the 21st century.

Jeffrey arranged to fly over from Boston to arrive on the first day of rehearsal and found lodgings in the Bayswater Road area. Each element of the production was falling nicely into place, and I began to feel that familiar buzz of excitement at the prospect of working on another of his plays. I remained convinced that this would be his masterpiece.

Rehearsals began on May 22nd. Jeffrey fought through his jetlag and, after hastily dropping off his bags in Bayswater, travelled over to Hammersmith, bringing with him his customary East Coast sense of style and dignity. The actors warmed to him immediately, and they were soon bringing the script to life. My sense was that this was a hugely talented cast. Everyone seemed excited and, from Day One, each was immersing him/herself in the play and discovering their character.

By Day Two, however, unable to swing even a kitten in the room he had rented, the whole Bayswater living situation was starting to get Jeffrey down. An unhappy writer was not what we needed. I managed to contact a friend with a flat in Berwick Street high above the fray, and with glorious 360° views across London. It was temporarily unoccupied and, with a sense of great relief, I delivered Jeffrey there half way through the first week.

By the time of the final run-through, that very mature and professional cast were giving the piece a thrilling interpretation. The performances were moving. They were passionate, intelligible and utterly compelling. Jeffrey was delighted; the British/American mix was working well; and the evocation of the period and lifestyle seemed to be achingly authentic.

So, as the director, I had no worries. As a producer, on the other hand, I was concerned. Even with all the publicity that Greg was achieving, and with the play's punchy new title, bookings were slim. It dawned on us all very slowly that we were in the wrong place. This was a play for Shaftesbury Avenue - for a regular, discerning, theatre going public. Sadly, that audience was not going to trek to the Riverside Studios with its bohemian feel, paint peeled walls; its bewildering layout of steps and lifts to different performance spaces; its cramped, airless and uncomfortable Studio 3 in search of a stimulating night out.

An excellent play... with an exceptional cast... would work well in a more sophisticated venue. A strong script, with a fine cast – will resonate with many theatre goers... Yes, we got reviews, we got plaudits, we got praise, and we got sympathy but the numbers out front were small, most nights. Any waves we made lapped only as far as the doors of the Riverside Studios.

After completing its run, the play closed and everyone dispersed - disappointed, but pragmatic. The transitory nature of every production means that its spirit continues to breathe only for a limited timespan, once it is no longer given the lifeblood of performance. We had a small window of opportunity. Jeffrey Beatty whose wife and two daughters had flown from Massachusetts for the opening night returned to the US, and waited.

Another disappointment for him was unthinkable. John Kraaykamp had crushed Jeffrey's episode in Holland. Unable to adopt a new style, or be magnanimous towards it, he more or less rejected it out of hand and it sank without trace. I was angry and embarrassed, whilst Jeffrey outwardly, at least was philosophical and ebullient.

This time, I was convinced that the play's pulse remained strong enough for it to have a renewed life. There were two options: another stage production… or a film version. There were murmurs of interest all around. Was Jeffrey prepared to write a screenplay on spec?

Now that the scam's history had been unveiled, there were others looking to hop on the bandwagon. We needed luck and we needed kudos. One name kept resonating in my head, a name that would not only provide renewed impetus, but would represent inspired casting: David Soul. We resolved to track him down and see if we could get him involved.

In the meantime, another name came forward - not as an actor, but as producer. His name was Bob Walsh, and he was getting together a prestigious summer season of plays for 2001. He was also interested in Jeffrey's play. We spoke on the phone, and I realised that he was keen for us to get together. We could discuss the play and I could look at his theatre, at the same time.

Unfortunately, both he and the theatre were on the other side of the Atlantic.

*   *   *   *   *

And so, on September 22nd, I was back at Heathrow, the venue for the start of so many exciting adventures. This time, I was travelling as producer/director, on behalf of Head to Toe. London to Boston: about 3,300 miles. Within less than a year, the city of Boston would become inextricably linked with the atrocities of 9/11, but that was another September. For me, in 2000, the only significance of September 22nd was as the autumn equinox, and the official start of the Fall. New England in the Fall was an added incentive for a stay with Jeffrey and his wife, Annabel. This was also an important business trip, but for once my luck deserted me.

As soon as I took my seat on Flight UA 999, I sensed the unmistakable early symptoms of a severe cold. I tried to clear my thoughts and let my mind attack the matter on its own. But, as the plane made its steady progress across the ocean, my throat was already suffering a raging pain, and I was constantly reaching for a handkerchief. My fellow passengers understandably looked steadily more uncomfortable.

By the time we touched down on the East Coast, my status as pariah had served only to increase my perspiration levels. Immigration controls in the US are painful enough, and the vast arrivals hall seemed to be teeming with aliens slowly inching forward with their documentation. By the time I was through and looking for Jeffrey's smiling face, I was feeling distinctly ill.

Typically, and anxious that I should have an unforgettable introduction to Boston, he whisked me off to Harvard Square for lunch. Actually, progress was grindingly slow, due to the city's ongoing and laborious Big Dig, and I had very little appetite anyway. I tried not to show how I felt. I would normally have been on a high, as I was given a tour of Harvard and Cambridge, of theatres and concert halls, and the River Charles.

But, after a late family meal with Jeffrey and Annabel and their two beautiful daughters, Daisy and Arrabella, I crashed - citing heavy jetlag as an excuse.

Next morning, I felt worse.

Even though we visited the *Cheers* bar and Beacon Hill, and enjoyed the occasional tourist thrill at new sights and experiences, I spent much of the day wishing I were in bed, yet trying not to spoil things for my host. In the evening, we went to the theatre where, enclosed in a fairly airless space for two hours, I continued to suffer.

The following day would bring the centrepiece of my visit, lunch with Bob Walsh, the man I'd primarily come to see. In accordance with sod's law, and after another night of fitful sleep, it also brought the peak of my cold.

I felt a wreck, nothing like a dynamic London producer, with exciting proposals for the production of a brilliant new play. In the event, the meeting went well, and Bob and I agreed to get together again the following evening, Monday.

By Tuesday, I was feeling better and visited Bob's theatre ASF at

Milford, and Nashua, the summer season venue. I was greeted enthusiastically by the staff at the theatre, and left feeling hopeful. I was also excited. That afternoon, I was due to drive through the New England countryside - leaf watching, in the early Fall.

I looked forward to fabulous colours and dazzling beauty but, once more, luck was not on my side. It poured with rain and, although I could see all of their potential, the images I hoped for were mostly obscured.

The following evening, I was back at the airport for my flight home. My cold was receding, but my mind was in turmoil. I had learned a horrible secret.

Throughout Jeffrey's time in London - the jollity of rehearsals; the intensity of the work; the concentrated levels of spontaneity and inspiration; the anxiety over accommodation; the triumph of the opening night - throughout all of that, he had kept a secret from us.

He had known, even then, that he was facing a battle with leukaemia. Now, I also knew of the diagnosis and, though the disease was in its early stages, and Jeffrey was getting the very best treatment, it was still a devastating blow. And here I was sitting in the departure lounge at Boston, Massachusetts, complaining about having had a cold.

Also, our overnight flight was delayed for no obvious reason, since the plane was clearly visible at its parking stand. Making enquiries at the desk, I discovered that there was a good strong tailwind that if we'd left on schedule would have had us back at Heathrow whilst the night-time curfew there was still in force.

I had no sooner landed on this speedy return than I was given the news that, within 2 weeks, I would be crossing the Atlantic again. This time, my destination was Cuba. I was invited as Guest Director at the International Academy of Film & Television.

A few days of dealing with the Cuban mind-set, and the chaos surrounding simple travel arrangements, led to some advance trepidation. The turbulence we encountered for much of the flight to Havana (4,600 miles) seemed like an omen of things to come and, on arrival in Cuba, my fears seemed well-founded.

It was late evening, local time, when I clambered off the plane and into a vast room, seething with a mass of humanity that stretched into the distance. Against the far walls, a few desks, manned by indolent officials, unhurriedly checking documentation and paperwork. My spirits plummeted, until apparently hallucinating I spotted a placard, held high above the heads of the crowd.

At first, all I could make out were the letters: "V.I.P. Mr. Tony CRAVEN." I gave a tentative wave, and was rewarded with a dazzling smile. "Follow me," the girl cried. I needed no encouragement, as she effortlessly cleared a passageway through to the front desks. A tidal wave of antipathy from all those waiting gave added impetus. Those tailwinds were behind me again.

Within seconds, I was processed and on my way upstairs, to the V.I.P. Lounge, where I was left with my driver, whilst the girl with the placard went off to locate my luggage. After midnight, word reached me that it couldn't be found. I returned to the arrivals hall.

Buried beneath an avalanche of assorted bags, scattered across an isolated stairwell, the elusive case finally revealed itself, and I rejoined my driver. The turbulence of the Atlantic was as nothing to the discomfort of hitting potholes on the road to San Antonio de los Baños, and my driver seemed able to find each one with pinpoint accuracy.

After almost an hour, we arrived at the imposing gates of the Academy, and made our way up a long drive, edged with palm trees. My spirits began to revive. Here would surely be a welcome. We pulled up outside the front door of a 3 storey building and a figure emerged from the shadows. By the time I had eased myself out of the vehicle, my case was parked on the grass and my driver was shaking my hand. It would be another 2 weeks before we would be reunited.

As he drove away, I turned to the small woman who now stood beside me. She introduced herself as my maid, and led the way inside to look at the apartment - my accommodation for the next 2 weeks.

We walked through a few sparsely furnished rooms, that clung with some embarrassment to their peeling, ancient décor. We reached the kitchen, and my maid opened the cupboards. "Anything there is not here I will get for you tomorrow," she announced, helpfully, "But here there is sugar."

She forced open the lid of an old tin. I saw the maggots before she did.

"Well…" she muttered, "… tomorrow." And she was gone. The bed looked possible, and I was ready for it.

The next day being Sunday, I was left to my own devices. In the light of day, and having rested, things looked more impressive and the apartment was not so bad. Set on a large and seemingly well fortified campus, the Academy sported a number of buildings, residential blocks, studios and lecture halls. There was also a self-service canteen, my first port of call.

Hungry, and determined to be positive, I spread some pale butter on a slice of bread and bit into it. The bread was very old, and the butter was a mashed coconut paste. To help it down, I reached for the coffee, but that was equally unpleasant. The combined mixture of watery brown liquid, greasy tasting coconut, and heavy stale crumbs banished my hunger immediately. I looked around and attempted a smile. No longer like a V.I.P., but feeling let down, isolated and lonely, I decided to go for a walk.

The lunchtime menu comprised black beans and rice. How I longed for Morino's restaurant, in Boston. Within the confines of the Academy complex, and the bare walls of my apartment, I tried to occupy myself as best I could for the rest of the day. There was nothing to drink but Cola. The fuzzy black and white picture on the apartment television came and went, and I nodded off in front of it. In the evening, I topped up with more black beans and rice.

First thing on Monday morning, I reported to the Academy Director's office - bright-eyed, as they say, and bushy-tailed. The mood did not last. I was informed that the bus delivering the staff, including my interpreter, to San Antonio had broken down. Since nobody knew how long it would take for people to arrive, perhaps I would "make a start"?

My students were on a TV and Film Director's course, and came from all over Latin America, mainland Spain and other parts of Europe and the US. The Spanish language was their common bond, and many of them spoke no English at all. So, I could not have been more relieved when after half an hour of confusion all round the door opened, and a gentle looking figure walked in and presented himself to me: "Ismael. Your interpreter." We were ready to start, and the next few days flew past.

Ismael and I got on wonderfully well. He had strong political views, and talked avidly about the situation in Cuba giving me a huge insight into what was happening there. I enjoyed the work and, as I sought out alternatives to black beans, rice and Cola, invitations came in from the British Council representative and others, for drinks and parties and general sightseeing.

At 9.00pm on Friday, I was delivered by car to the elegant Hotel Nacional, in Havana, where I was invited to attend an evening of Cuban Culture. The building stood in vast contrast to the rundown, poverty stricken areas that I had seen so much of since my arrival, and I was shown into a large ballroom, a dance floor, surrounded by tables. Here, were a number of short, fat, middle-aged couples eating, drinking and shouting loudly to each other, as a parade of musical combos took to the stage.

The centrepiece of the evening, however, was a particular orquesta that, once it was announced, received a rapturous reception and enthusiastic attention from everyone in the room. It was led by a man who claimed to have links with the inventor of the cha-cha-cha (I was

The group, filming in Cuba

introduced to him later).

Immediately, the musicians launched into the arresting sounds of the salsa. Slowly, the shapeless couples rose from their chairs at the edges of the floor and began to move to the rhythms of the music. The transformation was breathtaking. Each man and woman as they swayed effortlessly to languorous sounds from the orquesta exuded a sensuality, and sexuality, that had been unthinkable five minutes before. The whole of the next half hour was totally seductive, and I have been an ardent fan of the salsa ever since.

On the Sunday, Ismael devoted his day off to showing me around his native city. Politics, sights and sounds, the heavily beating pulse of Havana; the exotic mojito (supposedly discovered by Hemingway); the fascination of listening to my guide, as he talked of Castro and all that was happening beneath the social surface of Cuba; the architecture, the streets and the hillsides; hidden bars and tucked away treasures; and, above all, the colours and the rhythms, my Sunday took in the entire spectrum.

Ismael with a combination of pride and a scarcely hidden anger at his country's condition brought it all to life. But it will surely be the music, and the radiant, smiling faces that will remain with me for as long as I remember that trip to Cuba.

By the time I left, I could see the frayed organisation and chaotic bureaucracy that I had first encountered through the eyes of someone who had fallen in love with Cuba, and could forgive its people anything. I left San Antonio with gifts and thanks from all I had worked with, and pleas that I would one day return.

My driver was there to return me to the airport, and this time I watched the route by daylight, relaxed and rested. Then, 20 minutes from our destination, we were stopped by a line of police.

I was fortunate in not being aware that some Britons had been arrested and imprisoned in Cuba during my stay. My real concern was not to miss my flight.

My driver was passive, as we waited to see what would happen. The clock ticked past, and the tension increased. Perhaps those tailwinds would hold the plane? Word filtered through that Fidel Castro himself was passing by. Outriders approached. Security tightened. Anxious faces looked around, guns at the ready.

For thirty minutes, the world seemed to stop, as we waited. Finally, a vehicle trundled across in front of us. I saw nothing, but evidently that was it. Fidel Castro. After another five minutes, the atmosphere relaxed and we were allowed to continue on our way.

I returned to the UK, a stone or more lighter. Black beans and rice, alternated with an occasional hamburger, is a very effective diet.

*   *   *   *   *

Music is never very far away. Samuel Barber, one of the great American composers of the last century, was an extraordinary romantic. Much of his choral work is difficult, but his Adagio for Strings is a heartrending classic, known to millions around the world, instantly recognised, and rarely failing to hit its emotional target.

So, why should Samuel Barber make a brief cameo appearance in this story? The answer is that he had a nephew called Jeffrey Beatty, whose way with words could achieve a similar effect.

Another brilliant musician is a man called Alasdair MacNeill, one of the finest musical directors in the business. We first worked together in 1982, on *Oh! What A Lovely War*, in Basingstoke and, although I tried to use him on other shows afterwards, he tended to be busy. He was almost always involved in one of the major West End shows, or composing his own.

I have learned to forgive him for passing on my telephone number to John Robinson, so that he could call me in Spain in March 2000.

But, as I returned from Cuba, I had other things on my mind. *The Inheritance* and David Soul were back in my sights.

An iconic figure, David Soul will be forever remembered for his role as Starsky (or was it Hutch?) in the American TV cop series. He and Paul Michael Glaser were both charismatic and independent characters, with a sense of humour that singled them out from many of the other TV automata.

David had moved to London and, at the turn of the century, was already carving out a respectable career in his adopted city. But there were rumours.

Practically no one remains untouched in this business from a certain kind of gossip, innuendo or critical abuse and, generally, people at the heart of it learn to distinguish the truth from the fiction. I have heard a ton of it, over the years, spoken about a whole host of people and most can be dismissed as hearsay, wishful thinking or sheer fabrication. Some, on the other hand, is recognised to have substance to it - accumulated through reliable sources, personal experience or from colleagues with firsthand knowledge of working with the individual concerned.

However, any rumour travels like wildfire through the profession and, if it's not extinguished rapidly, it can take hold. So, even when the majority remains sceptical, the rumour still lies around and eventually embeds itself in the theatrical psyche. Suffice to say that Greg Day and I were treading cautiously in our approach to David Soul.

We'd already had some contact by phone, and arranged to meet in November. Predictably, the venue was Groucho's, that watering hole of so many braying media types. I expected David to breeze in, spend a little time, with regular interruptions to engage in loud chats with friends and other colleagues before making his excuses and dashing off.

The reality was quite different, and I warmed to the man immediately. On arrival at the Club, he came straight to the table where Greg and I were waiting, sat down at once, and made rapid eye contact with us both.

He looked good, it's important to say. He also exuded a genuine interest in our plans, always an attractive trait in someone who is meeting you for the first time. Having ordered a coffee for himself, we got down to business. The conversation was relaxed and flowed very easily.

At one point, he turned to me and offered some advice: "You should be doing voice-overs. With that voice, I'm surprised nobody's suggested it before." They had, of course - frequently, but the advice didn't usually come from actors. Especially not from those that have their own voice-over careers. In fact, David had his own appointment for a voice-over that afternoon, as he explained when he first ordered his coffee.

As the conversation continued, however, and we all settled into some critical, albeit positive discussion of the script, he joined us in a glass of wine. I decided that the time was ripe for my own piece of advice to our American star. He was perfect for *The Inheritance,* and he should do it.

He ordered more wine, and Greg and I both raised an eyebrow. Eventually, we ran out of time and David had to leave, in order to fulfill his contract at the studio. We'd had an excellent first meeting, and we agreed to keep in touch.

After he left, we mulled over the possibilities, and wondered whether we would be taking a risk with the man, even if - and it was a big if - he could be persuaded to go along with us. We had no confirmed production in mind, but we hoped that David Soul's involvement would make it easier to achieve.

Sadly, we lost hold of the reins. I heard from Bob Walsh, in Boston, that his plans for the following summer had been severely curtailed, due to a ballooning budget deficit. His Board demanded that he fill the season with well-established pot boilers and not risk any premières. Another road had reached its cul-de-sac. And after a couple more telephone conversations with David, warm, friendly and constructive, it became clear that this was not going to work.

Jeffrey Beatty agreed, however, to start work on a screenplay treatment. For our part, Greg and I had plenty of meetings with Plaza Films, in London, and I had telephone conversations with Sarah Pillsbury, in California.

But I must return to John Robinson. So much has been written about *Behind The Iron Mask*, and so many myths have established themselves over time, that this is a good opportunity to put the record straight. In context, the production represented a tiny moment in my career, and so I will not bore you with too much detail.

The whole story is too surreal, and concerns so much ego, that I can best tell it as a fairy-tale from a Brother Grimm.

*   *   *   *   *

nce upon a time, there was a man called John Robinson, who became known as the 'Mad Professor'. He lived in a big house in Devon and dressed in silly costumes, probably to show what a whacky and eccentric character he was.

He made a lot of money as an engineer but, on his wife's deathbed, he made a vow that he would give it all up to concentrate on his second great love, music. He didn't truly understand music, but spent a good deal of his time humming tunes to himself and accompanying them with his squeeze box. And then he started to write them down.

Every time he wrote a note, the Mad Professor etched the date and time that the note had come into his head, so that every line of music bore lists of strange numbers and symbols. He soon realised that he must find a man who understood what to do with these notes.

One day, he went out into the world and found a 'Great Man of Music,' and asked for his help. This Great Man was called Alasdair MacNeill, and he agreed to turn the notes into musical arrangements

for the Mad Professor. This made the Mad Professor very excited, and he decided that he would write a Show.

For this, he needed some writers and so once again he went out into the world and found a 'Melinda' and a 'Colin', who luckily lived together in the same house. The Melinda had hair like a wild pomegranate tree, reaching out in all directions, and she gushed and twinkled, all day long. The Colin, on the other hand, was a dour Scot, who spoke quietly and infrequently, and gave everybody the impression that he was ineffectual and unconcerned.

These two people agreed to be the Mad Professor's 'Writers', and set to work on a tale about the Man in the Iron Mask.

Then the Mad Professor began to realise that he would need a clever person to put the Show on the Stage. He asked the Great Man of Music if he knew a 'Director of Shows', and the Great Man of Music said, "Yes. I know a Tony Craven. He could be the Director of your Show!"

And so it was that, in March of a new millennium, the Mad Professor called the Director of Shows who was a long way away, in Spain, and invited him to his big house in Devon in April, so that they could talk. The Director of Shows agreed, and battled through torrential rain in his car finally arriving outside a large manor house. There he was greeted by a bizarre figure, a man in his late 60s, dressed in tweeds, plus-fours and with a greying, straggly beard.

They were joined by a lady called Ann, who seemed to be secretary / companion / general dogsbody and a defiantly ardent supporter of everything "John." She was also an amateur musician. The Director of Shows soon realised just how mad the Mad Professor really was, even though he gave him lunch and showed him where all his musical notes were kept. He took his leave, at the first opportunity and drove back to London, where he had better things to do.

But then, the Great Man of Music sent a demonstration tape of notes that he had arranged into Proper Music, and the Director of Shows was impressed. He agreed to meet the Writers and the Mad Professor, to see if he could help. They all arrived at the Catherine's Lodge Hotel, in Brighton, where the Mad Professor had booked a room. The Director of Shows tried to explain all the problems with the Book and the Music.

Everyone nodded very wisely and told the Director

of Shows that they could solve all the problems, and that everything would be alright. They agreed to keep in touch. In April, 2001, the Mad Professor again asked to meet with the Director of Shows - this time, at the Royal Bath Hotel in Bournemouth. They had lunch together. The Writers had not done a good job, according to the Mad Professor, who asked the Director of Shows if he could make his own changes to the book.

The Director of Shows taught the Mad Professor how to write a cheque and how to pay people. This was a very difficult job. He then agreed to put forward some limited suggestions.

In truth, I had no real intention at this stage of ever directing the show. It all seemed like a bizarre game of make-believe. In Brighton, we were all shoehorned into that small room. I think I eventually sat on the single bed, whilst Melinda slid to the floor. Sandwiches were produced out of John's case, together with flasks of soup. I expected to hear of progress on the script. Instead, I got a childish inventory of who was responsible for this, and whose brainchild was that.

Was that lyric Colin and Melinda's, or had it come from John? Which one could take the credit for that idea? And so on. When I finally got the discussion back to the script, I realised that John didn't actually understand a script, or how it works. For example, he took exception to the writers' stage directions for the simple reason that the audience wouldn't hear them spoken.

There were all kinds of tensions between them, and it seemed as though it would never happen. As if to underline my relaxed attitude, when Alasdair called me later and said, "I'll do it, if you promise to do it," I gave my word. The show was a fantasy. Until one year later.

Fast forward to May 14th, 2002. I had paid a courtesy visit to John at his new house, on the edge of Dartmoor, as I drove back from a weekend in Cornwall. He must have been fired up, because then: The Mad Professor hired a big London theatre, so that some big Musical Names could come and audition his music. He wanted to find out if they were good enough to make it sound better than it was. There was Mark Wynter, a highly experienced stage and recording star; and he was followed by Frazer Hines a name from television, and also highly experienced.

The Mad Professor asked the Director of Shows

and the Great Man of Music what they thought. They shook their heads and said that the search for The Star must go on. And then came Michael Praed…

In truth, as I listened to Michael sing those songs, I began to see the possibility, together with Alasdair's arrangements, for something respectable to emerge. Michael Praed was brilliant and, in June, after he'd read the script, I had a long meeting with him, in Victoria in sight of the burned out shell of the Westminster Theatre.

This was a 3 handed musical and, if each was of Michael's stature and had his talent, and his intelligence - he had an intuitive sense of how the script should change - then we were in with a chance. But John Robinson was now off the radar, and sent his music to anyone with a musical name: Elaine Page, Patti LuPone even Shirley Bassey. And then, Dave Willetts.

The Mad Professor was dazzled by the biggest Names in Musical Theatre, but even as he sent demo tapes and flyers around the world he began to accept the advice he was given that, without a theatre or a date for rehearsal, he had nothing to offer but his genius.

The Duchess Theatre, for Behind the Iron Mask

He went out into the big, wide world and looked for a Sympathetic Producer. And, after a few false starts, he arrived at a solution. Andrew Jenkins was his name.

Things were beginning to get serious.

Suddenly, the Mad Professor encouraged by all the attention that his chequebook was receiving, and propelled forward by the combustion from his own irrepressible ego made a pact with the Devil.

Otherwise known as Ms Nica Burns, this was a Very Important Person in the organisation known as the Really Useful Company and she made decisions in relation to the Duchess Theatre. The Mad Professor signed a contract.

In truth, this was no longer a fantasy or a children's fairy tale. We were all committed - trapped by the arrogant unstoppable thrust of John Robinson's ambition. The odds were still on a strong, professional cast with time to rewrite much of the script and, possibly, to sideline John Robinson himself. I banked on it.

I met with Dave Willetts, Alasdair MacNeill, Andrew Jenkins and John Robertson, at the National Theatre, at the end of October, 2004 and the mood was a very positive one. Andrew was a genuine producer, with sensible views. Dave Willetts, in particular, seemed keen. He'd apparently been seduced by Alasdair's arrangements, which he heard on John Robinson's car CD player, after a show, in a carpark... somewhere.

He arrived at that meeting, with quite a few ideas and much to say for his Brummie self though none of the chiefs, that afternoon, truly wanted to be Indians. They all had their say, but I was still unsure as to whether we should go ahead. I consequently bided my time.

Nevertheless, a cast was coming together. With Dave Willetts and Michael Praed (if he could be persuaded to commit), we stood a chance. From then on, events moved swiftly driven by John Robinson's obsessions.

We still needed to find the female, the young, sexy, dark skinned gypsy girl, who could dance up a storm and seduce the two males. It was for this part that John had chased Shirley Bassey, Patti LuPone, Elaine Page, Sarah Brightman... and many others, besides.

In August, that year, The Ambassador's Theatre had been mentioned, imagine my horror. Nica Burns was blowing hot and cold, and would not make a decision. We soon knew that Michael Praed was not going to be persuaded, but Michael Ball was in the frame, and thinking about it. Andrew Jenkins started to talk serious possibilities, and Alasdair emailed copies of all the arrangements to me reminding me of our pact.

At the end of the month, The Duchess Theatre became a contender, and I began to get the feeling that it was a case of any theatre, at any time. In the meantime, I had done another play in Holland, *Potasch*

& *Perlmoer*, and a new play in Brighton, *Naked Love*, whilst John Robinson was already contacting choreographers.

And then it all went quiet. It was the calm before the storm.

At my suggestion, a script had gone to Paul Nicholas. Or so I thought.

I had assumed it was rejected but, in truth, John had forgotten to send it.

Suddenly, in April 2005, I was tied in irrevocably. Paul Nicholas had reservations about the script and asked me to edit it, to change it. He didn't want the writers to get involved, because he wanted a different approach. Foolishly, in retrospect, I agreed.

Sheila Ferguson in rehearsal for Behind the Iron Mask

Everything hung in the balance, as I worked - reshaping rather than rewriting - since I didn't believe that it was my job to do that. Whatever I did, it seemed to work. On May 20th, Paul Nicholas agreed to do the show and, on the strength of his name and mine and the potential involvement of Dave Willetts, The Duchess Theatre was booked.

John ran amok. He went to see Sheila Ferguson, to pursue her interest in the show. Paul Nicholas disappeared to France and could not be contacted. Dave Willetts became unavailable. But John was playing West End producer Big Time.

Everyone was under contract; the theatre was booked; we were less than 3 weeks from rehearsal; and we had no cast. Two weeks after Paul Nicholas had agreed to do the show he then disappeared, he put his head above his French parapet and pulled out. We were doomed.

The show needed extraordinary voices to sing the score. The book needed miraculous actors to play the lines. Our producer was only interested in the music. He booked three singers: the 57 year old Sheila

Ferguson, Mark McKerracher, and Robert Fardell. Rehearsals started on June 20th, at Sadler's Wells.

Sheila Ferguson had been the lead singer of the 70s pop group, *The Three Degrees*, with hits such as *When Will I See You Again?* and *Take Good Care of Yourself*. Having moved to the UK in the early 80s, she was picking up bits and pieces on television and emerging as a kind of celebrity.

Within 10 minutes of our first meeting, she announced that she was relying on me: "Make me a Star, Tony!" She certainly behaved like a Star. A car was sent every morning to transport her to London from her home in the country. She was taken back every night to be with her twin daughters and, if one could believe all that she told me, to drink gallons of champagne. I have rarely encountered such false sincerity in a person.

As you will know by now, my book shelves carry a few editions, signed with gracious comments by their authors. These have usually come in recognition of work done together, and to demonstrate a genuine affection.

On just the second day of rehearsal, Sheila arrived with a copy of her book, *Soul Food* for me. Inside the cover, she had scrawled: *To Tony, with Love and Gratitude and Respect*. For what? I hadn't even CAST her.

Robert was fully out of his depth, but Mark was something else, a tower of strength and a very fine performer. He didn't deserve the onslaught that followed.

We all fought with our Producer. John Robinson was impervious to any alteration to his music. He would write more, if we wanted it, but would lose none of it. The writers resisted further changes to the script. The three actors struggled with their lines and the music. And, in the middle of it all, terrorists struck the capital's tube and bus network, in the notorious 7/7 bombings.

For once, I was not in danger, but a whole day of rehearsal was lost, and it seemed only fitting that the show should be dogged by disaster, from then on.

John increased the list of musical chiefs. Alasdair MacNeill was forced to leave the show. The writers wanted their names off it, and asked me to do the same. But you can't jump ship, in that way. I had agreed to do the show, and I was going to see it through, even though I knew it would flop.

But the way in which the vultures circled was insidious. Through the previews, the Press sent their scout. It's reprehensible, but it can't be stopped. We went through a golden age of theatre critics, some decades ago. The giants have since died off.

On this occasion, collusion led to communal prejudgment from the Press. The pygmies sharpened their knives and compared their notes. I watched them gather, on the first Press Night - huddling in groups and smirking. They didn't need to, but it was the time of year. Like schoolboys ready to break up for the holidays, they giggled and threw their stink bombs and farted in our faces, and then ran away with their inky fingers, to watch the carnage they wreaked from afar.

It was sad. The show deserved to fail, but the violence was gratuitous and offensive. In my world, fortunately, there was so much more going on. I had nothing to prove.

Afterwards, the Mad Professor was so delighted by everything that he had achieved, even though everyone else had let him down, that he decided to record it for posterity. The Bad Girl, Sheila, sulked and refused to come out of her house and sing. So, the Mad Professor found another girl who, with Mark and Robert, sang a lot of songs that all sounded the same, so that the Mad Professor could put them onto a CD and sell them to all the towns and villages in the land.

So excited was the Mad Professor by his own incomparable talents that he decided to take his shows to America. But nobody wanted them. So the Mad Professor wrote a NEW show, called *Too Close to the Sun* and put it on at the Comedy Theatre, in London because he got a big kick out of seeing his music flop. Which it did.

But he slipped further into denial, and lived happily ever after.

* * * * *

I began this story by suggesting I might be treated rough. In fairness, it's happened very rarely and, in contrast, the treats in store have been plentiful.

But, somewhere along the line - maybe because you were caught up

in fantasy and fairy tale, maybe too involved with gossip and intrigue -
you might have missed the fact of my novel. As I was able to step back
from the frenzy of life elsewhere and settle under the sun, in Spain,
this was a lifetime's ambition achieved.

I looked out over mountains and orange groves and the shimmering
almond blossom, and concentrated my thoughts onto writing a book. I
set much of it in Amsterdam and the apartment on the Prinsengracht
that I had come to love. Some of my experiences in Holland filtered in,
but the rest came from my imagination, stimulated by the tranquillity
and calm of my surroundings.

Slipping Out was finally published in 2004, and I am proud of it.
And that brings us back to reality, and the closing pages of this book.

Having worked closely with so many writers over the years, I have
become truly fascinated by the process. As early as 2002, other seeds
were planted that, in time, would flourish.

My old friend, Guus van der Made, came on a visit to Spain. By now
separated from his wife, he was travelling with his girlfriend and they
began to seriously consider settling in Andalucía. Having lost his job
with Endemol, he was looking for new horizons and new experiences.

Guus had worked with me on stage scripts, of course, and he'd done
a great deal of translation work for *Mills & Boon*, but out of late night
chats came the idea of creating a series for television and, by the time of
his return to Spain, we had a working title, *Bombing The Dykes*. Edward
Arthur was also fired up by the possibilities and became involved.

The idea was to make a comedy-drama series about a family who
moved to Spain, but who were also subjects of a fly-on-the-wall
documentary film. Interaction between members of crew and family
would provide a rich source of material.

There was a good deal of discussion about the different characters
and the slant that we would take, and the working title changed to *All
Behind*, suggested by everything the family would leave in the UK.

It became impossible to grow the series with any sustained continuity,
whilst Guus was only making the occasional trip to Spain, and our ideas
for it gradually went in opposing directions. A split was inevitable,
and Guus eventually disappeared off to Indonesia with his girlfriend.

Edward and I worked hard on this idea. We took a draft script to an agent and altered the title again. This time, it evolved as *Culture Shock*. In the meantime, we moved to a more sprawling property in Granada Province with olive groves, an orchard, a pool, stunning views and lots of private land, on different levels.

It was the perfect location, and encouraged by a variety of reactions to what we were doing, we decided to bite the bullet and shoot a pilot episode ourselves.

Of course, it was a huge undertaking but, in the summer of 2007, I flew to the UK for auditions. Recalls followed, in September, and we arranged for the shoot to follow, in October.

I contacted my pet cameraman from van den Ende days, Gert Zuydgeest, who flew over from Amsterdam; we got hold of two sound guys David Machado Dominguez and Daniel Fernandez who drove down from Santiago de Compostelo in the north of Spain, where they were based; we hired lighting and camera equipment; we rented accommodation for all concerned; we took on a driver and production runners; and we flew the cast from England. We then became the caterers, as well.

With yet another new title, *Sunstroke*, we spent a few days rehearsing, before filming the whole episode. The cast of seven included: Edward, Daniel Kruyer, Jason Courtis and a brilliant young talent called Daniel Attwell. The three ladies were Sophie Thursfield, Christina Schofield and Emma Hewitt, and we used some locals as extras.

Mostly, things went well. The male actors, in particular, did a fantastic job (though Jason brought a commune thinking with him), but Sophie didn't bother much - hardly learning the lines, preferring to wing it instead. There were times when she tested all our patience, particularly as the sound of her thunderous belly-flops in the pool interrupted our very concentrated rehearsals nearby.

Nevertheless, we wrapped on schedule and I then spent a couple of months editing what we had, before booking the Soho Screening Room in January 2008, for an unveiling for the cast, technicians and invited guests.

As I approached my 60th birthday, therefore, I could celebrate another achievement. Of course, the programme was made on a shoe-string budget, and everyone involved gave their services for free, but the BBC were quick to react: *It's very clever, and the taster is funny and charming, giving a great flavour of your show.*

An insider in America wrote: *The idea is original, creative and full of potential... never seen anything quite like it... enjoyed the characters, interested to know what would happen to them next, and believe they have plenty of room for amusing, and at times poignant adventures... original and natural – the English adrift, in the heat, an exotic location – all of it.*

Now we had to interest the right people. It went to agents - 'peripherals' - who either lost it, couldn't find it, or sat on it for weeks. It went to production companies, to David Morrisey, whose staff couldn't locate him, and to Robson Green, too busy fishing. A Spanish company offered to co-produce IF we could get a UK company on board...

Meanwhile, Jeffrey Beatty was writing another play, *Fixation* - a mystery, set in the Art world. He was coping with his illness as only Jeffrey could - with good humour, tenacity, courage and downright stubbornness. He used to quote Winston Churchill: "KBO," he would say. Especially when things were tough. "Keep Buggering On!"

Drafts of *Fixation* flew back and forth across the Atlantic. I was always on the lookout for those personalised jiffy envelopes of his.

He had backing for a London tryout, possibly the King's Head Theatre or the Jermyn Street Theatre. But both were now run chaotically, taken over by more 'peripherals', without the dedication or the passion of a Dan Crawford. On the other hand, amidst growing frustration with the London scene, Jeffrey was also considering an off-Broadway venue in New York. Perhaps my dream was about to come true.

*   *   *   *   *

Inevitably, this story has no dénouement. Only endings. The show goes on, the show always has to go on.

A wonderful actor called Nicholas Selby played Garry Essendine, in Noël Coward's *Present Laughter,* and he was magnificent. But it very nearly finished him off.

The Coward set was much smaller than some others in the repertoire and, whenever *Present Laughter* was scheduled, it made sense for the technical staff to leave much of the upstage area unchanged. They simply masked it off behind the Mayfair studio of Garry Essendine. It's a huge role and much of the time is spent on stage. However, one afternoon following one of his exits, Nick Selby took a wrong turning.

Masked off behind, and in darkness, was part of a larger set that included a massive hole. Gary lost his footing and plunged "gracefully, I hope" to his almost certain death. As he plummeted down, he recalled: "The astonishing thing was that I didn't see my life flash before me. I don't think I even thought of my family," he said. All that occurred to him, as he continued his descent, was "Who the hell is going to play my part this evening?"

The show has to go on, as long as it can. For Nick, a pile of mattresses stacked on the floor below allowed him to appear as usual that evening.

Jeffrey Beatty and his wife had bought an apartment in New York, a pied-a-terre for weekend trips to the theatre, or the ballet, or just to wallow in some jazz. The apartment was at an exclusive address: One Fifth Avenue and I was invited to use it whenever I was in town.

We decided to spend my 60th birthday in the city (I was treated), and to take the Beattys up on their offer. Ironically, this was also the NY home at the time of Sam Shepard and Jessica Lange, and I hoped to come face to face with them whenever the door of the elevator opened, so that I could introduce them to *The Inheritance*.

During our stay, we arranged to meet with Jeffrey in Newhaven. It was roughly halfway between Boston and New York. Jeffrey would drive, and we would take the train.

And so it was that we arrived at Grand Central Station, New York an adventure in itself. Majestic and magnificent, and straight out of so many movies, this was a hub that Brussels could only dream about.

As we rattled along, the guard brought a few smiles to our faces, with her "Listen up, folks!" lines. I remembered Jeffrey arriving at Waterloo Station, one time, rhapsodic about English politeness, just because of the speaker announcement, "We apologise to passengers arriving…"

At Newhaven, he was late. There had been a few holdups en route. But, suddenly, we heard the sound of a car horn. Across the way, a car sped past, the unmistakable figure of Jeffrey driving it. That welcoming grin. An arm manically waving. His excitement. It felt very emotional.

We bundled into a restaurant, a table reserved in his name. Jeffrey had altered physically. The disease was taking its toll, sapping his strength. In a rare moment of negativity, he confided that he didn't know how long he could go on.

But generally, the lunch was fun and stimulating, with lots of laughter and characteristic witticisms from Jeffrey. Afterwards, there were hugs. There were sad farewells. We knew, I think, what it meant.

I never saw him again. Over the next 12 months, he deteriorated. Though in pain, and constantly in and out of hospital he never complained and always returned with more plans for *Fixation*.

Jeffrey and Annabel Beatty, on Venice Beach, California·

*Courtesy: Annabel Beatty

In December, 2008, Jeffrey Beatty died. I remember exactly where I was and what I was doing when I got the news. We were born in the same year. I was just a few months ahead of him.

The Boston Globe newspaper called me, for my contribution to the obituary that they were planning. It wasn't easy. They probably expected a few fun anecdotes and colourful quotes. At that moment, all that I could summon up was his smiling face.

After 40 years in the business, I looked back. Who knows whether there are still footprints on the moon, or whether they faded over time? Or how many stars that seem to twinkle did in fact die long ago? Forty years is just a moment, a moment since I climbed those steps at the old Birmingham Rep, at the start of my adventures; just a moment until I stretch out under the sun, in 40° heat, to consider:

The world may not recognise my name, but I have had an astonishing time at the piano, on the concert-hall and in front of the cameras; at University, where I gained my Honours Degree, and a couple of film credits; and through a career in theatres and television studios. I have travelled the world, and met with dozens of unforgettable characters; I have a published novel already soon to be an audio book; I have co-written, produced and directed the pilot episode of a new television series; I have learned Dutch, French and Spanish; and I live in the most beautiful spot in the world.

And as for recognition? Let me put it into perspective.

Early in my career, I went to the theatre with a friend of mine, a very recognisable name from television. As we approached our seats, I was aware that he had been spotted - especially by a group of ladies, already installed in the row behind us. They whispered between themselves, nodded and pointed, and I was very relieved when the lights went down and we sat back to enjoy the first act.

Even then, it was clear that the eyes of those ladies were more on the television star next to me than they were on the drama being played out on stage. Every time my friend reacted, with a laugh or a whispered comment to me, there was a frisson behind us, as the ladies leant forward to try to catch what was being said.

By the time the interval arrived, I knew that we would have to run a gauntlet of adulation. We made for the bar and ordered coffee. Once we had been served, we moved to the far end and tried to cut ourselves off. It was never going to work. A spokesperson from the group was elected, and she made a very purposeful move towards us. Ignoring me, she pushed her programme at my friend, before turning back to the group and nodding, as if to say, "It's alright. He doesn't bite."

They all hesitatingly approached. I separated myself from my friend and went over to look at some paintings that hung on the wall. After autographs had been collected, and the ladies started to move away blushing slightly, and whispering their impressions to each other, the ringleader turned and stared at me. I pretended not to notice.

A second later, she was on the warpath, heading in my direction - a rolled-up programme wielded, challengingly, in her hand. A few feet away, she stopped and looked me up and down, before coming out with the immortal line:

"So," A sneer crossed her face. "Are you anybody famous?"

I was about to respond with an observation that if I was famous then surely she would know? But I just smiled, and shook my head. She was triumphant at her accurate assessment and, adopting a smug look, she returned to her group.

On another occasion, I was in the audience at a studio theatre, along with an actress friend of mine. At some point during the first half, she pointed at one of the actors on stage and whispered to me, "I recognise him. Who is he? Do you know?"

Since neither of us had had time to pick up a programme, I had to shake my head. "Why?" I whispered back.

"It doesn't matter. I've worked with him somewhere and just can't remember where."

The act continued and, by the time of the interval, my friend was kicking herself that she couldn't remember the actor's name. "I know I've worked with him. It's driving me crazy. Let's see if we can get a cast list."

Well, it proved impossible to find anyone to sell us a programme but, as we took our seats for the second half, I made a suggestion. "Why don't you go backstage afterwards and see him? He's bound to recognise you, then introduce you to the others and say 'I worked with her at...' Or else you might just remember where it was, when you get talking to him."

She agreed and, as I made my way to the bar after the show, she disappeared in the direction of the dressing rooms. I got her a drink and waited for some time. When she rejoined me, she was almost hysterical with laughter.

"Well?" as I gave her her glass.

"Oh, I know him alright. But I've never worked with him." And she lowered her voice. "I slept with him, though!" An easy mistake to make.

And finally, when we were in Egypt, a few years ago, we stayed at the famous Mena House Hotel in Cairo, overlooking the Pyramids. It's a magnificent place, with some very enjoyable restaurants. One, in particular, became our regular lunchtime choice.

Through diaphanous curtains that swayed in the midday breezes, there was a perfect view of the gardens from one particular table, and this was the one we gravitated to each day.

However, there was an occasion when we walked into the restaurant to find a camera set up pointing directly towards "our" table. It was obviously there for a commercials shoot, and we scoffed at it.

"What a crazy time to be making a commercial - in a restaurant at lunchtime. We'll just take our places, as usual." Which we did. After a few minutes, the director came over to ask us very pleasantly if we could possibly move to another table.

"Well, we understand. We're in the business, as well. Silly time, but… okay." And we reluctantly relocated.

As we started our lunch, the filming began. One simple sequence was repeated over and over. The actress merely had to cross, from one side to the other, in front of the table as the curtain billowed behind. She looked very inexperienced to my practiced eye, and I commented that she wasn't very good. The whole shot would take a long time.

Finally, they finished, and we breathed a sigh of relief, as we returned to our lunch. Before too long, the actress came over to speak to us, to apologise that we had had to move to another table. She also apologised that the whole thing had taken so long.

"You see, I'm really not used to doing this sort of thing." Well, that was obvious, but she was very amicable and friendly, and the conversation continued.

"So, what are you shooting? Is it a commercial?"

"No. We're actually going to a number of hotels around the world making a documentary."

"About what?"

"Well, it's a programme about some of the hotels where my grandfather stayed."

"And he stayed here. Clearly."

"Yes. With T. E. Lawrence. You know? Lawrence of Arabia?"

"Of course." I think we finally knew what was coming. "And who was your grandfather?"

"Winston Churchill."

Yes. We recognised the name.

Of that huge family that welcomed me with open arms way back in 1969 many have gone. Some of us are left. We all recognise each other instantly wherever we go in the world. Despite the memories, the ups and the downs, we are always looking forward, with eagerness and anticipation.

Under the Sun, at the house in Spain

Our stories continue. The pages still turn. The show goes on. KBO will be our motto.

Index

G

Gable, Christopher 168
Gardner, Ava 87, 114
Garland, Judy 94
Garrick Club, The 118, 145
Gee, Prunella 260, 266
Genet, Jean 54, 57
George, David 80, 130
Ghosts 19, 199
Gilbert, James 29
Gillham, Felicite 49-50, 59-60
Gill, James 226
Gittins, Jeremy 260, 266
Glasgow Citizens' Company 54
Glitter, Gary 76
Goldby, Derek 43, 44
Goldie, Hugh 103, 118
Goldman, Robert 27
Golightly, John 197
Goodson, Felicity 303, 308, 310
Gorchem 276
Granger, Lindsay 93
Grange, Robert 120, 122
Granger, Stewart 94, 140, 227, 344
Grantham, Leslie 299, 301, 303-304, 307
Grant, John 142
Grant, Russell 222, 228
Gray, Dulcie 23
Greco, Juliette 34-36, 53
Green, Benny 298
Green, Hughie 4, 47
Green, Robson 376
Greenwood, Joan 337
Gregg, Hubert 21
Gretton, David 135
Grey, Clifford 181
Griffin, David 93
Griffin, Helen 304
Grimaldi, Marion 154, 217, 228, 244
Groningen 269
Groucho's Club 118, 270, 361

H

Hague, The 263, 317
Hale, Binnie 182, 205

Hale, Georgina 209
Hall, George 77
Hamilton, Gabrielle 184
Hancock, Sheila 9, 98, 99
Hancock, Stephen 21, 27
Handl, Irene 256, 258, 259
Hanly, Jenny 87
Hardy, Robert 157
Harewood, Marion 34
Harlow 125-126, 282
Harper, Gerald 223-225
Harris, Anita 127
Harris, Joy 157
Harris, Julie 128, 329
Harrison, Wilfred 272, 274
Harris, Richard 145, 254, 256, 260
Harris, Rolf 280-283, 288, 291
Harvey, Laurence 17
Hatton, Stephen 80
Hauser, Frank 100, 102
Havana 355, 358-359
Hayes, Melvyn 280-281
Head to Toe Productions 338, 349, 353
Healy, Tim 118
Heath, Edward 25, 34
Henney, Del 43-44
Henry, Paul 9, 11
Henson, Nicky 202
Hepple, Peter 123
Herdman, Ronald 64
Hewitt, Emma 375
Hewitt-Jones, Brian 282
Hilary, Jennifer 37, 157
Hill, Daniel 168
Hilversum 318, 321-327, 333
Hines, Frazer 350, 367
Hinson, Claire 343
HMS Monkton 224
Hockey, Alan 64, 74
Hoffman, Dustin 193
Holland 88, 130, 262, 266, 268-269, 272, 276, 309, 318-319, 321, 325, 334, 338, 341, 353, 370, 374
Holt, Thelma 139, 209, 211-213
Hong Kong 222-225, 229, 248-249
Horne, Bill 77, 79, 82
Horseshoe Theatre Company, The 146, 157, 164

387

N

Napier, John 43, 45
National Youth Orchestra 15
Nawras, Nofel 162
Neagle, Anna 95, 196
Nedwell, Robin 87
Newark, Derek 301
Newcastle 57, 59-60, 63, 68, 70, 73,
     77-78, 106, 130, 135
Newell, Michelle 131
Newhaven 218, 377
Newman, Greatrex 181
Newspapers & Periodicals
  Boston Globe, The 379
  Daily Telegraph, The 123
  Evening Standard, The 123
  Financial Times, The 205
  New York Herald Tribune, The 190
  Scotsman 134
  Stage, The 5, 123
  Times, The 123, 158, 231
New York 17, 146, 190, 217, 237,
     239-241, 254, 351, 376-377
Nice 57, 104-105, 131
Nicholas, Paul 350, 371
Nicholls, Sue 74-75, 135
Nickson, Brenda 7
Nimmo, Derek 32, 39-44, 144, 184,
     186-189, 221-222, 226, 230-
     232, 246-248, 255, 295-296,
     301, 303
Norman, Monty 8
Norwich 316

O

Oates, Simon 126-127, 329
O'Brien, Patrick 79, 82
Ogdon, John 25
Ogilvy, James 194
Ogilvy, Marina 194
Ogilvy, Sir Angus 194
Oliver, Ian 287
Oliver, Jonathan 201
Olivier, Laurence 40, 119, 141, 205
O'Mahoney, Sean 207, 209, 213
Oman /Muscat 189, 299, 305-308
O'Mara, Dickon 150

O'Mara, Kate 149
O'Neil, Sheila 142, 211, 252, 275
Ono, Yoko 8, 267
Opera
  Arabella 228
  Marriage of Figaro, The 277, 285
Ortega, Ismael 357, 359
Osborn, Peter 132, 134-135
O'Toole, Peter 139, 141, 158-159, 162
Oulton, Brian 173
Oxford Festival 157

P

Pacey, Steven 190
Page, Elaine 159, 209, 350, 368, 370
Palante, Jean-Pierre 317
Pantomime
  Aladdin 277, 280, 282, 291, 316
  Cinderella 249, 253-254, 277-278,
     281, 284-285, 302, 311-314
  Humpty Dumpty 173
  Jack & the Beanstalk 284
  Peter Pan 5, 128
  Robinson Crusoe 292-293
Paris 35-36, 53, 57-58, 103-106,
     192, 208, 244, 287
Parnes, Larry 119
Parr-Burman, Pat 131
Paxton, Glenn 27
Pearson, Fred 72
Pederson, Fredie 260
Perkins, Geoffrey 342
Petit, Roland 36
Pilbrow, Richard 9
Pilgrim Players, The 18
Pillsbury, Sarah 362
Plays
  Amadeus 197
  Anastasia 91-96, 99-103, 118-119,
     147, 196, 217, 228, 248-249,
     348
  Antony & Cleopatra 13
  Arsenic and Old Lace 192
  Bed Before Yesterday, The 97, 100,
     115
  Bedroom Farce 146, 153
  Beggar My Neighbour 56, 130
  Beowulf 80

CPSIA information can be obtained at www.ICGtesting.com
Printed in the USA
LVOW13*1504070414

380669LV00002B/35/P